WHAT WORK MEANS

WHAT WORK MEANS

BEYOND THE PURITAN WORK ETHIC

Claudia Strauss

ILR PRESS
AN IMPRINT OF CORNELL UNIVERSITY PRESS
Ithaca and London

First published 2024 by Cornell University Press

Library of Congress Cataloging-in-Publication Data

Names: Strauss, Claudia, 1953– author.
Title: What work means : beyond the Puritan work ethic / Claudia Strauss.
Description: Ithaca : ILR Press, an imprint of Cornell University Press, 2024. | Includes bibliographical references and index.
Identifiers: LCCN 2023034436 (print) | LCCN 2023034437 (ebook) | ISBN 9781501775505 (hardcover) | ISBN 9781501775512 (paperback) | ISBN 9781501775529 (pdf) | ISBN 9781501775536 (epub)
Subjects: LCSH: Unemployed—California, Southern—Attitudes. | Unemployed—California, Southern—Psychology. | Unemployment—California, Southern—Psychological aspects. | Unemployment—Social aspects—California, Southern. | Work ethic—California, Southern. | Protestant work ethic—California, Southern. | Employee motivation—California, Southern.
Classification: LCC HD5708.2.U6 S77 2024 (print) | LCC HD5708.2.U6 (ebook) | DDC 331.13/797949—dc23/eng/20231106
LC record available at https://lccn.loc.gov/2023034436
LC ebook record available at https://lccn.loc.gov/2023034437

Contents

PREFACE

WFH (*working from home*) and *RTO* (*return to office*). *Quiet quitting. The Great Resignation.* These buzzwords show that work has become a hot topic.[1] The COVID-19 pandemic upended assumptions about where work occurs, and then labor shortages gave employees the leverage to negotiate better pay and working conditions—or to leave for a better job. Yet, at the same time, there is uneasy speculation about which jobs may soon be replaced by sophisticated AI programs.

I did not know any of these changes were on the horizon when I began my research with job seekers in California in the wake of the Great Recession of 2007–9. I wish I could brag that I had predicted these impending upheavals to working conditions, labor markets, and work meanings, but that would not be true.

I took a roundabout route to arrive at my topic of work meanings in the United States. For many years, I have been interested in how Americans think about the political and economic forces that shape their lives and the social policies that could address those forces. As part of my earlier research I talked to ordinary Americans about government social welfare programs and US immigration policies. However, few of these people were directly affected by the policies I asked them about.[2] For example, I asked Black and white North Carolinians about immigration, but none was an immigrant or had recent immigrants in his or her family. That made me wonder how Americans thought about policies and structural forces that mattered in their own lives.

It was 2011, and I had been living and working for a decade in southern California on the eastern edge of Los Angeles County. When I moved there, I felt an economic energy that contrasted with the East Coast metropolitan areas where I lived previously, which were still recovering from factory closings decades earlier. For those living elsewhere, Los Angeles may evoke images of beaches and Hollywood, but it and nearby Long Beach are also home to two of the busiest ports in the United States, the major points of entry for cargo containers from the Pacific Rim.[3] From my town of Claremont, I can see trains and trucks carrying what is currently 40 percent of the nation's goods to huge warehouses in the Inland Empire counties of San Bernardino and Riverside.[4] In 2009 Los Angeles County was the nation's leading regional center of manufacturing employment.[5]

Unfortunately, there is not enough housing for all the people attracted to southern California, and it was one of the regions hardest hit by the housing bubble that precipitated the Great Recession. Escalating home prices put pressure on potential buyers to purchase before prices rose even higher. Home buyers were vulnerable to shady lenders who were paid by the number of mortgages they processed, whether the borrowers could afford them or not. Everyone assumed that prices would keep rising, so no matter how much debt was incurred by buyers, it seemed as if they could always sell their homes for a profit. When house values plunged in 2008, jobs were lost in construction and finance and nearly every other sector due to the ripple effects of tight credit and of consumers having little disposable income.[6] Although the economy was no longer in recession by 2011 when I began my research, unemployment rates were still higher than 12 percent in southern California.[7] I decided to talk to unemployed southern Californians about the ways they coped with being out of work and the meanings of working and not working for them.

As a cultural anthropologist who conducts research in the United States, I had another reason for being interested in work meanings. I have encountered too many unfounded generalizations about Americans' values and beliefs—generalizations that are repeated to justify the policies that the commentators favor. Work meanings are highly susceptible to these tendentious cultural descriptions. Observers on the Right see declines in workforce participation rates as evidence that government social welfare programs are weakening Americans' work ethic.[8] For some on the Left, long average workweeks are proof that Americans have been indoctrinated into devoting their lives to producing profits for others. Many commentators on both the Left and Right assume that most people would happily stop working if they could support themselves by other means, but this assumption fails to consider the meanings that people's work has for them.

Work meanings are not a new topic for me. In my doctoral dissertation research in the mid-1980s, I interviewed employees of a Rhode Island chemical factory that had announced plans to close its doors, throwing nearly four hundred employees out of work.[9] It was a time when factories were closing all over the US Northeast and Midwest. Twenty-five years later, I found myself circling back to some of the same topics I explored then, including how displaced workers think about the place of work in a good life. In my previous research, I discovered that some of the factory workers declined promotions into management roles. They perceived these positions as likely to diminish their free time and pit them against their fellow workers. That research led me to question blanket cultural generalizations about Americans wanting to get ahead above all else.[10]

Finding my interviewees for this book required a multipronged approach because in southern California in 2011 unemployment was not limited to a single company or even a single sector of the economy. I searched for activist groups organizing the unemployed, but there were none. Later, in the fall of 2011, the Occupy movement arose, including a large encampment in Los Angeles, but that movement was not limited to the concerns of those without work. In the past, researchers could try to talk to people waiting at unemployment offices, but now most applications are submitted online. I needed a different strategy to find unemployed southern Californians.

Fortunately, there were many places where job seekers gathered. I recruited some participants by standing outside job fairs and handing out flyers describing my project. However, all-purpose job fairs generally offer only low-wage jobs. To find workers from other socioeconomic levels, I attended career counseling sessions, including some sponsored by a local nonprofit organization, and a job club run by the San Bernardino County office of the California Employment Development Department. Those sessions catered to middle-income workers. Someone I met that way invited me to attend her accountability and support group of job seekers, several of whom participated in my project. To find unemployed managers and executives, I visited career counseling sessions organized by an executive outplacement firm. At each setting, the organizer kindly gave me a little time to describe my project. I met a few participants through mutual acquaintances, which offered the opportunity to talk to people who were not working but lacked the knowledge, ability, or motivation to attend career counseling sessions and job seeker accountability groups. To enhance socioeconomic diversity, I recruited participants from different parts of the region around Los Angeles—from the relatively wealthy suburbs of Orange County and the San Gabriel Valley to the inland Riverside-San Bernardino-Ontario metropolitan area, which in 2012 had the highest poverty rate among large metropolitan areas in the United States.[11]

My participants were diverse in other respects as well. Many earlier studies of US culture examined the experiences of the white, native-born, middle class. Studies of work meanings typically focused on men rather than women. There is nothing wrong with a narrow demographic focus if the researcher intends to illuminate the outlooks of just that slice of the public. Indeed, there is considerable value in attaining a deep understanding of one group. My dissertation research was with white, working-class men because they were the workforce of the Rhode Island chemical factory that was the focus of my study. By contrast, my research for this book took place in an ethnically diverse part of the United States, where more than one-fifth of the population are foreign born, and with the goal of illuminating what is shared and what varies in meanings of working and not working for men and women from differing backgrounds.[12] For help in finding and interviewing first-generation Latino/a immigrants, I hired a research assistant, Claudia Castañeda, a recent UCLA graduate and an immigrant from Guatemala, who interviewed eleven immigrants from Latin America. I recruited and interviewed some immigrants as well.

Together, we interviewed thirty-six women and twenty-eight men who varied in occupation, income, ethnic or racial identity, and country of origin.[13] One was living in a homeless shelter when we met, and another would soon move to transitional housing for the homeless; by contrast, four had former annual household incomes of more than $500,000. The rest fell somewhere between these extremes of poverty and wealth.

Their previous jobs reflected the diverse local economy. The occupations of those without a bachelor's degree included administrative assistant, construction worker, contractor, machine operator, landscaping worker, cashier, auto parts salesperson, housecleaner, waiter, massage therapist, hairdresser, customer service representative, home health aide, warehouse worker, and roofer. One participant had been released from prison a few years earlier following a long sentence for drug dealing; another was an Air Force veteran recently returned from deployments to Iraq and Afghanistan. Some occupations of those with a college education were quality assurance supervisor, nonprofit program officer, plant manager, business-to-business salesperson, human resources executive, student adviser, grant professional, information technology recruiter, schoolteacher, special education teacher, loan underwriter, and financial officer (see the appendix for a more detailed description of the participants).

No one was looking for a first job, and most had a long work history. I discovered that career counseling sessions and accountability groups tend to attract middle-aged job seekers. Some of my participants were in their twenties and thirties, but most were in their forties or fifties. This method of recruitment also meant that my research underrepresents those who had withdrawn from the labor force. I interviewed just a few of them whom I had met through personal contacts; I did not interview adults who had never entered the labor force nor had any plans to do so.

Of the forms of diversity represented here, the inclusion of first-generation immigrants may raise the most questions for a study of cultural meanings in the United States. I included immigrants because they are a significant part of the nation. In 2010, 12.9 percent of the population of the United States was foreign born, a percentage nearing the high rate from 1900 to 1910 when immigrants comprised 13.6–14.7 percent of the US population.[14] Images of ships carrying European immigrants past the Statue of Liberty are central to the popular imagination of the United States as a nation of immigrants.[15] I hope that one day the current wave of immigrants from Latin America and Asia will be seen in the same positive light.

As it happens, all the immigrants in this book had lived in the United States for at least ten years. We did not ask about their immigration status, but everyone volunteered this information, from which we learned that all but two were either lawful permanent residents or citizens. Claudia C.'s interviews were conducted in Spanish; I conducted my interviews either in English or with the help of a friend or family member who translated.

Another reason I recruited immigrants for this research is that some of those who came as older teens or adults embraced what is called the "American dream," the ideal shared by many immigrants and native born alike that the United States is a land of economic opportunity. How were their dreams affected by unemployment?

The interviews averaged six hours per person, spread over two or more initial meetings (usually at a coffee shop or restaurant) between the fall of 2011 and summer of 2012 and another lengthy follow-up interview two years later.[16] Each of the first interviews began with the request, "Please tell me about your life, leading up to your situation now." In addition to biographical information, their stories were interesting for the varying ways they narrated their lives and the importance they gave to their jobs and unemployment in their life stories. After sharing these stories, which usually consumed much of the first interview, we discussed the financial, social, and psychological impacts of being out of work and how they were coping. The second interview delved into the meanings of work and a good life for them, their explanations for why the recession occurred, how they would deal with the bad economy if it were up to them, and their opinions on related topics. In addition to the interviews, I stayed in touch informally with several participants through email and social media.

I also observed the career counseling, networking, and accountability group meetings where I recruited my participants. Two participants invited me to attend religious services with them, and I observed a session of a ministry for job seekers sponsored by the evangelical Saddleback Church in Lake Forest, California. Those observations, along with earlier pilot interviews in Rhode Island and Massachusetts, informal conversations, and media commentary, all contributed to my understanding of Americans' work meanings.

Many of my participants said the interviews were their first opportunity to talk about being out of work. Some voiced their experiences for documentary purposes, so that others would know what they had gone through. Others seemed to see it as therapy, an opportunity to express pent-up emotions. Some participants treated our interviews as one more networking event, another contact that might be useful to them. The small honorarium and free meal I offered may have been an attraction for a few. At a minimum, the interviews were an excuse to get out of the house, to give some structure to their day, to do something other than keep sending their resumes into the black hole of online job websites. Whatever their motives, all helped me, and, in return, I tried to help them in any way I could. Some asked me for advice about their resumes. I would explain that I was no expert, but I passed on tips I heard at the career counseling sessions I attended. Several were curious to hear how my other interviewees were coping, information I was happy to share while preserving confidentiality.

Even with their varied occupations and backgrounds, my participants had one thing in common: being unemployed gave them an epistemological break from working as a daily routine. As the political theorist Kathi Weeks comments, "When we have no memory or little imagination of an alternative to a life centered on work, there are few incentives to reflect on why we work as we do and what we might wish to do instead. Rather, our focus is generally confined to how, to draw on a famous phrase from another text, 'we shall set to work and meet the demands of the day.'"[17]

The long-term unemployed did not have to imagine an alternative to a life centered on work; they were living it. Out of work for many months or years, they were forced to confront what work meant for them.

I had once been in the same situation as them, but strangely, it took me a while to remember that. In the summer of 2011, I was busy with preparations for this project, applying for funding and conducting pilot interviews.[18] As I drove to a networking group meeting, I thought about how I should introduce myself. I suddenly remembered that twelve years earlier, I had been out of work myself. A tenured college professor, as I am now, has an unusually secure job. The tenure system protects teachers so they cannot be fired for expressing unpopular views. However, untenured professors—and the increasing number of adjunct faculty not on the tenure track—have insecure jobs. In the late 1990s I did not receive tenure in my first job, and I was out of work for a year before I was offered my current position.

Amid the minutiae of preparations for this project, I had forgotten that I had lived through the experiences I was planning to ask about. But then those memories started coming back to me. The letter announcing I had not received tenure, which seemed to come out of the blue when I thought I was doing very well. The injury to my self-esteem and threat to my professional identity. The much-appreciated courtesy appointment at another university, which did not provide a salary but gave me the cover of professional standing, like the consulting businesses some of my college-educated interviewees started—which, as one of my participants explained candidly, was just smoke and mirrors to make it look like she was working. The camaraderie with other anthropologists who reached out to tell me that they too had been denied tenure in their first job. And the stories I told myself, and which others told me, that there was bound to be a silver lining in these experiences. Perhaps losing my job was a lesson in humility that would make me a better person.

I did not delve into personal details that summer day when I introduced myself to the networking group. However, those difficult memories come back to me now as I am writing, and they help me better understand some of my interviewees' thoughts and feelings. Some of our reactions, including the impulse to put a positive spin on a negative situation and seek larger meanings in it, draw on ways of interpreting difficulties that are widely shared in this society but are not found everywhere. In other words, they are cultural. The fact that I had forgotten that I too had experienced long-term unemployment reminds me to put job loss in perspective as only one chapter—and not necessarily the most important one—in a life story.

My experience also underscores the fact that cultural meanings are not uniform. Many of my participants thought about being out of work differently from the way I did when I was unemployed. Not only were their income needs and job prospects unlike mine but so were their previous experiences, career goals, life projects, and understandings about the forces that govern our lives.

I now have another personal connection to my topic of the meanings of working and not working. My son, who is in his early thirties, has not had a steady job for several years because he is spending all his time trying to start an online business. His path is an entirely different way of launching a career from my more conventional get-a-graduate-degree-then-look-for-a-job route.[19] The differences between his work goals and mine are a reminder I live with every day that meanings of work vary—even within families. My primary goal in this book is to illuminate some of the key differences I found in Americans' cultural meanings of working and not working.

Acknowledgments

This research would not have been possible without the generosity of sixty-four unemployed southern Californians and of a dozen pilot interviewees in Rhode Island and Massachusetts. Thank you for taking the time to talk to me or to my research assistant Claudia Castañeda. I am sorry it took so long, but here, at last, is the book we promised you would appear in. Even though your life has probably changed a great deal, I hope you feel this is a faithful account of the thoughts and experiences you shared when we spoke.

In the summer of 2012, Claudia Castañeda recruited and interviewed eleven unemployed or underemployed immigrants from Latin America who varied in education and income. Her sensitive interviews enriched this research considerably.

I am fortunate to have worked with many smart and helpful undergraduate student research assistants from the Claremont Colleges: Mathew Barber, Elena Breda, Kiana Contreras, Karen Eisenhauer, Grace Fan, Rylie Fong, Ciauna Kui-Chavez, Liliana Mora, and Javid Riahi. I look forward to seeing the work you do someday.

This research was funded by the National Science Foundation under Grant Number 1230534 and the Wenner-Gren Foundation, as well as several Faculty Research Award grants from Pitzer College. Those grants made it possible to pay my wonderful assistants, provide small stipends to my participants, hire transcriptionists, and cover other research expenses.

Although only my name appears as the author, this book is the product of many minds. I benefited from the insightful evaluations of Cornell University Press's well-chosen reviewers, Carrie Lane and Christine Walley, as well as from the comments of my colleagues Susan Seymour and the late Lee Munroe. I can never give sufficient thanks to my SIS (Sisters in Scribbling): Alma Gottlieb, Beverly Haviland, and Susan Scheckel. Your comments forced me to explain myself better and to question what I had taken for granted. Above all, your edits made my writing easier to read and more interesting. Our regular deadlines, your critiques, and the example of your own work transformed this book from its awkward adolescence into a more polished grownup. Everybody should have a writing group this good. I also learned from audience feedback at talks at the Claremont Colleges Library's Claremont Discourse series, MIT, the University of Maryland-Baltimore County, Northern Illinois University, Queen Mary University of London, Sun Yat-sen University, and too many academic conferences to name.

I am grateful to Fran Benson, who suggested I submit this manuscript to Cornell University Press. Although she retired as the editorial director of ILR Press before I was ready to submit it, Jim Lance, Clare Jones, and the team at Westchester Publishing Services capably saw it through to completion.

My husband, James Van Cleve, has an impeccable ear for the best way to phrase a thought. Thank you, Jim, for being my 24/7 editorial consultant. I am fortunate that my life partner, like me, is happy to devote a good part of every vacation and weekend to reading, thinking, and writing. According to the definitions I give in this book, that means we live to work. However, like many of my participants, we enjoy it. One of my interviewees said it well: "If you ever do make a living from your passion, you're truly blessed."

NOTE ON TERMINOLOGY

Terms for those with a Latin American heritage are contested at present. There are good reasons to choose Latino/a, Latina/o, Latinx, or Latine. Following common usage among those with that background in the United States, I settled on Latino/a.[20] I chose to follow thoughtful journalists in using "Black" and "white" to refer to those socially constructed racial categories.[21] When I speak of "women" and "men," I do not assume that gender identities are binary or fixed.

I struggled with the best adjective to describe the people and characteristics of the United States. The problem with "American" is that the United States is only one country in the Americas. For ease of exposition, I usually resort to the shorter, more common term "American," with occasional switches to "US American" as a reminder.

For the same reasons—ease of exposition and because they are the locally preferred terms—I use "work" and "working" to refer to waged work. Meanings of "work" are central to this project and were contested by some of my participants, so I write more about alternative definitions of "working" and "unemployed" at the end of chapter 1.

Transcription Key for Interview Excerpts

Speaker's emphasis = *italics*

My emphasis = <u>underline</u>

. . . = pause

[. . .] = deletion

[*italics*] = added for clarification

() = nonverbal features

WHAT WORK MEANS

CHAPTER 1

Multiple Meanings of Work in the United States

For almost two hundred years, commentators have described the people of the United States as having an outsized devotion to work. This common cultural description is perfectly summed up in a Labor Day op-ed celebrating "one of the most fundamental values of American society: our love of work." That commentator, like many others, repeats the well-known theory that Americans' work ethic had its origins in the theology of the nation's Puritan settlers: "Call it the Protestant work ethic, the Puritan work ethic, or just a work ethic, Americans are driven."[1] This book will explain why I disagree with this assessment.

The simplistic notion that Americans are driven by a Puritan work ethic exemplifies all that is problematic about glib cultural generalizations. It equates a "work ethic" with a "Protestant work ethic," and a "Protestant work ethic" with just one of its forms, the hard-driving, self-denying "Puritan work ethic." To reduce all work ethics to a Protestant work ethic or a Puritan work ethic overlooks other work motivations in the United States and homogenizes diverse meanings of work. Describing Americans as joyless worker bees also distorts the elements of play and pleasure many Americans find in their jobs. Finally, a reductive explanation of why we work is dangerous because it underlies the assumption that people either have a work ethic or they do not. The truth is more complicated because there are multiple work ethics.

This book presents the observations of people in a wide range of occupations who shared what their jobs have meant to them. They had time to talk and a pressing concern with these issues because they had been without full-time work for many months—in most cases, more than a year—when we first met during the period of high unemployment that followed the Great Recession of 2007–9. Thus, this book is about the meanings of working and not working in the twenty-first century, not thirty or a hundred or two hundred years ago, and it is about ordinary people's understandings, not experts' theories, although some of these ordinary people had relevant expertise. Given that so much has been written about the cultural meanings of work in the United States, this book is also about whether those time-worn descriptions are accurate.

Beliefs about the place of waged work in a good life are central to debates about the kind of society we want. For example, do we want a society that provides a good job for all adults capable of working, or do we want a society in which adults can work less and have more free time? How should life partners divide responsibilities for income earning and the unpaid labor of taking care of their home and dependents? Is anyone responsible for providing financial assistance if adults cannot support themselves? Those debates are not new, but they are especially pressing now, amid concerns about the replacement of human workers by intelligent machines and questions raised by the COVID-19 pandemic about the value of going to a workplace and the place of work in a good life. These policy discussions often rest on unexamined assumptions about people's reasons for working. Do people have to be forced to work out of fear of starving, or would they want to work even if it were not necessary for their survival?

Portraits of Five Unemployed Americans

My arguments in this book rest on interviews with sixty-four unemployed southern Californians. Here are five of them. Their stories illustrate the diversity of Americans' lives and work meanings.

Terrance West

Terrance West, who worked as a shipping/receiving clerk in a warehouse in his last job, told me, "Right now I don't really feel very important to anything or anyone" because he was then unemployed.[2] Terrance came from a family in which steady work was valued. After his mother escaped from an abusive relationship, she worked two or three jobs at a time, when necessary, in human services. She provided a supportive environment for Terrance and his sisters. He said he was "nerdy" as a child; after he finished reading the dictionary, his mother bought him a set of encyclopedias, which he read through the letter S. When Terrance was still in high school, the mayor of his town announced that he wanted more ethnic minorities to become involved in city government. Terrance, who is Black, said he was interested, and he began working at City Hall. He aspired to become a mayor himself someday, and although he is gay, he even entered a brief sham marriage to a woman to further his political career. However, he could not afford to continue his education beyond community college. Terrance took technical school courses in accounting and bookkeeping and then obtained an unrelated job as an auto parts buyer. Terrance is smart, hardworking, and dedicated, and he rose to become the youngest and only Black supervisor in the company. Two years later he showed up to find the building padlocked and chained because the company had run out of money.

That became the story of Terrance's life. He would find one of the jobs available to workers without a bachelor's degree (customer service for another automotive parts company, installation coordinator for a telecommunications company, shipping/receiving clerk in a warehouse, convenience store clerk), and throw himself into it. Whatever he did—whether it was working in a warehouse or a convenience store—he wanted to be an excellent worker. It was as if he took his desire to be of service and focused it on his jobs. As he explained, "Once I'm working somewhere, I want to be the best at it. I don't want to be mediocre." He was proud that "at most of the jobs that I've had in the past, I've been the one that they call when no one else will come in, the one that they'll call in the middle of the night and ask, 'Well, how do you reboot the system?' or 'How do you cash out for the night?' or whatever. I've always been that guy."

One of Terrance's favorite jobs was working as a shipping/receiving clerk in a warehouse for a company that made sweet snacks. The smell of chocolate filled the warehouse, which was kept dark and cool to preserve the candy. Although he never earned more than $15 an hour, he had an affordable, comprehensive health insurance plan and was eligible for bonuses. All workers were respected at that company, regardless of their position, and Terrance's supervisors recognized his multiple skills and devotion to the company, calling on him to fill in for security or accounting or to help train temporary workers. He said, "I really loved that place. I mean, I would get up in the morning happy to go to work." However, after he had been there three years, the company moved out of state. Terrance had a criminal conviction, which closed off some job possibilities. Sometimes he lost his job because he would react angrily to racial or homophobic harassment; one time he walked off a job rather than be goaded into a fight with a racist coworker. Terrance is tall and looks imposing; he thinks some of his supervisors were afraid of him.

When we met, few companies were hiring, and Terrance had been out of work for two-and-a-half years, which made him feel "lazy" and "kind of like a bum." He detested laziness in others, and he hated feeling that way about himself. Having a steady income also mattered for his romantic life and gender identity. When we first met, he had just turned forty, and he was worried that his young boyfriend would leave him for someone who could afford a nice car, concerts, and other fun activities that were beyond his means while he was out of work. Terrance told me, "I feel less of a person and less of a man because I'm not working" and that not working "emasculates you." He also confessed that without a job, it was hard for him to be romantic with his boyfriend because "I feel like I don't deserve it." To get by, they relied on food stamps and relatives who found a place for them in their already crowded housing.

At the time of our initial interview, Terrance had never earned more than $42,000 dollars a year. As the years passed, Terrance found work again, and he took courses to move into somewhat higher-paying jobs, but money was still tight. He could not afford to buy a home in southern California, but that did not seem important to him. When I asked what income he would be satisfied with in the future, he chose the $40,000–$65,000 range. Over the years I have known Terrance, he went from thinking it was his role to provide for their household to being frustrated that his boyfriend did not share the value he placed on steady work. Still, Terrance's dedication to work is limited to his assigned working hours. In his free time, he avidly follows local, state, and national politics and frequently posts on social media.

Isabel Navarro

Unlike Terrance West, the meaning of work for Isabel Navarro is shaped by her drive to improve her economic standing. Getting ahead is a persistent theme in Isabel's life story, one she traced back through two generations of women in her family in Mexico. She talked about her mother's mother, "a woman who pushed to move her children forward," and her parents, who "always got ahead" despite little formal education. They started a profitable business in Mexico City selling meals to factory workers and sent their children to private schools. Isabel had not planned to emigrate, but in college she fell in love with a US football player who was then working in Mexico. He proposed, and she moved with him to the United States. Once there, he stopped talking about marriage, but then she became pregnant and vowed, "I am not going to go back to Mexico as a failure with my big belly; I'm staying here. And in order to stay, I need to be married." Their marriage did not last long, but it enabled Isabel to obtain a green card, making her a lawful permanent resident.

Isabel found a job taking appointments at a large health maintenance organization, and members of her family helped watch her young son. As she explained, "I loved it, but I said, 'Well, which is the next stage?' So, there was a position that was at the top of the clerical ladder. Above all other office positions." It paid more than $21 an hour and required statistical training, so Isabel devoted all her vacation time to taking the necessary courses. She obtained the job, but it was stressful. Isabel started getting stomachaches. Worse, her coworkers did not accept her, especially one woman who constantly made derogatory comments about Mexicans. Isabel said, "I went to tell the supervisor about this lady, and in front of the supervisor she [*the coworker*] said to me, 'You know what, you *mexicanita* [little Mexican]? If you want, we can fix this out in the street.'" The supervisor did nothing, and eventually Isabel had a nervous breakdown. Her therapist suggested that she become a beautician, and as compensation for the harassment she had suffered, her former employer paid for Isabel's training. Once again, Isabel wanted to be the best in her field. She studied advanced techniques in skin care, attracting a large clientele at the spa where she was working, but again, she encountered a supervisor who put her down. She went into business for herself, and after a rocky start, her business was flourishing until she fractured her foot while caring for her nephew. This injury prevented her from working, and then her parents became ill. Isabel went to Mexico to care for them and tried to start a business there, but she could not attend both to the business and to her parents, who died within weeks of each other.

Isabel was in her late fifties, depressed, and still mourning the deaths of her parents two years earlier when she first met with my research assistant Claudia Castañeda. Although Isabel's new partner was not as loving and considerate as she would like, she said under such circumstances you have to "swallow your pride." She was living with him and letting him support her. Her now-grown son, who had enlisted in the military, provided some financial support as well. Isabel received disability payments after she fractured her foot and Medi-Cal (California's version of Medicaid, government health insurance for low-income adults), but when Claudia C. asked her whether she had applied for government-subsidized housing or food stamps, Isabel answered emphatically, "I have never wanted to ask for it." Although she was not sure what she wanted to do next, Isabel still described herself as "a success-driven woman."

On the form we gave participants to indicate the income they would be satisfied with in the future, Isabel first picked the $65,000–$80,000 range, then crossed that out, and chose the top category of over $500,000.

Katarina Spelling

Katarina Spelling is straight, white, and US born, so she did not have to deal with the same discrimination as Terrance West and Isabel Navarro, but she hid her religion from potential employers who might be prejudiced against Mormons. When we met, her main problem was that she was in her late twenties and unsure of what kind of career she wanted or whether she should even be thinking about a career at that point.

Katarina had two dilemmas. The first was that she was newly married and trying to decide how to balance a job with devoting time to the children she hoped to have soon. Her father had earned enough as a medical professional to support the family, and her mother had been "a very, very excellent home-maker" but had not provided a model for balancing work and family. Katarina found such models through Women at Work, the nonprofit organization where she had a part-time job and where I recruited several of my participants. There, Katarina came to understand "how you're able to do both [*paid work and raising a family*] and be balanced": she did not have to find her identity just in a career or just in being a homemaker. Still, when her children were young, she wanted to spend most of her time home with them, which meant postponing a demanding career.

Katarina's other dilemma was that her heart's desire was to become a professional singer, but she had been unable to earn a living that way. Katarina had started college as a vocal performance major, then switched to what she thought would be a more marketable major in communication studies. After graduating, she took unfulfilling office jobs (bank teller, administrative assistant) where she felt "like a flower in a closet." An enjoyable position as a music and dance instructor at a summer camp in Europe when she was in her mid-twenties gave her hope that she could make a living as an artist, but to be safe she applied for other jobs and considered law school. Katarina landed some music and acting gigs. After she recorded a couple of tracks for a friend's independent film, she told her husband that she had made more money for two hours "not even working" than she did in a whole day at the office at the nonprofit. Singing never felt like work to Katarina. Unfortunately, those opportunities were rare.

By the time we met, Katarina had decided against law school because it was too expensive, and she was completing a master's degree in public administration in hopes of working for local government someday. In the meantime, she needed to help pay the bills. Her husband's family had been unable to pay for his college education, so he came to the marriage with almost $100,000 in student loan debt. Katarina's father had paid for her undergraduate education, but he made it clear that after that, she was on her own. She should not expect to live at home or receive any other financial assistance, and so she took out loans to finance her master's degree. Katarina told me she had gone from "wanting to just explore and play and also learn, to, okay, now I want to make money. And so I feel like it's like this mental shift of, okay, I just need to categorize myself for eight hours, and then after that I can do whatever I want." Katarina told herself, "Work is work," meaning it is just a way to make money and does not have to express her identity or be fulfilling. Still, without any reason to choose one occupation over another if she could not be a professional singer, Katarina was rudderless. In our initial meetings she agonized about her job choices. She was going to start a part-time job as an assistant in an accounting firm right after our first interview, a job that she did not expect to like or be good at.

When we met for a follow-up interview two years later, Katarina had a toddler and was still working part-time for the accounting firm. She told me that this position was just a "job" and not a "career," but she liked it. She could do some work from home and some at the office. She hired a sitter one day a week, and her husband watched their daughter in the evenings and some afternoons. Going to the office gave Katarina other adults to socialize with. The day before our follow-up interview, Katarina had had an enjoyable day at the office, talking to her coworkers, joking with her boss, and having "that part of your brain used" that is not engaged by childcare. The job made her feel valued. While she kept an eye on her adorable toddler, Katarina explained, "As much as I love this work [*of being a mother*], it's not as rewarding as having somebody need you as an adult." Katarina said that job kept her from postpartum depression. She had figured out that data entry could be enjoyable if she treated it as a computer game like Tetris. Still, Katarina had not given up on her dream of becoming a professional singer. She is a devout Christian, and she hoped that an impending move to Los Angeles for her husband's new job was part of God's plan to put her in the center of the entertainment industry.

In our initial interviews, Katarina could not decide what income bracket to choose for the household income she would be satisfied with in the future: she checked both $80,000–$120,000 and $120,000–$150,000. During our follow-up interview she chose $150,000–$200,000. Two years after that conversation, Katarina became an accountant at the same firm.

ReNé McKnight

When I first met ReNé McKnight outside a job fair where I was recruiting participants, she was a thirty-two-year-old mother, although with her slight frame and sweet face, she looked younger. From our very first meeting, I was amazed by her restless energy. She had big dreams fueled by her devout Christian faith and by her desires to help others and become wealthy.

ReNé was eager to escape the poverty she had experienced growing up. She is Black like Terrance West, but her childhood was much harder than his. ReNé's mother is mentally ill and left the family when she was young; her father was seriously injured working on an oil rig in Texas many years earlier. He became an alcoholic and drug user who partied away the financial compensation he had received for his injuries. By the time ReNé was in high school, there was no money left, and she, her brother, and their father were living in a small trailer where they had to wash dishes in the bathtub. ReNé began working when she was sixteen. She left home right after high school and began slowly paying for her own college education, taking a few courses at a time while she worked and took care of her daughter, born when she was in high school.

ReNé arrived in southern California from Texas a few months before we met. She hoped, in vain, that her daughter's father, who had moved there, would start providing more financial support now that she and her daughter were in the area. He was a police officer who dated her when she was in high school. He never told her he was married until she was seven months pregnant. ReNé attempted suicide but survived. After her daughter was born, ReNé's father said, "Your life is over." That made ReNé angry. "I was like, 'You know what? I'm going to prove you wrong.' That's probably another reason I'm still in school. I was, like, 'No, my life is not over. I can do it.'"

ReNé had considerable experience providing care for the elderly and disabled, as well as customer service work. She was willing to take any job, but for nearly a year, she could find nothing. In the fall of 2011, the Los Angeles and Riverside, California, metropolitan areas were two of the three worst areas in the country to look for a job, with high numbers of job seekers and few openings.[3] As a new arrival in California who had voluntarily left her last job, ReNé was not eligible for unemployment benefits. ReNé did not try to find a romantic partner who would financially support her because she did not want any man to think she only cared about his money. While ReNé looked for work, she and her daughter barely subsisted on food stamps and a $490 monthly CalWORKs (Temporary Assistance to Needy Families) cash grant. Her rent for a guest house without heat, hot water, or a working stove was $500 a month. To have a habitable place to live, they had to move to a military barracks that had been converted into transitional housing for homeless families. Eleven months after moving to California, ReNé obtained a job caring for residents and training other workers in a group home for adults with developmental disabilities, but only a few months later, she was rear-ended by a truck at a traffic stop. She was then terminated from her job because the resulting injuries left her unable to lift the residents. By the time she found a part-time, in-home care job with no heavy lifting required, her car had been repossessed, and she had to walk two miles in each direction to get to work.

ReNé had written a draft of her life story, but she had not tried to publish it. Wanting to understand why God was keeping her out of work for so long, she figured out that her difficulties in finding and keeping a job were God's plan to get her to finish her book. She told me that God came in her dreams, showed her step by step how to self-publish the book, and sent her people to proofread and edit it: one of those people was me, the professor who, out of nowhere, appeared at the job fair she had attended.

ReNé felt she had a calling to share her life story because she had had a traumatic childhood and adolescence. She believed she could inspire others who hurt and feel like they may "explode." That was another reason for her hard work. After I heard her life story, I asked her how she carried on. She answered, "I think, staying busy. 'Cause I've always worked. I've always been active with things." She became tearful as she described how psychologically difficult it was for her not to have a steady job. While she was looking for work, she stayed busy promoting her book through her social media accounts, and she started a business helping others self-publish. Staying busy with such self-employment schemes helped ReNé block out having been sexually assaulted when she was in her teens, her mental health struggles, and other life traumas.

Her long-term plan was to start group homes to help troubled young women or the disabled elderly, like her mother. She also hoped that her business would make her wealthy, a hope encouraged by the prosperity gospel teachings of her church. For her, a good life was one in which she made at least $100,000 a year, owned homes in different parts of the country, and had several successful businesses. Still, when I asked whether work was central to her identity, she replied piously, "No. What's central to my identity is God. I put him first in all that I do. So, I can't really say, 'Work.'" She added, "However, I love working. I'm a workaholic"—an accurate description, from my observation.

When we chatted recently, I learned that ReNé had found a steady job as a social worker and had earned a master's degree in social work. She had also started a nonprofit to help faith leaders who are dealing with trauma, and she hoped to develop wellness centers for them.

Robert Milner

Robert Milner was a supply chain strategist for a cosmetics company earning between $80,000 and $120,000 a year before he lost his job in a corporate restructuring. He was in his early fifties and had been out of work for more than a year and a half when I met him at a support group for unemployed managers and professionals. I noticed that throughout the meeting he was consistently kind and encouraging.

Robert, a grandson of European immigrants on one side of his family and of Mexican immigrants on the other side, considered himself a "baseball, hot-dogs, apple pie, Chevrolet" American. He was proud of having fulfilled classic American middle-class ideals, which he explained as follows: "We got married. We bought the home. [. . .] We have two kids. That whole—you know?"[4] These achievements were especially meaningful because his father had left the family when Robert was a young child.

Robert had held jobs in a variety of businesses by that point in his life, including at an auto dealership where he learned to "hustle" for commissions. He said, "That has been my work ethic all along. I just work hard." He described his last job as a supply chain strategist as "real fun" because it was intellectually challenging. However, Robert hated that, between the job and his commute, his work occupied twelve hours a day, which left him little time to enjoy life. When I asked whether there was anything he was not proud of in his life, he mentioned subconsciously blaming his wife for her not working. She used to earn some money helping a relative in their small business, but that business failed, and her poor health prevented her from taking another job.

In our first interview, Robert shared that he wanted to earn at least $80,000 in his next job, but when we met again, he decided that he should be satisfied with less. With fervor, he described his conversion, while he was out of work, to being "happy with just the simplest things." He was learning to be content to "be with your family, read a good book, take a walk," and watch the birds in his yard build a nest. Robert admired Europeans' more relaxed schedules: "They take off two, three weeks, sometimes a month out of the summer." By contrast, in the United States, "Here, we're so go, go, go. We're chasing that almighty dollar." He said Americans should be less "greedy," not only "the people at the top" but "even the regular people like me." When I asked whether work was central to his identity, he explained, "Although I work to live, I don't live to work."

In addition to being out of work, Robert was dealing with health problems he could not afford to get diagnosed or treated because he had no health insurance. Still, his religious faith helped him persevere. In between pauses to manage his pain, he said, "I don't believe God wants this for me" because "He only wants what's good for me." Robert tried to see the positive side of his unemployment and health problems: "To go through the pain and the struggles and everything—I believe it'll only make me stronger. And in some way, down the road, I might be able to share this with somebody else, if they're having problems."

Each of my sixty-four participants had an interesting life story, and I share more of them in subsequent chapters. For now, these five examples suffice to illustrate the variety of meanings of work and unemployment that I explore in this book.

For example, productivist work meanings like Terrance West's dislike of feeling lazy are different from consumerist work meanings like Robert Milner's goal of earning enough to afford a single-family home and other accoutrements of a middle-class life. Isabel Navarro and ReNé McKnight wanted to get ahead, but for Terrance West and Robert Milner later in life, it was more important to have a steady job and pay the bills.

Some of the men, like Terrance West, felt like "less of a man" because they were not working. Yet none of the unemployed women said she felt like less of a woman while out of work, even though they were as likely as the unemployed men to suffer emotionally and feel diminished as persons. Still, gender roles are changing, as was evident in Robert Milner's secret resentment that his wife was unable to contribute financially. Those changes played out differently in relationships depending on the interviewees' class, gender, sexuality, and prior work histories.

These five stories also show the culturally constructed ways my participants thought about their jobs and occupational paths. As I will explain, some, like Isabel Navarro, cared about getting ahead more than which occupation took them to that destination; others, like ReNé McKnight and Katarina Spelling, felt a "passion" or "calling" to pursue an occupation that was especially meaningful for them. However, available cultural categories like those of a "passion" or "calling," or the difference between a "career" and a "job" that Katarina also drew on, fail to describe what I call a "good-enough occupation," which Terrance, Isabel, Katarina, and Robert all found. Many participants, like Robert, described at least one of their jobs as "fun"; I will explore the implications of their considering their jobs "fun" for how they thought about paid work.

Their experiences of being unemployed were also shaped by their values and beliefs about how to obtain financial assistance while retaining their self-respect. Isabel Navarro proudly refused to apply for food stamps, but she "swallowed [her] pride" and let her boyfriend support her, even though she would not have lived with him if she could have supported herself. ReNé McKnight made the opposite choice: she did not want any man to think she only cared about his money, so she did not date while she was unemployed. Instead, she obtained food stamps and a small welfare cash grant to support herself and her daughter. Interestingly, Isabel accepted financial assistance from her son, unlike many others who were horrified by the idea of asking their grown children for financial help.

Finally, my participants differed in the discourses they used to make sense of their troubles and talk about them with others. The Christian faith that sustained Katarina Spelling, ReNé McKnight, and Robert Milner provided a framework, shared by many Americans, for putting their struggles in a larger context. As I explain later in the chapter, their religious beliefs and other popular discourses in the United States provide alternatives to individualistic explanations that foster self-blame.

I would not say that my participants are representative of all Americans. My aim is not to claim representativeness, which few qualitative studies can achieve, but rather to explore diversity. By considering Americans in a wide range of occupations and of varying backgrounds, we can begin to see the inadequacies of descriptions of work meanings that do not take account of culture or that take a society's work meanings to be homogeneous and unchanging.

Cultural Meanings Matter

It is easy to find theories of work meanings that ignore cultural differences and changes over time. One place to look for such theories is in speculative commentary about what life would be like were AI and automation to displace much of human labor. Some writers imagine that a mostly work-free future would be a paradise; others depict it as hellish.[5] Although the predictions are starkly different, they rely on presumed universal meanings of working.

The utopian visions postulate a future in which the necessities of life are inexpensive and can be obtained with the assistance of a universal basic income, leaving people free to spend most of their time doing whatever they want to do instead of being forced to earn a living. People could devote more of their time to caring for others, lifelong learning, politics, or pleasurable pursuits. Post-work theorists Stanley Aronowitz and William DiFazio claim, "When they are given the opportunity, workers—skilled and unskilled alike— are pleased to be relieved of participation in the labor process provided they are guaranteed an income adequate to the current 'decent' standard of living."[6]

As the sociologist Peter Frase puts it succinctly, "Wage labor sucks, and a lot of people will only do it if the alternative is destitution."[7]

By contrast, another group of theorists view a future in which most adults do not work for a living as a dystopia of stunted lives shorn of material comforts, purpose, and dignity. For example, in *The Second Machine Age*, management theorists Erik Brynjolfsson and Andrew McAfee are awed by the productive potential of new digital technologies but worry about the consequences for workers displaced by machines; they believe people do not want to be liberated from working. Brynjolfsson and McAfee write, "It's tremendously important for people to work not just because that's how they get their money, but also because it's one of the principal ways they get many other important things: self-worth, community, engagement, healthy values, structure, and dignity, to name just a few." Based on a cross-national Gallup survey, they conclude, "It seems that all around the world, people want to escape the evils of boredom, vice, and need and instead find mastery, autonomy, and purpose by working."[8]

The dystopian theorists draw on important research by the social psychologist Marie Jahoda, who argues that humans need paid work in their lives. Jahoda was the lead author of a classic ethnographic analysis of unemployment, *Marienthal*, a study of the consequences of shuttering a factory that had been the main employer in a small Austrian town in the 1930s. Drawing on such research from the Depression, as well as studies of the effects of unemployment during the deep US recession of the early 1980s, Jahoda argues that unemployment deprives adults in modern society not only of money but also of psychologically important immaterial benefits: "time structure, social contacts, the experience of social purposes, status and identity, and regular activity."[9]

Utopian images of a creative, leisurely post-work future are diametrically opposed to the dystopian images of boredom and vice. Yet, both assume that work means the same thing for all humans. Based on their assumptions about either the inessential or essential place of waged work in a good life, theorists from these opposing camps arrive at confident predictions about how all (or, at least, most) people everywhere would react to a work-less future. Both approaches fail to consider that, in this imagined society of the future, there will probably arise new ways of living and thinking about a good life. The result will be new subjective meanings of working and not working, ones that differ from subjectivities formed under industrial capitalism in the global North.

The very idea of unemployment is new in human history. As the historian John Garraty points out, unemployment was not considered a social problem until the late nineteenth century. In his words, unemployment is a disease of capitalism because it depends on an economic system in which most people sell their labor to an employer to sustain a living.[10] Only people who enter into an ongoing contract to work for someone else can become unemployed. In societies that depend primarily on foraging and hunting, hunters do not think of themselves as unemployed when they rest between hunting expeditions.[11] Farmers working on their own land or peasants bound to a lord can harvest too little to survive, but their problem is not a lack of employment. Nor would a self-employed artist, craftsperson, shopkeeper, or other business owner ever be considered unemployed, even if their business was unprofitable. As Garraty puts it, "Only those who work for wages or a salary, who are at liberty to quit their jobs yet who may also be deprived of them by someone else, can become unemployed."[12] Thus, unemployment is only conceivable in societies in which most people work for wages.[13]

Employment in a formal economy of regulated, continuing jobs is not the global norm; at present, 61 percent of the global population works in the informal economy.[14] Given current digital information and communication technologies that enable new forms of self-employment and hybrid forms of employment—for example, independent contractors who work for others, such as ride-hail drivers—unemployment could cease to be a meaningful social construct in the future, as I explain in chapter 7.

Work has not always been considered necessary for dignity and purpose. In the 1830s, Alexis de Tocqueville traveled from France to the United States to study Americans' values and institutions, which he expected would spread to Europe with the rise of democratic institutions. Among many other observations, he was struck by the fact that because there was relatively little hereditary wealth in the United States, it was common for men of all classes to work: "Everything therefore prompts the assumption that to work is the necessary, natural, and honest condition of all men. Not only is no dishonor associated with work, but among such peoples it is regarded as positively honorable."[15] Notice Tocqueville's surprise about the high value placed on work. Coming from the aristocracy, he did not assume that working is a necessary source of self-esteem and dignity for all people. Instead, the social respect accorded to working for pay struck him as a curious new development. He commented that some rich Americans moved to Europe because "there they find the relics of aristocratic societies in which leisure is still honorable."[16] As Tocqueville clarifies, among the European aristocracy, work can be honorable but only "when inspired by ambition or pure virtue." What was dishonorable was working just to earn money, and that too was a contrast with the attitudes he observed in the United States in the 1830s, where making money seemed to be the point of all work.

When Tocqueville writes, "Work is the necessary, natural, and honest condition of all men" in America, he may have meant "men" to be gender inclusive; more likely, he was not thinking about women, given the gender roles in the United States at that time. Adult women are not always and everywhere expected to engage in waged work, so how can work meanings be universal?

Subjective meanings of not working also depend on social expectations about when one's working years begin and end. In some societies and in some economic classes, preadolescents are expected to help contribute to the family's income, and by their late teens and early twenties young adults are expected to be self-supporting; in other societies and classes, working years typically begin later. There is also variation around the world regarding the end of the working years; that is, the age when adults are allowed, expected, or legally required to stop waged work. Thus, cultural conceptions of the life course and mandatory retirement age laws or job stipulations affect meanings of not working, as do accepted nonmarket ways of sustaining a living through assistance from kin, local communities, and the state.[17]

In sum, the meanings of working and not working could never be the same for all humans throughout time.

Multiple Cultural Meanings of Work

Some commentators do take culture into account when they contemplate the prospect of a possible future in which adults would not spend most of their time at paid work. They argue that a future without steady work would be especially difficult for US Americans because hard work is venerated in this society. In a thoughtful examination of the cultural effects of automation's predicted displacement of large numbers of American workers, the journalist Derek Thompson writes, "The transition from labor force to leisure force would likely be particularly hard on Americans, the worker becs of the rich world." He notes, "Richer, college-educated Americans are working *more* than they did 30 years ago, particularly when you count time working and answering e-mail at home." He states, however, that this dedication to work is not new: "Industriousness has served as America's unofficial religion since its founding. The sanctity and preeminence of work lie at the heart of the country's politics, economics, and social interactions."[18]

Observations about Americans' devotion to work have been offered for nearly two centuries, as we saw in Tocqueville's surprise that among the Americans he observed in the 1830s, work for pay "is regarded as positively honorable" and is not limited to those who are forced to work by economic necessity.[19]

Political philosopher Judith Shklar argues that in the United States paid employment is necessary for full social standing and inclusion. She writes, "The dignity of work and of personal achievement, and the contempt for aristocratic idleness, have since Colonial times been an important part of American civic self-identification."[20] A 1980s guide for international visitors to the United States explains that Americans are "known as 'workaholics,' or people who are addicted to their work, who think constantly about their jobs and who are frustrated if they are kept away from them, even during their evening hours and weekends."[21] Recent cultural descriptions echo these themes.[22]

These standard descriptions of American cultural meanings of work are voiced by ordinary Americans as well. We saw that in Robert Milner's comment: "Here, we're so go, go, go. We're chasing that almighty dollar." In an online comment on a news article about skimpier economic protections for workers in the United States compared to other wealthy countries, someone wrote, "In the US, I think we believe life is for working hard. We are always trying to make that extra dollar thinking it will buy happiness. I'm not sure it will ever change in the US. The Protestant work ethic is part of our cultural DNA."[23]

I explain the problem with speaking of "our cultural DNA" shortly. At this point, notice that these commentators are all saying that Americans work hard, but they give different reasons for it.

One motivator for long work hours could be the desire to afford a better standard of living. That seems to be what the commentator meant by this statement: "We are always trying to make that extra dollar thinking it will buy happiness." Working hard for the sake of "buying happiness" is also what Robert Milner meant when he said of Americans like him, "We're chasing that almighty dollar." However, that is just one reason why Americans could be driven to work hard.

Another motivator for hard work can be the desire to be self-supporting. Americans are often called "rugged individualists" because adults try to avoid financial dependence on other people or the state. Those who work low-wage jobs may need to work long hours out of necessity if they want to be self-supporting.

Sanctifying paid employment, and making it a prerequisite for full social standing, means that one has a social duty to be a waged worker; yet one can value holding a job and being a conscientious worker without wanting to work all the time. Robert Milner said he worked hard while at his job, but he did not like working long hours: "Although I work to live, I don't live to work." Furthermore, not everyone has the kind of job in which work can be completed on evenings and weekends; there would have been no way for Terrance West to bring home his warehouse or convenience store work, even if he had wanted to do so. He could answer occasional phone calls at night, but most of his tasks required his onsite presence.

Finally, there are those "who think constantly about their jobs and who are frustrated if they are kept away from them, even during their evening hours and weekends." They willingly work long hours because their work is central to their identity and interests. These people certainly exist—they were among the participants in my study—but they are only a portion of US workers, not the majority. However, this unusual minority who lives to work may be more visible to commentators than the quiet majority of those who are conscientious but not obsessive about their jobs. Furthermore, only some of those who live to work are "workaholics" in the clinical sense. As I explain in the next chapter, "workaholism" has a technical meaning of work addiction driven by feelings of anxiety or guilt, and it differs from fulfilling work engagement.[24]

One of my key points in this book is that when people speak of Americans' work ethic—that is, their willingness to work hard—they can mean four things: (1) working hard to be self-supporting—which I call *working to live*; (2) working hard to afford a comfortable or affluent standard of living—which I term *working to live well*; (3) willingly working long hours because work is central to one's identity and interests—which I call a *living-to-work ethic*; and (4) being a conscientious worker during regular work hours—which I term a *diligent 9-to-5 work ethic* (figure 1.1).[25]

With the first and second work motivations—working to live and working to live well—the primary goal of working is to earn money. Working hard to support oneself, or to live well, is not what Max Weber meant when he wrote about the "Protestant Work Ethic."[26] For Weber, the Protestant work ethic made work a moral duty, hence an end in itself. (To avoid any connotation that it applies to Protestants only, I prefer the term "productivist work ethic.")

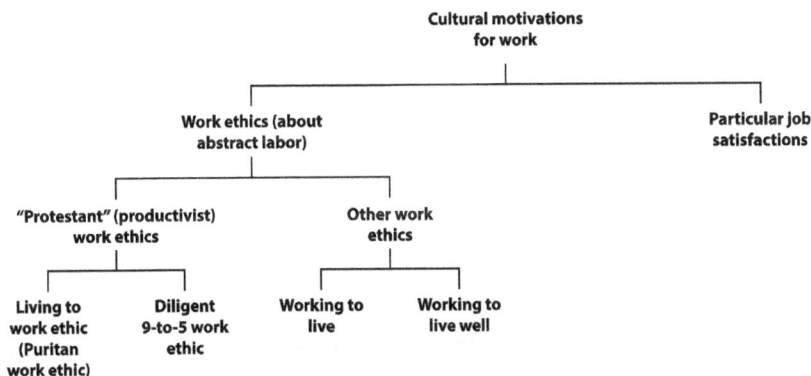

FIGURE 1.1.   Work motivations

Weber's important insight was that work valued for its own sake is not the same as work valued for the sake of the income it brings. However, as I explain in chapter 2, Weber never clearly differentiated two forms of a productivist ethic: a moral duty to be a conscientious worker during one's assigned work hours (a diligent 9-to-5 work ethic) and the restless urge to keep working all the time (a living-to-work ethic). Only the latter should be termed a Puritan work ethic. These distinctions matter because they lead to different ways of working, different ways of balancing waged work and the rest of life, and different feelings and behaviors when one is unemployed.

These work motivations are not mutually exclusive: many of my participants were motivated by more than one of them. For example, ReNé McKnight walked two miles to her job as a home health aide and two miles home to support herself and her daughter (working to live), and she threw herself into business ventures that would make her prosperous (working to live well). She valued doing her job well (both productivist work ethics), and she thought up new business ideas because she was a high achiever and because staying busy all the time helped her deal with her mental health struggles (a living-to-work ethic).

ReNé was also driven by a sense that there was a certain kind of work she was meant to do: helping others who were mentally ill or had experienced trauma. She had a passion for that field of work; for her, it was a calling in the original religious sense. She was not only dedicated to working generally but was also driven to perform a particular kind of work—which is not covered by any of the work ethics I listed, for reasons that are interesting to explore.

The "work ethic" construct is not about a passion for a particular occupation or simple enjoyment of one's job, for two reasons. First, a "work ethic" connotes devotion to labor in an abstract sense—that is, devotion to paid labor in general—rather than engagement with a specific job. Second, having "a good work ethic" suggests having the fortitude to do something that is intrinsically unpleasant. However, not all work is unpleasant. Some jobs, like Robert Milner's, are stimulating; some offer the satisfaction of being needed by one's employers, contributing to a team, and being recognized for one's contributions, as Terrance West and Katarina Spelling experienced; some are fun because they include enjoyable social interactions with coworkers, as Katarina also found. Most have both enjoyable and unpleasant aspects. It is meaningless to ask whether "work sucks" or instead is a source of "mastery, autonomy, or purpose." Some jobs are the pits, and people are happier unemployed, at least for a while, than having to do those jobs every day. Other jobs are enjoyable or even deeply meaningful, and losing such work is a blow. Terrance was heartbroken when the job he loved so much at the sweet snack company ended; he spoke of it like a jilted lover. He did not feel the same way about the jobs where he was harassed. Yet, too often commentators talk about a "work ethic" as a character trait separate from people's feelings about the specific work they are doing.

Most of this book is devoted to describing these differing ways my participants thought about their work and how each cultural model affected their experience of being unemployed. Chapter 2 discusses the two Protestant (productivist) work ethics; chapter 3, working to live well; chapter 4, working to live; and chapter 6, work motivations related to specific occupations and jobs. As I will explain, these different ways of thinking about work also provide distinctive ways of constructing a class identity. Is one's class defined by being a productive worker, rather than someone who is idle? Or by one's level of consumption or by being able to pay for one's living expenses and be financially self-reliant? Or is it defined by the kind of tasks required in one's job?[27]

Describing Cultural Meanings

Cultural anthropologists have long recognized that folk cultural descriptions, the ones that circulate as popular national self-understandings, are subject to distortions. There is a cultural politics of representation: only some commentators are recognized as having the expertise to offer up cultural pronouncements, and those representations often serve political purposes. Contemporary cultural anthropologists have criticized essentializing descriptions and their baleful political effects, although their criticism is usually focused on homogenizing, static descriptions of non-Western societies.[28] However, essentializing descriptions of the United States are just as problematic.

For example, a 2018 White House Council of Economic Advisors report begins, "The American work ethic, the motivation that drives Americans to work longer hours each week and more weeks each year than any of our economic peers, is a long-standing contributor to America's success."[29] This rhetorical invocation of "the American work ethic" served a specific purpose in the report—to support stricter work requirements and so diminish reliance on government-funded health insurance, food stamps, and subsidized housing. True Americans, it seems, work long hours; everyone else has no desire to work, leaving out the vast middle ground of all those who do want to work but not to the exclusion of everything else they care about.[30]

Contemporary cultural anthropologists question the generalizations implied in a phrase like "the American work ethic," and they definitively reject the assumptions underlying the statement that any value is part of a "cultural DNA." That biological analogy assumes that a culture is a singular entity, a bounded organism that reproduces itself over time. That is not how we anthropologists currently think about culture. "Culture" is not a singular thing, nor should we imagine it like a vapor suspended over a nation or social group. Instead, it is a gloss for a messy collection of things, from the "Sunday best" values trotted out for special occasions to unexamined everyday assumptions that may be quite different. I use "culture" as shorthand for referring to public artifacts, discourses, and shared practices, along with people's learned understandings, which are the basis for constructing those public elements and are in turn constructed by them. It follows that this bundle of different things we call culture cannot have boundaries. Nation-states have defined borders, but the various things that constitute culture are not bound by international treaties. Artifacts, practices, and discourses spread across political borders and have differing meanings for various social groups within them.[31] Some artifacts, practices, discourses, and understandings are long-standing and mutually reinforcing; others clash and change over time.[32] Someone living in the United States may hear speeches extolling the dignity of work, positive or negative comments by relatives and friends about their jobs, thought leaders urging high ambitions and thought leaders who promote inner peace, dramas that glorify heroic exciting jobs and sitcoms set in dysfunctional offices. If we are to describe cultural meanings of work in the United States, we must include them all.

My concern about essentializing cultural descriptions is amplified by the theories and methods I follow as a psychological anthropologist. Psychological anthropologists examine the subjective meanings of shared discourses and institutions. Our approach is person-centered, meaning that we begin with how particular people think, feel, remember, experience, and act.[33] Thus, for the most part, my primary sources are not books, speeches, movies, or television shows, even though studies of public culture are invaluable and I include some examples of sources that mattered to my participants. The sources that mattered to them were usually ones I would never have thought to examine.

Yet, if one examines only the public side of culture, it is easy to make assumptions about the meanings they impart. Not all cultural anthropologists would agree about this, but I have argued that meanings do not reside in public discourses, artifacts, and practices. Instead, those things are endowed with meanings by persons whose interpretations are socially learned but selectively filtered and colored by their personal histories and values.[34] Thus, I speak of "Americans' cultural meanings" rather than "meanings in American culture." "Americans' cultural meanings" can be diverse, whereas "meanings in American culture" implies that American culture is a single thing.

To analyze people's meanings, I paid attention not only to what they said but also to how they expressed their views. For example, when Robert Milner stated proudly, "We got married. We bought the home. [. . .] We have two kids.

That whole—you know?" he assumed that this cultural model of a desirable life needed neither further elaboration nor defense. Similarly, he did not explain or defend his comment, "I don't live to work." In both comments, his wording suggests he believes his attitudes about what matters in life have a strong *cultural standing*. The cultural standing of a view is its perceived acceptance in a social group.[35] My participants treated some ideas about working and not working in the United States as commonsensical and others as more debatable or controversial. Through cultural standing analysis, which I illustrate in subsequent chapters, we can see not only which views were frequently stated by my participants but also, and more importantly, which views they thought were widely shared in their social circles.

My discourse analysis also considered what my participants left unsaid, including the implicit cultural models they drew on to understand their experience. A cultural model is a shared schema, a simplified holistic mental representation.[36] These schemas furnish much of the taken-for-granted assumptions everyone acquires while growing up. They include cultural models of a good life, cultural models of a normal life for someone like you, and cultural models of the social categories that underlie judgments about who is "like you" and who is not. In ordinary conversation, it is rarely necessary to make all these understandings explicit. Researchers can ask about them, but people always leave unspoken more than they say. Thus, my analysis attends not only to what my participants said and how they said it but also to what they implied rather than stated.[37]

Types of Unemployment

Being out of work is not a uniform state. The experience depends on the political and economic system, as well as typical labor markets for different types of workers. As I already discussed, the experience of being out of work also depends on the availability of options for sustaining a living—assistance from the state, community, and family—other than daily waged labor. Gender roles matter. Are both men and women expected to hold paying jobs? Is regular waged work a prerequisite for having a committed life partner or beginning a family? At a larger level, what is taken as normal in the society for different social groups at different life stages, and what is the place of work in a good life?[38]

The experience of unemployment also depends on whether there have been wrenching changes in local labor markets. These affect whether the worker planned or foresaw being out of work; how long they are out of work in relation to how long they had expected to be out of work; and their prospects for occupational continuity—that is, whether they expect to be able to find the kind of work in which they have experience or training or instead will need to train for a new occupation. Subjectively, it also matters to the unemployed whether they are hearing sympathy for their situation in the current public discourse or instead are being publicly blamed for their plight. When unemployment is widespread and generally understood to be due to causes beyond the control of the displaced workers, as was the case at the beginning of the COVID-19 pandemic in the spring of 2020, there is usually greater public sympathy and more financial assistance from the government. That kind of unemployment is easier to bear than the isolation, stigma, and inadequate assistance experienced by those who cannot find work during a time of generally low unemployment.[39]

These varying conditions matter for unemployed people's ability to imagine the future and plan for it financially and psychologically. Fundamentally, these varying conditions shape the very sense of self for those not working and the way other people see them.

We can see those differences when comparing ethnographies of unemployment in the United States. Some of these studies depict the human costs of factory closings in the late 1970s and 1980s, which were devastating for the permanently displaced workers. By contrast, more recent descriptions of managerial and professional workers in well-paid but insecure postindustrial jobs show them as unconcerned—or even relieved—by short periods of unemployment.

The experience of my participants that I describe in the rest of this book does not fit either of these scenarios. They did not feel that life as they had known it was over, but they did not take their unemployment in stride as normal and expected either. It is important to understand how these contexts differ just in one country, never mind in entirely different political and economic contexts, which I discuss as well.

Factory Closings in a Fordist Economy

Descriptions of displaced workers' reactions to the wave of factory closings in the United States in the late 1970s and 1980s highlight their shock at the crumbling of all they had taken for granted. They had little experience with unemployment and few prospects for another job similar to the one they lost.[40]

Economists call this *structural unemployment*, which "occurs because of a geographic or skill mismatch between workers and employers."[41] One type of work ends, and the displaced workers do not have the right skills to qualify for other available jobs in the area with similar or better pay. Most economists see structural unemployment as a normal market problem, requiring only a better matchup of those out of work with available positions.[42]

Yet, what appears to be a relatively untroubling situation from a bird's-eye view of the economy can feel like a disaster to those who lost their jobs. There are many heart-wrenching accounts of workers devastated by the closure of factories that had furnished well-paid blue-collar jobs. Middle-aged and older factory workers could not easily relocate across the country or suddenly transform themselves into knowledge-economy workers.

The anthropologist Christine Walley provides a moving depiction of what happened to her father after the steel mill where he worked in Chicago closed in 1980. Charles Walley and the other steel mill workers thought they would work at the same plant until they retired, because that had been the norm in their industry as far back as they could remember. It was not that the work itself was so wonderful; it was dirty and dangerous. However, it paid well. The closing of the steel mills was the permanent end to a way of life, and it was unclear what the displaced workers could do next. The jobs Charles Walley eventually obtained—tollbooth attendant, janitor, security guard—did not pay nearly as well, were not stable, and for the most part did not offer the same camaraderie as his shear operator job at the steel mill.[43] Initially, Charles Walley fell into a depressive stupor, refusing to shave, change his clothes, or leave the house. Others he had worked with became alcoholics. Some ended their lives.[44]

Those factory closings in the US Northeast and Midwest marked the end of the Fordist period of industrial capitalism. During that period, if workers submitted to dull, repetitive factory work, they could receive a wage sufficient to buy cars and household appliances, followed by a secure pension after they retired. Fordism refers to "mass production, relatively high wages, and mass consumption" leading to predictable, increasing incomes, with predictability partly insured by the state through assistance to the unemployed, permanently disabled, and retirees.[45] That predictability started to end in the late 1970s. Subjectively, factory workers thrown out of work at that time were still Fordist in a world that was changing, upending the life course they had expected.

High-Churn Fields in a Post-Fordist Economy

The post-Fordist period began following the mid-1970s recession in much of the West.[46] Global competition and automation weakened workers' bargaining power, as did the rise of neoliberal ideologies about the importance of "flexible labor" practices. Flexible labor is not (as one might think) about workers' ability to adapt to new jobs or tasks. Instead, for economists, "flexible labor" means that firms are free of regulations about hiring and firing workers and setting their wages and working conditions. To achieve this flexibility, large corporations and their ideological allies attacked mandated labor protections and replaced full-time, permanent employees with ones hired on short-term contracts.[47] As Karen Ho explains in an illuminating ethnography of Wall Street investment bankers, job insecurity was also exacerbated by the shareholder revolution of the 1980s and 1990s, when the focus of corporations came to be not just making a profit but also continually increasing the value of their stock. Mass layoffs often improve a company's stock price because they demonstrate that the company is committed to a "lean, mean operation."[48] All these forces gradually made jobs less secure, and in some fields, workers now accept job insecurity as normal.

Ho describes Wall Street analysts working in "a culture of insecurity and competition" in which they rarely last at their positions more than a couple of years. They are seldom promoted; more often, they leave or are fired. When Ho and the other analysts in her group were laid off in the late 1990s, two of her coworkers commented, "On Wall Street, everyone is rather desensitized to layoffs." The analysts quickly found other well-compensated jobs. Ho writes, "Though constant, their experiences of job insecurity were so seemingly well tolerated and expected that it hardly seemed as if it had happened."[49]

The anthropologist Carrie Lane found the same relatively untroubled acceptance of layoffs when she interviewed high-tech workers in Texas who lost their jobs during the recession of the early 2000s. Among software developers and other information technology professionals, neither employers nor the workers expected a long-term commitment, so workers were used to periodic bouts of unemployment.[50] Some had found their jobs stressful and appreciated what they anticipated to be a short break. Being unemployed under those circumstances can be an opportunity to relax a bit between stints of high-pressure work and to enjoy "funemployment," to use a term I heard recently.[51] They experienced no stigma for alternating between periods of lucrative employment and short periods of unemployment. Lane quotes a high-tech worker who contrasts his tough-minded readiness to manage his own career through the vicissitudes of short-term jobs and periodic layoffs with "the 'suckers' and 'victims' who perceive job security as a possibility, let alone a right."[52]

This is a kind of unemployment that economists call "frictional": the typically short-term unemployment that occurs when workers first enter the job market or are looking for a new job because they left their old one or were let go.[53] If this period of unemployment does not last much longer than the job seekers expected, and if they find another job in the same field or one they like better, the layoff becomes a short detour in their life's journey, rather than the end of the road.

Still, not all frictional unemployment is the same. It seems to be easier to bear when it is relatively short and is commonplace in their field. It is also easier to bear when the unemployed workers had been well paid and had savings, a severance package, unemployment compensation, or a spouse or partner's income to help them through their time out of work.[54]

The Limbo of Post-Fordist Long-Term Unemployment

My participants' unemployment in southern California following the Great Recession of 2007–9 does not fit either of these scenarios. They did not react to being out of work with the complete shock of displaced workers when their factories closed in the 1980s following decades of post-war economic growth, but nor did they take losing their job in stride with the "So what else is new?" nonchalance of those accustomed to post-Fordist short-term jobs. Instead, they described an unemployment experience that was subjectively distinct.[55]

Economists term unemployment during a recession as "cyclical." Cyclical unemployment "rises during economic downturns and falls when the economy improves; it is the extra unemployment that occurs during recessions."[56] It furrows economists' and policy makers' brows more than does structural or frictional unemployment because there are not enough jobs for all those who want them, and without aggressive government intervention, reduced consumer demand leads to even more job losses.

Yet, although cyclical unemployment is the most worrisome kind from a larger perspective, for my participants, it was easier to bear than structural unemployment (to translate their narratives into economic jargon). For one thing, they did not have to deal with the crushing finality experienced by those whose factories closed and had no hope of finding work that was even remotely the same. None of my participants was in an occupation or industry that was ending; all expected, at first, to be able to find another job in the same or a similar field.

Furthermore, unemployment occurring long after the onset of post-Fordist flexible labor practices did not come as a complete shock, as other studies of unemployed US workers conducted at the same time found as well.[57] Nearly all my participants had been laid off before, as had others in their social circles. Furthermore, their job loss occurred during or shortly after a recession when official unemployment levels reached 10 percent nationwide and even higher in southern California.[58] Some had anticipated losing their jobs.

Yet, their unemployment was challenging. None of my participants was in a high-churn field like finance or software development, so frequent bouts of unemployment were not routine in their occupations. They were also out of work much longer than anticipated. Although my participants knew the economy was sluggish, their expectations for how quickly they would find another job were based not on the current state of the economy but on their experience the last time they had looked for work, which had occurred under different economic conditions.

In the United States, if someone has been out of work and on the job market for more than six months (twenty-seven weeks or longer), they are classified as long-term unemployed. Employers discriminate against an applicant who has been out of work that long because they figure that if no one else has hired the job seeker in that time, there must be something wrong with them. There is experimental research showing that employers are more likely to interview applicants with no relevant experience but less than six months of unemployment than to consider applicants who had relevant experience but more than six months of unemployment.[59] Thus, cruelly, long-term unemployment begets even longer-term unemployment.

The Great Recession—the most severe economic downturn in the United States since the Great Depression of the 1930s—created unprecedented levels of long-term unemployment.[60] From 1948 through 2008, the average length of unemployment in the United States never exceeded twenty-two weeks. By July 2011, it was nearly double that, at close to forty-one weeks.[61] What made the Great Recession and the years that followed so difficult for those out of work were how long it took them to find another job and the fact that they were unprepared for long-term unemployment. For most job seekers, the past provided no precedent to be out of work for three-quarters of a year or longer.

Of course, forty-one weeks is only an average; some of the unemployed were out of work a shorter time, whereas others were unemployed longer—sometimes much longer. I am writing in the aftermath of the COVID-19 pandemic when there is a tight labor market, making it easy to obtain entry-level jobs, but it was quite different after the Great Recession. In that slack labor market, anyone with a strike against them might be out of work well beyond a year. Experiments have found that fictional applicants in the United States who are well qualified but have a nonjob-related disability (for example, applicants for an accounting position with a spinal cord injury or who are on the autism spectrum), who are age fifty or older (especially women in that age group), who have what appears to be an African American or Asian name, who mention leadership in an LGBTQ organization (depending on the state where the employer is located), or who indicate they are Muslim, Catholic, or pagan are less likely to be called for interviews than those without such a disability, who are in their late twenties or early thirties, who have what employers interpret as a European American name, or who leave no clues about their sexual orientation or religious beliefs.[62] In a slack labor market, anyone with a criminal record may be ruled out right away.[63] A poor credit score also hurts. This is another example of a vicious circle: losing income can result in a poor credit score, and then a poor credit score can make it harder to find another job.[64] High-income earners also tend to be out of work longer because it can be hard for them to adjust their salary expectations to the buyer's market during a recession. Any of these factors could lead to long-term unemployment, which as mentioned earlier is also a strike against a job applicant. Most of my research participants had one or more of these strikes against them, which is why they were out of work for a long time and were interested in talking to me.

When my participants shared their life stories, they seemed not to consider their unemployment as a life-altering event. Being out of work felt like a suspension of normality, not a radical disjuncture—at least, not right away. Still, they did not know how long their unemployment would last, which made it hard to plan. When Claudia C. and I conducted our initial interviews from the fall of 2011 through the summer of 2012, nearly every participant had not had a full-time job in more than six months, three-quarters had been out of work for more than a year, and about a third had not had a full-time job in more than two years. They were financially and psychologically unprepared to be out of work that long.

Yet, by 2012 there were some job openings in their fields, the recession was officially over, and experts kept predicting that hiring would pick up again soon. This left my participants in a fog of uncertainty. Should they hold out for their ideal job, take any job that was available and for which they qualified, or re-train for another field? Should they sell their house and move to smaller quarters, or were such drastic measures unnecessary because, surely, they would find work again soon? Maybe they could hold on by drawing down their retirement savings. One of my participants described her feeling of not knowing what to do: "It's like I'm doing a term paper, but I don't have any footnotes. I have no references. I have no guidelines. I have nobody telling me where to go, or how to do it, or this is the precedent. I have nothing." There has been too little attention paid to this limbo-state experience of unemployment that drags on for months and years.

So far, I have only described historical change and varying types of unemployment in the United States. Anthropologists of unemployment elsewhere depict additional forms it can take and other ways of thinking and feeling about not working.

As the anthropologist Jack Friedman notes, economic precarity as a new situation for the individual is more disruptive of one's place in society and sense of self than precarity normalized as "the violence of everyday life."[65] Disruption was severe after postsocialist societies like China and Romania privatized state-owned enterprises. Under state socialism, workers in those factories and mines had been glorified as the hardworking proletariat, but when they became unemployed or precariously underemployed in the new market-dominated economy, they felt cast out of society and betrayed by the state.[66] Many reacted with anger because the loss of their livelihood could be traced to specific political actors rather than invisible market forces, which dominant US discourses offer as an explanation for layoffs. By contrast, in Scandinavian social democracies there is relatively generous support for the unemployed. In return, they feel an immense obligation to return to work so they can pay taxes that fund the welfare state.[67]

Precarity is more normalized in societies with chronic, high unemployment rates. In urban Ethiopia in the 1990s and early 2000s, the unemployment rate among young men was estimated at more than 50 percent, and on average they were out of work for almost four years.[68] When one anthropologist asked some of these jobless men whether there was any shame in being out of work for so long, "They were usually surprised by this question. They explained that a condition shared by so many people could not be considered shameful."[69] Similarly, in South Africa, where unemployment rates have never been lower than 20 percent since record keeping began in 1994, many have learned to find sources of self-respect and a meaningful life in ways other than through a steady job.[70]

In sum, the political and economic context shape the experience of those without work. Dominant discourses do as well, as we can see from these examples. What other discourses (beyond those about market forces) are available to those facing economic adversity in the United States?

Cultural Resources for Making Meaning and Coping

It is common for those who study the ideologies available to unemployed Americans to divide them into two alternatives: individualistic ideologies and collectivist ideologies.[71] As I explain shortly, those are not the only alternatives, but let us start with them.

Individualistic ideologies are more common than collectivist ideologies in the United States due to the common discourse that anyone can get ahead with talent and hard work. According to this discourse, it is up to you whether you end up rich, poor, or somewhere in between. Some researchers have found that this ideology of meritocratic individualism makes long-term unemployment psychologically more difficult for the unemployed because they blame themselves for their situation.[72]

Surprisingly, I found only occasional self-blame among my participants for their continuing unemployment. Some blamed themselves for the missteps that led to their job loss, but they tried (not always successfully) to avoid self-blame in understanding why they had been out of work for so long.

One reason they tried to avoid self-blame is that it could impede their job search. Career counselors advised not blaming yourself for being out of work because doing so would undermine the self-confidence that job seekers need to project to potential employers. To sell yourself, you must build yourself up, not tear yourself down. If you start believing something is wrong with you, that it truly is your fault you are not working, it will make the job search much harder. When I asked Stephen Smith, a displaced executive, whether he ever blamed himself, as his wife did, for being out of work for nearly three years when we met, he replied, "I can't go there. I'd give up the fight." This "no shoulda, woulda, coulda" mindset discourages regrets. It is resolutely forward looking.[73]

Selling yourself also means protecting yourself emotionally, because you are the product you are selling, as I heard a career counselor explain. Thus, it means taking time for self-care, such as listening to upbeat music, meditating, and exercising. These self-care practices helped my participants cope with long-term unemployment.[74]

It also helped that my participants knew that unemployment rates were high at that time following the Great Recession and that they were not alone. I met many of them through career counseling sessions and support groups for the unemployed. Those meetings helped my participants build a shared identity as morally worthy people who worked hard at trying to find another job.[75]

Widespread economic insecurity received a political framing when the Occupy movement spread throughout the country shortly after I began my research in the fall of 2011. Occupy protestors shifted blame away from individual job seekers, focusing instead on the commercial lenders and investment bankers whose predatory mortgage lending practices and financial instruments had caused the Great Recession. I noticed a sharp uptick in my participants' collectivist interpretations of the Great Recession after the Occupy movement began. However, their political views varied, and only two became active with Occupy or related movements at that time.[76] For the majority, what proved to be more meaningful than a political-economic framing were their spiritual outlooks and positive thinking discourses.

Some of the most important cultural resources for my participants were their religious and spiritual beliefs, which are neither individualistic nor collectivistic. Katarina Spelling, Robert Milner, and ReNé McKnight were not alone in drawing on their Christian faith to understand their circumstances. I had not anticipated this phenomenon—perhaps because I am not religious myself. At that time, some southern California churches hosted support groups for the unemployed, but I found only one participant that way. Still, many of my participants said that their unemployment was part of God's plan for them. For example, Ann Lopez, an unemployed IT worker, explained, "I believe in God. So, I do believe that he has a plan for me and I leave it in his hands." That did not mean that she, or anyone else, sat back and waited for a miracle. Devout Christians engaged in the same job search efforts as everyone else, but with the balm of believing their time out of work was meant to be. Some saw their extended period of unemployment as a spiritual trial. They took comfort from the belief that ultimately the Lord has "plans to prosper you and not to harm you, plans to give you hope and a future" (Jeremiah 29:11), as a discussion leader explained when I attended a Career Coaching and Counseling Ministry lecture at an evangelical megachurch.

Contemporary Christian preaching in many churches departs from earlier theological interpretations of economic misfortunes. In Edward Wight Bakke's comprehensive study of unemployed working men during the Great Depression in the 1930s, Protestants were inclined to think that their economic hardships were God's punishment for their sins. Catholics believed that the greater their suffering in life, the greater their reward in the next life. Neither group spoke of a loving God who would redeem their troubles in this life.[77] By contrast, much Christian teaching at present portrays God as personal and loving—not distant and judgmental.[78] If a benevolent and all-powerful God puts you on the path of unemployment, it must be for a good reason. Believing that being out of work for many months or years is part of a loving God's plan helped many of my participants not give up in despair. This view was usually voiced by Protestants, but I heard it as well from Catholics and members of the Church of Jesus Christ of Latter-Day Saints. Several other recent ethnographies of the unemployed in the United States note the same current Christian interpretations.[79] It is another way in which older descriptions of the Protestant work ethic, according to which not working is a personal moral failing, do not apply very well in the contemporary United States.

To be sure, other Christians among my participants, like Terrance West and Isabel Navarro, did not give a theological interpretation of their unemployment. Nor are all my participants Christian. Although only two have no religious affiliation or spiritual beliefs, there is some diversity among the rest: two are Jewish, two are Buddhist (of radically different sects), and one is Hindu. My participants also included several New Age spiritual seekers who sought the meaning of their unemployment in the workings of the universe, rather than the intentions of a deity. They typically spoke of lessons they were supposed to learn from economic adversity. As one such spiritual seeker put it, "This [*being out of work*] was here for a reason." In total, about one-third of my participants drew on their religious or spiritual beliefs to find a reason why they were meant to be out of work at this time.

These views are an example of positive thinking, which is focused on the bright side of negative circumstances and expecting a change for the better. Some commentators worry that such positive thinking can lead to self-blame for job loss or serious illness: the reason you are down on your luck is that you were not thinking positively.[80] I saw some examples of that. Two of my New Age participants worried that they were sending thoughts about what they lacked into the universe, thereby continuing to attract lack into their lives. For most, however, the belief that they were meant to be in this situation and that they needed to focus on the positive to be successful in their job search led them to eschew self-blame for failing to think positively.[81]

That does not mean that my participants were always upbeat. By letting my participants talk at length for at least two initial interviews, I would hear not only about their determinedly positive takes but also their depression, anxiety, and, in a few cases, suicidal thoughts. Still, most tried to stay positive. ReNé McKnight, for example, never complained; it was only after she had found other living quarters that I learned that the guest house where she and her daughter were living when we first met had no working stove, heat, or hot water. The way I discovered her car was repossessed and she had to walk two miles to work was by asking about the road noise I heard when I called her one time. She tried to focus on what she could do to make a better future for herself and her daughter. She stated, "Things are going to be better. So, I just started thinking about the positive things and focusing on what I can do, instead of looking at the problem and my weaknesses." As Robert Milner explained, from being out of work he learned "to be happy with just the simplest things," and his debilitating pain and struggles to find another job "only make me stronger."

These coping resources were necessary because their unemployment lasted for many months—in some cases, for years. They would need every possible source of encouragement, hope, and self-care to sustain themselves.

"Working" and "Unemployed"

"Work" has two meanings. One definition is "to perform work or fulfill duties regularly for wages or salary," but another is "to exert oneself physically or mentally especially in sustained effort for a purpose or under compulsion or necessity."[82] As feminists, welfare rights activists, and those who study labor cross-culturally have long noted, it is dangerous to conflate those divergent meanings. Women caring for children, the disabled, and elderly in their families are engaged in necessary sustained effort, but they may be accused of lacking a good work ethic because they are not working for wages. What is the work ethic of dedicated community volunteers? Groups who sustain themselves through foraging, hunting, or subsistence farming or in economies where most people scrap together livelihoods from informal ways of making money do not "fulfill duties regularly for wages or salary," but they still labor "under compulsion or necessity."[83] In Germany, in response to cuts in the duration of unemployment benefits in the early 2000s, a movement arose of the unemployed who described themselves as *erwerbslos* (without income) rather than *arbeitslos* (without work) to emphasize that they still performed labor to find another job, contribute to their communities, and sustain themselves and those they cared about.[84]

Several of my participants challenged the assumption that "work" is restricted to paid exertions. As I show in chapter 2, my participants often told me they "worked harder" looking for a job than do many people with jobs. I saw a hint of a broader way of thinking about "work" when Katarina called watching her toddler, as she was doing when we met for a follow-up interview, "this work." For Sam Lennon, who had lived in communes, raised children, and taken a variety of retail and food service jobs before she became disabled, work did not have to be paid: "You work at brushing your teeth or your hair, or making dinner, or going through the trash cans looking for a can to recycle it so you can buy some food, or raking the yard, or feeding your animals. Everybody has to work. It's just [that] some work pays money, and some work feeds your spirit." For Gabriella Gomez, a yoga teacher and massage therapist, work is the way you share your "gifts, talents, attributes." It is the way you "occupy yourself" so you can "be of service." Their broader understandings of work are supported by thoughtful scholars such as John Budd, who defines work as "purposeful human activity involving physical or mental exertion that is not undertaken solely for pleasure and that has economic or symbolic value."[85] To avoid repeating the phrase "waged work," I will use "work" in its usual meaning of paid work. However, we would do well to question the artificial divide between paid and unpaid life-sustaining activities.

"Unemployed" is an ambiguous term as well. The US Bureau of Labor Statistics only counts as "unemployed" those who are not working at all at present and who have actively looked for work in the past four weeks. Unemployment rates thus omit the "discouraged workers" and others "marginally attached to the labor force," who had not applied for jobs in the last four weeks but who had looked for work within the past year. Nor do unemployment rates count anyone who did any work at all for pay or profit in the week before the employment survey, even if it was just for one hour. The self-employed who received no income in the week before that survey are also left out; they are still officially considered to be employed.[86]

The government needs fixed cutoff points for its statistics, but for the people I talked to, there were no such hard-and-fast lines. Exhausted by month after month of applying for jobs and not getting interviews or often any response at all to their application, they would ease up on their job search. However, if someone they knew gave them a tip, they would follow up on it, and nearly all still had hopes of returning to work even as years went by and their objective chances of being hired dwindled. In the meantime, many took any odd jobs they could find—yard work, modeling, grading for an online course, editing, chores for friends—to earn a little cash, but those occasional gigs were insufficient to pay their bills and they still considered themselves unemployed. Anthropologists of unemployment have talked to people who were earning a regular income, but who said they were unemployed because they were still looking for a job in their desired field. There are also many people who work hard in the shadow economy but would not be considered part of the labor force in official statistics.[87]

Some of my participants were underemployed, rather than unemployed, meaning they were working part-time when they wanted to be working full-time or had jobs for which they were overqualified.[88] Katarina Spelling, for example, had part-time jobs when we met, but she was looking for a full-time job. Others were independent contractors, including a housecleaner and hairdressers who had lost many clients during the recession. They lacked sufficient work, but the government did not consider them to be "unemployed." In the research for this book, I included anyone who considered themselves to be unemployed, even if they did not fit official definitions.

Overview

I did not design this study with the aim of comparing work meanings in different social subgroups in the United States. I prioritized multiple, in-depth interviews with a moderate number of people willing to meet repeatedly for lengthy interviews instead of shorter interviews with a larger number of randomly selected participants. Still, throughout the book, I will point out any patterns I noticed.

For example, I found no correspondence between race or ethnicity and work meanings. Thus, I do not routinely state each participant's race or ethnicity, although this information is available in the appendix. More important than race or ethnicity was the divide between those who had a bachelor's degree and those who did not. Education affected previous earnings, how they expected to live, and how they approached their job search.

The education, occupations, and outlooks of my immigrant participants varied as well: there was no one shared set of immigrant meanings of working and not working. One interesting pattern, however, is that immigrants who had not attained citizenship tended to be highly reluctant to apply for historically stigmatized government social welfare benefits like food stamps, even if they were legally entitled to receive them, as I explain in chapter 4.

Although I noticed few differences between most work meanings for unemployed women and men, gender mattered together with education when my participants spoke of the effects of unemployment on their relationship with a life partner or potential life partner. Many participants took for granted a contemporary version of a male breadwinning model that was shaped by the need for two incomes, given the high cost of living, but still assumed that men have the greater obligation to be household providers in heterosexual couples.

Despite the potential importance of the trends that I observed in my interviews, I worry that describing these patterns takes the life out of my findings. The contribution of this study lies in its qualitative details—the ways my participants described thoughts and feelings that resist easy categorization. Their stories and differing ways of thinking about work are the heart of this account.

The next three chapters are devoted to differing work ethics. Chapter 2 details the two current forms of Weber's Protestant work ethic that I sketched earlier: a living-to-work ethic versus a diligent 9-to-5 work ethic. Chapter 3 examines the value of working to live well and how my participants felt when they became "flawed consumers," as one social theorist puts it.[89] That chapter also describes varying meanings of unemployment for immigrants who were motivated by "the American dream" of a materially better life. Chapter 4 considers the motive of working to live; that is, to be self-supporting. Being self-supporting was not possible for many of my participants. The sources of support they turned to or ruled out were shaped by cultural understandings about what parents owe their adult children and what adult children owe their parents, whether other family members (for example, siblings) have any obligations to each other, limitations on the help one could request from friends or local communities, and prevalent social discourses about the meanings of different government social welfare programs.

Chapters 5 and 6 explore other meanings of being out of work beyond those associated with these work ethics. Chapter 5 considers the effects of unemployment on my participants' gender identities and their relationships with their life partner, potential partner, and any children. Chapter 6 explores the meanings of specific jobs and occupations, an aspect of work meanings that is usually ignored in descriptions of Americans' work ethic. There, I also consider what my participants meant when they said one or more of their jobs had been "fun." When were they able to find pleasure from their job?

Finally, in chapter 7, I consider the social policy implications of my research. For example, are generous unemployment benefits a work disincentive? Would a universal basic income be desirable? At stake are clashing values about the place of paid work in a good life and a good society, values that cut across standard ideological divides. For example, the laborist Left and the socially conservative Right both believe waged work is necessary for a morally good and satisfying life. By contrast, post-work theorists on the Left and libertarians on the Right think it is more important to ensure that people are free to choose how to spend their time. I will explain why my ethnographic research leads me to a position that is neither laborist nor post-work.

In that final chapter, I also discuss the implications of this study beyond the United States at the present time, including work meanings in the future. By exploring the social and cultural factors shaping the meanings of work, we have a better understanding of how they might change. As the anthropologist Christine Jeske points out, one way to "challenge problematic dominant narratives" is "by uncovering counternarrative that already exist in a society."[90] I hope to challenge problematic folk cultural descriptions of Americans' work ethic by portraying the great variety of work ethics in the United States and quite likely in other societies as well.

Work seems like a serious topic. Some authors depict it as a site of alienation and exploitation. Others sanctify work as necessary for a meaningful life. However, the outlooks of my participants were more nuanced than these portrayals. Some did find their jobs very meaningful, but not all did. When they talked about their jobs as fun, they revealed a less serious way of looking at work. Furthermore, work was hardly all they cared about. Sometimes they preferred to talk about their health, hobbies, politics, spiritual concerns, or relationships with other people. This book is all about their meanings of work, but work is not all that made life meaningful for them, as we will see.

CHAPTER 2

Two Protestant Work Ethics (Living to Work or Working Diligently)

In *The Problem with Work*, the political theorist Kathi Weeks asks, "Why do we [*in the United States*] work so long and so hard?" She argues that Americans often work long hours not for the sensible purpose of making enough money to pay for our expenses. Instead, most Americans are driven by a less rational motivation: we have been socialized to believe that our job should be central to our identities and an all-consuming interest. The result is that Americans do not simply "work to live" but we "live for work." Weeks argues that despite all the economic changes over the last four centuries, Americans are still haunted by the Protestant work ethic described by Max Weber.[1]

Yet, do all Americans "live for work?" Who is the "we" Weeks assumes as her typical American?

Weeks may have in mind the sorts of people she encounters at her university—professors like her or me. Professors not in a tenure-track position and those who do not yet have tenure labor feverishly to compile an excellent record of teaching, scholarship, and service so they can keep their jobs. Later in life, many professors who have the job security of tenure continue to devote their weekends and vacations to research and publication, new course preparation, or administrative work. I know that I am typical of many academics in choosing to work far more hours than I need to.

Many of our students also work hard. Some faced considerable competition to get into college, and they have uncertain prospects after they graduate. One of my students told me it is common for students at our selective liberal arts college to announce that they had stayed up to 3:00 A.M. to get all their work done. She felt there was a competition to see who could work the hardest.[2] To illustrate her point, she showed me this tweet, "How to know you've internalized capitalism":

—you determine your worth based on your productivity
—you feel guilty for resting
—your primary concern is to make yourself profitable
—you neglect your health
—you think "hard work" is what brings happiness.[3]

This tweet received thousands of retweets and likes. My student said she had to fight off her guilty feelings when she took time for herself, and she thought that description applied to many of her peers.

Successful entrepreneurs work long hours as well, and they proclaim that their 80+-hour workweeks are necessary for anyone who wants to achieve what they have. For example, Elon Musk, the founder of Tesla, tweeted to his millions of followers, "Nobody ever changed the world on 40 hours a week." The correct number of hours "varies per person," he continued, but is "about 80 sustained, peaking about 100 at times." Marissa Mayer, the former chief executive of Yahoo, said a 130-hour workweek was possible "if you're strategic about when you sleep, when you shower, and how often you go to the bathroom."[4] There is a popular t-shirt worn by Silicon Valley employees proclaiming, "9 to 5 is for the weak."[5] One contestant on a reality television show, *Planet of the Apps*, on which app developers compete to win venture capital funding, stated, "I rarely get to see my kids. That's a risk you have to take."[6] Recently, Alexis Ohanian, the founder of Reddit, warned the tech community that such comments are "one of the most toxic, dangerous things in tech right now." He said, "This idea that unless you are suffering, grinding, working every hour of every day, you're not working hard enough" was what led him to neglect the depression he was suffering while he was building his business. He called bragging about hard work "hustle porn."[7]

From a cross-cultural and historical perspective, it is unusual for the well-off to boast of working constantly. As the late nineteenth-century economist Thorstein Veblen observed, "conspicuous leisure" conventionally signaled wealth and conferred greater status than constant work.[8] Recently, however, researchers have observed the opposite norm among upper-income salaried workers in the United States: a "conspicuous consumption of time" devoted to paid work.[9]

Average work hours of full-time, nonagricultural workers have fallen considerably over the last hundred years in Europe, Australia, and the United States from about sixty-five hours a week in 1870 to a little fewer than forty hours a week in 2000.[10] However, many US workers receiving a fixed salary rather than an hourly wage are currently working at or near nineteenth-century levels. In a recent survey, one-quarter of US salaried workers reported working fifty to fifty-nine hours a week, and another quarter said they worked sixty or more hours a week. Although eighty-plus-hour workweeks are unusual, there are "time-greedy professions" like law, finance, and consulting, where sixty- to eighty-hour workweeks are expected if employees want to get ahead.[11]

What about everyone else? In the same survey, only 26 percent of those paid hourly in full-time jobs worked fifty or more hours a week. Over two-thirds of full-time hourly wage earners worked a more moderate forty to forty-nine hours a week, compared to just under half of salaried employees.[12] Many workers could not work at their jobs at all hours even if they wanted to. If you are a sales associate, or meat-processing plant worker, or work in an online retailer's fulfillment center, you cannot bring your work home. You may work extra shifts to earn a living wage or to afford a higher standard of living, but those are instrumental reasons for working (what I call *working to live* or *working to live well*), rather than working because your work is central to your identity and interests (*living to work*). Or you may work long hours only because it is a job requirement, and you would work less if you could. If that is your situation, you are not working long hours because you live for your work.

Living to work is one version of a productivist ideology, and that broader ideology does have a strong hold in the United States.[13] Like the social theorist Anthony Giddens, I define *productivism* as the ideology that one's self-esteem and social worth should depend on one's work effort.[14] If you hold productivist values, you feel guilty when you are not productive. You admire hard workers and look down on those you consider lazy. If you are successful, you attribute your success to your hard work, rather than to any advantages you had from your family, social connections, or lucky opportunities. Many of my participants judged their moral worth by their work effort. Many also valued staying busy. However, I noticed that they practiced two distinct ways of valuing productivity and busyness. Some believed they should work conscientiously or stay busy in other ways during fixed, regular hours; others willingly worked longer hours because they aspired to high levels of achievement in their careers. I call the first a *diligent 9-to-5 work ethic* and the second a *living-to-work ethic*.[15] These two versions of a productivist work ethic set different life priorities when workers had a job, and they fostered different feelings and approaches to their job search when they were unemployed.

Those who had a diligent 9-to-5 work ethic took pride in being good workers, disdained lazy people, and missed the routine of going to work. Still, they were not workaholics: it was important to them to maintain boundaries between work time and the rest of their lives. While they were unemployed, they tried to keep busy and productive during working hours to maintain a division between work time and nonwork time.

By contrast, many of those who had lived to work before they lost their jobs discovered through their unemployment that they could find fulfillment from other activities. They said that their journey of unemployment made them reconsider their priorities. Contemporary values of work-life balance and wellness helped these formerly high-achieving participants adjust to not working.

It is paradoxical. Those who had previously guarded their private time missed the daily routine of working. Those who had spent most of their waking hours working were more likely to say they appreciated taking a break. You might think that those who had a living-to-work ethic would be more upset by being out of work than those who had a diligent 9-to-5 work ethic, but that is not what they reported.

I have implied that these work ethics correlate with the kinds of jobs people hold: entrepreneurs, as well as salaried managers and professionals, have a living-to-work ethic, whereas hourly workers have a diligent 9-to-5 work ethic. That is close but not completely accurate. What makes this distinction a good first approximation are the regulations of the Fair Labor Standards Act (FLSA), which classify workers as either *exempt* or *nonexempt*. Employers are required to pay overtime to nonexempt workers if they work more than forty hours a week, but exempt workers do not receive overtime pay. (They are called "exempt" because the FLSA provisions do not apply to them.) Exempt workers have a fixed salary rather than an hourly wage, and they have supervisory and management duties, so their jobs are at a higher level in the organization than nonexempt workers. At present, employees who are paid less than $35,568 per year are nonexempt.[16] If nonexempt workers "lived to work," they would be entitled to a 150 percent pay rate for their extra hours, so many employers limit their overtime opportunities (or force them to work off the clock). By contrast, employers can demand that their exempt employees work longer than forty hours a week without having to pay them more. Ideal exempt employees, from the employer's perspective, voluntarily work extra hours because they are devoted to their job.

Still, not all managers and professionals have a living-to-work ethic. In chapter 1, I gave the example of Robert Milner, a supply chain strategist earning more than $80,000 a year, who was unhappy with the long hours expected of an exempt employee. Robert even stated, "Although I work to live, I don't live to work." Several other managers and professionals I talked to also explicitly rejected a living-to-work ethic. Conversely, one does not need to be a manager or professional to have a living-to-work ethic. Consider the example of Isabel Navarro in chapter 1. Isabel began as a low-paid clerical worker, but she devoted all her vacation time to taking coursework that would qualify her for the best-paid clerical position. When she was forced out of that job, she again devoted her free time to learning advanced techniques in her new occupation of skin care. Isabel went on to start her own skin care salon. Business owners, regardless of the size of the business, often devote long hours to their work. Isabel had a living-to-work ethic. The same was true of ReNé McKnight, whom I also described in chapter 1: she was a self-described "workaholic" and would-be entrepreneur who had been working as a customer service representative and as a home health aide.

Other participants did not have a productivist work ethic in either the diligent 9-to-5 or living-to-work senses. That does not mean they had no interest in working. A productivist work ethic is about devotion to abstract labor; that is, devotion to being a good worker regardless of the particulars of the job or how much money one makes. Some of my participants did not care about work in this abstract sense. For them, what mattered most was earning money to support themselves and others in their household at the standard of living they desired, socializing with coworkers, or being occupied with meaningful or enjoyable assignments. They will be described in later chapters. Earning enough to support oneself and others, afford a desired standard of living, socializing with coworkers, and enjoyment of the tasks were also common motivations for those with a living-to-work or diligent 9-to-5 work ethic.

Why should one be devoted to being a good worker, regardless of the job or how much money one makes? Kathi Weeks and many others trace productivist thinking to the Protestant work ethic described by Max Weber. Thus, we need to revisit Weber's description of this work ethic to understand not only what it illuminates but also what it obscures.

Weber on the Two Protestant Work Ethics

In *The Protestant Ethic and the Spirit of Capitalism,* published in 1904 and 1905, the German sociologist Max Weber attempts to explain "the origin of the Western bourgeois class and of its peculiarities."[17] By "bourgeois class," he means business owners, whose greatest peculiarity was the way they used their time, devoting all of it to their business without relaxing to enjoy the fruits of their efforts.

Weber contrasts this ethos with what he calls a traditionalistic spirit, which he illustrates using the example of European cloth merchants in the pre-industrial putting-out system. In the putting-out system, cloth merchants bought fabric made by farm families in their homes and sold it to middlemen. The relationships between buyers and sellers, the prices paid, and the expected quality of the cloth were set by custom. Weber's description of these traditionalistic merchants emphasizes their plentiful free time: "The number of business hours was very moderate, perhaps five to six a day, sometimes considerably less; in the rush season, where there was one, more. . . . A long daily visit to the tavern, with often plenty to drink, and congenial circle of friends, made life comfortable and leisurely."[18]

Then, as Weber tells the story, "this leisureliness was suddenly destroyed" by one or more hard-driving young men who upped the ante by asking cloth buyers what they wanted, closely supervising the cloth makers to ensure they provided what the buyers wanted, and selling a higher volume of fabric at lower prices, which forced the other merchants to do likewise or go out of business: "The idyllic state collapsed under the pressure of a bitter competitive struggle . . . The old leisurely and comfortable attitude toward life gave way to a hard frugality in which some participated and came to the top, because they did not wish to consume but to earn."[19]

The competitive new merchants would not have been popular, and their approach required "infinitely more intensive work."[20] Weber asks what motivated those new merchants.

You may be thinking at this point that what motivated them was the desire to make more money and that no further explanation is needed. Weber would reply that you are thinking with a modern capitalist mindset. Why should people prefer to earn more and more money, without end—especially if their goal is not to have more money to spend but only to reinvest in their business? He considered the traditionalistic ethos more natural: "A man does not 'by nature' wish to earn more and more money, but simply to live as he is accustomed to live and to earn as much as is necessary for that purpose."[21]

Weber's surprising explanation for the rise of the competitive business spirit is that these new businessmen were adherents of the ascetic Protestantism of the sixteenth-century theologian John Calvin. Calvinists believed that only those chosen by God for salvation could work effectively to increase the glory of God through their worldly callings; thus, success at work is a sign that one is among the elect who have been saved and will go to heaven after they die. For the ascetic Protestants, including the English Puritans, "Waste of time is . . . the first and in principle the deadliest of sins."[22] The seventeenth-century English Puritan minister Richard Baxter said one must do God's work "'as long as it is yet day'" because idle hands can get into mischief and one has only a short life-time to labor for God's glory on earth: one can rest all one wants in the next life. In Weber's explanation of this view, "Not leisure and enjoyment, but only activity serves to increase the glory of God."[23] As a result, "Loss of time through sociability, idle talk, luxury, even more sleep than is necessary for health, six to at most eight hours, is worthy of absolute moral condemnation."[24]

Weber did not think a concern with salvation motivated Western business owners much beyond the 1600s, although for at least two more centuries they continued to believe they had a moral duty to devote all their time to their business. That version of productivism was summed up by aphorisms like "time is money" published by Benjamin Franklin in his *Poor Richard's Almanac* in the mid-eighteenth century. What Franklin meant is that someone who could earn "ten shillings a day by his labour" but takes off a half-day has "thrown away" five shillings. Not working has an opportunity cost. That attitude lives on in metaphors of "saving," "spending," and "wasting" time, which reflect a cultural model of time as a scarce resource we ought to conserve, as George Lakoff and Mark Johnson point out in *Metaphors We Live By*.[25] Franklin also advised appearing to be busy from early in the morning until late at night to give lenders the confidence their loans would be repaid.[26]

Weber believed that an internalized duty to work was waning by the beginning of the twentieth century when he wrote about the Protestant ethic. By that time, he felt that personal values and beliefs no longer mattered because industrial capitalism had become so entrenched in the West that everyone had to conform to its discipline: "The idea of duty in one's calling prowls about in our lives like the ghost of dead religious beliefs," and "in the field of its highest development, in the United States, the pursuit of wealth" had been "stripped of its religious and ethical meaning" and had "the character of sport."[27]

Weber also observed a shift from Puritans' reluctance to spend their hard-earned money. Their suspicion of consumerism was based on their belief that "man is only a trustee of the goods which have come to him through God's grace" and thus should not "spend any of it for a purpose which does not serve the glory of God but only one's own enjoyment."[28] Attitudes about consumerism had changed by the beginning of the twentieth century when "material goods . . . gained an increasing and finally an inexorable power over the lives of men," becoming an "iron cage."[29]

Despite these changes, a key feature of modern Western bourgeois culture persisted: the centrality of work in a businessperson's life. They lived to work rather than working to live. No longer motivated by concern for their salvation, these modern businesspeople could not explain what drove them: "If you ask them what is the meaning of their restless activity, why they are never satisfied with what they have, thus appearing so senseless to any purely worldly view of life, they would perhaps give the answer, if they know any at all: 'to provide for my children and grandchildren.' But more often and, since that motive is not peculiar to them, but was just as effective for the traditionalist [*who worked to live*], more correctly, simply: that business with its continuous work has become a necessary part of their lives."[30] In other words, their habits, values, identities, and self-esteem all depended on constantly working, being productive, and achieving success. Weber realized that wealth could bring influence and higher status, but his ideal-typical businessperson (the owner of a small business, not a tycoon) "gets nothing out of his wealth for himself, except the irrational sense of having done his job well."[31]

Weber uses words like "irrational" and "peculiar" to describe the ethic of living to work, in which the goal is "the earning of more and more money, combined with the strict avoidance of all spontaneous enjoyment of life."[32] In Weber's description of this ascetic ethic, work itself is not expected to bring happiness nor is the point to earn money that will be enjoyed later. Weber asks why people should devote all their time to something that does not increase their happiness. That was the irrationality Weber saw at the heart of the Puritan work ethic. Weber thought the ethos of Western businesspeople was strange, and among Western businesspeople, he thought that ethos had reached its apogee in the United States. *The Protestant Ethic and the Spirit of Capitalism* reflects Weber's culture shock as a German intellectual contemplating the values and life choices of American businesspeople.[33]

As an explanation for the rise of modern capitalism, Weber's story is controversial. There is no shortage of historical, theological, sociological, and anthropological studies showing problems with his analysis.[34] Nor is a hardworking, entrepreneurial ethos limited to Protestants or to the West.[35] And yet, *The Protestant Ethic and the Spirit of Capitalism* remains an incomparable, searing description of a consequential mindset. Kathi Weeks is just one of many influenced by "Weber's brilliant study of how . . . we came to be haunted by the legacy of this Puritan ethic."[36]

I, too, am fascinated by Weber's depiction of this ethos. My late father-in-law fit his description of a businessperson with few interests in life other than making and saving money, and Weber helped me understand him. Moreover, Weber's emphasis on people's values and meanings influenced the kind of anthropology I do. However, an ambiguity lies at the heart of his description of this work ethic. Did Weber mean to describe only the mindset of businesspeople, or did he intend to include their employees as well? In most enterprises, workers do not share in the profits of the business: Are they as driven as those who derive greater financial benefits from unceasing labor? Given Weber's interest in "the origin of the Western bourgeois class and of its peculiarities," he devoted scant attention to the inner life of ordinary working people. Yet, in *The Protestant Ethic and The Spirit of Capitalism* there is a suggestion of another, less driven, work ethic that is more relevant for ordinary workers. That hint is Weber's description of an earlier stage in the development of Protestant attitudes about work, beginning with the pre-Calvinist Protestant theology of Martin Luther. Weber's treatise is really a description of two Protestant work ethics, not one.

In Weber's account, the Protestant ethic began with Martin Luther. Luther rejected the then-prevalent Christian theology that the best life in God's eyes was one devoted to religion. Instead, Luther preached that "the fulfilment of worldly duties is under all circumstances the only way to live acceptably to God . . . hence every legitimate calling has exactly the same worth."[37] Thus, Martin Luther expanded the notion of a "calling" from a religious vocation to one's God-given work in the world. As Weber explains Luther's ideas, "Labour must . . . be performed as if it were an absolute end in itself, a calling."[38] In other words, workers in every occupation should perform their work as if they had been called to do it by God, even if they fell into their occupations because they had no choice.

Weber stated that among ordinary workers, as with entrepreneurs, treating one's job as a calling led to a move from traditionalism; that is, from being content with one's customary standard of living and working only as needed to maintain it. Traditionalistic workers receiving a piece rate had the tendency to quit when they had earned what they needed, even if they had not finished their assigned task. Even when they put in a full day, they might not have put much thought or effort into their work. By contrast, devout Protestant employees in the seventeenth century took it to be their duty to work hard and well in their worldly vocation.[39] Weber noticed that inculcating workers with this work ethic fattened the business owner's bottom line: "The power of religious asceticism provided him . . . with sober, conscientious, and unusually industrious workmen." With heavy sarcasm, Weber commented, "It appears here that the interests of God and of the employers are curiously harmonious."[40]

Being conscientious during normal working hours is not the same as devoting most of one's time to one's job: these two forms of productivism do not lend themselves to the same kind of exploitation. Luther's conception of a worldly calling was "fulfilment of the obligations imposed upon the individual by his position in the world."[41] "Obligations" suggests an agreed-on, fixed set of tasks. Once workers discharged those obligations, their work was done, and they were free to enjoy the rest of their time. That is completely different from the anxious, restless Puritan work ethic with its suspicion of leisure. In the Puritan work ethic, there is always more work one could do.

Although Weber focused on the Protestant departure from Catholicism, he also made distinctions among Protestants. When he spoke of "the Protestant ethic," he really meant ascetic Calvinist Protestantism, best represented by the Puritans in England and in what became the United States. He noted "the lesser degree of ascetic penetration of life in Lutheranism as distinguished from Calvinism."[42] Lutheranism was the largest Protestant denomination in Germany, in contrast to the United States, with the result, according to Weber, that Germans were more relaxed than Americans. Weber believed that even facial expressions of Germans and Anglo-Americans were different, with German facial expressions reflecting "*Gemütlichkeit* (good nature) or 'naturalness,'" while Anglo-American facial expressions reflected "narrowness, unfreeness, and inner constraint" shaped by their Puritan heritage.[43]

To sum up, although it was not his main point, Weber in effect described two Protestant work ethics, an early Protestant work ethic and a later, Puritan work ethic. Even though the stringent Puritan work ethic is what Weber and subsequent scholars emphasized, it is not clear that it ever motivated most workers, even in the United States. Both work ethics are productivist, but they espouse different versions of productivism, as I explain in greater detail.

I see in my participants' diligent 9-to-5 work ethic the continuing influence of the early Protestant work ethic. This ethic calls for workers to be industrious during their normal working hours. It is an ethic held by employees who value doing their jobs well but are happy to stop at the end of the workday. By contrast, my participants with a living-to-work ethic share the drive for high achievement, work centrality, and long hours of Weber's businesspeople driven by the Puritan work ethic.

That is not to say that either version of Weber's Protestant work ethic is completely apt at the present time. As Weber explained, attitudes about consumerism changed quite a bit (and perhaps earlier than Weber thought, as I explain in the next chapter). What is also missing from Weber's account of Puritans' "avoidance of all spontaneous enjoyment of life"[44] is any possibility that workers could enjoy doing their jobs. What are the contemporary forms of the early Protestant work ethic versus the more extreme Puritan work ethic?

Unemployment among Those Who Live to Work Today

Lisa Rose had worked her way up in the nonprofit sector. When she was in her mid-forties, she was hired to be the vice president of a well-known Los Angeles nonprofit. She loved being in that world and was dedicated to the goals of the organization, even though she encountered resistance from the longtime professional staff she was supposed to lead. She earned a six-figure salary, more than her husband made, and they had no children. Lisa estimated that "probably 85 percent of it [*my time*] was work." During the Great Recession, the organization's endowment lost much of its value, and they let her go. When we met for the first interview, Lisa had been out of work for a year and a half.

As Lisa got to this point in her life story, she surprised me by saying, "Being laid off was the best thing that ever happened to me." I replied, "*Really?*" She then explained why she felt that way:

> Because it gave me a chance to take a look at what was the role of work in my life. It was too strong, too big a dimension. I'd let work become too big a part of who I saw myself to be. And in the absence of having a job, you see this much more starkly than when you're working. You don't realize how much of your identity gets invested in who you are and what you do and all of that. [. . .] it's like you've got this pie chart, and probably 85 percent of it was work. I mean, don't ever let that happen again. That can't happen again.

This is a remarkable statement from someone who had previously lived to work: it is a repudiation of putting one's career ahead of all else.

One of the negative outcomes was neglect of her health: "I wasn't taking good care of myself. So, I immediately leapt into regular exercise every day, eating better, spending time with friends and family, taking long walks with my dogs." Being "healthy" required more than regular exercise. It also meant changing what mattered in life. The jolt of long-term unemployment led Lisa to believe that, by devoting 85 percent of her time to work, she had lost her true identity and needed to regain it to "remind myself of who I was when I was younger and try to recapture that essence of who I was." She talked about establishing a "healthy" relationship to work: "Getting my strongest sense of who I am from work is something I have to change. And that's a good thing to change, so if I've lost a sense of identity because I don't have the same work anymore, I think it's healthy for me. Not easy but healthy."

There was a moral element to her new priorities. Lisa was ashamed of having neglected people she cared about. She said, "I also started to think about people whom I hadn't seen in a long time, where I needed to strengthen those relationships, so I did. People I needed to apologize to, people I needed to make amends to." She hoped that by making amends she would "feel more worthy in a way." Lisa was grateful that while she was unemployed, she had time to care for her mother-in-law who had moved nearby. She also went on a retreat to try "to recover some elements of spirituality in my life."

Lisa is a good example of someone who used to have a living-to-work ethic: work was very central to her interests and identity, and she willingly and regularly devoted long hours to her work.[45] "Work centrality" is a standard term in occupational psychology, inspired by Weber's description of the Puritan work ethic: it refers to how important work is in someone's life. Psychologists measure it by seeing how much someone agrees with statements like "the major satisfaction in my life comes from my work" or disagrees with statements like "my work is only a small part of who I am."[46]

Lisa's repudiation of making work her highest priority was repeated by several others who had previously had a living-to-work ethic. These are people who said of themselves, "My career was my life" or that they had been "such a workaholic." Pepper Hill, another former nonprofit administrator, could find only part-time work for more than six years. In the past, work had been central to her identity, but she was trying to change. She appreciated her therapist's advice, "We're human beings, not human doings." In other words, her core identity should not depend on what she does. When I asked Elizabeth Montgomery, who had sold high-end office furniture, if she agreed with the statement, "Work is central to my identity," she responded, "It was extremely central to my identity. This time off has made me look at myself differently." She started to question whether putting "100 percent" of her time into her job might be out of balance. She said she had to learn, "Don't be the workaholic. Put it in perspective." She mused, "I lived in the future," always "yearning to do better, better, better." Now she was trying to "live in the day to day," to appreciate "the journey" instead of striving to reach a set destination. When I asked Stacie McCarthy, a former loan processor, whether there was anything she was not so proud of in her life, she said, "Maybe I'm not so proud that I made it [*my career*] my life," instead of spending more time with her parents and siblings. Abel Jimenez lost his successful produce market when he failed to pay all the taxes he owed. Although that was a financial disaster, he saw a benefit of not working so hard: "Life is so beautiful, and one doesn't know how to live it. You understand? You get too deep into work, you think work is everything. You think that everything will be solved just by working and nothing else. Now I'm looking at it from a different life, which I might have missed previously." He was spending time with his grandchild, a luxury he did not afford himself when his children were young.

Not everyone who had lived to work when employed later repudiated those priorities when they were out of work. Several participants said work was still central to their identity. They had held demanding jobs that probably required long hours, but they did not label themselves as reformed workaholics nor say they now regretted the time they had devoted to their jobs.[47] Still, it is striking that many others did express those regrets.

It has probably occurred to you, as it did to me, that Lisa Rose and the others I quoted might be saying they learned important lessons from losing their job as a way of finding something positive about their situation to help deal with the stress of long-term unemployment. In chapter 1, I discussed the positive thinking ideology that is common in the United States, which encourages looking for the positive aspects of negative circumstances. Lisa's and others' "blessing in disguise" framing of their job loss is a form of positive thinking I heard frequently in this study.[48]

That may be true, but it does not make their new outlook any less sincere. Lisa, for one, did change her priorities. Initially she was forced to work less because her first regular job after her long period of unemployment was non-exempt. Her employer restricted her work hours to forty hours a week so they did not have to pay her overtime. Later, Lisa was promoted into an exempt position, and I wondered whether she would return to devoting 85 percent of her time to work. I got in touch to ask how she was balancing work with the rest of her life following her promotion, and Lisa replied at length. When she had been in the nonexempt position, she had to electronically punch in four times a day, which conflicted with her self-image as a professional: "As a professional it's annoying because I don't think of myself as being on the clock." Yet, she acknowledged the benefits: "At the same time it kept me from working too many hours. Now that I'm in charge of my time I have to be more vigilant about my hours and watch the weekend work." Still, she was proud that she had recently taken two weeks off in the middle of an important work project to deal with a family matter. She realized, "Family first and asking for help is OK."

Similarly, Stacie McCarthy said she no longer spent her free time on her loan processing work in the new job she obtained after her long period of unemployment. It had never been expected in her position, but she had been devoted to her previous job and her boss. Now, she said, "I just wanna go in and do my job and go home."

Living to Work Meets Self-Growth and Self-Care

Those who had lived to work and then questioned their former priorities did not have to invent a new way of thinking. In the contemporary United States, there are popular discourses that critique putting work above all else. Discourses of wellness and "work-life balance" provide respected alternative cultural models in which work plays a reduced role. We can see the influence of those discourses in my interviewees' comments about establishing a "healthier" relationship to work.

In *The Hearts of Men*, Barbara Ehrenreich describes a shift in psychother-
apy that began in the 1950s. Proponents of humanistic psychology, like Abra-
ham Maslow, aim to maximize psychological health, not just cure mental
illness. Humanistic psychotherapists believe that human growth requires fulfilling your individual potential instead of blindly conforming to conventional
social obligations. Fritz Perls advocates, "Do your own thing," see life as an
adventure and reject guilt as an "obsolete emotion." From this humanistic psy-
chotherapeutic perspective, losing one's job can be a "growth experience."[49]

Although "do your own thing" now rings of the countercultural movement
of the late 1960s, broader ideas of "health" and "wellness," which go beyond
the absence of disease to encompass life satisfaction,[50] are now widely accepted
in the United States. So are some elements of New Age beliefs and practices,
such as meditation.[51] Indeed, many of my participants practiced meditation
and yoga.

Concerns with wellness can be co-opted by corporations seeking to improve their employees' productivity.[52] Managers hope that encouraging employees to do yoga or take a walk during their lunch break will make them
more willing to work late and will reduce health insurance costs. Still, there
are influential discourses that reverse those priorities, making health the master value instead of work productivity. The very term "workaholic," a port-
manteau of "work" and "alcoholic," pathologizes people who work long hours
and cannot stop thinking about their work. According to one psychologist
quoted by the health website WebMD, "A workaholic is someone who is on
the ski slopes dreaming about being back in the office. A healthy worker is
someone in the office who dreams about being on the ski slopes."[53] Workaholism is considered an addiction, an "'uncontrollable need to work inces-
santly'" according to one definition,[54] just as alcoholism is "continued excessive
or compulsive use of alcoholic drinks," according to the *Merriam-Webster Dictionary*. Workaholics have their own twelve-step programs.[55]

A "healthy" relationship to work means creating "work-life balance."[56] This
term gained favor in the 1990s as more inclusive than "work-family" policies
because workers who do not have family responsibilities still want time for
activities outside work. Calls for work-life balance "capture a widely felt need
to prevent paid work from invading too much into people's lives," especially
for white-collar workers who are expected to be digitally available to their employers at all hours.[57]

Although concerns with work-life balance are not limited to parents of
young children, they are especially acute for them. For such parents, pressure
to spend long hours at their jobs competes with expectations that they also
devote considerable time to parenting. One of my participants, Anastasia Tang,

was fired from her HR manager job a few months after she finished maternity leave. She believes she was let go because she declined to attend two after-hours company functions, including the annual company dinner, because she wanted to be home with her sons, who were younger than two years old. Parents like Anastasia and her husband face difficult choices, especially given current parenting norms. Today, parents are expected to closely watch their young children. Furthermore, especially among members of the middle and upper-middle class, worries about their children's uncertain future drive parents to give their children enriching experiences that will later give them an edge in entrance to top colleges.[58] Anastasia told me she did not have reliable childcare for events after work, but her decision not to obtain a backup sitter for such events also reflects her preference for limiting her work hours so she could spend more time with her sons. Like Anastasia, several of my participants appreciated having more time to become involved with their children's activities while they were unemployed.

In sum, there are many contemporary discourses and practices that reject long working hours. Still, if those counter-discourses and practices are so influential, why did my participants spend so much time at their work before they lost their jobs?

Why Work Long Hours?

To be sure, many Americans do not work long hours because they live to work but because they must do so to keep their jobs. As I explained earlier, the United States has no overtime protections for exempt workers. The result is many unhappy workers like my participant Robert Milner, who was "bitter" about having little free time after his ten-hour-or-longer workdays and minimum hour-long commutes in each direction. The United States also has no regulations on the length of a workweek. By contrast, the European Union mandates an average workweek of no longer than forty-eight hours in all member states, with exceptions for only a few occupations.[59]

One researcher studied a consulting firm, one of the "time-greedy professions" in which sixty- to eighty-hour workweeks are expected. Employees who asked for less travel or a lighter schedule would be punished with a poor performance evaluation or denied a promotion. Instead, some employees "passed" by teleworking, taking on more local clients, collaborating with others on their team to jointly manage their hours, and controlling information regarding their whereabouts. They were as productive as those who worked longer hours, and they received good performance evaluations and promotions.[60]

Women in male-dominated fields and people of color in white-dominated organizations may feel particularly strong pressures to work long hours.[61] My participant Caroline James rose to be a senior vice president of HR for an entertainment company in which there were only three female executives in a workforce of more than two thousand. She said she had to deal with being dismissed by bigwigs whose attitude seemed to be, "Oh little girl, you're funny. Go away. Don't bug me." She had been working seventy or more hours a week in an effort to be taken seriously. Eventually she realized this was hurting her marriage, and she stopped trying to base her self-worth on her bosses' opinion of her.

Yet, none of the participants I quoted earlier who said they now regretted having devoted so much time to work—Lisa Rose, Pepper Hill, Elizabeth Montgomery, Stacie McCarthy, and Abel Jimenez—gave any hints in their life history of having disliked their long hours while they were immersed in their jobs. Their narratives suggest what some occupational psychologists would term positive *work engagement*, rather than guilt or fear-driven *workaholism*.

Some psychologists define workaholism as "the tendency to work excessively hard in a compulsive way."[62] As one source explains, "For workaholics, the need to work is so exaggerated that it endangers their health, reduces their happiness, and deteriorates their interpersonal relations and social functioning."[63] Workaholism is work centrality driven by anxiety and guilt. It is assessed by agreement with statements like "I feel guilty when I take time off work" or "Do you immerse yourself in activities to change how you feel or avoid grief, anxiety, and shame?" Work engagement, by contrast, describes interest in one's current job. It is a positive form of work centrality assessed by agreement with statements like "I am enthusiastic about my job" and "I am immersed in my work." Some organizational psychologists find that those with high work engagement put in long hours just like workaholics, but they enjoy work more, have better mental and physical health, and describe higher life satisfaction.[64]

As my participants narrated their life stories, the way they talked about their prior jobs made me think that work engagement was a better explanation for their long hours than workaholism. Still, it is hard to know for sure or to untangle their mix of motives. Even if I had administered the standard psychological scales, these results would have provided an unreliable retrospective account of how my participants felt a year or more earlier when they were working full time. After they were out of work, some rethought their priorities. That new perspective could prompt them to reframe what may have been a perfectly healthy dedication to a challenging job as an unhealthy obsession. Thus, I define a living-to-work ethic to include both workaholism and work engagement without having to choose one or the other.[65]

For example, Elizabeth Montgomery, the successful high-end business furniture saleswoman, speculated that her work efforts stemmed from her difficult-to-please mother: "You could come home with straight As, and she didn't think it was good enough." Elizabeth was trying to accept that "you're perfect in your own right" and "just be okay with who you are, what you're doing and where you're going." Yet, when she gave her work history, she described how much she had enjoyed her jobs. For example, in one of her early jobs she was a buyer for a department store chain of forty stores, which gave her a lot of clout at trade shows: "So that was really, really fun." She "had a blast" when she grew online sales by 500 percent in another job. (In chapter 6 I give an in-depth analysis of my participants' accounts of the fun they had on their jobs.) That sounds like enthusiastic engagement rather than a compulsive addiction. Elizabeth had been a standout athlete in high school and college, and she used sports analogies to explain why she liked concrete ways of measuring achievement: "In the athletic part you set the goal. You go out and achieve it. If that means hiking to Mount Whitney, getting a trophy or that, okay. And so, I think that's who I am." Winning the trophy, literally or metaphorically, is pleasurable.

Similarly, Abel Jimenez said he had enjoyed his work when his produce market was doing well. In her interview with Abel, Claudia C. added some of her own wording to our standard question, "What is the meaning or importance of work for you?" She asked Abel instead, "There are people who live to work, because the only way they know to enjoy their lives is working. What does work mean to you?" Her wording illustrates the cultural standing of the idea that it is bad to "live to work." Abel may have picked up on that cue because he replied, "At some point I was also dedicated exclusively to my work. The more you have, the more you want to have." He went on to deliver the lines I quoted earlier about having gotten "too deep into work," which kept him from spending time with his young children. Yet, as Abel kept talking, his story changed. He said he used to sleep in his truck because he was constantly on the go: "Why? Because one gets deep into business. Well, at least I did. Because the more you get into it, the more you enjoy it, and more business brings in more business, and so on." He explained, "And so you get yourself deeper into work, and you feel fulfilled by work. And you like more and more the product of your work, what you get out of it, what you do, what you start achieving." To me, it sounds as if Abel had been deeply and pleasurably engaged by his work.

It seems that those who hold a living-to-work ethic want to be high achievers and are willing to work long hours to attain their goals. The psychological and material rewards of achieving challenging goals make this ethic more understandable than Weber's depiction of a joyless, nose-to-the-grindstone habit. What is missing from his description is that at least some of those who live to work take pleasure in doing so.[66]

Job Search with a Living-to-Work Ethic

How do high achievers accustomed to devoting much of their time to their work approach a search for another position? Typically, they do not take the first job that comes along just to keep working. Elizabeth Montgomery's drive for success makes her job search quite different from one colored by her blue-collar parents' view that one job is as good as another, which I discuss in chapter 6 as the "work-is-work" approach to choosing a job or occupation. That difference came to a head after she had been out of work for many months, and her father said, "'Just go get a job. Even if that's McDonalds.'" Elizabeth was incredulous: "I'm like, '*What?*'" If someone cares about career success, it is not that all work has dignity: some jobs are worthwhile, and others are not. Thus, many of those who had lived to work ended up staying out of work longer than those who had invested less of their time and identities in their jobs. This was partly because those who had lived to work typically had greater financial resources (savings, severance payments); yet they were also selective about what job would be an appropriate next step in their career.[67] Instead of taking the first job that came along, some of those who had lived to work threw themselves into the challenge of finding another job that would fit their high goals.

And a challenge it was. In the United States, it was more than six years before the numbers of jobs returned to their levels just before the Great Recession, which hit southern California particularly hard.[68] However, US labor market practices also made the job search onerous.

Job hunting in the United States can be extremely time consuming at present. The minimum that job seekers need to do is stay up to date with postings on numerous websites, which can occupy several hours every day. Applying for those jobs is also done online, which can be a lengthy process, especially for someone who is not computer-savvy. Yet, learning about job openings and applying for them just scratch the surface of job search efforts.

First, job seekers need to decide what kind of work they want. Nearly everyone I interviewed wanted to find another job like the one they had before. Except for my participants in their twenties, very few were formulating their career goals from scratch. However, as the duration of their unemployment grew longer, some reconsidered their career goals. A handful obtained additional education or skills, although free retraining programs were in short supply.[69]

Second, all aspects of one's self-presentation must be carefully managed. Each application requires tinkering with the wording of your resume so that it includes the keywords that will highlight your suitability for the opening and will ensure it will pass through automatic filters. There are strategic choices to be made about the resume, such as whether it should be organized chronologically or functionally, whether to include testimonials, and how to hide embarrassing gaps between jobs. Although I heard varying opinions about whether employers read cover letters, some of my interviewees put a lot of time into crafting those as well.[70]

Job seekers also must always be ready to promote themselves one on one, as I heard from Heather Wieshlow, a career counselor who spoke to a job club meeting organized by a county office of the California Employment Development Department. She asked the job seekers to refine their "thirty-second commercial" (a.k.a. the "elevator pitch," because it is short enough to be delivered in an elevator ride). This two- to three-sentence job pitch is used to describe a job seeker's work experience and goals to someone staffing a table at a job fair or to acquaintances who might be able to suggest someone they could talk to. She also suggested listing fifty accomplishments in a spreadsheet. Fifty was a bare minimum; she said her clients could come up with a hundred or more, once they thought about it. They did not all have to be work accomplishments, but all should be in the PAR format: What was the **P**roblem, what **A**ction did you take, and what was the **R**esult? Results should be quantified if possible. After job seekers created a list of their accomplishments, they could turn them into effective "power stories" to share in a job interview.

The part of the job search that *really* consumed a lot of time was networking. Job seekers were told over and over that the only way to get an edge in the job search was to talk to people who might know about openings. Career counselors estimated that at least 70 percent of job seekers find a position through networking, because many of those positions were not advertised.[71] To learn about unadvertised jobs, the diligent job seeker must constantly reach out to new people to ask if they know of any openings. Anyone could potentially have a lead, so one always must be ready to deliver a thirty-second commercial. Networking can be done in person or through social media. Social media connections, and all one's other acquaintances, can be solicited for job leads or for names of someone else who might know of a job lead. In-person networking can take place through planned group networking events, professional meetings, everyday encounters, and informational interviews. One's presence on professional websites can be boosted by increasing the number of one's connections, obtaining endorsements, joining online groups, posting comments that get liked, and so on.[72]

Doing volunteer work was also a popular job search strategy. Several of my interviewees worked as volunteers in the hopes that the agencies for which they volunteered might eventually have a paying job for them. Others took freelance jobs to continue using their skills, even if they were unpaid.

Career counselors also recommended that job seekers meet once a week with a small group or accountability partner to set goals and discuss their job search efforts. At the meetings of one accountability group I attended, members delivered progress reports each week and gave each other emotional support, as well as practical advice.

Some of my interviewees were skeptical about the value of the large networking events where you spent your time talking to other people who were out of work, but others attended them regularly. That strategy could be useful because even within networking groups for people in the same field—for example, for IT workers or for finance and accounting executives—attendees had different specialties, so they were not necessarily in competition. Probably of greater value, if they could afford the registration fees, were trade and professional association meetings where they could chat up employed colleagues in their field.

Elizabeth Montgomery went to many kinds of networking events. She had attended four in the week before we met for the first time. At these networking meetings, she gave other job seekers names of people they could talk to, and she hoped they would reciprocate. She liked talking to people, and networking fit with the skillset she had as a successful sales representative. Still, it was tiring to continue that outreach for the two-and-a-half years she had been out of work. She commented wearily, "I know something will happen. It's just, it's kind of like sales. We gotta throw so much up there, and something'll land. But I'll be honest, I did—how many events this week? Four. And I'm tired." At each of these events, it was "like keeping your face and smiling." She had also belonged to four accountability groups, although by the time we met, she was down to two.

Lisa Rose also put a lot of effort into her job search. She told me, "When you've been doing, doing, doing, doing, doing, my goodness, it's hard to just come to a grinding halt. So, I was probably overly ambitious, but I got out and I met with, like, 110 people in the space of four months. So, every day I was meeting with usually two people, sometimes three." Lisa preferred doing one-on-one informational interviews rather than networking in large groups. An informational interview is a prearranged meeting with someone working in one's desired field. Its ostensible purpose is to learn more about the person's work, but everyone knows that the hidden agenda is to impress someone who will keep you in mind for a job opening. When Lisa finally got a job, she sent me an email that cataloged her efforts during her twenty-nine-month job search. Here is her list, verbatim:

4,000+ emails
252 networking meetings
430 connections on LinkedIn (started at 0)
34 resumes
25 positions for which I was interviewed
4 times a finalist
3 temporary jobs
2 training/skills development programs

Job searches are not conducted this way everywhere. Ofer Sharone compared the process of looking for white-collar jobs in the San Francisco Bay area with the process in Tel Aviv, a high-tech hub in Israel. In Israel white-collar job seekers submit their credentials to staffing agencies rather than to employers. The agencies consider the applicant's work experience, salary requirements, and interpersonal skills, as revealed by tests. The result is that Israeli job seekers worry about the screening tests and still must put the right buzzwords on their resume, but they only submit it once and do not spend their time on coffee dates with strangers who might know about a job opening. Nor do Israeli job seekers send cover letters when they apply for jobs or thank-you notes following an interview. When Sharone conducted his research in 2006, there were no networking events in Israel, and Israelis did not use online professional social networking sites like LinkedIn. Israelis did not understand why anyone would expect someone they barely knew to help them get a job.[73]

How useful is this never-ending job search activity in the United States, especially the optional networking? One of Lisa Rose's 252 networking meetings, an informational interview, eventually led to her new job. The same was true, however, for only one other participant in my study. Everyone else I interviewed eventually found work in conventional ways: through job websites, employment agencies, and tips from people who knew them, rather than by networking with strangers.

I was struck, however, by the psychic and social benefits of networking. Networking was an optional activity with no upper limit on the amount of work one could do. For some of those who had lived to work, like Lisa Rose and Elizabeth Montgomery, it may have been an opportunity to really kill it at the job search, just as they had on the job.

Attending networking events enables the job seeker to stay busy. Pepper Hill, a nonprofit administrator, described the social pressures to be busy all the time, mimicking a typical conversation with other professionals: "You know most people: 'I'm busy, busy, busy.' 'How are you?' 'I'm busy, busy, busy, busy.' People never say, 'Gee, I got nothing going on this weekend.'"[74] Many of my participants wanted to stay busy. In addition to attending networking meetings, Elizabeth Montgomery had taken an MBA course while she was out of work, and she attended alumni events for the university. She explained why: "'Cause I just can't sit idle. So, I wanted to be doing stuff." Some stayed busy with sports and exercise. Elizabeth completed long-distance bike rides; Pepper Hill took up water aerobics and even taught classes in it.

Notice, however, that a stay-busy ethic is not the same as a work ethic. That is evident in Pepper Hill's mimicking the words of her professional peers, who "never say, 'Gee, I got nothing going on this weekend.'" If it is shameful to have nothing planned for a weekend, then perhaps work is not what matters. What matters is constant activity.[75]

Unemployment among Those with a Diligent 9-to-5 Work Ethic

Many of my participants distinguished living to work from a different kind of work ethic. This would sometimes happen when I asked whether they agreed with this statement: "Work is central to my identity." Several responded by saying "no" or "not now," but they would immediately add that when they had a job, they had been a conscientious worker:

> CHARLIE MIKE ROMERO (unemployed database administrator): My work—no [. . .] For me, it is my family. My work is important—I mean, I will do it, of course I will always deliver in the best possible manner, it is always my pride when I finish a job well done. I enjoy doing well what I know, but, still, it is not the center of my life. The center of my life is my family. And then comes my work.
>
> NATALIE HARPER (unemployed grant professional): "Work is central to my identity." I might have said that years ago. No, it's just that—I mean, I do a good job. I'm professional.
>
> JIM WADE (former worker in an auto parts store, among other jobs): I'm not a workaholic, but I do believe in hard work.

The quick additions of "I mean I do a good job"; "My work is important—I mean, I will do it, of course I will always deliver in the best possible manner, it is always my pride when I finish a job well done"; and "I do believe in hard work" suggest that these participants did not want me to draw the wrong conclusion when they said work was not central to their identity or they were not a workaholic. Even if their work was not their central concern or what they wanted to do all the time, they still were good workers. Being a conscientious worker has high cultural standing.[76]

Yet, they also spoke as if the common view in their opinion community was that one should not go overboard and become a workaholic. Views that are perceived as representing the common opinion can be stated without qualification.[77] Jim Wade did not explain or defend his statement, "I'm not a workaholic." Nor did Robert Milner when he stated, "Although I work to live, I don't live to work." He made that comment when I asked for his thoughts about the statement, "Work is central to my identity." He said it was, but then he clarified his response so I would not get the wrong idea: "Yes, um . . . by saying—although I work to live, I don't live to work."[78] He reacted as though I might think less of him for agreeing that work was central to his identity. It was as if he had read Weber and did not want me to think he was one of those dull businessmen who was preoccupied with his work to the exclusion of all else. Robert's and Jim's wording implies that *of course* one should not be a workaholic or live to work.

Listening to these participants and others like them, I realized that there was a different kind of productivist work ethic, one that emphasizes pride in one's work effort without making one's job the center of one's interests. This is what I call a *diligent 9-to-5 work ethic*.[79] ("9-to-5" should not be interpreted literally; the actual work hours could be different.) Four key characteristics of a diligent 9-to-5 work ethic are pride in the quality of one's work; needing paid work to feel productive and worthwhile, hence drawing self-esteem from having a job and being a good worker; criticizing those who do not want to go to work; yet believing work time should be contained.

The first three features define a productivist outlook and are also typically held by those with a living-to-work ethic. It is the last feature—believing that work time should be contained—that differentiates the two groups: they differ in their working rhythms and boundaries. For those with a living-to-work ethic, the boundary between work time and nonwork time is porous. Achieving at a high level comes first, and everything else fits into whatever time is left or it is postponed or dropped. By contrast, those with a diligent 9-to-5 work ethic appreciate the rhythm of going to work, focusing on their job, and doing it well—and then leaving the workplace and immersing themselves in the rest of their life. They believe one should be a good worker on the job, but one's job should not be all-consuming. In other words, there should be a division between work time, when one should be devoted to one's job, and nonwork time; this separation is missing for those who live to work. Those with a diligent 9-to-5 work ethic had already erected boundaries between work and the rest of their life that some of my living-to-work participants only began to construct after they lost their jobs.

As I describe the features of a diligent 9-to-5 work ethic, it will become clear that the experience of being unemployed was different for those with this ethic than it was for those who said they had lived to work. Ironically, although those with a diligent 9-to-5 work ethic want boundaries on their work time, when they were unemployed they talked about missing the intangible benefits of work more than did those who had lived to work.

Work Pride and Diligence

At the beginning of this section, we heard from Natalie Harper and Charlie Mike Romero that, although work was not central to their identity, "It is always my pride when I finish a job well done," as Charlie Mike put it. Similarly, Terrance West, who had held a variety of jobs, including working as a shipping-receiving clerk in warehouses and a convenience store clerk, spoke of taking pride in being a good worker: "I take my work very seriously, and I take a lot of pride in what I do." Theresa Allen, who had worked as a waitress and in other jobs in the hospitality industry, was proud to recall, "I would work the Monday through Friday and always be there. [. . .] I remember my boss, I worked at Embassy Suites for about seven years and my boss would say, 'I'm okay. I have the A-Team.'" Emily Quinn remarked, "Nobody can take away my history as an executive assistant." She added, "I was fabulous."

Summer Carrington, who handled foreclosed properties for a big bank, and her sister Krystal Murphy, an administrative assistant at the bank, said they had learned the importance of being conscientious workers growing up, when they went into the office to help their mother, a medical chart clerk: "We learned, all of us, a good work ethic. [. . .] Mom said, you know, 'These are people's lives. These are not just paper. You have to remember that. When you look at a chart, it doesn't matter who they are, anything else. That information needs to be put in there because that's their life.' [. . .] Working and doing the work correctly [*is something*] we learned at an early age."

This pride in being a diligent worker was the first shift from traditionalism that Weber described: it stemmed from Luther's preaching that workers should consider their worldly duties as a sacred calling. Weber spoke of employers' frustration with traditionalistic workers who put little thought or energy into their jobs, and he pointed out that it served employers' purpose for workers to believe they had a religious duty to work hard and well.

It would be a mistake, however, to view work pride as entailing quiet subservience. Summer Carrington had raised hard questions at company meetings and mocked one of her bosses to his face. Terrance West did not hesitate to speak up when he thought he was not being treated properly. Someone with a diligent 9-to-5 work ethic is motivated by pride in their work, not by loyalty to the organization and its management.[80] Workers who master their jobs may realize that they know operations at that level better than their bosses do. The very nature of the diligent 9-to-5 work ethic limits their commitment because workers only agree to be conscientious during their stipulated workday. Terrance was willing to go beyond that, to be called occasionally to answer questions in the middle of the night, but this work ethic only commands doing a good job during one's contractual work hours.

Upholding a duty to be a conscientious, reliable, professional employee explains *how* my participants with this ethic worked. It does not explain *why* they worked and what many of my participants missed when they were unemployed.

Needing Paid Work to Feel Productive and Worthwhile

The eminent social psychologist of unemployment, Marie Jahoda, identified as a key intangible benefit of work that it links individuals to "goals and purposes that transcend their own."[81] We could ask why someone needs paid employment to work to achieve larger goals and purposes. Certainly, those who volunteer their time for a good cause can feel a sense of purpose and make a social contribution. Some participants realized this. Ichabod Jones, an unemployed human services program director, pointed out, "You could be productive doing something else that is not work." However, most of my participants felt they needed paid work to contribute something of value.

My participants' belief that paid work gives them a purpose, and a way to be useful, would often be expressed in response to one of my standard questions, "What would you say is the meaning or importance of work for you?"

> GINGER THI (unemployed administrative assistant): It gives you meaning to life, I feel worthwhile. And it pays the bills.
> JAGAT BODHI (unemployed telecommunications technician): It's a purpose in life. To be able to work. And to contribute. And to be rewarded for your efforts.
> EMILY QUINN (unemployed executive secretary): I miss being valuable.

Without a job, some saw little reason to get up in the morning. Terrance West stated that he hoped to "get back to the workforce and feel like I'm a productive citizen." He hated feeling "lazy" and "kind of like a bum because I'm not working." During his more than two years out of work, he told me, "There's times where I don't even feel like getting out of bed, because I'm like, 'Well, if I get out of bed, what am I gonna do?'" Terrance had many other interests: a boyfriend, a dog, a close family, and a strong interest in politics. Yet, without a job and after months of fruitless job searches, he did not know what to do with his time.

As another participant, Ralph Edwards, put it, "We have to have a purpose in order to sustain life, to get up in the morning. So, the most important reason for work is purpose, and not the monetary one." Ralph was an unpaid lay minister, and he found some purpose in that. However, most of my participants needed a regular, paying job to feel they had a purpose in life and were productive.

Applying Productivist Values to Others

Those who hold a productivist ideology are likely to criticize adults who do not work regularly. Terrance West applied his productivist values not only to himself but also to others. From his mature perspective as a forty-year-old, he criticized young people like his niece and nephew, who were unwilling to work hard for their goals. He said his nephew wants to be a rapper and pretends he had a hard life, which Terrance disputed. He recounted his attempt to set his nephew straight: "'No, kid. Your mom had a hard life. She had to get up at the crack of dawn and take care of your black ass,' you know? 'You didn't have no hard life. Your life is hard now because you didn't put in work.'" Terrance held up his niece and nephew's mother (his sister) as an exemplar of hard work: "I remember her car broke down and she couldn't drive to work, so she went and bought a bike, and she was riding on her bike at 3:00 in the morning. Riding her bike through Rialto to go to work. She would ride it in the rain. Then someone stole her bike, and she was walking, but that's how dedicated—that's how strong her work ethic is. My mother's work ethic is like that." He added, "My work ethic is like that." Terrance's disparaging comments about young people's poor work ethic were common among those in their forties, fifties, and sixties, regardless of their racial identity. I heard similar complaints from middle-aged whites and Latinos about younger family members' or coworkers' lack of diligence.

The topic of government social programs was particularly likely to evoke a productivist discourse. When I asked whether the government should guarantee food, housing, or health care to everyone whether they are working or not, Jake Taylor, a young veteran who returned from deployments in Iraq and Afghanistan, said it depended on why they were not working. He did not currently have a job, so he could understand that someone might not be working even though they wanted to and that others are physically or mentally disabled. Yet, he shared, "People who are lazy, or lackadaisical, just don't want to do anything with their freakin' life or anything like that, I mean, I would make them work for it." This attitude was common among my participants, and other research shows it is common among the US public.[82] As I describe in chapter 4, my participants were grateful for the food stamps and other programs that helped them, and they thought those programs should be available for others who could not find work in a bad economy. They drew a moral line, however, between those who wanted to work and could not find a job, and those who were able to work but not willing to do so. The latter should not receive government support, in their view.

This productivist judgment of those who did not want to work could also be the basis of a class identity: we, the middle class or "working class," are hardworking, unlike the idle poor and the idle rich. For example, Charlie Mike Romero, who had been a database administrator, sketched a pyramid in response to a request to draw an image of society and his place in it. He placed himself in the middle layer of the pyramid, which he labeled "working class." He described his class as "all of us who work" and "make an effort," unlike the "rich and famous" at the top and the "welfare recipients" at the bottom. In his view, a work effort also includes efforts to afford a college degree. He commented that the rich "can go to any university they choose" because they can easily afford the expense, unlike the working class who "work hard in order to be able to get an education."

Yet, this conventional discourse about lazy people was a double-edged sword for the long-term unemployed. They could take pride in having been good workers in the past, but after going months without working, they were keenly aware that others might perceive them as loafers. About a year into my project, I attended a job club reunion. One of the attendees had helped run her family's pharmacy, but after it closed, the only job she could get was as a part-time cashier at a chain drugstore where she earned less than she was receiving from unemployment benefits. She took the job anyway. Another attendee jokingly invoked a common stereotype of the unemployed: "You could be sitting on a couch, with your feet up, watching TV, and eating bonbons." Everyone there understood that was far from the truth, but they suspected that it was what other people thought.

Jim Wade felt that stigma from some older members of his church who had been employed at a time when it was easier to find a job: "I've had problems with people thinking that I was unemployed, you know, because I don't wanna work, I'm not trying to find work." Some of those who had the living-to-work ethic shared their worries about this perception. In our interview, Stacie McCarthy referred to a *Sixty Minutes* segment on employers' reluctance to hire the long-term unemployed. She wondered whether employers "think we're lazy." Pepper Hill commented, "I don't think it's bad to be unemployed, but we put a connotation to it as a negative, and unemployed is seeing someone sitting home just looking for jobs or doing nothing. And number one, as we know, most unemployed people aren't doing that."

Wanting Regular Work Hours

The culture theorist Lauren Berlant writes of the way post-Fordist uncertainty creates "aspirational normalcy"; that is, "the desire to feel normal, and to feel normalcy as a ground of dependable life, a life that does not have to keep being reinvented." Going to work, she explains, is one way of constructing a dependable, normal life.[83] Less poetically, the social psychologist Marie Jahoda proposed that having a "time structure" is one of the intangible benefits of working.[84]

As I have argued, that is an overgeneralization: those with a living-to-work ethic do not need dependable work patterns or a fixed time structure. After experiencing working from home during the COVID-19 pandemic, many may find that a fixed time structure is less important. Still, most of my participants with a diligent 9-to-5 work ethic in the pre-pandemic period missed their regular working hours—leaving home in the morning and returning at night—and the sense of normalcy that this routine had provided.

Fixed work hours are not universal; some argue they are a malign invention. In Lucien Febvre's evocative terms, industrial capitalism brought about a shift from lived time (*le temps vécu*) to measured time (*le temps mesuré*).[85] In an influential article, the historian E. P. Thompson wrote about the shift from the irregular schedules that are common in pastoral and agricultural societies—where work rhythms depended on requirements of the task, the season, and the hours of sunlight—to industrial time set by clocks. He saw chaining work to the clock as contributing to the rigid Puritan attitude about wasting time described by Weber. Thompson appreciated the earlier task orientation because it required the "least demarcation between 'work' and 'life.' Social intercourse and labour are intermingled—the working-day lengthens or contracts according the task."[86] At the end of his article, he called for a return to the earlier rhythms: "Men might have to re-learn some of the arts of living lost in the industrial revolution: how to fill the interstices of their days with enriched, more leisurely, personal and social relations; how to break down once more the barriers between work and life."[87]

Yet, as Thompson realized, "No culture re-appears in the same form."[88] He wrote this article in the late 1960s as leisure time was increasing, but that trend has since reversed. Thompson wanted to let some personal time back into working hours instead of maintaining their separation, but the reverse has been happening: work is infiltrating personal time, especially for white-collar workers.[89] It matters whether breaching barriers between work and the rest of life will give workers more personal time and greater flexibility, or less personal time and thus fewer options about how to spend their time.

Many of my unemployed participants in the early 2010s aspired to return to regular, dependable daily and weekly rhythms of work time alternating with time outside work. They did not want unending free time during their weekdays while they were unemployed, nor did they want their jobs to spill over into their evenings and weekends once they were working again. They also preferred a spatial division, with work and the rest of their life occurring in different locations.

Several participants spoke about missing the routine of getting up and going to work:

> DELLA JONES (unemployed teacher): Since I don't have a job, I kind of don't know what I'm doing. It's not that you just don't have any money. It's also you get up and you're not going to work. You miss that whole thing.
>
> AMBER WASHINGTON (unemployed social service agency administrator): I need structure. I need something to get up and go to every day and know I'm gonna be there [. . .] 9:00 to 5:30 or 9:00 to 6:00 every day.
>
> MICKEY MULLER (unemployed engineer): Work would get me up in the morning, go someplace, have relationships with my coworkers.
>
> MARY BROWN (unemployed student adviser): I've always worked. So, you know, it's kind of weird not getting up and going to work every day.
>
> TERRANCE WEST (unemployed shipping-receiving clerk): I hate the not having somewhere to be every day and the being on a set schedule.

Defined work times also create a distinction between idleness and leisure. For those with a diligent 9-to-5 work ethic, leisure is enjoyable when it contrasts with and refreshes one from work. Idleness during normal working hours is something else entirely. Day and night, weekdays and weekends, flow together without distinction. Terrance West said, "Sure, I like to sleep in from time to time, but not all the time. Yeah, sure, I like to watch TV, but I don't want to watch it all the time." My participants appreciated that being out of work gave them more personal time than their previous overfull work schedules had allowed, but they did not need or want as much free time as they had.

Some spoke of work as necessary for their health and well-being. Summer Carrington and Krystal Murphy attributed their father's untimely death in his late fifties to the closing of the Kaiser steel mill where he had worked, leaving him nothing to do but hang around the house and clean his guns. Hillary Edwards, who had been a banker, said, "Work is a stress buster." She explained, "You can sit at home and be depressed, but if you go out to work and around other people, you don't have that problem." When I asked Miguel Vargas, an unemployed business operations manager, what he thought about the statement, "Work is central to my identity," he replied that he did not work for his identity: he worked "to be healthy. If you're working, your body will still continue to work." Not going to work, he said, was like leaving a car on the street to rust. In that sense, regular work can be a form of self-care, if it is properly bounded.[90]

Boundaries are important for those with a diligent 9-to-5 work ethic. In their view, work time should not intrude on nonwork time. Celeste Rue, an administrative assistant, was clear about this. She recounted telling a coworker in a recent job, "I said, 'I love doing this.' I said, 'But once I walk out the door at five o'clock, my day begins. I can't wait to get to work, and then when I'm at work, I can't wait to get home to family stuff.'" Miriam Ramos loved being a hairdresser, but time away from work was equally important to her. She recounted being incredulous when another hairdresser said the salon owner was forcing her to work six days a week. Miriam said to her, "'Well, the whole point of working is not just to work. It's to have a balanced life so you feel good about your work and what you're doing.'" Jorge Paiz, a construction worker, corrected his wife's translation when he talked about his ideal job. Initially she thought he had said, "It doesn't matter if you have to work extra hours or hard work." He explained that, no, he was happy to do hard work, but he did not want to work extra hours.

Ichabod Jones is an interesting example because he had the opportunity to pursue higher-level jobs but chose not to do so to preserve his free time. After he received his master's degree in public health, he held program director positions in human services for nearly thirty years. He was not interested in moving up to an executive director position because "I want to be able to go home at five o'clock. I don't like the thought that I've got to meet with this group, I've got to meet with that group, the board, the foundation." He acknowledged that anyone looking at his resume would say, "'Well, Ichabod, that's a natural progression.'" His response was, "I know the bus is going there, but I want to get off the bus sooner." When I asked the salary he would be satisfied with in the future, he said he would be satisfied with a large pay cut from the $80,000 a year he had earned before, if it were a secure job that would give him "peace of mind."

Wanting to Belong

Taking part in those rhythms of going to work and coming home is a way not only of structuring one's time but also of forming human connections and being part of mainstream society.[91]

Emily Quinn, a former executive secretary, said that work meant for her a sense of "belonging." Without a job, she felt left out. She depicted this feeling when I asked her to draw a picture of society and her place in it. Emily drew a fence, on one side of which were people laughing, talking, and going together into and out of a workplace and a restaurant. She was on the other side of the fence, alone (figure 2.1). The weekly job club meetings and accountability/

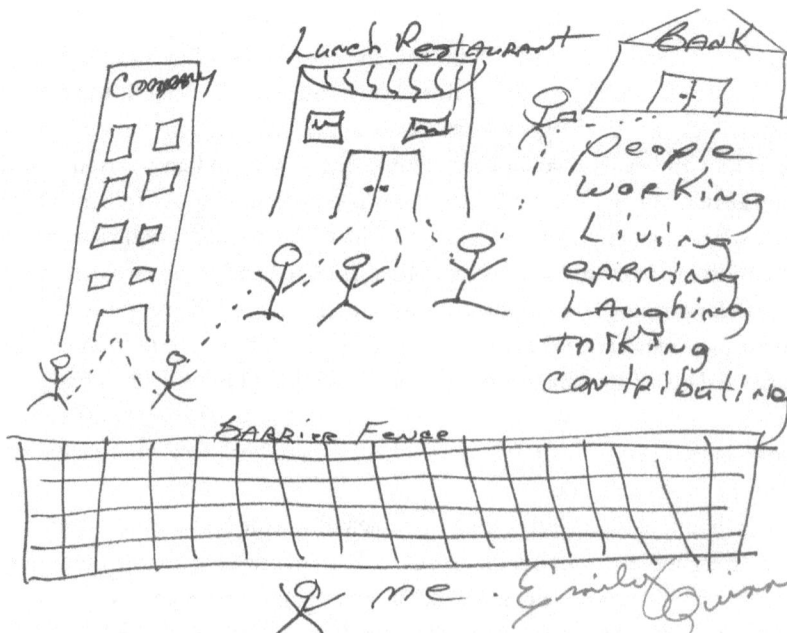

FIGURE 2.1. Emily Quinn's drawing in response to the question, "How do you see society and your place in it?"

support group meetings she had attended were not a substitute for going to work every day.

Part of what Emily missed was socializing with coworkers. In chapter 6, I discuss how socializing with coworkers contributed to making a job "fun." However, the feeling of belonging goes beyond socializing. For those with this productivist work ethic, what matters is a broader sense of having a place in society.

Two people spoke of being jobless as akin to being homeless. Natalie Harper, the grant professional I quoted earlier as saying her work was not central to her identity, still said she felt "marginalized" by being out of work. While she was unemployed, she felt, "I'm not in the mainstream of America." She said she would think of that when she saw people wearing work badges: "I see people walking around [. . .] with little ID badges. Maybe work isn't my identity, but having that badge distinguishes somebody in a traditional way. It's like having a house key means you have a door to unlock. Homeless people don't have to have a key."

Ann Lopez, an unemployed IT worker, also used the metaphor of being homeless and feeling "misplaced." This came to a head when she tried to keep busy while she was out of work by helping her sister, only to displease her. Ann said, "I really wanted to cry and get depressed 'cause I felt misplaced." Searching for words to explain her feeling of being "misplaced," she said, "Like a homeless [*person*], because you're jobless, basically. You don't have a home to go to every day. You don't have a routine." For Ann, a "routine" is more than a structure for her time. It also provides a place to go and belong.

My participants' desires to belong, to be healthy, and to return to the routines of going to work were not morally loaded the way that their values of being productive and conscientious were. They spoke of what they needed and wanted, not only of what they ought to do.[92]

It is significant, however, that what my participants enjoyed was work that was organized in a certain way—with regular hours that were not onerous and at a shared workplace where they could socialize with others. All of that changed for the 42 percent of Americans who worked from home during the early months of the COVID-19 pandemic in 2020.[93] Suddenly, many had more flexible working hours, with greater opportunities to take care of personal or family needs during the hours they had previously been expected to be at the office focused on their job. Those who used to spend an hour or more commuting between their home and their office gained precious time to use to meet their own needs and those of their family. On the downside, however, some had to work longer hours during the pandemic, and many parents found trying to combine childcare with their work unbearably stressful. Workers under the age of fifty reported having difficulty being motivated to do their jobs remotely.[94] Earlier research found that, after an initial honeymoon period, those who work from home full time miss human contact.[95] If working from home were to become the dominant way of organizing work in the future, a normal life would no longer be defined by a fixed workday or by leaving home and then returning to it. The new normal could have its own pleasures, but they would be different.

The Diligent 9-to-5 Job Search: Re-Creating a Normal Workday

Earlier I described the psychic benefits of the elaborate, time-consuming rituals of contemporary job hunting in the United States for those who had held a living-to-work ethic. For those with a diligent 9-to-5 work ethic, the career counseling, job club, networking, and accountability group meetings also yielded psychic and social benefits.

For one thing, going to these meetings enabled them to defend against any perception that they were just kicking back and enjoying their free time. My interviewees rebutted suspicions that they were loafing by reciting their job search efforts: "I'm up there, Employment Resource Center, on a regular basis. I'm checking, using all the methods of job search" (Jim Wade); "I'm doing what I can. I check my websites every day [and] I'm going to the networking [meetings]" (Daniel Horn). Mona Childs's conscience was clear: "I really have to ask myself truthfully, were you dedicated in using your time wisely and looking for work, in networking, and doing as much as you can? And I do. People that know me have told me, 'Mona, let's just put it this way. We can't fault you for trying. You try harder than anyone we know.' I do try really hard."

Like other researchers, I often heard the refrain that finding another job was a job in itself, which it certainly could be.[96] Robert Milner said, "I've been telling people we probably work harder at trying to find a job than most people do that are already working." Linda McDaniel made the same point: "My full-time job right now is finding new employment, and so, every Monday morning [attending the Employment Development Department job club], that's my way of reminding myself and goal setting for what I want to accomplish that week. Who do I want to talk to? What do I want to change on my resume? What interview skills can I gain? How do I need to tweak my thirty-second commercial?"

Not all unemployed people fill up their time with job search activities. My sample was biased toward those who did, because I met many of my participants at career counseling sessions, job clubs, and accountability group meetings. By contrast, those I met because they were referred to me by friends included a discouraged worker who may also have been suffering from depression and spent his days watching television; someone who was physically disabled; and a woman who had quit full-time work many years before we met and only returned to the job market when her husband lost his job. These people did not feel the need to stay so busy. However, they were the exceptions among my participants.

Like those with a living-to-work ethic, those with a diligent 9-to-5 work ethic found ways to stay busy in addition to attending those meetings, such as by doing volunteer work and taking occasional freelance jobs. However, those who had lived to work and those with the diligent 9-to-5 work ethic stayed busy in different ways. At least some of the former, like Lisa Rose and Elizabeth Montgomery, went all out on the optional aspects of the job search like networking, trying to stay almost as busy as they had been when they were working. By contrast, for many of those with a diligent 9-to-5 work ethic, one goal (in addition to finding another job) seemed to be to re-create the routines of a normal workday. The job search rituals were a form of what Michael Flaherty calls "time work": "ways in which people attempt to control or customize their own experience of time."[97]

That was clear in the way Robert Milner responded when I asked about his daily routine while he was unemployed. He said he got up early, checked his email, and took a walk before he left the house at 8:00 or 9:00 A.M. Then he went to Starbucks, which he used as his office. There he would look at job openings online and go through his social media to see whom he could contact for leads. He belonged to two accountability groups, each of which met weekly. ("I'll go there, spend some time, just to talk to people who are in the same situation as I'm in. Try to help each other. Try to set some goals.") He had two friends in business whom he helped without pay so he could keep his skills up to date, and sometimes he did research in the town library. He returned home around 4:00 P.M. and then would work out in the community center's fitness room. In this way he managed a semblance of a normal working day.[98] Going out to Starbucks was an important part of that: "It's just a great way to be amongst people who are kind of doing the same thing." Also, it helped him and his wife, a full-time homemaker, maintain their separate realms: "My wife is at home. That's her space. That's her time."

Note that exercise was also part of Robert Milner's daily routine: a walk to start the day and a workout at the community center to end it. Exercise was a regular part of many of my interviewees' daily routines. Few could afford a gym membership, but they could take advantage of the warm southern California climate by biking, walking, and running outdoors. When he was not looking for work or taking odd jobs, Daniel Horn, a former contractor, would run for three miles every other day and was up to 190 pushups, which he explained by saying, "I can't just sit around."[99]

Regular exercise, of course, contributes to both physical health and mental health because it relieves stress. It also is a way of staying busy, of structuring time and filling it. As Ann Lopez said, "People think I don't do nothing. But, you know, hey, I do things. I keep myself busy." However, those with a diligent 9-to-5 work ethic did not describe social pressures to be "busy, busy, busy"—the unending busyness of those who live to work. Instead, the social pressure they faced was to do something productive during conventional working hours.

Thus, Americans' time work is not limited to work time. As I explained, a busyness ethos is not necessarily a *work* ethic; for example, exercise is one of many ways of staying busy. Nor does a stay-busy ethos require living to work, although these have been equated. For example, a guide for international visitors to the United States links Americans' valuation of staying active to workaholism and identifying with one's occupation:

> People think that it is "sinful" to "waste one's time," to sit around doing nothing or just to "daydream." Such a "no nonsense" attitude toward life has created many people who have come to be known as "workaholics," or people who are addicted to their work, who think constantly about their jobs and who are frustrated if they are kept away from them, even during their evening hours and weekends. The workaholic syndrome, in turn, causes Americans to identify themselves wholly with their professions.[100]

This cultural stereotype ignores the legions of diligent 9-to-5 workers who like to stay busy but who reject workaholism.

The Two Productivist Work Ethics Now

The two groups I have described here, those with a living-to-work ethic and those with a diligent 9-to-5 work ethic, share some productivist values and beliefs. Members of both groups take pride in the quality of their work and judge themselves and others by their work effort. However, these believers in hard work found these same productivist values were turned against them when others judged that their long-term unemployment indicated a deficient work ethic. Putting considerable time into their job search was one way to defend against those negative judgments and to stay busy—another value they shared.

However, it is also important to recognize the differences between a diligent 9-to-5 work ethic and a living-to-work ethic. Those with a diligent 9-to-5 work ethic want fixed working hours that leave them time for other things, whereas those with a living-to-work ethic are willing to work as long as necessary to reach their goals. With the forced interruption of unemployment, several of those who had lived to work began to question their former values. Nevertheless, some of those same people put long hours into their job search, even beyond the considerable effort expended by those with a diligent 9-to-5 work ethic, for whom it was more important to replicate a regular workday while they searched for another job.

Weber's *Protestant Ethic and the Spirit of Capitalism* turned a spotlight on those who live to work. However, I suspect from my interviews in this project, my earlier research, studies of workers who "pass" as working longer hours than they do, and surveys of Americans' working hours that workers with a diligent 9-to-5 work ethic are more numerous in the United States than those who willingly devote all their time and attention to their job.[101]

These two productivist work ethics may not be fixed orientations. Some of my participants' ways of structuring their time changed, usually going from a living-to-work ethic to a 9-to-5 work ethic. When I asked Natalie Harper, an unemployed grant professional in her early sixties, whether work was central to her identity, she replied, "I might have said that years ago." Stacie McCarthy, the loan processor who used to bring work home even though that was not expected in her position, stopped doing that in her new job. It is possible that younger workers might change in the other direction, perhaps taking on a living-to-work work ethic if they found work that inspired them to set aside everything else.

It is also possible for social and cultural values to change. One analysis of Americans' holiday letters found a dramatic increase in references to the writer's hectic schedule since the 1960s.[102] Perhaps this "conspicuous consumption of time" will lessen. Some observers hope that the COVID-19 pandemic, which disrupted so many social habits, will lead to a greater appreciation of leisure and relaxation instead of being "crazy busy."[103]

Some of my participants were not especially motivated by either work ethic described in this chapter. Rather than being shaped by productivist attitudes, their work choices were driven primarily by consumption desires (working to live well), by the desire to be financially self-sufficient and care for their families (working to live), or by their gender identities and intimate relationships. In addition, work motivations and experiences are shaped by specific occupations and workplaces. I discuss these alternative ways of thinking about work and the problems they created for those out of work in the next several chapters, beginning with working to live well.

CHAPTER 3

Working to Live Well

In the last chapter, I showed that holding productivist values of being a hard worker can be the basis for claiming a middle-class identity in the United States. Another way of signaling a middle-class identity is through one's consumption. As the anthropologist Anna Jefferson puts it, being middle class in the United States "has also always been about appropriate consumption."[1] Yet, just what constitutes *appropriate* consumption, and how do those who are out of work judge themselves by that slippery standard?

According to Weber, in the seventeenth and eighteenth centuries, an entrepreneur motivated by the Protestant ethic worked tirelessly to earn a high income but did not spend it: "He gets nothing out of his wealth for himself, except the irrational sense of having done his job well."[2] By the time Weber wrote at the beginning of the twentieth century, he thought that had changed: "Material goods have gained an increasing and finally an inexorable power over the lives of men," becoming like an "iron cage."[3]

Weber's account, which argues that productivism was a reigning motive in the seventeenth and eighteenth, centuries in Western Europe and the United States, only to be displaced by consumerism at some point in the late nineteenth or early twentieth centuries, has been challenged by many historians. There are debates about whether a European "consumer revolution" began as early as the 1400s, or was triggered by inexpensive fabrics imported from

India to England in the late 1600s, or truly took off with the creation of department stores in the 1800s.[4] I do not have the historical expertise to contribute to debates about key shifts in the history of consumption in the West, and certainly not for the rest of the world.[5] What matters for a discussion of contemporary work meanings is Weber's insight that working hard because one values being a good worker is not the same as working hard to earn money to spend as one chooses.

My participants worked to earn money to spend, in addition to any other motives they had, such as wanting to do well at their jobs or because they enjoyed them. With only a few exceptions, they sought not just a bare living but also a higher standard. They also had pressing immediate needs, and in chapter 4, I discuss how they met them. Still, my participants had not worked just to meet their basic needs. They did not work just to live; they worked to live well. Their long-term unemployment imperiled their consumption dreams.

Carl Mathews is a prime example of someone who worked long hours, but not because he was a workaholic or especially engaged with his job. He worked hard because he wanted to earn enough money to live well. Carl's class identity rested on his level of consumption. As he saw it, a nice home, car, and clothing were what made him middle-class. Spending on luxuries at home and on vacation also made life more pleasurable. Unlike many of my participants, Carl freely expressed the pleasure he had taken in his prior level of consumption. However, once he lost his job and had no income for nearly a year, he harbored dark fears of becoming completely destitute. Oddly, so did many others who had worked especially hard to earn high incomes—more so than the unemployed who had formerly earned middle-range or lower incomes. His story raises many questions about the conflicting messages Americans hear about consumption and their differing ways of defining "appropriate consumption."

Carl had been a security officer working for the city of Los Angeles. When this book was written, the average salary for security officers working for the city was only a little over $48,000 a year, but when Carl was working, there were overtime opportunities that paid double the usual hourly rate.[6] Carl said he used to work seventy hours a week to obtain overtime pay. Sometimes he was so tired that he nearly fell asleep driving home. He recalled, "I used to work so much overtime, either before shift or after shift, I was actually killing myself 'cause I was taking medicine to go to sleep, but I was taking medicine to wake me up. I'd be drinking a lot of coffee to wake me up because, sometimes, I, literally, would come home, shower and lay down for two hours, get up and go right back out, or, I'll just sleep at the job in my car 'cause it wasn't worth it [to drive home]." Carl was able to make between $120,000 and $160,000 a year this way, and he earned additional income serving in the National Guard.

His wife had a good salary as well. He estimated that at its highest, their annual household income had been between $200,000 and $250,000.

Why did he work so hard? Carl explained, "I was putting in, sometimes, over twelve hours a day just so I could make my home a palace." He saw no reason why he and his wife should only enjoy comfortable, beautiful furnishings when they were on vacation: "Hey, you ever went on vacation and you said, 'Oh! This is beautiful. Man! I like this.' You told your husband, 'We gonna come here again! Look at the couch, look at the chairs, the bed! I could live here forever!' But, see, that's how you should [*always*] feel, in my mind. Why do I need to go someplace else to feel that way when I could feel that way in my house? I want everybody to come here and feel like they was on vacation, 'cause it's gonna be a palace, here." When I asked why that was important to him, Carl replied, "You only live once . . . live the best you can. If God give it to you, do the best you can." He went on to reminisce about the time his wife had just had an operation so he treated her to a vacation in a villa that "cost me, like, four Gs [*$4,000*] for five days. But it was worth it . . . we had massages every day. I was in a shower with over thirty shower heads. I was in a pink bathtub with jets, drinking champagne." He also described the luxurious cruise they took in which they stayed in a private suite where he could look out over the ocean, drink cognac, and smoke cigars.

I was confused by his responses because Carl is a devout Christian, and I recalled Bible verses such as the well-known passage, "It is easier for a camel to go through the eye of a needle than for a rich person to enter the kingdom of God." Both in that interview and in an earlier one, Carl told the New Testament story of the rich man who lived in luxury, refusing to share food with the beggar Lazarus at his gate. After they died, Lazarus went to heaven, and the rich man was tormented in hell. The moral, Carl explained, is that "money can't buy you eternity. It can't put you in a better place." I explained my confusion to him: "That's what I'm trying to put together . . . you know, those two sides 'cause, on the one hand, you want Lazarus's afterlife, but you want the rich man's life now?" Carl replied, "Why not?" He explained, "God doesn't hate rich people." The lesson to be learned from the story of Lazarus and the rich man is not that it is bad to be rich but that it is bad to be selfish: "If you're blessed to have it, enjoy it. Just remember how you got it, who let you get it, and [. . .] help others." In other words, if God blesses you with wealth in your life, there is no sin in enjoying it so long as you are also generous. As Carl explained, "While I'm male or female, I'm gonna do that same thing that male and females do . . . I'ma get married, I'ma go around the world, I'ma eat lobster and shrimp. In the next life, I'll be living outside the realm of time. . . . I won't need food." He agreed that "money can't buy happiness," because true happiness was an eternal reward; however, money "can buy fun."[7]

When Carl had money, he generously shared it with his family, friends, and strangers. At the time we met, however, he was broke after eleven months out of work. Carl had been searching diligently for another job, but it was difficult for someone in their early fifties to find another security officer job. One prospective employer told him the company did not hire anyone over thirty-seven years old. Carl had been fired from his city job for what he considered to be false charges, and being fired made him ineligible for unemployment benefits. Yet even before he lost his job, the city had begun to limit overtime opportunities, and in response Carl tried to cut his expenses. He had contacted his bank to see whether they would modify his mortgage, but despite government programs requiring banks to work with homeowners in danger of foreclosure due to the recession, the bank refused to do so.[8] Carl was in arrears on his mortgage, and he had declared bankruptcy, ruining his credit rating. He was also expecting his wife to leave him; their marriage had been strained because he had worked nights when she worked days, and they had spent little time together aside from their vacations. Carl anticipated that she would be unwilling to stay with him once he stopped earning an income. Nor could he get any financial help from others whom he had helped in the past. He used to pick up the check when he and his friends got together. Now that he was penniless, no one returned the favor: "Now that I need the meal or the friendship or whatever, you don't get it. You don't get the camaraderie. You don't get the 'Hey, glad to see you.' You don't get that." It made Carl feel that his friends had only valued him because of his generosity.[9]

In our first interview, Carl spoke of his financial difficulties as a spiritual test: "It's a test of faith, you know? Just to see how I'm going to do." He emphasized staying positive and counting his blessings. The second time we met, however, his comments were darker. While talking about how his spending had changed, he shared the following story:

> You know your whole situation changes. For a person that worked all the time to come to this [. . .] I was going on a job interview one time, I was right down the street at the Jack in the Box. And I seen this white guy [Carl is Black], he was—it's the daytime, he's in the trashcan in the daytime pulling out food and eating it. And he don't care who's looking at him; he just pulling it out, eating it and eating it. And all the food he couldn't eat, he's putting it in his pocket. And I almost didn't want to buy anything to eat at that point, not because he disgusted me but

because I saw myself in his shoes. He didn't disgust me because I've seen people do that before. I just figured, "God bless them." I hate that he had to do like that. Ordinarily, I'd be the kind of guy to go out and buy him something to eat. But I looked at him and it shook me up so bad because I said, "I'm one step from that. That could be me eating out of that same trashcan, having those same people look at me." [. . .] How long it going to be before I probably get divorced? Or whatever. Won't have no benefits and won't have nowhere to go, nowhere to hide.

I asked Carl whether he could stay with his parents, if need be, but he did not think they had room because other people were living in their house. Imagining himself homeless and eating from a trashcan brought intense shame. He said, "I can't stay here because too many people know me here. I don't want to be homeless here." He said he was not thinking of killing himself, but he could understand why someone in that situation might do so: "I used to always say, 'How could somebody kill theyself?' But I can understand why. Sometimes it's better to die than go through all that. You know, and I don't wish death on nobody, but everybody knows what they can take. If this is what it is. . . . You know, I ain't gonna be eating out of garbage cans. Dead people don't have to worry about eating. Dead people don't have to worry about nothing no more."

Carl's wife did leave him, he did lose his home, and physical ailments from his National Guard service made it hard for him to take another job. However, Carl's situation took a turn for the better. Two years later, when we met for a follow-up interview, he was buoyant. After he lost his home, he was able to stay with his parents. He had begun to receive retirement benefits from his military service, which would soon be bolstered by pensions from his city job and Social Security disability. He was wearing a spiffy new shirt, and he was thrilled to show me his new, full-size SUV. They were a stark contrast from his description of the embarrassing signs of his poverty when we had met two years earlier. He said he was "middle-class, now," unlike when I had first met him and "my car was bad, my clothes were bad." He was in college studying business with the goal of going into business for himself. He was also hoping to meet someone and marry again someday. Carl said his story had "a happy ending."

Carl's story raises many questions about Americans' work meanings in relation to their consumption goals and how they may change under financial strain. Listening to Carl, it is easy to understand the appeal of a luxurious home and fabulous vacations. Yet, his unbridled pleasure in such spending was rare among my participants. How did others think about working to live well and about the unemployment that reduced them to poverty? Many of my participants were also on the brink of financial ruin, but did they share Carl's feelings of shame? Why were fears of destitution especially common among those of my participants who had previously had the highest incomes?

In this chapter, I address these questions by showing, first, the mixed messages about consumer spending in contemporary US society and then the differing ways in which my unemployed participants drew on those mixed messages. I found a continuum of attitudes—from those who seemed relatively indifferent to material possessions, to those who spoke of their reduced spending as a profound and beneficial change, to those who had conflicting feelings, to those who spoke only of negative aspects of their reduced spending, and to those, like Carl, for whom drastically reduced consumption created intense shame and fear. The financial setback of long-term unemployment or underemployment was especially complicated for immigrants, who could compare their current living standard with others in their country of origin, with native-born US Americans, or with other immigrants in the United States.

Mixed Messages about Consumption

My claim that there are conflicting discourses about consumer spending in the United States may seem surprising. "The American dream" is commonly imagined as the opportunity to live at least a comfortable, middle-class life and perhaps to achieve great wealth. For example, the sample sentence provided by the Merriam-Webster dictionary to illustrate the meaning of "the American dream" is, "With good jobs, a nice house, two children, and plenty of money, they believed they were living *the American dream*."[10]

Many commentators have proposed that concern with material acquisition was developed early and to an unusual extent in the United States. Alexis de Tocqueville contrasted Americans' desires for "the comforts of life" with the indifference to physical comforts that he believed was common in Europe in the eighteenth and early nineteenth centuries: "In [*European*] nations where an aristocracy dominates society, the people finally get used to their poverty just as the rich do to their opulence. The latter are not preoccupied with physical comfort, enjoying it without trouble; the former do not think about it at all because they despair of getting it and because they do not know enough about it to want it."[11] By contrast, in a society like the United States where the middle class has predominated,[12] concern with such comforts becomes a common preoccupation, according to Tocqueville: "But when [. . .] education and freedom spread, the poor conceive an eager desire to acquire comfort, and the rich think of the danger of losing it. . . . They are therefore continually engaged in pursuing or striving to retain these precious, incomplete, and fugitive delights. . . . The passion for physical comfort is essentially a middle-class affair; it grows and spreads with that class and becomes preponderant with it."[13]

Writing in the late-nineteenth century, the economist Thorstein Veblen agreed with Tocqueville that class boundaries were permeable in modern societies. In contrast to Tocqueville, however, Veblen emphasized the aspirational influence of upper-class lifestyles on the middle class.[14] Rejecting a view of humans as driven to maximize economic utilities, Veblen focused instead on status seeking through "conspicuous consumption":

> In modern civilized communities the lines of demarcation between social classes have grown vague and transient, and wherever this happens the norm of reputability imposed by the upper class extends its coercive influence with but slight hindrance down through the social structure to the lowest strata. The result is that the members of each stratum accept as their ideal of decency the scheme of life in vogue in the next higher stratum, and bend their energies to live up to that ideal. On pain of forfeiting their good name and their self-respect in case of failure, they must conform to the accepted code, at least in appearance.
>
> The basis on which good repute in any highly organized industrial community ultimately rests is pecuniary strength; and the means of showing pecuniary strength, and so of gaining or retaining a good name, are leisure and a conspicuous consumption of goods.[15]

Veblen saw the need to show outward signs of wealth as especially great in urban, mobile environments where people did not know much about their neighbors other than what they could infer from their houses, furnishings, dress, ornaments, and leisure pursuits.[16]

If Veblen is right, then consumption ideals in the twenty-first-century United States would be influenced by the huge gulf in incomes and discretionary spending that has opened both between the rich and the upper-middle class, and between the upper-middle class and everyone else. From 1947 through 1979, US incomes grew at the same rate at all income levels. However, from 1979 to 2016, the average after-tax income of the top 1 percent of US families increased by 226 percent versus only 47 percent for the middle 60 percent.[17] Writing in a Veblenesque vein, Juliet Schor suggests that "to compensate for the growing chasm between their lifestyles and those of the rich and famous, these upper-middles also began conspicuously acquiring . . . luxury symbols," even if that meant, for example, "leasing luxury vehicles they often couldn't afford."[18] The examples set by the upper-middles then affected norms for what constituted appropriate consumption for everyone else and changed the types of products available for consumption (larger houses, more expensive appliances). "Upward comparison" also occurred as families with one earner observed neighboring families with two earners. Taking inflation into account, the average American's spending increased by at least 30 percent and by as much as 70 percent between 1979 and 1995.[19]

The importance of consumer spending is hardly limited to the United States, as social theorist Zygmunt Bauman notes in describing a global shift from producer societies to consumer societies. For Bauman, the difference between a producer society and a consumer society lies in which role is socially most important. He argues that during the industrial period, being a good worker was what mattered; in the present, late-modern period, what matters is being a good consumer. Good consumers must never remain satisfied with what they have. They must be ready to spend to get something new, better, or at least different.[20] An important corollary of the shift to a consumer society is that poverty is interpreted differently. Being poor in a producer society is equated with the shameful status of not working. By contrast, being poor in a consumer society is shameful because one cannot spend. It means becoming "a flawed consumer."[21]

Bauman's distinction between productivist values and consumerist values helps us understand Carl Matthews. He did not work seventy hours a week because he lived to work; he worked that hard to earn money to spend. His understanding of his class identity rested on being a certain kind of consumer. In Bauman's terms, the shame Carl felt about his old car and clothes while he was unemployed could be perfectly summed up by saying that Carl saw himself as a "flawed consumer."

However, Bauman's typology is too sweeping. As I showed in the last chapter, productivist values are still strong in the United States. Many of my participants valued being a good worker beyond the income they earned. Furthermore, having a productivist work ethic and having consumer desires are not mutually exclusive. It is possible to take pride in your work and believe in working hard and, at the same time, to enjoy spending the money you earn. American mythology celebrates those who work hard and become wealthy through their own efforts. Riches are considered the just reward for hard work. That cultural model joins prosperity and consumption to hard work.

Yet, although there are strong consumption pressures, there are also forces pushing the other way. It is too simple to say that Americans' values are materialistic and that their vision of a good life requires conspicuous consumption. In the United States there are also widespread critiques of excessive consumption.[22] It is perhaps unsurprising that a society with strong consumption pressures would generate counter-discourses critiquing excessive consumption. Critiques of material excess condemn this spending as immoral, imprudent, unhealthy, unsustainable, and ineffective in promoting happiness.

The first criticism is that materialistic priorities and excessive consumption are morally suspect. In this cultural model, materialistic excess is blamed in part on the bad example set by the dissolute lives of rich celebrities. Both in my interviews for this book and in my earlier research, my participants excoriated celebrities for self-indulgent spending when they could be giving away more of their wealth. Parents were blamed, as well, for "spoiling" their children by handing them money and toys, as the participants compared the extravagant present with an imagined simpler, more wholesome past. Other analysts have seen in Americans' concerns about the immorality of excessive consumption the survival of the Puritan suspicion of self-indulgence.[23] I would also point to long-standing populist critiques of the rich. In American popular culture, the rich are often portrayed as immoral villains who prey on the moral middle class.

That second criticism of excessive materialism—that it is imprudent to spent more than one can afford—was widespread during the Great Recession. Although many in the public blamed that recession on the greed of commercial lenders and Wall Street investment bankers, a conflicting narrative blamed consumers for taking on excessive debt. In one famous example, the CNBC reporter Rick Santelli criticized the Obama administration for proposing to help homeowners facing foreclosure, accusing it of "promoting bad behavior" among "losers."[24] Although Carl Mathews and others of my participants who were facing foreclosure on their homes did not see themselves as "losers," many criticized their own previous spending habits after their unemployment made it impossible for them to carry their debt load.

An alternative critique of excessive consumption sees it not as a moral failing but as a disease. As Anne Meneley's overview of recent scholarship on the anthropology of consumption points out, "Excessive consumerism . . . is increasingly medicalized."[25] Although "compulsive shopping disorder" (or "compulsive buying disorder") has not been listed in the *Diagnostic and Statistical Manual of Mental Disorders*, it is considered by many therapists to be an addiction or possible variety of obsessive-compulsive disorder.[26]

Another late twentieth-century and early twenty-first-century critique is that excessive material consumption is unsustainable, both because of the resources required to produce the products consumed and the waste that accumulates when unwanted products are discarded.[27] Concerns about sustainability and the environment contributed to the countercultural ethos of the late 1960s; at present in the United States, young adults' concern about the environmental and human costs of cheap clothing has helped popularize buying used clothing instead of new clothes.[28]

Finally, there is a long-standing conventional discourse advising that material consumption is ineffective: having more money and more "toys" will not provide the happiness that consumers desire. Founding father Benjamin Franklin is reported to have said, "Money never made a man happy yet, nor will it. There is nothing in its nature to produce happiness. The more a man has, the more he wants. Instead of its filling a vacuum, it makes one. If it satisfies one want, it doubles and trebles that want another way."[29] Or, as the popular saying goes, "Money can't buy happiness."

Several of these arguments are offered by the organization New Dream (formerly the Center for a New American Dream). Its mission statement begins, "We envision a world in which the values that enhance well-being—relationships, service to others, spending time in nature, community building, and personal growth—are the primary drivers of societal behavior, resulting in reduced consumption and a healthier planet." That center asks Americans to "join us in challenging the idea that our worth or happiness is represented by what we buy."[30]

If all these pro- and anti-consumerist pressures in the United States were not already confusing enough, they are further complicated by different spiritual and religious outlooks, especially in Christian theology. On the one hand, Christian religious and spiritual values are often contrasted with materialistic values. The New Testament is full of verses like "Do not lay up for yourselves treasures on earth, where moth and rust destroy and where thieves break in and steal, but lay up for yourselves treasures in heaven" (Matthew 6:19–20) and "the love of money is a root of all kinds of evils" (Timothy 6:10). However, for preachers of the Christian movement known as "the prosperity gospel," the pursuit of wealth and enjoyment of what it brings are entirely consistent with the teachings of Jesus.

As Kate Bowler's history explains, the Christian prosperity movement began with the preaching of Pentecostal ministers in the mid-twentieth century that good health and great wealth were the rightful due of those who had strong faith. The movement exploded in the late 1970s,[31] the same period when incomes began to climb more steeply for the top 1 percent of Americans than for everyone else. Much as in the Calvinism of seventeenth-century Europe, material success is an outward sign of piety for prosperity ministers. Unlike the early Calvinists, however, the prosperity gospel says there is nothing wrong with enjoying one's wealth. The prosperity gospel has been particularly empowering in Black churches.[32] According to the African American prosperity preacher T. D. Jakes, the message that one can have a life of abundance is preferable to traditional Christianity, which was "taught 'by slave masters to pacify their slaves.'"[33] As Carl Mathews put it, "If you're blessed to have it, enjoy it."

This theology is fine when you are blessed with wealth, and it can motivate striving for economic gains. What is confusing for devout Christians like Carl Mathews who were unemployed for many months or years is why God chose to withhold financial blessings for them at that time, even though they tried hard to find another job and their faith was unchanged. It is a variant of the perennial problem: Why does a loving God permit suffering?

A similar tension outside Christian theology exists among followers of differing New Age spiritual philosophies. Some New Age spiritual leaders stress the unimportance of material possessions; others believe that both material and spiritual abundance can be attained by harnessing the power of thought. As Rhonda Byrne explains in her bestselling book, *The Secret*, "Thoughts are magnetic, and thoughts have a frequency. As you think, those thoughts are sent out into the Universe, and they magnetically attract all *like* things that are on the same frequency." This is the law of attraction. The tricky part of the method is that if you are thinking about lack, that will be attracted to you as well: "When you *need* money, it is a powerful feeling within you, and so of course through the law of attraction you will continue to attract *needing* money."[34] It is very important not to feel lack because your negative thoughts will block good things from coming to you. For example, if your goals are to purchase certain material items, do not entertain doubts about whether you can afford them: "As you see your dream car drive past, say, 'I can afford that.' As you see clothes you love, as you think about a great vacation, say, 'I can afford that.' As you do this you will begin to shift yourself and you will begin to *feel* better about money." Giving away money for charitable purposes is recommended too—not on the grounds of what it does for others but because it makes you feel rich and will attract more money into your life.[35]

New Age beliefs and Christianity are not the only religious or spiritual belief systems in the United States, but they are widespread, as I found from hearing these ideas expressed by many of my participants.

In sum, there are powerful consumption pressures in contemporary US society alongside widespread critiques of problematic consumption. One way of integrating these messages is by idealizing *appropriate* consumption, consumption that is neither too much nor too little for a happy life.

White Picket Fences and More: Aspirations for the Good Life

When I gave my participants paper and markers and asked them to write or draw their idea of a good life, one item was mentioned or drawn more than any other: a house.[36] Everyone, of course, needs some dwelling place, but in the United States from the 1950s on, the ideal dwelling place has been commonly imagined in the way my participants did: as a single-family home. Typically, my participants drew a car as well.[37]

Celeste Rue drew God in the form of a sun, a home with curtains on the windows and a piano inside, a yard with flowers, and a smiling family made up of a husband, wife, and three children, each holding one or more dollar signs (figure 3.1). "Everybody should have some money," she commented. Jake Taylor wrote, "The good life is a hot summer day, playing in the front-yard sprinklers with my friends and family while drinking a few beers and relaxing in the sun." A yard where one can relax is part of the cultural model of a single-family home. For Mary Brown, a good life is "a house, a car, my family. And then being able to also help people in the community." Ichabod Jones drew a home with cars in the driveway for himself and his wife near homes for his grown children and granddaughter. Fred Hernandez drew a family and a house surrounded by a picket fence. Many participants depicted their home in a beautiful natural setting. Theresa Allen drew a cozy house with a red front door and a view of the mountains (figure 3.2). Maria Carrera did the same.

What strikes me about these images and my participants' discussions of them is that their ideas of a good life were neither entirely material nor

FIGURE 3.1. Celeste Rue's drawing in response to the question, "What is a good life for you?"

FIGURE 3.2. Theresa Allen's drawing in response to the question, "What is a good life for you?"

entirely immaterial: they were a mix. A home and a car often went with smiling faces, children, or pets. A home could be where one enjoyed nature. In some of the anticonsumerist public discourse, as that from the New Dream center, material consumption ("what we buy") is opposed to "relationships, service to others, spending time in nature, community building, and personal growth." For most of my participants, however, these goals are intertwined.[38] A comfortable home is the foundation for a happy family. It is where one socializes with friends, as Jake Taylor imagines ("playing in the front-yard sprinklers with my friends and family while drinking a few beers and relaxing in the sun") and where one can relax and enjoy nature. One can want those things and still care about contributing to their community and society, as Mary Brown does.

That mix of material and immaterial desires is typical in definitions of the "American dream," such as the one in the Merriam-Webster dictionary: "a happy way of living" that is best illustrated by having a family, a home, and prosperity. In the crowd-sourced Urban Dictionary, one definition of the American dream is "to marry that perfect someone, move into the classical suburban house, with a front yard, a garage & driveway, a white picket fence. You have a dog, a cat, and several kids. On weekends and summers you barbeque in your yard while your kids play on a tire swing and build a tree fort."[39] The author of this definition further states that this is "an image originally created in the late 1950s and 1960s," adding that it is "innocent by nature but commonly deplored by those who cannot achieve it or don't agree with capitalism."[40] Despite recognizing the contested cultural standing of these desires, this contributor still sees them as "innocent by nature."

That Urban Dictionary definition I quoted of the American dream home includes having a yard with "a white picket fence." A white picket fence is what William Gamson and Andre Modigliani call a "condensing symbol"; that is, "a deft metaphor, catchphrase, or other symbolic device" that sums up a cultural model.[41] A house surrounded by a white picket fence is a recurrent trope in descriptions of the American dream one might hear or read, and it was invoked by some of my participants as well. Jake Taylor said, "Pure happiness" for him is "having a wife and kids, little picket fence, all that stuff." Anastasia Tang explained, "You just want to live the American dream; you want to have the house and a picket fence and maybe the dog and have your car, and that's it."

Why a yard with a white picket fence?

Yards with white picket fences are not actually all that common these days. I suspect that is the point. The house with a white picket fence nostalgically evokes the post–World War II era. The cover illustration of Jim Cullen's book, *The American Dream*, shows a 1950s-style image of a father coming home to his wife and young son outside a small, 1.5-story home on a yard surrounded by a white picket fence (figure 3.3) That image harkens back to a period when the typical American house was smaller than it is today. In 1950 the most common new American home was 1,000 square feet. In 2020 the median new home was more than double that size at 2,333 square feet on a lot too large to easily enclose with a white picket fence.[42] Perhaps the white picket fence persists in descriptions of the American dream precisely because it represents the imagined simplicity of an earlier period. For many people, the white picket fence version of American dreams represents "innocent," appropriate consumption as the setting for a happy (traditional nuclear) family.[43] As Jake Taylor put it, "Don't spend money on stuff you don't need. [. . .] I think back to like the 'forties and 'fifties [*1940s and 1950s*] and stuff; we had a really simple outlook on life. Like the American dream kind of thing and everything. And that's like the complete opposite of material kind of wants and needs."

Unlike Carl, who reveled in the pleasures of making his home "a palace" and of luxurious vacations, many of my participants contrasted what they took to be their own right-sized, white-picket-fence consumer desires with others' excessive spending. For example, Jim Wade, who had worked in the parts departments of auto dealerships, said, "I believe in modesty." He explained that if he could afford a home, he would want only a three-bedroom house, not a five-bedroom one; his preferred car was a Ford Focus, not a Mercedes, BMW,

or Porsche. He recounted a discussion with some other job seekers at the employment resource center. One man was saying he wished he could have a Porsche, but Jim said he found agreement among others there that a Ford Focus was more practical. Theresa Allen, who had been a waitress, said the "haves" in society "put a lot of emphasis on things, to me, that aren't that important. A lot, a lot of money, jewelry, cars, trips." She saw them as driving Jaguars, whereas she preferred a Ford Focus or Toyota Highlander. Theresa criticized the values of those who flaunted their possessions: "I don't think they think about what's really important."

Of course, cultural models of modest, appropriate spending depend on one's social reference group and on the norms of a historical moment. A Toyota Highlander is a midsize SUV, and Theresa recognized it was "extravagant, but I would keep that for ten or fifteen years," so she saw it as a good value over the long term. It was certainly less extravagant than a Jaguar. Someone who bought a house in 1950, when the average American home was 1,000 square feet, might consider Jim Wade's ideal three-bedroom home to be excessive if Jim was imagining the 2,400 square foot home that was the average size at the time we spoke.[44] An upper-middle-class family's 3,500 square foot home would be unexceptional in a neighborhood of similar homes, although it would stand out as a risible "McMansion" if plunked down somewhere else.

I noticed that my participants tended to set the bar for excessive consumption above the level at which they lived at present or hoped to live in the future. A standard of living up to their own accustomed or desired level seemed reasonable; above that was just showing off and so was subject to all the critiques of excessive materialism—it is immoral, imprudent, unhealthy, unsustainable, and ineffective in producing happiness—that are conventional US discourses. Jake Taylor, in his twenties, was living with his father, who earned about $55,000 a year. Jake said, "You don't need all kinds of stupid electronics and iPods and a whole bunch of computers, big screen TV's, huge stereo systems, nice cars that are all luxurious." Charles Toppes, who had earned between $150,000 and $200,000 as a factory manager, may have owned such consumer electronics, but he said he and his wife would make fun of other people who "own a big motorhome and they're pulling a trailer with Ski-doos on it." Charles and his wife liked recreational vehicles too, but they just rented them for a week rather than try to own "all those toys." Phoenix Rises, a teacher married to a former broadcast engineer, at one time enjoyed an annual household income of more than $500,000. She used to drive a Mercedes, but she was critical of those who "view the world through being in a Maybach Rolls Royce and all these gold chains and diamonds and gold on your teeth, all this ridiculousness."

As Juliet Schor has noted, "Surveys show that people are more likely to attribute materialism to others than to themselves."[45] The same goes for me, and possibly for you, the reader of this book. Academics, in particular, need to consider that our own ideas about excessive consumption are likely to be shaped by what Meneley insightfully describes as "a new prestigious piety of conspicuous nonconsumption, an aesthetic asceticism desirable to those who can afford . . . high-quality, durable goods such as sleek marble countertops and hardwood floors, adorned only by distinctive objects."[46] Of course, this is hardly "nonconsumption": it is merely a different style of consumption, a different way of achieving distinction.[47]

Not everyone described their consumption desires as modest. For example, when I asked ReNé McKnight to depict a good life, she first replied, "What America told us—the white picket fence, puppy." But when I asked if that was really what she wanted, she laughed and said no: she actually wanted multiple homes in different parts of the country and several successful businesses. Paula Jackson's image of a good life included a New York City penthouse. Elizabeth Montgomery's idea of a good life included "make enough money to be able to do the things I deem important." She explained what she meant by "enough money": "It may be a million versus someone else wants ten million." Some, like Paula and Elizabeth, had grown accustomed to high household incomes. Others, like ReNé, fervently hoped for such prosperity in the future. A few enjoyed dreaming of possible wealth and the fun it could bring, without investing their hopes in these dreams. As one immigrant day laborer put it when imagining a good life of a house with a pool and traveling around the world, "Dreaming is for free."

Others would fantasize about being a wealthy celebrity, but then describe celebrities' unsuccessful marriages, substance abuse problems, and other indications that wealth and fame were no guarantee of happiness and could loosen the moral restraints needed for a good life. For example, when "Ann Lopez" was choosing a pseudonym for this study, she decided to take the name of someone she wanted to be like: "Who would I like to be? Jennifer Lopez? She's so beautiful. She's got beauty and money. Of course, that doesn't always bring happiness, as you can see. She has not been happy with all the different husbands she's had." When Jim Wade imagined a good life, he told me, "I dreamed about John Wayne today. I would not like a life like him." Celebrities have to deal with paparazzi, "and you know what happened to him smoking and drinking; he killed himself off." The pattern was the same in both cases: expressing a fantasy of being a wealthy celebrity and then disavowing that wish while explaining why lots of money and fame do not add up to a good life.

For most of my participants, the white-picket fence version of a good life is freighted with moral approval, unlike a wealthy lifestyle, which may be desired but repudiated. Despite all the variation in my participants' specific consumer desires, they could draw on widespread American discourses that criticized excessive consumerism—however "excessive" was defined on their sliding scale. Those discourses condemning excessive consumerism were especially meaningful when my participants were forced to curtail their consumption.

Meanings of Curtailed Consumption

Widespread home ownership no longer looks so innocent. In the housing bubble of 2000–7, which particularly affected California and a few other states, house prices rose rapidly because more and more people felt they had to buy before prices rose even higher. Everyone figured that home values would continue to rise, so buyers could always sell at a profit. Predatory lenders took advantage of the desire for home ownership, enticing low-income buyers with affordable teaser mortgage rates that jumped after a year or two to unaffordable levels. In turn, the commercial lenders were goaded by financiers who sold bundles of these bad mortgages. When homeowners could not pay their mortgages, the resulting foreclosures and consequent steep decline in home values led to a precipitous drop in consumer spending that triggered the Great Recession, which led to many of my participants losing their jobs.[48]

During the Great Recession, family incomes of long-term unemployed workers across the country fell 40 percent or more.[49] Like other Americans dealing with long-term unemployment at that time, my participants were hard hit. Before they lost their jobs, most of my participants had a household income above the regional median, which was a little over $52,000 at that time (figure 3.4).[50] After they lost their jobs, their household income fell drastically, with a median decline of $42,500, according to my estimates.[51] Some of the wealthiest participants saw their income decline by more than $100,000 (figure 3.5).

Income losses of that magnitude drastically limited their consumption. Wealthier participants usually had savings and other assets, but some had to downsize to smaller homes and less expensive cars. Many middle-income participants had to start drawing from a retirement account if they had one, limiting their future life prospects to meet their pressing present needs. As I explain in the next chapter, many could no longer afford to pay rent or a mortgage, and they had to move in with a relative. Everyone curtailed travel and sought less expensive forms of entertainment. Even a modest middle-class version of the American dream was out of the reach of most.

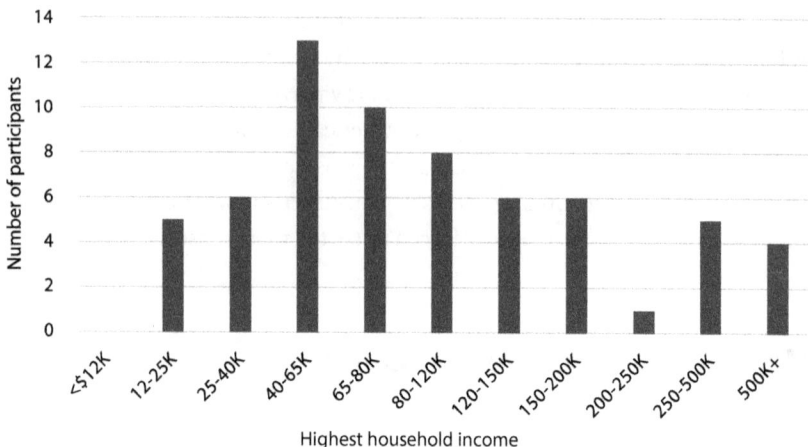

FIGURE 3.4. Highest household income in the past (number of participants at each income level).

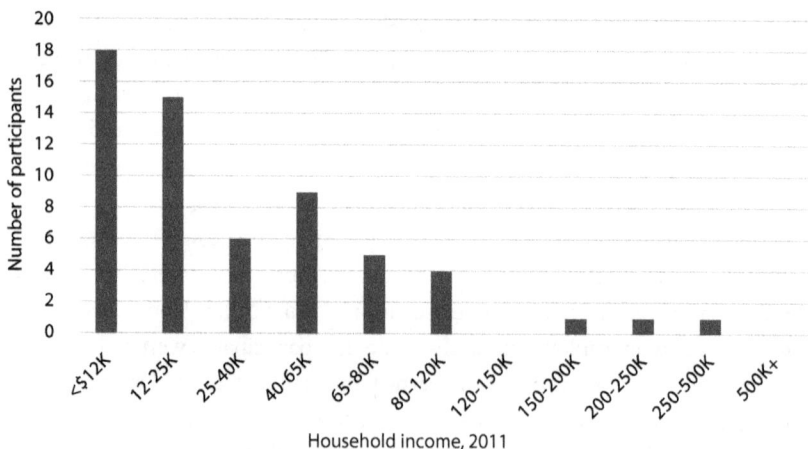

FIGURE 3.5. Household income in 2011 (number of participants at each income level).

The long-term unemployed lost access to credit, as well as income. In 2010 nearly one in ten of the unemployed declared personal bankruptcy, immediately giving them a very low credit score and making it difficult for them to borrow.[52] Right in line with national statistics, among my participants 9.5 percent had filed for bankruptcy. Before the recession, homeowners had another way of obtaining credit, which was to borrow money secured by the equity in their homes. However, with the bursting of the housing bubble, home prices plummeted, and many owed more than their homes were then worth, which meant they could not obtain a home equity loan. With little to no income and unable to borrow money, it was difficult for them to fulfill their consumption desires without emptying their savings. The only other option was to slash their spending. How did they feel about that?

A few of my participants seemed genuinely uninterested in spending money beyond the minimum they needed to sustain themselves. Their ideas of a good life did not center on their level or style of consumption. For example, after Ginger Thi became sick, she lost her administrative assistant job in the Bay area and became unable to pay her rent. Her friends paid to put her belongings in storage, but Ginger felt uncomfortable about accepting their help with the on-going storage fees. She decided, "It's just stuff," and gave up her storage locker key. She said that for years afterward she grieved for some of her things that she lost—her books, music, pictures, a pair of Calvin Klein suede pumps she could have used for job interviews—so she was not indifferent to their loss, but she still let them go. Ginger drove back to Los Angeles, where she had been raised and where most of her friends lived. When I first met her, she was living in a homeless shelter, but soon afterward she moved to a subsidized apartment building. Ginger obtained a part-time job that paid a pittance, working for the homelessness agency that had helped her. The rest of her time she was busy with spiritual and political activities. She identified as middle class because her family was educated and she was well read and knowledgeable. Ginger was one of the happiest of the people I spoke with. Neither her class identity nor her life satisfaction rested on her minimal consumption.

For Kham Sy Phouphan, an unemployed machine operator and a Buddhist from Laos, all things of this world, including material possessions, are transitory. No possessions belong to you: they are all part of nature. The things you own are no more yours than the scenery you fly over in an airplane. Even "your body not belong to you." He declared, "I don't worry nothing in here. It's car or house, whatever. [. . .] I have money or not, I'm not worried." His content-ment was contagious. I felt very relaxed as we chatted at the picnic table in his carport under a sign that read "Save Water. Drink Beer."

This apparent indifference regarding discretionary spending was not lim-ited to those with lower incomes. For example, Caroline James had earned more than $250,000 a year as a senior vice president of HR for an entertain-ment company. In our first two lengthy interviews, she did not mention any spending that she had greatly missed during the year and a half she had been unemployed, beyond her desires to travel a little more or have more money to go out to eat. When I asked her to draw her image of a good life, she drew a raft floating on the water with a little barrel representing the resources she needed to stay afloat, a door for other people to come and go, and a sun representing a "life force" or "inspiration."

I say "apparent indifference regarding discretionary spending" because it is difficult to know for sure what my participants really thought about having to spend less, as I found out near the end of my second interview with Auguste Salander. Auguste had been a dancer and a personal trainer, done desktop publishing, sold vacuum cleaners, and delivered pizza. When we met, he had been fired from the pizza delivery job for having too many traffic accidents, and he was living with his sister. His sister was trying to get him interested in becoming a medical assistant. Auguste said he understood her motivation: "The idea is to be self-supporting, and to have a good life, and all that sort of stuff," but "I am not at all interested." His passion was to start a business that would combine his interests in movement and art. He was also deeply knowledgeable and concerned about national politics. From our first three hours of conversation over two meetings, I would have categorized him as not caring about money. That changed when I asked him to describe what was a good life for him. Among other things, he wrote, "Known as artist, unlimited wealth, prosperity, successful business, travel." So much for my assumption that he did not care about money.[53]

The best evidence of my participants' priorities are the choices they made. Ginger Thi's choices demonstrate a relatively low level of concern about her standard of living, and a handful of other participants seemed to share her outlook, based on their life choices. However, they were outliers.

Among the rest, I found that the mixed messages about consumption in the United States provided ways for some of my participants to see a good side to their reduced consumption. Others tried to see a good side but remained conflicted. Then there were some for whom there was no silver lining about reduced consumption. That was especially true for my formerly wealthy participants whose identities and social relationships depended on a high standard of living they could no longer afford. Surprisingly, several of the formerly well-off were like Carl Mathews in being fearful of tumbling down to the lowest economic rungs in society and becoming homeless. For immigrants, there were additional complications created by multiple frames of reference, as I explain later in this chapter.

Less Is More

A few participants said that being forced to curtail their spending was a jolt that radically reshaped their priorities for the better. In contrast to those who had never cared greatly about consumption and did not discuss their spending habits in our interviews, this "less is more" group wanted to talk about their new perspectives on life.

Emily Quinn, a former executive secretary, had enjoyed clothes shopping. She joked, "I think I kept Nordstrom's in business." Emily told me that when she had been working, there were times when she ran up more credit-card debt in a month than her take-home salary. Listening to the popular financial adviser Suze Orman and obtaining only low-paid temp jobs helped her reduce her imprudent spending. Still, she continued to pay only the minimum due on her many credit-card bills each month, hiding them so she did not have to look at them. She did not completely change her habits until her last job ended. By the time we met for a follow-up interview, she had been out of work for more than four years. Her unemployment benefits had long since ended, and she was getting by on money borrowed several years earlier against the equity in her home. Although that was difficult, Emily was proud that "I don't owe anything. I have no credit card bills. . . . I feel really good about straightening that up. I feel real good I finally have it straight in my head." She spoke of the change in her spending in almost religious terms, announcing, "I finally saw the light." She also commented that she appreciated her rare discretionary purchases more: "If I let myself buy a lipstick, it is so fun. It is so fun, whereas before I would just throw it in the basket and never even give it a second thought."

Robert Milner, an unemployed supply chain strategist described in depth in chapter 1, was proud to rise from poverty and fulfill the American dream ideals of buying a home and raising a good family. Although that was still a source of pride, Robert spoke of a profound transformation in his priorities after he was laid off. He became willing to earn less and spend less. Like Emily Quinn, Robert spoke as if he had been converted:

> ROBERT: There were times I've said to myself, "Yeah. I'm a lot wiser now." And there were tears rolling down my eyes. Because I've been so happy that now I finally see it. You see so many things that you didn't see when you were working. So, this has given me the opportunity to see what was always there, but I didn't see.
> CLAUDIA: Like what?
> ROBERT: What's important? It's not all about money. It's not all about trying to work those extra hours. You know? [. . .] Because, at the end of the day, it doesn't matter anyway. You know? So, what it's allowed me to see is—is just to be happy with just the simplest things.

For Robert, the idea that money cannot buy happiness inspired him to live a life he considered more meaningful.

In the previous chapter, we met Lisa Rose, the nonprofit vice president who told me, "Being laid off was the best thing that ever happened to me." A large part of the reason why was that she learned not to let work take so much of her time. Another reason she mentioned, however, was a change in her class identity. She realized this after some of her colleagues suggested they meet for dinner at an exclusive club. When Lisa was vice president of the large non-profit organization, constantly interacting with wealthy donors, she routinely met donors and colleagues at that club and attended work-related retreats at expensive resorts. After being out of work for a year and a half, she saw more starkly the luxuries she and her colleagues had taken for granted. She mused, "I've hopefully gotten a little tougher in good ways and a little less privileged and a little less having such high expectations for what I'm going to get all the time. I think I'm becoming more regular again. So, it's almost like I'm coming back to—I grew up solidly middle class. I hope to somehow remain in the middle class." For Lisa Rose, living a middle-class lifestyle had moral value: it would make her a better person.

Unemployment changed Mona Childs's values about personal spending as well. When I first met Mona, whose last job was handling the marketing for an assisted living facility, she told me that work had been important to her identity. When I asked why, she explained, as if it were self-evident, that in the United States, "We're kind of capitalists" and "so a lot of our self-worth is how much can you make." She explained, "There's a big void in my life not having a job because so much of my identity, so much of what I've accumulated in my life, have a lot to do with how much I made." When I asked her what she had accumulated, she mentioned her home and her savings account. She said she did not care so much about her car "because I'm not a superficial person," but her family and friends had "called me a damn cheapskate after all these years working that I won't buy myself something better than a Honda," so she purchased a BMW. She said, "At that point I did it because I thought, 'You're approaching fifty. You've worked hard. You maybe deserve it. Maybe everyone's right. You need to break down.'" After being unemployed for a while, however, she worried about the extra expense of maintaining an imported vehicle and whether she could "keep up with making a certain salary expectation to live the lifestyle that I was comfortable with." Mona was anxious about the impending end of her unemployment benefits and seemed tense.

When we met again two years later, Mona was much more relaxed. Even though she could obtain only occasional freelance jobs, she had figured out that she did not need much money to live. Mona was one of a very few participants who had paid off her house and car and had accumulated considerable savings. She knew how to shop for bargains and find inexpensive ways to socialize with friends as a single woman. She said, "I have invested in myself. I've taken the time to look at my life spiritually," and she had found new friends now that she was home during the day. She appreciated having more time for her hobbies of gardening and cooking, and her extra time allowed her to help her mother recover after being hit by a car. Mona still hoped to return to full-time work, but for the time being she was content with her occasional part-time gigs. She mused, "I'm much more grounded and centered, and I know myself better than when I was working." She commented that money does not necessarily buy happiness: "I have friends that are successful, they make damn good money, like $150,000-plus a year," but "they are so unhappy."

Emily Quinn, Robert Milner, Lisa Rose, and Mona Childs were the best examples of participants who had previously appreciated the lifestyle their job had supported but later came to value some aspects of a simpler life. Although they still wanted to find another job, and all had appreciated more about their work than the income it provided, once they became accustomed to living on less, they approached their job search with a different set of priorities. In addition to these four participants, there were others who did not speak of a great change in their priorities but shared that they had learned to be content with less and to make a budget and stick to it, which they saw as valuable lessons.

Still, the "less is more" perspective was not the most common reaction among my participants. What was more common was either ambivalence or unmixed displeasure about curtailed spending.

Ambivalence

Some participants declared that material goods were not important, drawing on conventional American critiques. However, they did not seem completely convinced by these discourses, and their feelings were conflicted.

Sam Lennon had lived in communes and been a Hare Krishna devotee, living with other followers of this movement. After she left the Hare Krishna, Sam held a variety of service-sector jobs, including as a barista and a cashier. Workplace injuries left her unable to continue working. Sam's household income had never been above $25,000, but she used to love to shop. In our first interview, she said she recognized that in the past she had been "trying to fill some kind of gap in my life with things," pathologizing her shopping as a personality disorder:

> One thing I have learned, and I'm really actually proud of myself, is that I'm satisfied with what I've got. And it's the first time I've ever been like that, because if I had any money at all I would go out and buy something.

My ex-husband, he always told me, "Save that money," because I used to get tips when I was a barista, and I used to get $50 a day in tips and I would go out and spend that money. I'd go to T. J. Maxx or buy clothes that would hang in my closet with the tags on them. I was trying to fill a hole, you know? I was trying to fill some kind of gap in my life with things. I don't have to do that anymore.

Sam still had several thousand dollars in credit-card debt from her previous shopping sprees, but she was grateful that the physical disability that forced her to stop working had also ended her shopping habit, and she was slowly selling her unneeded purchases at swap meets (flea markets). She felt that her earlier experiences with communal living had taught her how to adjust to low consumption, a capacity others lacked: "I've always learned how to live on nothing most of my life, and most people haven't 'cause they've been acquiring more and more things and more debt. And so, it makes it worse, because most people don't think they can live without this or that, and I've already learned how to live without it. Our society, I think, is—it's just based on getting more and more stuff. It's bad." In these comments Sam sounds like Emily Quinn and Robert Milner, who spoke of their conversion to a less materialistic way of life.

When we met again two weeks later, Sam sounded different. She said she missed shopping: "I'm trying to be less of a consumer, but still, everybody wants to go out and buy something. People say money doesn't buy happiness. That's a lie. That's a total lie. If you have money, you are happy. Believe me." For reinforcement, she added, "And all my friends say that, too. It's not just me." Sam could not really convince herself that she ought to forego the pleasures of shopping when her personal experience and that of her friends, was that shopping was fun.

Others alternated between anti-materialist discourses and hopes for a wealthier future. Tom Dunn, who had been an IT recruiter earning between $80,000 and $120,000 a year, rejected my exercise of drawing an image of a good life because, as he explained earnestly, material things do not guarantee happiness, so a good life could not be drawn:

I don't mean to push back, but I have to tell you, my life in general, but more specifically the last three years [while he was out of work], has taught me something that's not a picture. It's nothing tangible. Happiness really doesn't have much to do with material [things]. It really doesn't. Happiness has to do with how you feel about yourself and the people around you and not the kind of car you drive or the house you live in, the size of the house you live in, the size of your bank account. Those things, they just don't mean that much to me.

To illustrate how little material things mattered, he said that if were to win $20 million in the lottery, he would give away half the money to those in need and use the rest to buy land that would someday go to his children. Talking about winning the lottery led him to comment on the dangers of coming into a lot of money. Evoking the cultural model of the rich having bad values, Tom said, "I worry to death that money and having money would pollute me and my values" and his children's values as well. I coded this as a strong anti-materialist statement.

Two years later when we met again, we were discussing the income he would be satisfied with in the future. That prompted Tom to wonder whether it "would change your opinion of me if I told you that I actually daydream about being a lottery winner and what I would do with it." He said he regularly bought lottery tickets using the money he saved from switching to a cheaper brand of cigarettes. His plans if he won a large prize were unchanged: he would divide the money in half, using one half to help others, while the rest would go into real estate that would someday go to his children. He would not just hand that money over to his children. They had to work with him in the philanthropic organization he would create with his lottery winnings because "I'm not gonna give them anything until they can get their heads around the fact that money isn't free." His altruism—coupled with his desire to leave an inheritance for his children and his belief that too much money obtained easily can have harmful effects—had not changed. But my understanding of the importance of these material goals to Tom flipped 180 degrees when I realized that winning the lottery was not just a hypothetical example for him. Instead, it was a goal in which he invested his money and hopes.

Paula Jackson's husband had been an executive in a financial services corporation with an annual salary of more than $500,000. They and their children used to live in a five-bedroom, million-dollar home in an upscale suburban community, and Paula had a Mercedes and a BMW. When the company ran into problems and her husband was let go, they had to downsize to an average-sized home in a poorer city and turn in their high-end leased cars for less expensive ones. Paula's husband found a lower-level, less-well-paid position, and Paula went back to work for the first time in fifteen years as a medical assistant. However, the on-call hours and other working conditions were difficult because she also had to drive her teenage sons to their many activities, so she quit and considered starting a small business. I met her when she and a friend were planning a possible business venture over a meal at a restaurant, and they became interested in the interview I was conducting in the next booth.

In my first meeting with Paula in her pleasant, downsized home, she went back and forth between mourning her old life and expressing that such possessions are not important:

> CLAUDIA: So, you downsized the car too, you said?
> PAULA: Oh, yeah. We have a 2002 Volvo that we bought used, and I drive a PT Cruiser.
> CLAUDIA: And what did you have before?
> PAULA: I had a 650i BMW, and I had a 500 CLK Mercedes.
> CLAUDIA: Yeah. So, all that's a change.
> PAULA: Yes, it was a change, but it's okay. I mean, as long as I have a car to get me from point A to point B, I'm okay.
>
> PAULA: [*Talking about her current home, where we held the interview*] It's an old house but it's nice.
> CLAUDIA: It's very nice. Yeah. It's perfectly nice.
> PAULA: They remodeled the whole kitchen and that's what I like because I like to cook. My kitchen's remodeled and that's all you need. You need somewhere for your family to be together. And—I had three family rooms [*in her former home*].
> CLAUDIA: Wow.
> PAULA: I had a formal living room, two family rooms. A formal living room and a family room for the boys and a family room for me.
> CLAUDIA: Wow. Wow.
> PAULA: Where the boys were on the other side of the house.
> CLAUDIA: Oh my gosh.
> PAULA: But all those things don't matter.
> CLAUDIA: Yeah.
> PAULA: They really don't.

I am sure that one part of Paula believed that all that should matter in a vehicle was whether it took her "from point A to point B" and that what was really important for a home was that it provided "somewhere for your family to be together." The happiness of her family was what was truly important to her. When she asked how my other interviewees were doing, and I described in a general way another participant whose wife was very angry with him for losing his job, Paula was shocked and saddened. She responded, "I think people just harp over the money. Money, money, money, money, money." Instead, what matters is "happiness." Although she was pained that she could no longer provide spending money to her teenage boys, she saw an upside: "I think it's making them more men."

Still, from the loving detail with which she described her former home and cars, it seemed as if those things still did matter. Indeed, when I asked how she was feeling about her situation, she said, "Downsizing? It's tough. I think I'm still trying to get over it right now. I'm still like in a big dream. That, you know, I'm not driving my car anymore. My Mercedes." She believed that all these things should not matter, but they really did. As a devout Christian she recognized that "I have to feel blessed" for what God chose to provide, but rather than become adjusted to her new way of life, she hoped it was temporary: "I read my Bible every morning, and I'm very spiritual. Very spiritual. And I do believe things will get better. I know things will get better." She had faith that God would restore her family's income and the things that money could buy.

The objects of these three people's material desires varied: shopping for Sam, wealth for Tom, and consumption for Paula. All, however, were caught between desires to have more money and discourses that counseled them to abjure such desires.

Others of my participants were less torn between material desires and critiques of materialism. They still had some inner conflicts, but their dominant emotion was unhappiness about their economic struggles.

Less Is Less

Some of those who were less conflicted about their desires for more money saw their consumption goals as reasonable, not excessive. They seemed to feel that all they wanted was what any normal American would want.

Jim Wade had worked in the parts departments of car dealers and auto parts stores for many years, never earning more than $40,000 a year. His wife Connie, who joined him in the interviews, was a part-time medical assistant. In our follow-up interview when I asked Jim what would be a good life for him, he replied, "I'd say, for me, the American dream." That dream would be to "have a decent job with decent pay" and "being able to afford a decent house and a decent car." Earlier in this chapter I gave Jim's definition of a decent house ("a modest three-bedroom") and a decent car (a Ford Focus, not a Mercedes or BMW). He explained, "I believe in modesty." All he wanted was "just basic middle class—or wealthy, fairly wealthy."

Jim did own a Ford Focus, which was in danger of being repossessed when we first met, but he was able to make his car payments with help from his church. However, his housing was more precarious. After he was laid off from his job as an auto parts salesman, he was only able to obtain short-term census jobs, followed by sales jobs on commission. When I caught up with him two years after we first met, he only had a part-time job, and he and his wife could not afford their rent. When I asked Jim to write or draw his image of a good life, the first thing he wrote was, "Relationships are more important than posses-sions." He pointed out, however, that it was difficult to have a successful rela-tionship with his wife when they were under so much financial strain. He said he understood shooting rampages: "People are so desperate because of their eco-nomic situation; they're going off the deep end." Jim was impatient with plati-tudes that money does not buy happiness. Two years earlier, when I had asked him what social group he would put himself in, he said, "Poor." Connie thought they were "low medium, tending to poor." She shared, "I don't want to be rich," but Jim said, "I do." Every time he had come into a little money—for example, from an insurance settlement after a drunk driver hit him—that money made him happier. Much like Sam Lennon in our second interview, Jim commented, "People in my church wouldn't like me saying this, but I do not agree with the idea that money does not buy happiness. [. . .] Money does buy happiness. It does make a life a lot happier."[54] He added, "People like to tell other people that to try to dissuade them from being interested in money. Health is important, but if you don't have money, you don't have much of anything in today's life."

All that sustained Jim was "faith in God, trusting God." He explained, "I know that God is in control. [. . .] Proverbs says, 'A man plans his ways, but God directs his steps.' God works in our lives." When I asked, "Why do you think God would be making life so difficult for you?" Jim replied immediately: "Testing my faith." Later in the same interview, however, he confessed to con-fusion about God's intentions:

> My situation now, and this is a challenge of my faith, is, I feel like God has abandoned me. I feel like Job. I don't understand—I feel like, "Why doesn't God give me an opportunity? I wanna work hard. I wanna be successful. Why doesn't God give me an opportunity? Why?" But if you read the Bible and God tells you he doesn't bless people with material wealth. That's not the idea. There's an afterlife coming, but one of my problems, faults, is I tend to think if God really loves a person, he blesses them with wealth and prosperity. But not necessarily. Right now, I'm struggling with the idea that God has abandoned me, but Hebrews, I think it's 15, anyway, "God will never forsake you." But then I feel like, "Well, then why am I going through this?" I mean, I do struggle with the idea that God has abandoned me. Where is he? I don't understand what he's putting me through or why.

Jim's Bible studies had taught him not necessarily to expect wealth in this lifetime, which was the point Carl Mathews had also made with the story of Lazarus and the rich man. However, it was hard for Jim to square that with promises that God will reward the faithful with a good life. Although there was some ambivalence in his attitudes about living well (he had fantasized about being a rich celebrity like John Wayne but then pointed out that Wayne had smoked and drunk himself to death), for the most part he was clear that earning enough for a "decent" life would make him much happier.

Similarly, Theresa Allen saw her consumption dreams as modest. Earlier, I included her image of a good life (see figure 3.2): a cozy house with a cheerful red door and mountains in the background. I asked how big her dream house was, and she said 1,500–1,600 square feet would be perfect. She and her husband had lots of pets but no children, and they did not need anything larger. When I asked her next to draw what groups there were in society and which group she was part of, she divided the sheet in half. On one side were "the Haves" with lots of dollar signs, fancy cars like Jaguars, and jewelry. Theresa also wrote "In the red?" because she suspected that they had gone into debt to finance that lifestyle. On the other side of the sheet were "the Work Fors": "people that try to live within their means" like her husband and her. He had been a woodworker; she was a waitress earlier in her life. Their highest annual household income in the past was in the $80,000–$120,000 range. As I mentioned earlier in the chapter, she said at that point that she would never want to buy a Jaguar—only a Ford Focus or a Toyota Highlander, which she had owned until recently.

Theresa's husband lost his manufacturing job at the same time that their mortgage payments jumped from a low initial interest-only payment to a much higher interest-plus-principal payment. After the housing market crashed, they could not sell their beautiful home; what had been a lifestyle they could afford became out of reach. Between what they owed on their home, unpaid medical bills, and credit-card debt, they owed between $400,000 and $500,000 when they declared bankruptcy. They walked away from their home as the bank began foreclosure, and they rented an apartment. Theresa missed not only their home but also the identity of being a homeowner. She confessed, "I always considered myself a homeowner, and then I rented in my fifties. I was mortified. I was, like, 'Oh, my God, I don't even wanna go to my high school reunion, I'm too embarrassed.'" For Theresa and many other participants, it was reasonable to want to own a small single-family home and a typical middle-class vehicle, and there was no upside in losing possessions so important for one's identity and happiness.

The Fears and Shame of the Formerly Wealthy

If Theresa Allen, whose household income had formerly been between $80,000 and $120,000, could feel shame at having to rent instead of owning a home, it is understandable that those who previously had much higher incomes would feel an even greater threat to their identities and everything they had worked for when long-term unemployment drastically curtailed their consumption.

Phoenix Rises was in severe distress when we first met. She had been a special education teacher; her husband had been a highly paid broadcast engineer. At one time their annual household income had been more than $500,000, and they had owned a nearly 5,000-square-foot home in the hillsides: "Big house, decks, beautiful view of the Rose Bowl and all this stuff, big, huge gourmet kitchen, you know, that stuff." In the mid-1990s, Phoenix's husband suffered a traumatic brain injury on the job, and he had to stop working and go on Social Security disability. Phoenix took on consulting jobs to earn more money, but then she too suffered a workplace injury and was unable to teach for more than two years. By the time she had recovered, the Great Recession was underway, and she could not find a job. For a long time, they relied on their savings: "So I'm paying the mortgage out of my savings; I'm paying car notes out of my savings." By the time they realized they could no longer pay for their house and cars, more than half their savings were gone and they had to move to a small apartment. Phoenix took odd jobs to help pay the bills, but in 2011 she estimated their income as only $25,000 for the year, and she had just under $4,000 left in her bank account. She was highly anxious and had symptoms of clinical depression.

Phoenix tried to look on this setback as a life lesson that would make her a better person: "Sometimes it's a gratifying feeling to be humbled. Life is humbling me. Yes, I've had the Mercedes, the Louis Vuitton, the Rodeo Drive, yeah. But now I get to know what it's like to eat those soups that are ten for a dollar with way too much salt and stuff like that. I get to know what the 99 cent store is all about." She said it had helped her empathize with the poor: "I won't go back to that person that I was. I was arrogant, I felt that I worked hard, 'I got mine, you can get yours.' I looked at people that were struggling, like, 'I don't know why, all you got to do is get out here and make it happen.' That's not me anymore."

Still, as much as Phoenix tried to find something positive in the life lessons learned from economic adversity, she had not changed how she thought of herself and her place in society. When I asked her to draw groups in society and where she placed herself in those groups, she wrote, "Haves vs. Have nots." She was frightened of crime from the "have nots" because "their thinking skills are not our thinking skills. Our thinking skills are more grounded from more of a have place." She also talked a lot about "winning" versus "losing": "I may be down but I'm not out of the game. I'm going to win. [. . .] If it's a game of win or lose, if I give up, then I automatically lose."

Phoenix struggled to hang on to her identity as a "have" and a "winner" in the face of judgments she read into looks and comments from her former friends. She felt that, in urban California, especially, "We don't want to be associated with those of our friends that have lost their jobs and lost their homes and that are having hard times. It's like we're the *plague*." She said, "I found in bad times you will really find out who your friends are: slim and none. The first thing that they're going to think of is, 'Oh, they're going to ask me for money.'"

The most painful consequence of Phoenix's economic straits was her younger daughter's anger and contempt. When Phoenix and her husband had to move to a small apartment, they did not have room for their college-aged daughter, so her boyfriend's parents offered to let her stay with them. Through tears, Phoenix recollected, "Then, to have her call us losers, she hated us: 'Why did I have to have you as my parents? I counted on you all my life, and now I can't count on you' was probably the worst thing that I've ever had to endure." Phoenix kept herself going by expecting that "I will in the end not only survive, but I'm going to win big." That is why she chose her pseudonym; she wanted to be the phoenix that rose from the ashes.

The other thing that kept Phoenix going was her spiritual practice. She is a follower of Soka Gakkai Buddhism. In mainstream Buddhism one strives for nonattachment to worldly desires, an outlook exemplified by my Laotian American participant Kham Sy Phouphan. However, just as there are different sects of Christianity, so are there different sects of Buddhism. The Soka Gakkai movement developed from Japanese Nichiren Buddhism, which emphasizes obtaining proof of the teaching's power by chanting and seeing the results in the here- and-now. In that respect, this form of Buddhism has many parallels to the Christian prosperity gospel.[55] In the words of Soka Gakkai International's president, Daisaku Ikeda, "Those who have experienced great suffering must win in life and become happy. If you're always losing and miserable, then you are not practicing Nichiren Buddhism correctly. You are not following the true path in life."[56] As Phoenix explained it, "Buddhism is win or lose." The key was to discipline her thoughts: "I will lose if I don't stay in control of my mind. I have to master my mind every single day." Although Phoenix did not refer to the New Age law of attraction, some of her beliefs were similar. For example, she had considered replenishing her nearly depleted bank account by selling some of her expensive handbags and watches, but a friend scolded her for her bad attitude, saying "'Where is your faith? Where is your head right now, that you think that you're not gonna win? You're accepting defeat again.'" Phoenix realized her friend was right and that it was necessary to keep those symbols of wealth to bolster her certitude that she would win.

Phoenix had experienced a steep class descent and had come to rest, for a while, in a stable, if much lower, income bracket. She and her husband had an apartment, even if it was small, and they had food, even if it was minimal. Others who formerly had the highest incomes worried they would fall even farther and find themselves on the streets.

Paula Jackson, whom we met earlier mourning the Mercedes and large home she used to have, at one time enjoyed an annual household income of more than $500,000, like Phoenix Rises. Then her husband lost his executive position and had to take less well-paying jobs. In 2011 their household income was at the national median, in the $40,000—$65,000 range. It enabled them to live in a comfortable ranch house, but when I asked Paula about her fears for the future, she said, "I'm afraid of being *broke*. Not having a home. That's really scary." Elizabeth Montgomery, whose household income had also been more than $500,000 a year, likewise spoke of her fear of falling into poverty due to long-term unemployment. Stephen Smith, a former upper-level corporate manager, lost his income and stock options when he was forced out due to his company's plunge in sales following the 2008 financial crisis. Yet, he and his wife, who then retired from her own high-level corporate job, still had a substantial retirement fund and a large home, and they could afford to spend thousands of dollars renovating their home while he was out of work. He said that nonetheless his wife "is very fearful":

> She's horrendously fearful that she will be like Scarlett O'Hara in *Gone with the Wind*. [*Putting on his wife's voice*], "I will be a poor destitute individual after having aspired for such greatness and worked my tail off for years and years and years. [. . .] I will end up with nothing at the end of the day. Sitting on the side of a road having somebody care for me as they push me along in a wheelchair next to a drainage culvert because I have no house. I have no money left. No insurance. And I'll be dead shortly after that."

This may not have been an accurate representation of her views; Stephen might have exaggerated his wife's concerns to make fun of them. Still, she was clearly worried about falling into extreme poverty. We also saw the same fears expressed by Carl Mathews, who at one time had an annual household income of more than $200,000 but was very shaken by the sight of a man eating out of the trashcan near a Jack in a Box fast food restaurant. What was so upsetting for Carl was the thought that "I'm one step from that. That could be me eating out of that same trashcan having those same people look at me." In short, I kept hearing fears of destitution from those who seemed the least likely to fall into it. This is a mystery. Why were some of my formerly well-off participants so anxious?

My first thought was that these fears revealed the underbelly of the American economic system. As I explain in the next chapter, there is a woeful shortage of affordable housing throughout the country. As a result, homelessness is all too common in the United States, especially in southern California. In 2018, Los Angeles County had the second highest number of homeless people in the country.[57]

Still, anxiety about homelessness and other forms of extreme poverty did not loom so large for all my participants. To be sure, not all the highest-income earners expressed such fears, nor were these fears limited to the formerly wealthy; yet they were disproportionately common among those who formerly had annual household incomes of $200,000 or more. Forty percent of my participants from that upper bracket expressed fears of complete destitution, compared to just 11 percent of the rest.[58] I found it surprising that those who voiced the greatest fears of extreme poverty and homelessness were not only the people at the lower rungs who were realistically in the most danger of experiencing them but also included those who had earned the highest incomes.[59]

When I met Carl for our follow-up interview, he thought it was just obvious that someone who had lived in luxury would hate to become poor. At that point he was no longer so afraid for himself because he was staying with his parents, and he could joke about it. He laughed throughout the following comments:

> When you're poor, it's easier to accept a better lifestyle. I don't think a poor person out there wouldn't mind saying, "Pass the Grey Poupon." [. . .] It's easy to adapt from being on the streets to a home with warm water and air conditioning and heat, and the lights, and a nice bed instead of a concrete sidewalk to sleep on. Who couldn't adapt to that? Now, take that same person who was rich, all their life . . . let the bottom fall out. It's hard to adapt the other way, huh? You went from a Sleep Number to a sidewalk. You know what I'm saying? You don't understand why your world is changing.

That seems just like common sense, but why would not someone who had been accustomed to a middle-class life also have trouble adjusting to living on a sidewalk? I know I would. Why should someone who had been wealthy be especially fearful of this fate? There are several possible explanations.

The fears of some of the formerly well-off may have been realistic because (as Theresa Allen suspected) they were living a lifestyle they could not afford. Phoenix Rises and her husband kept trying to maintain their lifestyle for ten years after he became disabled. Even when Paula Jackson's husband was earning more than $500,000, her Mercedes and BMW had been leased. Carl Mathews and his wife had to declare bankruptcy after he had been out of work for less than a year, which suggests that he had not put much aside in savings. However, fear of destitution did not seem realistic for Stephen Smith and his wife, who had considerable assets to cushion their loss of income.

Another part of the explanation seems to be how important a high income had been for my wealthy participants' sense of self and how hard many of them had worked to achieve that status. Tocqueville observed the same pattern in nineteenth-century America: "The poor conceive an eager desire to acquire comfort, and the rich think of the danger of losing it." He proposed that the possibility of a rapid change of fortunes in the United States at that time made the rich anxious: "Most of these rich men were once poor: they have felt the spur of need; they had long striven against hostile fate, and now that they had won their victory, the passions that accompanied the struggle survived. They seemed drunk on the petty delights it had taken forty years to gain."[60]

Tocqueville's insightful description fits Carl Mathews, Elizabeth Montgomery, and Stephen Smith's wife, all of whom grew up poor and had a strong drive to escape from poverty. Elizabeth was one of six children in a poor Midwestern family that had to abandon their farm and move to town. Carl's parents had steady jobs, but money was tight. I did not interview Stephen's wife, but he said that being poor while she was growing up made the thought of moving down the class ladder unbearable.

Their desire to maintain what they had was not just about enjoyment of those possessions but also an attempt to maintain their social status and previous patterns of socializing. Phoenix lost friends when her economic difficulties became uncomfortably obvious. Paula used to treat her friends to spa days, restaurant meals, and parties at her house. That changed when her husband lost his executive job. Now, "since I don't have my social status—I used to always have nice little get-togethers and parties at the house, wine parties and so on. Since I stopped having those, I don't have any friends." Carl Mathews had the same observation. Perhaps the loss of supportive relationships contributed to the fears of some of the formerly wealthy that there would be no one they could turn to in need.

Recalling the man eating from the trashcan at the Jack in the Box restaurant, Carl said, "That could be me eating out of that same trashcan having those same people look at me." What bothered him was not just that he would have no other source of food but also that he would be seen by others eating from a trashcan. That is why he could not bear the thought of being homeless where people knew him. The anticipated shame of having fallen so low would make someone who had been wealthy especially anxious, whether their fears were realistic or not.

Finally, I was struck by Phoenix's depiction of society without a middle class—only the haves and the have-nots, the winners and the losers. Her dichotomous image of society was not shared by all those who had been well-off, but if Stephen's wife, for example, thought of the US class structure in the same way, it would explain why she saw no viable socioeconomic status between a household income of more than $250,000 and living by a drainage culvert.[61]

Immigrants' American Dreams

Another group who had worked to live well were immigrants to the United States. Although some came to the United States as political refugees or for other reasons, many left their homelands because they were drawn by the image of the United States as a land of opportunity where anyone could work hard and achieve a comfortable life. If they migrated for economic mobility, how did they feel when their unemployment or underemployment imperiled their achieving their American dreams?

First, one might ask whether immigrants tend to return to their native country when they face severe economic challenges. Many do. There was considerable return migration even during the late nineteenth and early twentieth centuries, the period that shaped the mythology of grateful immigrants sailing into the New York City harbor past the Statue of Liberty to make a better life for themselves in the United States. Alejandro Portes and Rubén Rumbaut estimate that during that period up to half of southern Italians returned home or migrated back and forth depending on labor demands in the United States and in their home region.[62] Estimates of return migration following the Great Recession in the United States vary considerably, but some research found there were more return migrants than new entrants from 2009 to 2014.[63]

My research was limited to those currently living in the United States, so I do not know the perspectives of those who chose to return. All my immigrant participants had lived in the United States for at least twenty years, and most had children who had only known life there, making it difficult for them to uproot themselves and return to their country of origin. How do those who remained in the United States feel about long-term unemployment or under-employment? We might expect two possible reactions.

The first possible reaction is that, however difficult things are now, immigrants would feel that they are still better off than they would have been if they had stayed in their country of origin. Migrants have what researchers call a *dual frame of reference*. As they think about how well-off they are, they are comparing themselves with other people both in their new and old country.[64] This complicates feelings about whether they are getting ahead. Comparing themselves to those better off in the new host country could cause feelings of relative deprivation, but if they think they would be worse off had they remained in their native country, they could still feel they improved their fortunes. In those situations, we would expect them to feel satisfied with their life choices and hopeful about the future. Another reference group consists of other immigrants in the new host country. If an unemployed immigrant feels they are still better off than other immigrants—especially, other immigrants of the same ethnicity—they may not mind their economic straits as much.[65]

However, another reasonable supposition is just the opposite. Some researchers propose that, throughout the world, international migrants are likely to be much more strongly motivated to get ahead economically than compatriots who do not migrate.[66] They further propose that even if immigrants were not especially motivated to live well when they migrated, after experiencing discrimination in the receiving society and the difficulties of adapting, migrants then come to place greater weight on material rewards than on intangible satisfactions such as a sense of belonging.[67] Alternatively, getting ahead economically and being able to afford the same kinds of commodities as others in their new community can bring a greater sense of belonging.[68] For example, Fred Hernandez said that when he arrived in southern California from Tijuana, Mexico, at age eight, he was teased by the second-generation Latino students who made fun of him for his accented English, for playing barefoot outdoors to preserve his shoes for school, and for his unfashionable clothes. As we talked about why, when he was a truck driver in his twenties, he bought a big house with a pool and a driveway wide enough to park a recreational vehicle, he said his desire "to be accepted" was part of the explanation. If a better life in material terms has heightened importance for most migrants for any of these reasons, then we might expect them to be especially frustrated by economic setbacks.

I found examples of both reactions—of being glad they immigrated, despite their unemployment, and of second-guessing that decision—as well as some reactions that did not fit either pattern. There was no single shared interpretation of their economic difficulties among my sixteen first-generation immigrant participants.

Jorge Paiz, who came from Guatemala, exemplified the first reaction of being glad he immigrated despite his current unemployment. He was the middle of seven children. His mother was a nurse and his father a sometime carpenter. Jorge says he came to the United States as a teenager against his parents' wishes "because of the poverty." Jorge never attended college, which he regrets, but he was eager to begin working. He arrived without papers but was able to obtain a green card through the Nicaraguan Adjustment and Central American Relief Act. He met and married Isela, who joined us for the interviews to help translate, and they had three children. Isela is a clerk in a local school district. The factory where Jorge found his first job moved to Mexico, but Jorge was immediately hired by a construction company. The work was new to him, but he is a hard worker and a quick study. He got yearly raises; in 2011 he and Isela had a combined income in the $65,000–$80,000 range, which was above the median income for Latinos in California (combining immigrants with nonimmigrants).[69] He and Isela bought a house in the working-class city of Pomona, and he became a US citizen. However, in early 2012 the construction company decided to hire outside contractors who could do the work more cheaply, and Jorge and many other long-term workers were laid off. When we met, Jorge had been out of work for five months, which was distressing because being a worker is so important to him. Isela was not paid by the school district when schools are closed during the summer, so it was hard to pay their mortgage and car note. Jorge would not find a full-time job until a year later. Still, he was glad he immigrated. He said he is "really grateful to United States" because "it's like a window that was opened for a lot of us."

By contrast, Anastasia Tang had started to question her decision to immigrate to the United States. Anastasia's material circumstances were considerably better than Jorge's, but she was unhappier about them. Anastasia came from what she describes as a middle-class family in southeast Asia. Her father was a horse trainer who privately traded stocks on the side. He never went to college, so it was important to him that Anastasia do so; he sold some property to pay for his daughter's college education in California. Anastasia received her bachelor's and master's degrees and for many years was an HR manager at a midsize manufacturing company. Her husband was an accounting manager; together they had an income of $180,000 in 2011. Still, they did not own their own home. With their incomes, I suspect they could have easily afforded a home like Jorge and Isela had in Pomona, but Anastasia had set her sights on buying in the upscale community of Irvine in Orange County because of its excellent public schools. As of this writing, the average home value in Irvine is just over a million dollars, double the average home value in Pomona.[70] After Anastasia had two children and began prioritizing family time over after-hours company events, she was fired. At that time, her husband was on family leave; when his leave ended, he decided he did not want to return to work. All the burden of supporting their household fell on Anastasia, and for three years she was only able to obtain temporary contract jobs.

In both the first wave of interviews in 2012 and when I talked to her again in 2014, Anastasia was feeling sad and stressed. She had not been able to achieve her own goals, and she felt she had let down her parents, as I explain further in the next chapter. In the twenty years since Anastasia first came to the United States, the GDP per capita in her home country had doubled.[71] The money she and her husband had saved was unremarkable compared to what many others back home had. Her husband thought that the fact that they were both immigrants (he is from India) gave them options; they could move back to one of their home countries if they desired. But Anastasia did not feel good about returning home with nothing to show for it: "When people leave their country, sacrifice their family life, their childhood, everything to come here for a better life. Then I go back, I feel I'm going back empty-handed. What did I accomplish?" She has a 401(k) with $300,000–$400,000, but "frankly more people have money like that in [*her country*] in their savings." She felt that now the grass is "just as green on both sides"—that is, in both her country of origin and the United States—and that she could not return as a success unless she had a million dollars. Nor did she feel she had achieved what others had in the United States. She said, "My hopes and dreams were to just have whatever you guys [*US Americans*] have." As she explained, "You just want to live the American dream; you want to have the house and a picket fence and maybe the dog and have your car, and that's it. I always wanted to just settle down and be stable. That's what I pictured here. Just American dream; everybody dreams of that." Whether Anastasia compared herself to peers who stayed in her home country, to return-migrant success stories, or to other managers and professionals in the United States, she came up short.[72] Furthermore, after living in the United States for twenty years, Anastasia no longer felt at home in her home country: "Home is where your heart is, right? Where you feel the most comfortable. Now I'm feeling uncomfortable everywhere."

Alfredo Reyes was unhappy with his family's decision to immigrate to the United States when he was twenty; as soon as they arrived in the United States, he wanted to return to El Salvador. Even though he became a skilled baker earning about $1,000 a week, he was never able to afford a home in Los Angeles, where his family settled, because housing is extraordinarily expensive there. He had to go into debt to buy a new truck. When Claudia C. asked

Alfredo whether the United States is still a land of opportunity, he said no. He felt immigrants had always been exploited. As Alfredo's example shows, comparisons of material advantage are not based on income alone ($1,000 a week in the United States versus maybe $125 a week in El Salvador).[73] A higher income means little if your living expenses are greater, and if you cannot obtain the kind of life you expect or want without incurring tremendous debt.

As mentioned, the immigrant participants' reactions to the material setbacks created by long-term unemployment were not limited to the possibilities of feeling they were better or worse off. Comparison of lifeways is tricky when one goes from farming one's own land to selling one's labor. Luis Segura grew up on a farm in Michoacán, Mexico. When Claudia C. asked him why he migrated, he said it was to earn more money and help his family. After he came to the United States, he worked for landscaping companies, earning, at the most, nine or ten dollars an hour. He was satisfied with that and, when necessary, moved to different cities to find work; yet after returning to Los Angeles in 2010 in the middle of the recession, all he could obtain were occasional jobs as a day laborer. He and his long-time partner had broken up, and he was living with four other men in quarters with only one bedroom. His green card had been revoked for a DUI arrest many years earlier, so he was not eligible for food stamps even if he had been willing to apply for them. As I explain in the next chapter, many immigrants we talked to did not obtain food stamps even if they qualified for them. When he needed food, Luis and his friend Feliciano, who participated in the interviews with Luis, asked local restaurant managers for a meal. Despite these difficult circumstances, Luis said that even when times were hard in the United States, he could earn more money than in his rural area of Mexico.

Yet, he struck a different note when Claudia C. commented, "You were telling me that in Mexico, you were in agriculture with your dad and your family. And times in Mexico were hard when you were growing up." Luis responded that at least food had not been a problem then: "Well it's always been hard in Mexico," but by "planting their corn, their beans, lentils, there is a way to eat. You have your cow to drink milk and all that." When Luis compared incomes, the United States was much better, but when he compared the availability of food, living on a farm in Mexico was preferable. When Claudia C. asked Luis to picture a good life, he thought of cows grazing.

Another complication is that many immigrants care not only about living well for themselves but also about improving living conditions for their family of origin. Luis Segura was proud that he was able to send money to his parents in Mexico and that they used those remittances to fix the family home: "Above all, I fixed the house [. . .] I would send money and they fixed it up and we got into a better state." His consumption desires were more for his family of origin than for himself. *He* may not be living well, but *their* circumstances improved because of his decision to come to the United States.[74] He said he had been born poor, and if he died poor, that was okay. By contrast, a large part of Anastasia Tang's frustration stemmed from the fact that her family had sacrificed to send her to the United States, but she was unable to repay them because their material circumstances were now better than hers.

To be sure, not all my immigrant participants had come to the United States to achieve upward economic mobility. Alfredo Reyes and Kham Sy Phouphan were political refugees, not economic migrants. Alfredo's family came to the United States in 1980 to escape the civil war in El Salvador. His family had some relatives in the military and others among the FMLN guerillas, so they faced threats from both sides. Kham Sy Phouphan left Laos after the communist Pathet Lao took power in the mid-1970s. Another two of my immigrant participants were women who had not planned to leave their home countries but had fallen in love with a man from the United States.

I earlier described the anti-materialist discourses that helped many of my participants cope with the disappointments of material setbacks. Those discourses could be helpful for immigrants as well. For example, some expressed the conventional discourse that money cannot buy happiness:

> MIGUEL VARGAS (unemployed operations manager, immigrant from Mexico): I've seen people that, they have money, and they're considered high class, but they're not enjoying their life.
>
> MARIA CARRERA (unemployed quality assurance supervisor, immigrant from Ecuador): I think that also there is people who have money, but they don't have health, or they are not happy. [*Goes on to talk about the singer Whitney Houston, who had died shortly before that interview.*]

One discourse that I heard from two immigrants, but from none of my native-born participants, is that the poor may not have money but they have God's favor. In one part of the interview, we asked for reactions to several statements, including "Poverty can be a blessing." Few of my participants, native born or immigrant, agreed. Some were mystified by it: How could poverty possibly be a blessing? However, Luis Segura and his friend Feliciano Salas, both immigrants from Mexico currently working as day laborers, endorsed it. Feliciano said that God "loves the poor more than the rich. He protects you more, takes care of you more." Luis chimed in, "We're going to heaven, and the rich go to hell."[75] For them, at least, belief in an ultimate reward in the afterlife helped them deal with their current economic struggles.

Another option available to some immigrants disappointed by their economic setbacks was to blame their family. Often the decision to immigrate is a family, not an individual, decision. Alfredo Reyes said he had never agreed with his family's decision to move to the United States to escape the civil war in El Salvador. Lucy Guerrero, who came to the United States in the early 1990s after she met and married a US citizen, and her younger sister, La dama de abril, had different stories about why La dama de abril migrated to the United States. Lucy and La dama de abril grew up in Colombia. Their father abandoned the family when they were young, and their mother struggled to support them. Then La dama married and moved to Venezuela. This was in the 1980s, before Hugo Chavez came to power. There she began an exciting and fulfilling life as a cosmetologist at a salon with celebrity clients. Lucy moved to the United States, only to find out that her husband had deceived her about his economic circumstances. He did not have a good job, and his credit rating was ruined from his first marriage. Lucy and her husband were living on charity from their church when she became pregnant, and La dama de abril, who by this time was divorced, and their mother joined Lucy in the United States. The move did not work out well for La dama de abril, who came on a tourist visa and up to 2012 had not been able to regularize her status. Salons in the United States did not recognize her certifications from Venezuela, and La dama lacked both the English competence and the money to get her license. She had studied acting in Venezuela and landed parts in soap operas in the United States, but she could not continue without documentation. She ended up doing what so many Latina immigrants without green cards do—working as a housekeeper and nanny—but even those jobs were scarce during the recession.[76]

At the time of her interview, La dama de abril was miserable that she had not achieved any of her goals. Her frustration, along with Lucy's guilt about what had happened to her sister, probably explain their divergent explanations for why La dama had come to the United States. According to La dama, "I had a really good life, but my sister decided to come with her husband to [the United States]. [. . .] We are a really small family; then my sister wanted me to come here, too." Lucy, who was interviewed separately, remembered that differently. She claimed that she did not know why her sister came to the United States because "I didn't want [her] to come." However, Lucy admitted that she did not warn her sister about what her life was really like because La dama would not have believed her: "I thought, if I tell her not to come, she will say I am selfish, because the United States, wow! Right? [. . .] One thinks that in the United States, dollars grow in trees." Claudia C. responded, "Everybody was headed to a paradise that didn't exist." Lucy agreed, "To a paradise that didn't exist."

Many Dreams Hiding in One

In chapter 2 I argued that a productivist ("Protestant") work ethic is made up of two distinctly different ethics: a living-to-work ethic and a diligent 9-to-5 work ethic. These ethics motivated different groups of workers, although someone could switch their orientation from one ethic to the other.

Working to live well is different from either of those work ethics. It did not motivate everyone; some of my participants seemed largely indifferent to the form or level of their consumption so long as their basic needs were met. Most of the rest, however, were in general agreement on the essence of "living well": they worked, in part, to pay for a single-family home, at least one car, and money left over to spend as they wished. These desiderata for a happy life are captured by standard descriptions of "the American dream." It is materialistic, but the material things are only part of a larger cultural model that usually includes happiness with a life partner, children, or pets.

I also found widely shared (although not uniform) agreement that consumption should not be excessive. This is the "white picket fence" version of the American dream. "Not excessive" means that one should strive for the size of house, vehicle price range, and type of leisure pursuits that are currently typical among the speaker's peers. Anything beyond what the speaker considers normal spending may be censured as immoral, imprudent, unhealthy, unsustainable, or ineffective because it leads to less happiness, not more. These critical discourses are as American as materialistic images of the American dream: they are the counter-discourses evoked by economic striving among observers alarmed by what they see as its nightmarish side. To be sure, some of those criticisms are less established than others. Only one participant, a young woman in her twenties, raised the relatively new unsustainability critique. All the other criticisms of excessive consumption, however, were common to the point of being clichés, like the saying "Money can't buy happiness."

Still, the same conventional anti-materialist discourses had different meanings for my participants. Some found genuine comfort in a shift in their priorities based on the idea that money cannot buy happiness. Others were annoyed by such platitudes, which contradicted their experience that life was less pleasurable without any discretionary income or—as we see in the next chapter—even enough for their basic needs. Still others ambivalently flip-flopped between wanting to live well and telling themselves those things should not matter.

Some of my participants desired a life of luxury or wealth, not just a modest middle-class life. Their ambitions certainly have been encouraged in contemporary American culture, with reinforcement in recent years from some

New Age writers and Christian prosperity gospel preachers. Yet, in the end, what struck me most were not categorically different images of a good life but rather that they can be ordered along a sliding scale. Although there was broad agreement that it is justifiable to want "normal" forms of consumption, "normal" covers a wide range once you get into the details. One person's "modest" consumption looks like an ostentatious display to someone else. Anastasia Tang described her American dream as what "everybody dreams of": "You just want to live the American dream; you want to have the house and a picket fence and maybe the dog and have your car, and that's it." However, only a few of my participants aspired to own a million-dollar home.[77] The same formulations could cover a wide range of consumer desires. We talk of "the American dream," as if there is just one. But the American dream is fantasized and lived in different ways.

CHAPTER 4

Working to Just Live

At one level, work has a universal meaning, in that humans must expend effort to provide life necessities for themselves and others who depend on them. I call this "working to live."

Waged work to obtain life's necessities, however, is neither necessary nor universal. People have not always lived in money-based market economies, and even in the contemporary United States, there are other possible ways of sustaining a living. Some life necessities could be obtained outside market relations, as they are on a family farm or through barter or reciprocal assistance—or they could be socially provided instead of individually purchased, like health insurance.[1] Nor do all people work to support only themselves and perhaps a life partner and their children. They could live in multigenerational family households or communally with unrelated individuals or families. Moreover, societies have differing norms regarding who is expected or even permitted to earn an income.[2] In the United States, for example, undocumented migrants are excluded from formal employment. We could also ask, What are the necessities of life? Everyone must consume sufficient calories to sustain life, but beyond that basic minimum, social groups differ regarding what they consider necessary. The seeming naturalness of working to live dissolves when you look at it closely.

Just as "working to live" varies, so do the implications of not earning a living in a market economy. What it feels like when you are unable to meet your household's expenses depends in great part on the fallback options. How well do those safety nets meet your needs? Are you able to accept this assistance and still think of yourself as being a good person living a proper life? What feelings are created by receiving—or giving—this assistance?

One might think that there would be few good fallback options in the United States because it is known for extolling self-sufficiency or "rugged individualism." Many observers have argued that, to an unusual extent, American society leaves individuals to succeed or fail on their own. They point both to the absence of a feudal tradition of interdependence between a lord and the people on his land and to the myth of equal opportunity that fosters the belief that anyone should be able to get ahead through ingenuity and hard work. Those who oppose "collectivist" state welfare programs justify their position by claiming that any such government assistance runs counter to the "rugged individualism [that] has defined American character and uniqueness."[3] In addition, there are relatively loose kin obligations in US families compared to societies with a tradition of joint family households or strong ties to ancestral property. As the philosopher Nancy Fraser and historian Linda Gordon write in their history of the meanings of *dependency*, "The United States was especially hospitable to elaborating dependency as a defect of individual character."[4] Yet, what it means to be "independent" or "dependent" is historically contingent, as Fraser and Gordon also show. Even in the United States, financial "self-sufficiency" is not practiced the same way in the twenty-first century as it was in the seventeenth century.

It is particularly difficult to be self-supporting in a deep recession. By the fall of 2011 when I began my research, nearly one-third of the unemployed in the United States had been out of work for a year or longer.[5] Among my participants, three-quarters had been unemployed for a year or longer when we met, and two-thirds of them had been the sole or primary income earner in their household. Even if they had prudently followed financial advisers' recommendations to put aside enough money to cover their expenses for three to six months, they would have exhausted their savings in the year or longer they were out of work.[6] Still, they survived thanks especially to assistance from their families and state programs. In practice, Americans do not expect their compatriots or family members to be rugged individualists if that means starving.[7]

Yet, although my participants found ways to get by, shifting norms for what family members should expect from each other and what citizens should expect from the state created stress in families and challenges to the values and self-understandings of some of those out of work. Others, however, forged positive new forms of interdependence with family members and rethought their relationship to the state.

None of my participants questioned the ideal of being self-supporting. Unlike the cultural battles I described in the last two chapters of living to work versus maintaining a balance between work and the rest of life, or of consumerism versus anti-consumerism, all my interviewees assumed that adults ought to be economically self-sufficient. Therefore, the question is not whether that ideal exists but what "self-sufficiency" currently means in the United States and what are the most acceptable fallback options when it is not possible.

The unemployed faced more than just the material problem of how to stay alive. They had to do so in a way that had meaning and aligned with their values; that is, they had to figure out how to stay alive with self-respect. That was clear when I asked Ann Lopez, "What would you say is the meaning of work for you? The meaning or importance of work?" Ann, who was divorced and had been an IT worker for a large telecommunications company until it fired many of its employees and gave the work to outside firms, replied, "To make a living. To feed my face. (*laughs*) To enjoy life. Work is to provide. You know, I don't want nobody to provide for me. I've never—again, I'm not asking for handouts. It's real hard for me to go say, 'Hey, I want some food stamps.' No, I've always been able to provide for myself."

As we can see, Ann began by saying she worked to meet her biological needs: "To make a living. To feed my face." But she did not stop there. When she said, "To enjoy life," I thought of the pride with which she told me about being able to provide nice vacations and leisure activities for her children when they were growing up, which her struggling family had not been able to give her as a child. In other words, Ann also worked to live well. Finally, she explained another meaning of work for her: "I don't want nobody to provide for me. I've never—again, I'm not asking for handouts. It's real hard for me to go say, 'Hey, I want some food stamps.' No, I've always been able to provide for myself." She said "again" because earlier in the interview we had discussed her feelings about applying for food stamps. If Ann were only concerned about meeting her material need "to feed my face," she would have accepted food stamps without hesitation. The last temporary job she had been able to obtain had ended nine months earlier; her unemployment benefits had recently ended as well. Still, she hesitated because of the stigma that accepting food stamps means "asking for handouts" instead of providing for oneself.

In the rest of this chapter, I explain some of the psychological and social effects of my participants' forced financial reliance on family members, friends, faith communities, local nonprofits, and the state. When I get to the section on state support, I will reveal whether Ann Lopez ever did apply for food stamps. First, however, I need to explain the material consequences of long-term unemployment early in the second decade of the twenty-first century in one part of the United States.

Material Needs of the Unemployed in Early Twenty-First-Century Southern California

For my participants living in the suburbs of southern California in the early 2010s, some of the socially defined basic necessities of life included food, a dwelling place and utilities (gas, electricity, water), health care, a car and fuel, a phone, and internet access. They could postpone personal clothing expenditures, but if they had a baby, they needed diapers, and older children needed clothes that fit their growing bodies. Without an income, the unemployed had to make hard choices among these needs.

Food insecurity was widespread at that time. In the fall of 2011, a national survey of adults who wanted to work, but who had not had a full-time job for a year or more, found that 44 percent had problems paying for food.[8] As important as food is for life, however, when money is limited, groceries may come second to other demands.

For example, when Jackie Gallardo lost her job at a furniture warehouse, she had many harrowing months of having to choose between buying food for herself and her children or buying gas for her car. She could ignore her own hunger, but she did not want to do that to her children, nor could she tell her car to try to get along without gasoline. The suburbs of southern California, as is typical in suburbs throughout the United States, are poorly served by public transportation. Without a working vehicle, it would be difficult for people living in this area to get to the grocery store or their next job. When ReNé McKnight's car was repossessed, her daughter had to wake up at 3:45 A.M. to get ready to catch the first of the three buses she had to take to get to her high school. Making car payments and keeping their old vehicle running were constant preoccupations for many of my participants, as were worries about the cost of gas.

Housing was, and still is, a major concern for the unemployed. There is not enough housing in southern California, and its scarcity leads to high prices for both renters and would-be homeowners.[9] In 2011 the median rent in the greater Los Angeles area was among the most expensive in the country, at $1,214 a month. In the greater Riverside area inland, rents were only a little more affordable, with a median of $1,076 a month in 2011.[10] Nationwide, renters in the bottom fifth of earners spend nearly two-thirds of their income in rent.[11] The number of public housing units has shrunk by nearly one-quarter since the early 1990s, and vouchers to help renters in the private housing market are so hard to obtain that many public housing authorities have closed their waiting lists.[12] In Los Angeles County, there were 40,000 people on the waiting list in 2017.[13]

Mortgages were even more expensive. The Great Recession was created by a housing bubble fueled by a toxic brew of predatory, subprime-rate mortgages and feverish home buying that drove home prices ever higher, especially in California and a few other states.[14] Jackie Gallardo, whose gas-versus-food dilemma I just discussed, had been paying a mortgage of $3,200 a month for the large home she and her husband had bought during the height of the housing bubble. While they were working full time, they could meet those payments (barely), but during the Great Recession, their work hours were reduced. They, like so many others, could no longer pay their mortgage and so lost their home.

The unemployed had fewer options than other homeowners to reduce their housing costs. Once they were out of work, no bank would let them refinance their mortgage when interest rates dropped, even if they had faithfully kept up on their mortgage payments. There were national programs that were supposed to help homeowners, but the mortgage lenders did everything they could to avoid fulfilling their legal obligations.[15] Nationwide, nearly half of those who had not had a full-time job for a year or more in 2011 had trouble paying their rent or mortgage.[16] Forty percent of my participants had not been able to pay rent or mortgage at some point during the time they were out of work, and almost one of five lost their apartment or home and had to move in with a family member or friend. One was living in a homeless shelter, and another moved to transitional housing for the homeless during the first year I knew her. Those numbers do not include those who were already living with another family member to save money before they lost their jobs.

Health care was also unaffordable for many of my participants at that time, and that could be deadly. National provision of health insurance in the United States is still politically contested, although it is popular with majorities of the American public.[17] In 2000, I interviewed an elderly man who was nostalgic for the time when patients directly paid doctors in any way they could, perhaps by giving them a couple of chickens. Those days are long gone. Few doctors would accept payment in chickens now, and the costs of health care are so high that only a full-time chicken farmer could amass enough birds as payment. Many Americans are dependent on their employer to contribute thousands of dollars a year toward their premiums, which keeps the costs manageable.[18] Those employer contributions are in turn subsidized by the US government, which exempts the cost of employer-sponsored insurance from federal income and payroll taxes, forgoing $273 billion in revenues in 2019.[19] What does self-sufficiency in health care mean under these circumstances?

In any case, those relatively affordable employer-sponsored health insurance plans were largely unavailable to the unemployed. Their former employers were required by law to continue to offer them access to their health insurance plan for a while (typically, eighteen months), but the employers were not obligated to pay for any portion of it, making medical insurance unaffordable for all but the wealthiest of my participants.[20] At that time, Medicaid was only available to low-income children, their parents, and the disabled with few resources.[21] The Affordable Care Act, which provided funding to states that chose to expand their Medicaid coverage, passed in 2010, but when I began my interviews in 2011 and 2012, its benefits had not yet kicked in.

Many of the middle-aged participants in my project were worried about how they would afford health care because they had no health insurance. Charity care was available at overcrowded county hospitals, but trying to obtain health care in such spaces could be a horrific experience. In one Los Angeles County hospital, a woman died writhing and hemorrhaging on the floor of the waiting room while nurses stepped around her.[22] Community clinics did their best to meet the health care needs of those with low incomes, but some of those clinics lacked funding to keep their doors open. When my participant Phoenix Rises learned that her community clinic was closing for lack of funding, she told the clerk who gave her that bad news, "It's like you just threw me in the bowels of hell. That's how I feel." "The bowels of hell" meant the local public hospital where she would have to wait for hours for charity care in the emergency room when all she wanted was a prescription for medication to control her blood pressure.

When I asked the unemployed how they would pay for health insurance, a response I often got is that they planned not to get sick. That plan did not work for one of my participants. When we met, he was dealing with persistent, debilitating back pain. During our interviews, he would frequently pause to breathe deeply and try to manage the pain. He did not have health insurance, so his brother-in-law gave him some money to go to a chiropractor. The pain turned out to be caused by a malignant tumor that killed him a year after our interview. I always wonder whether his cancer would have been detected sooner and he would have survived had the United States made health care available to all.

Compared to food, shelter, and health care, a phone would hardly seem to count as a life necessity. However, it was essential for job seekers, because they needed a phone number at which potential employers could reach them.

They also needed internet access, either through a smartphone or a computer (their own or in a public setting) because of the way labor markets work today. Jobs are frequently posted online, and applicants are almost always required to submit their application online.

Some people might add or remove some items from my list. However, the ones I just outlined were a nearly universal core of nonnegotiable needs for southern Californians and, indeed, most Americans at the time of my research.

This, then, was the material context for my unemployed participants: what they needed, their difficulties affording those items, and some of the hardships they faced when they could not afford them. What were the social and psychological consequences of asking for assistance to pay for these necessities?

When Is the Family a Safety Net?

Anthropologists have shown that family structures vary around the world. One way in which they differ is in expectations about how economic resources will be shared.

In chapter 3, I introduced Anastasia Tang, who grew up in southeast Asia. Her parents sent her to the United States for her college education. After receiving her bachelor's and master's degrees, she obtained a managerial job in a mid-size manufacturing company in California; her husband also had a managerial job. Their life plans were disrupted when she was fired because she had chosen to go home to take care of her young children instead of attending two after-hours company events. At almost the same time, her husband, burned out from his corporate job, decided to take a long break from working. In the last chapter I explained that because neither had an income, the couple had to postpone fulfilling Anastasia's American dream of buying a house. That was not all that bothered her about being out of work, however. What made her so emotional that it became hard for her to talk was how she had let down her parents. She explained that her father had done so much for her, including selling a house they owned that would be worth millions of dollars in the current real estate market, to fund her education. She had no way to repay them: "All those things, and I feel like I can't even give them two dollars to help."

I had trouble understanding why this was so upsetting and asked whether her parents needed money from her. Not at all, she told me, but that was what was so distressing. They were well off now, and she was the one struggling financially. As she explained, in Asian families like hers, the parents will sacrifice for their children; in return, adult children should provide for their parents when they are older.[23] Anastasia was unable to fulfill her part of this bargain: "And here we are, I'm forty-plus, I can't even support my parents." That statement gave me culture shock. To my US way of thinking, I have no obligation to support my parents if they do not need my financial support. For Anastasia, however, the very fact that there was no meaningful way for her to support her parents because they were better off than she was meant she had failed in her responsibilities.

In many parts of Latin America as well, grown children expect to give their parents financial support. In the last chapter, I described Luis Segura and Feliciano Salas, longtime US residents from Mexico, who were barely supporting themselves as day laborers after they lost their regular jobs during the recession. Nonetheless, if Feliciano's mother called and said she did not have enough money for food, Feliciano said, "I have to borrow it from friends or something, but I have to send her some." Luis had never made much money working for landscaping companies, but he sent remittances to fix his family's home.[24]

In the United States, several researchers found that "patterns of giving back among whites are nearly purely unidirectional, flowing downstream from parents to children, and continue in this vein even after children reach adulthood."[25] It is uncommon for the flow to go from grown children to their working-age parents. Yet European Americans are not the only group who do not expect to support their parents or other family members. Jody Agius Vallejo studied middle-class, second-generation Mexican Americans living in southern California suburbs. Among other questions, she asked whether they have financially supported their parents and relatives and whether they feel an obligation to give back to their family. She found that their family's circumstances when they were growing up determined whether members of the second generation felt that obligation and gave back. All but one of those who grew up in a low-income family in the United States helped support their parents and siblings. By contrast, Latinos who grew up in middle-class families in the United States exhibited the more typically white pattern of financial support from parents to children, but not the reverse. Of course, among those who grew up in middle-class families, parents usually do not need their offspring's assistance, but Agius Vallejo noted that members of the second generation from such families also do not feel obligated to help other, less affluent relatives. She argues that what is relevant is not ethnic heritage but rather a firsthand experience of economic struggles—an experience that creates the desire to give back.[26]

The normative one-way flow of financial assistance from parents to their children in the United States created an age divide among my participants in the availability of family support and their feelings about it. I describe the implications for my middle-aged and older participants shortly. First, however, we need to consider the fraught question: At what age are Americans expected to be self-supporting adults? There is no clear answer at the present time—neither in the United States nor in many other parts of the world.

Ambiguous Adulthood

In an earlier study, I interviewed a man born in the late 1950s who grew up in a small town in North Carolina. He explained that when he graduated from high school in the mid-1970s, his parents gave him an ultimatum: he had one week to relax but then was supposed to start working full time. At that time, eighteen-year-olds with no more than a high school education could get well-paying jobs that would enable them to support themselves. In the decades since, automation and global trade have led to increasing job competition, and many stable, full-time jobs have been replaced by part-time or contingent jobs. Increased competition created "degree inflation" (or "up-credentialing"): to limit the pool of applicants, many entry-level jobs that had not required higher education in the past began to require a college degree.[27] In the United States, obtaining a college degree may require borrowing thousands of dollars to cover tuition and other expenses, leaving college graduates deeply in debt.

The difficulties of making a living, longer years of schooling, and high costs of housing have contributed to later ages at marriage, especially in wealthy countries.[28] The median age of first marriage in the United States is now over thirty for males and over twenty-eight for females—compared to just over twenty-three for males and just under twenty-one for females in 1970. Although more people are living together without marriage, that still leaves a significant number of unmarried singles in their twenties who are in no hurry to establish their own households.[29]

The result is an international trend of "boomerang kids"—grown children who live in their parents' homes—as Katherine Newman documents based on international statistics and interviews in Italy, Spain, Japan, and the United States.[30] In the United States in 2016, nearly one-third of young adults ages eighteen to thirty-four lived with their parents, and one-quarter of them were neither working nor in school.[31] Moreover, 60 percent of people in that age group were receiving financial support from their parents, a very large increase from their parents' time.[32] Although it is less common for those in their thirties to continue living with their parents, there has been a 50 percent increase since the 1970s in thirty- to thirty-four-year-olds who are doing so.[33]

Boomerang children are contributing to a rise in multigenerational households in the United States; that is, households with more than one adult generation living together. In 2021 almost one in five Americans lived in such a household, more than double the share fifty years earlier.[34] The numbers would be even higher if they included adult siblings sharing a household. Adult sibling households are not included because they are of the same generation.

These new trends are changing the age when one is considered to be an adult. Newman found that in the countries she studied, adulthood used to be marked by clear milestones such as turning twenty or twenty-one, working full time, becoming financially independent, and having a child. Currently, particularly for the middle class in those countries, adulthood is defined subjectively as a state of mind.[35] The psychologist Jeffrey Jensen Arnett argues that there is now a new stage of development, "emerging adulthood," which occurs between the late teens and late twenties.[36]

To be clear, not all Americans have the option of being financially supported by their parents. My participant ReNé McKnight left home as soon as she could to escape her substance-abusing father, who had spent what was supposed to be her college fund and left the family in poverty. Her parents were divorced, and her mother was mentally ill. ReNé was forced to be self-sufficient at a young age.

Other emerging adults have loving families who have the means to support them but do not believe in doing so. For example, Katarina Spelling's parents made their position clear: they would pay for her education through college, but she should expect no financial assistance after that. Katarina had imbibed their values; she supported herself and lived away from home from her college years onward. A devout Mormon, she went abroad on a mission after she graduated from community college in her early twenties. When she returned home eighteen months later, she recalled, "All I wanna do is stay with my mom, and they're like, 'No.'" Two weeks later she moved out while she continued her education.

By contrast, some of my participants in their twenties had parents who let them live at home. Jake Taylor described his father as an easygoing roommate. Jake joined the Air Force out of high school and served in Iraq and Afghanistan. He returned to civilian life in his early twenties and moved in with his father. I met Jake at that point, after he had held a series of poorly paid, unpleasant short-term warehouse jobs, which were one of the few positions in the part of southern California where he lived for someone with neither a college degree nor a skilled trade. His father, a mechanic, was in no position to demand that Jake be more independent because he also needed financial assistance. He was living with his ex-wife's wealthy aunt, who charged him only a nominal rent; Jake and his father shared a room on the top floor of her large house. Jake had been paying some rent to his great-aunt when he was working, but while he was out of work and looking for another job, he explained, "She's being lenient since she's my aunt, and she's obligated to love me." The only problem was that she was from a still-earlier generation and not as comfortable with Jake's unemployment as his father was. A month before I met Jake, they had gotten into a fight: "She was like, 'You just expect to kick your feet up and have everybody take care of you,' and this is while I was out helping her run an errand because she needed my help." Jake thought that possibly she was upset because neither he nor his father spent as much time talking to her as she would have liked.

Chipper Goodman's situation was a little different. He had been dividing his time between the homes of each of his parents, who were divorced and had new partners. I had the sense that neither Chipper nor his parents or stepparents had clear expectations about the terms under which living with them was acceptable after he finished college. Chipper's life had not lived up to his early promise. He was an outstanding football player in high school and had been offered a football scholarship to the University of Southern California, but he lost that scholarship because he had incurred too many concussions. After he graduated from college elsewhere, he had enlisted in the Navy but was rejected when a medical review showed that, as a teenager, he had been prescribed Depakote. He had been given this prescription for a possible bipolar disorder, even though Chipper thinks his only problem was that "I was going through puberty and didn't know how to deal with getting angry and sad." Chipper had been an Eagle Scout in high school and still wanted to serve others. He hoped to join the Los Angeles Fire Department, but a DUI arrest ruled that out. When I met him, he was in his mid-twenties, and he could only find part-time work as a bouncer at a club and occasional jobs preparing the grounds for outdoor sporting events. He spent time in both of his parents' houses but mostly lived with his father. In lieu of rent, he had been doing odd jobs around the house like replacing the sprinkler system.

His father and stepmother's expectations changed over the time Chipper was living with them. Shortly before our interview, his father had decided that Chipper should start paying rent. Chipper replayed that conversation: "He said he needs to start charging me rent to make me accountable, or whatever." In addition, his father wanted him to wash his own dishes, start making dinner once a week for the family, and sit down and talk with them. I asked Chipper whether those conditions were acceptable to him. He said they were. The only problem was that he felt he was being asked to choose between his parents, but he understood his father's perspective that he was "kinda freeloading between two places. Crashing here, crashing there, not really having any ties to one or the other." Both Jake's great-aunt and Chipper's father and stepmother wanted something in exchange for providing shelter to the emerging adults in their families—not just money but also nonmonetary forms of assistance and social interaction.

I am not surprised that expectations were unclear in Chipper's family about whether he should be paying rent and what should be his other household obligations. This is new territory for twenty-somethings and their parents, and everyone is feeling their way forward. The absence of shared understandings was expressed by the writer Jennifer Boylan in a thoughtful column about the dilemmas she faced after her son graduated from college. She noted that there are books, articles, and websites galore about how to raise young children but few about parenting an adult. Her friends gave her conflicting advice: "'I'll tell you what your job is now,' one friend said. 'You keep your mouth shut, and you write checks.'" But Jenny's hairdresser "couldn't have disagreed more strongly. 'Don't give them a dime once they've graduated, Jenny!' she said. 'If you love them, you let them fend for themselves. You let them fail. You let them be hungry.'" There is no cultural consensus.[37]

Clashing expectations about supporting grown children can also occur within a family. I should know. My husband and I were in accord in fully supporting our son through his graduation from college. However, once he graduated as an environmental studies major at the age of twenty-three without a job and moved back home, we found ourselves at sea with differing notions of which direction to steer. Our son found a job after a while, then quit the job after a year, and spent several years trying to start an online business—all the time still living at home. By day, I was teaching and writing this book. By night, my husband and I debated issues such as whether we should charge him rent. If so, how much? How long should we let him stay in our house if he was not earning an income? We felt tugged and pulled between love and concern for our son, on the one hand, and the disquieting feeling we should be pushing him to be more self-sufficient, on the other—the same mix Newman found in other American households with boomerang adult children. She notes that when grown children return to live with their parents as "in-house adults," this new role "has to be carefully negotiated on both sides of the equation."[38]

Still, it seems that most of the angst is felt by parents who grew up when "we couldn't wait to get out of the house," as two friends said to me, puzzled about the younger generation. For many young people in their twenties, living with or being financially supported by their parents is not so strange or hard to understand because it is becoming common in their cohort. The greater social acceptance of twenty-somethings living at home makes it easier for many of those in that age group to be unemployed. Not everyone has that option, but those who do are less likely to be stigmatized for failing to be self-supporting than they would have been in earlier decades.

Middle Aged and Broke

My participants in their forties, fifties, and sixties who were unemployed and unable to pay their bills faced a different set of cultural constraints. There is no ambiguity in the social expectation that they should be self-supporting at that age, but a confluence of forces made that difficult.

The Great Recession was particularly brutal for middle-aged job seekers in the United States. Unlike previous recessions, job seekers aged fifty-five or older faced longer periods of unemployment during and after the Great Recession than did their younger counterparts.[39] A government investigation found that older job seekers attributed their problems finding another job to perceptions that they had high salary expectations, would not want to work for a younger boss, lacked computer and other technology skills, would have higher health costs, or would want to retire before employers got a good "return" on their training.[40] Even though older workers are thought to have good "soft" skills (etiquette, communication, listening), the kinds of jobs for which they are preferred are low-wage service positions, for example, in fast-food restaurants.[41] My middle-aged participants wanted a more challenging and better-paying job than working in a fast-food restaurant.

Hiring managers who expect someone in their late fifties to retire soon have outdated assumptions. The number of Americans continuing to work from the age of sixty-five onward doubled from 1977 to 2007 for many reasons other than the size of the Baby Boomer cohort: they include better health, postindustrial jobs that are easier on an aging body, and unpredictable retirement savings that fluctuate with the stock market instead of defined-benefit pensions.[42] Employers may think a job applicant in their late fifties is getting ready to retire, but the applicant may be planning to work for at least another ten years.

Although I should know better, I too succumbed to ageism when I met my oldest interviewee, seventy-eight-year-old Alice Joyner. As a teenager, she was pressured to accept a marriage proposal because her mother was worried that, as a dark-skinned Black woman, she would have trouble finding a husband. Alice went on to raise eight children and divorce her first and second husbands because neither fully appreciated her desire to study and do more with her life. She was in her early seventies when she finished college. A daughter living in southern California suggested that Alice live with her and help with care of her child (Alice's grandchild). Alice accepted this invitation mainly because a local university had a master's program in psychology she hoped to enter. When I met Alice, she was looking for a job in family counseling to pay for her intended graduate work and to enable her to live on her own. Two years later, as I was driving to a restaurant to meet her for a follow-up interview, I fully expected her to say that now that she was eighty, she was ready to retire. I was wrong. Before we had even finished scanning the menu, she burst out with her exciting news: "I'm working!" She had a job offer to be a holistic counselor. Although the position only provided a stipend for her expenses, rather than a salary, she was happy to do it because it was a first step in her long-range plan to become a licensed marriage and family therapist. Alice commented, "I've had people say, 'Oh you've done enough. You sit down. You've done enough.' But see, they don't know what my 'enough' is. They can't measure me by age." For her, working meant being useful, "and it's good to feel useful all your life." Another participant began a new career in IT in his mid-sixties, after losing his previous job delivering pizza six years earlier.

For my middle-aged and older participants who wanted to keep working, the reluctance of many employers to hire them created enormous frustration. It also left them with the dilemma of how to afford life necessities during their long-term unemployment. When they could not support themselves, could they rely on their families?

The dominant US norm of a one-way flow of support from older to younger generations largely ruled out the option of the middle-aged unemployed receiving financial assistance from their grown, employed children. One national survey found that 39 percent of Americans said it is "not really a responsibility" for adult children to take into their home an elderly parent who wanted to live with them. Note that this question asked about an "elderly parent."[43] The percentage of those who do not see helping an unemployed parent as a family responsibility would surely be even higher if that parent is not elderly.

Phoenix Rises, for one, never considered asking her grown daughters for help. As I explained in chapter 3, Phoenix was a special education teacher, and her husband had been a broadcast engineer. At one time they had a combined income of more than $500,000, and they owned a large home. When both became disabled—her husband permanently, she for a few years from a workplace injury—they were nearly impoverished. They had to move to a small apartment with no room for their younger daughter, who was then in college. After Phoenix recovered, the recession slowed hiring, and she was unable to find another teaching job for almost three years. Their younger daughter went on to become a fashion buyer, and their older daughter was a secretary. At one point during Phoenix's job search, when she was ready to take any gig to bring in some money, she applied to be a product demonstrator at Costco. Her daughters were aghast: "My kids are, like, 'Seriously, Mom?' They're, like, 'Mom, you know you can always count on us.'" Phoenix proudly refused that offer: "I had strong women in my family to be great examples to me, and I'm gonna be a great example to you. I'm gonna show you."

Phoenix may also have doubted her daughters' sincerity. When we met for our third interview, Phoenix explained why it had been an especially bad week for her. She and her husband could no longer pay their younger daughter's cellphone bill. This daughter, who was then twenty-six, was making an excellent salary as a fashion buyer, but when Phoenix informed her that they could not pay her phone bills, "She got really mad. It brought up all of our past and it went into, 'I'm just so tired of you and Dad being such a disappointment, and it's just sad that you can't manage this.'" Phoenix felt "devastated." The conversation reminded her of when they had to move to a small apartment with no room for that daughter, who then called Phoenix and her husband "losers" for not being able to manage their finances better. Her younger daughter's contempt no doubt strengthened Phoenix's resolve to "show you" and become successful again. Under such circumstances, she certainly would not want to ask either daughter for financial assistance.

The disdain of Phoenix's younger daughter was unusual among my participants. No one else said their adult children were so critical of them for being out of work and in financial need. Still, few expected or received help from their grown children. Although some of my immigrant Latin American middle-aged participants received such financial support, among my native-born middle-aged or older participants, only two, Sam Lennon and Alice Joyner, had grown children who helped them financially—and neither was confident that they could rely on that assistance. Sam was disabled after working many years in low-wage food service and retail jobs. Her four children, then in their late thirties and early forties, helped provide for her. Sam's oldest son called twice during our first interview out of concern for her, and he had set up a bank account for her that was linked to his. However, Sam worried that because he had a girlfriend, the assistance would stop: "I'm afraid he's not gonna help me too much longer, 'cause that's what happens when you get a girlfriend." Alice, the seventy-eight-year-old who wanted to be a family counselor, had a son who was very well off. When she asked him for money, he started sending her $200 a month. But beyond that, "he don't want me asking for anything." Alice could not rely on him because "he just wants to be able to do it if and when he wants to do it." Living in a society without an established norm of supporting one's parents, even those of my interviewees who were receiving financial assistance from their grown children could not count on it.

To be fair, Alice wanted her independence as well. Her daughter had offered to share her home in return for Alice's help with childcare, but at our follow-up interview I learned Alice had moved out because she loved to study, and in her daughter's house there was no place to spread out her books. She added, "When I'm living with someone else, I'm kind of at their convenience. And, it's been okay, but I need my own space." Just as my younger participants chafed under the restrictions that came with living with others, so did some of my older participants.

Even though Lucy Guerrero, in her early fifties, was facing eviction because she had not been able to make mortgage payments for four years, she ruled out living with one of her grown daughters. In part, she did not want to be a burden on them, but another part of her reluctance stemmed from her desire to have more freedom: "Oh, Heavenly Father! This is very hard to say, but, actually, my dream is to have at least a one-room house. [. . .] This is the only thing I aspire to in this life, at this moment. That I have my own independence, that I may move, that I may cook my meals and not to be with them. They may visit me, but not to stay." I found Lucy's reluctance to live with either of her daughters especially interesting because her mother was living with her. Lucy and her sister were immigrants from South America who had lovingly cared for their disabled mother for many years. Lucy denied that caring for her mother was a burden on her, but it seemed that during her twenty years in the United States she had adopted the mainstream US norm of greater autonomy and looser family obligations.

Loose family obligations in the United States extend to siblings. The anthropologist Daniel Mains found that in Ethiopia it was common for young women to take jobs as domestic servants in the Middle East, sending remittances home that help support their unemployed brothers.[44] In the United States, there is no established expectation of sibling support. Some of my middle-aged participants reported siblings (in every case, a sister) who let them move in with them to save money, or siblings who generously sent them money. However, about an equal number never considered asking their siblings for financial assistance or said their siblings were unsympathetic. Several said their siblings were also struggling and were in no position to help.

That leaves the elderly parents of the middle-aged unemployed as being their most likely family safety net for monetary assistance or providing them a place to live. How did my middle-aged participants weigh their need for financial assistance and a place to live, if they could no longer afford their rent or mortgage, against their belief they should be financially independent at their age?

Several avoided becoming dependent on their parents. Some had a strained relationship with their parents, which made them highly reluctant to share living quarters or ask for assistance. Others did not want to worry their elderly parents, who had their own problems. There were also those who so strongly believed they ought to be self-sufficient that they ruled out that option. Phoenix Rises was no more willing to ask her widowed mother for assistance than she was to ask her grown daughters. Even though her stepfather had left her mother well off, Phoenix, who was in her early sixties, did not see that money as hers: "My dad did not work all those years to provide for *me*; it was to provide for my mother and my sister, who is developmentally delayed. You know what I mean? My brother and I are supposed to be able to take care of ourselves. So, I refuse to be a burden. On anyone." Similarly, Rebecca Robinson, also in her early sixties, hated the fact that she had to rely on an inheritance from her deceased mother to pay her bills. As Rebecca explained, "It bothered me because I was using my mom's money to support myself. And it made me just feel like, 'Good grief, you can't even care for yourself.'"

At the other extreme, some of my middle-aged participants had no problem at all accepting financial assistance from their parents. Mickey Muller lost his job as an engineer when he was in his mid-fifties. He gave up looking for another one because he assumed no one would hire him at that age. To help him and his family, his mother gave him $24,000, which he seemed to take for granted. He mentioned it casually: "Of course, that two months from August [to] September, my mom gave me $24,000 and I was paying the mortgage, paying all the bills." His mother was in her late eighties, and he was looking forward to the share of the inheritance he would receive when she passed away. He commented, "There'll be a lot of money coming out of my mom if she doesn't spend it all" to pay the fees at her assisted living residence.

Most of my participants fell between these extremes. Accepting financial assistance or a place to live from their parents was an option they turned to out of necessity but with complicated feelings. Moving back home to live with a parent was especially sensitive for some. Financial assistance can be hidden, but moving into their parent's home was a visible sign of deviance from the dominant script in the United States. Emerging adults can live with their parents without changing this script; they are only delaying the expected trajectory. However, for some in their forties or fifties, returning home after living on their own was shameful.

In chapter 3 we met Theresa Allen, who was embarrassed to attend her high school reunion when her husband's unemployment meant they could no longer pay their mortgage and had to rent an apartment. He had been dismissed from his job in a furniture factory after he recovered from a heart attack because the company did not want to be liable for any continuing health insurance costs. It was difficult for either of them to find another job in their fifties. Theresa had worked as a waitress in the past among other jobs, but she had not worked in many years and she also had health issues. Their situation became even more desperate when his unemployment benefits ended and she was unable to find a waitressing job because restaurants were not hiring during the Great Recession. They applied for and obtained General Relief (a cash grant for childless adults), but it only paid a pittance, and as I explained, government-subsidized housing or affordable housing of any sort was in extremely short supply in southern California. They could either live in their car or move in with Theresa's mother, and they chose the latter. Theresa has no children, but she has four younger siblings. She did not mention the possibility of moving in with any of them, nor did I ask, which shows that both of us took for granted that parents are a more acceptable safety net than sisters or brothers. Theresa was grateful to her mother for giving them a place to live, but returning to her childhood home was terrible for her. In part, that was because it was a symbolic regression to being a dependent child: "I hadn't lived with her for thirty-three years. Okay? So, you can imagine. Nice lady, nice home in Claremont Heights [*upscale neighborhood*], but moving back with your mom in your fifties is so unbelievably depressing, with your husband." What was far worse, however, was the condition her mother imposed: they could have only one pet because "she's really picky about her house." Theresa's passion had been animal rescue, and she had to make the wrenching decision to give away or euthanize all but one of her three remaining dogs and ten cats, who had been like children to her. The part of her life story in which she described what happened to each of them was heartbreaking.

However, living with one's parents does not have to be viewed as a return to childlike dependence. Several other participants framed the situation differently: instead of depending on their parents, they were helping them out in their old age. For example, Daniel Horn, a divorced, formerly successful contractor, moved back home from a neighboring state in his late forties to help out when his father was dying; then he stayed after the Great Recession hit and struggled to find work. When his father was dying, he told Daniel to "take care of your mom.'" Daniel then concluded, "So that's what I'm doing, is taking care of my mom." His mother was a healthy, independent eighty-year-old but she probably appreciated Daniel's companionship and help around the house. Similarly, Fred Hernandez, who like Daniel was divorced, moved back home in his early fifties when he was unable to find another job as a substance abuse counselor. I asked jokingly whether living with his parents put a crimp on his romantic life, but he responded seriously, "You know, even if I had the funds, and the ability to move, I don't think I would." I asked him, "Why not?" and he replied, "Because they're really old, and they need somebody there."

Alternatively, some of my participants brought their parents to live with them. That arrangement worked out well for Hillary Edwards and her husband Ralph, both of whom were unemployed finance-sector professionals in their sixties. After struggling to pay their bills, they invited Hillary's mother to live with them. Hillary's mother's Social Security checks helped pay the rent for their apartment, and Hillary and Ralph provided companionship and care for her.

These arrangements of mutual support could be emotionally satisfying because they enabled my participants to see themselves as playing a valuable role in their family. They could respect themselves and be respected by others. Another middle-aged participant, Stacie McCarthy, who was single and in her late fifties, received financial assistance from her mother during the three and a half years she looked for another full-time job as a loan processor. In return, she helped her eighty-year-old mother, who was starting to experience memory loss, with her daily chores. As Stacie put it, "We're helping each other. She helps me financially, and I help her physically." Stacie found their mutual support satisfying because "I feel like I'm paying her back a little bit."

Several other participants said that it was providential that they lost their jobs just as their parents or in-laws needed their help. Some spoke of their unemployment as a blessing in disguise because it occurred when an older family member needed them. For example, Mona Childs, an unemployed marketing professional in her mid-fifties, "saw it as a blessing" that she was out of work so she could help her elderly mother when she was struck by a teenage driver and badly injured. Mona devoted herself to her mother's care, not expecting anything in return, but Mona's grateful mother later gave her money she and her husband had planned to leave Mona as an inheritance.

Anthropologists would not be surprised that my participants wanted to give something to their parents in exchange for their parents' financial assistance. In a canonical text in our field, *The Gift*, the early twentieth-century French sociologist Marcel Mauss argues, "The gift not yet repaid debases the man who accepted it."[45] In other words, receiving a gift creates an obligation to give back. As I will show, this was a repeated theme when my participants spoke of receiving financial assistance, whether from their parents, friends, or faith community.

These examples of closer family ties do not fit the description of Americans as "rugged individualists"—a model in which even parents and children have few obligations to each other after the children are grown. The rising number of multigenerational households may be changing norms of family relations. I do not want to romanticize these arrangements; some of my other participants reported serious tensions in their multigenerational households. Still, for some, being forced to develop deeper ties of mutual dependence with their parents was a rare benefit of being out of work.

Neither Family nor the State

The primary safety nets for my unemployed participants were their families and the state. However, those were not the only options. Sometimes friends, faith communities, and charitable organizations such as food pantries were sources of economic assistance. For my participants, that aid could come at a cost to personal relationships, or it could foster deeper ties.

Alexis de Tocqueville observed in the nineteenth century that one way in which Americans combat the fragmentation of their individualistic society is by forming voluntary associations.[46] There is considerable debate about whether such associations are currently in decline, but those civil society groups can be sources of assistance in times of need, as can religious communities and friends.[47]

The forms of assistance that seemed to bring the most pleasure to my participants were voluntary gifts from peers that they could reciprocate in some way. Two mentioned such gifts from members of their church. When I met ReNé McKnight for our second interview, she said she was "in high spirits" because members of her dance team at church had asked her what she needed, and she was looking forward to obtaining winter clothes for her daughter and herself. Her experience in her previous church was different: "You were always for yourself. People would always be like, 'Oh, if you need anything, just let us know!'—you know how people just say?" However, when she asked for something, they never followed through. Similarly, Marcus Walker was grateful that his church gave him money to repair his used car and pay taxes on it. Both volunteered many hours a week at their church. Like my participants who gave their time to help their parents and received financial assistance from them, there was mutuality in their relationship: both felt they belonged to a supportive community to which they gave in their own ways.

It was the same with friends. A few participants reported a comfortable reciprocity with some of their friends while they were out of work. For example, Daniel Horn, the unemployed contractor who was living with his mother, had a middle-income friend who would pick up the restaurant tab when they went out to eat. In return, Daniel helped him with yard work. Paradoxically, he was more reluctant to ask his wealthier friends for financial assistance, even though they could better afford to help him, because he could not reciprocate.

By contrast, Della Jones, an unemployed schoolteacher, had needed to ask her friends for money so often, without being able to repay them, that she could no longer bear the lack of reciprocity in their friendship: "Every time I talk to them, it was like I was *getting* something from them, and I could *never* give back." She had needed assistance after her divorce, during her unpaid summer breaks, and after she was laid off during the Great Recession when schools had to cut their budgets. She could not afford to socialize with her friends because their get-togethers required spending money. She was so ashamed that she changed churches and stopped communicating with her friends. She said they were still willing to give her money, but she could no longer accept it. As Mauss would have predicted, Della felt wounded by this one-way charity. She missed her friends terribly, but "I just feel really yucky about always, just—I only see you when I want something. That's not a good *friend*." She also felt she was failing to live up to American self-sufficiency norms: "Maybe I'm asking for it because it's too easy. Maybe if I learned to live without it, then I'd be a better person."

Other gifts from peers were problematic because they came with condescending advice or conditions. Jim Wade's church was ready to give him financial assistance, but this assistance was accompanied by lectures from older, wealthier members, who had come of age when it was easier to find a stable, full-time, well-paid job. One said to him, "Your situation now—it's your fault because you didn't get a master's degree and you didn't further your education and you didn't apply for jobs I applied for." Jim, who had worked in the parts department of a car dealer and at auto parts stores, resented these lectures. The older church member giving Jim these lectures did not understand that the economy had changed, and he was ignoring the advantages he had because of his family's socioeconomic class. Jim came from a working-class family in which money was tight, and he had worked at lower-wage jobs that did not pay for higher education—unlike that church member, who had wealthy parents who could pay for the college education that enabled him to obtain a corporate job that then funded his master's degree. When Jim could no longer afford to pay his rent, his church offered to pay for his housing but only if he and his wife lived separately. They did not want to provide for her housing because she did not attend church due to her work schedule.

Charitable organizations such as food banks that made donations with no questions asked were less intrusive. My participants did not mind the lack of reciprocity in accepting their aid because helping those in need was those organizations' primary purpose, and accepting their assistance did not threaten any social relationships.[48] The problem was that their donations often had a "beggars-can't-be-choosers" quality. My participant Sam Lennon noted that one of the food banks she frequented had healthy food, but another primarily provided processed foods and odd items like chocolate-covered licorice. You cannot make a meal out of chocolate-covered licorice.

In sum, not everyone can count on assistance from their family or feel comfortable accepting their help. Occasional assistance from friends, faith-based organizations, and other nonprofit agencies may feel like a loving sign of belonging and support, or it may create feelings of failure to live up to cultural ideals and may imperil relationships based on mutuality. In any case, sporadic gifts are not enough to pay the bills. That leaves government social welfare benefits.

Navigating the Deserving/Undeserving Divide in the US Social Welfare Regime

At this time in the United States, it is better in some ways to be jobless and broke during a recession than when the economy is stronger. Although it is harder to find another job, there is more public sympathy and greater state support. ("State" in this context means government, whether federal or for each of the fifty states in the United States.) Still, those unemployed during the Great Recession had to deal with shifting regulations that left it unclear which forms of assistance were available to them or could be taken without public opprobrium. They were also caught between the binary cultural categories that oppose the "deserving poor" to the "undeserving poor"—categories that could not easily accommodate the long-term unemployed like my participants, who had been self-sufficient wage earners in the past but who had been unemployed for a year or longer. At first, those who lost their jobs during the Great Recession were considered deserving of state benefits by most members of the public, but during the slack labor market that continued for several years after this recession, those who were still unable to find work contended with comments that cast them as undeserving of continued public assistance.

The United States has never institutionalized universal "social citizenship," meaning the right for all "to live the life of a civilized being according to the standards prevailing in the society," as the sociologist T. H. Marshall famously formulated it.[49] Instead, the structures of public provision for those in need perpetuate a distinction, taken from the English poor laws of the late sixteenth and early seventeenth centuries, between those treated as the deserving poor ("orphans, widows, handicapped, frail elderly," along with the "involuntarily unemployed") and those treated as the undeserving poor (the "drunkards, shiftless, lazy").[50] The deserving poor are imagined as having good morals and a desire to be self-supporting but are prevented from helping themselves by incapacity or circumstances beyond their control. The undeserving poor, by contrast, are imagined as perfectly able to support themselves by their work but choose not to because it is easier and more enjoyable to depend on others. Deservingness is thus tied to productivist values that people's social worth depends on their work effort. The deserving poor are considered worthy of assistance, at least for a short time, but the undeserving poor should be forced to work. In the late twentieth century, this moralistic distinction was updated with an economistic argument that "free money" from the government is "a disincentive to work" because (these theorists assume) any rational person would choose the free money instead of the effort of working.[51]

The widespread unemployment, poverty, and potential social unrest caused by the Great Depression created pressure to pass the Social Security Act of 1935, which established minimal financial assistance for some of the unemployed, as well as the elderly, the blind, and dependent children.[52] Still, the distinction between the deserving and undeserving poor continued in the structure of US social welfare programs. As the historian Michael Katz notes, by the 1950s, "most elderly people, workers disabled in accidents, and the unemployed (not to mention veterans, always a special category) could claim help as a right through social insurance."[53] These government social insurance programs are ones to which workers and employers contributed, along with the federal and state governments, and from which all could claim benefits if they fell into one of those categories, even if they were not needy. These groups—the elderly, disabled, and unemployed—were generally considered deserving.[54]

For those in need who do not fall into any of these categories, there are other government programs, but their benefits are restricted to compel a return to waged work. As one European analyst, Stephan Leibfried, put it in the 1990s, the US social welfare regime shares with England and other Anglophone countries a conception of the welfare state as a mechanism to provide minimal subsistence while compelling waged work in the private sector. In Leibfried's words, these nations consider "the welfare state as a work-enforcing coercive mechanism."[55] He contrasted that coercive approach with three types of welfare-state regimes, including that of the Scandinavian welfare states, which also emphasize work but provide training for workers and jobs in the public sector to make full employment possible. The Scandinavian approach, in Leibfried's categorization, helps the unemployed go back to work instead of stigmatizing them for being unable to support themselves in the private-sector labor market.

We can see work-enforcing welfare state mechanisms in the United States in the two best-known examples of assistance targeted to the poor: small cash stipends to low-income families with children (Temporary Assistance for Needy Families [TANF], popularly termed "welfare") and nutritional assistance (Supplemental Nutrition Assistance Program [SNAP], commonly called "food stamps"). Benefits in those means-tested programs are intentionally low to discourage dependence on them. Despite the myth of the "welfare queen" living a good life on government benefits, in nearly every state, TANF benefits leave a family of three people below *half* the federal poverty level.[56] These benefits also have time limits: since the "welfare reform" laws of the mid-1990s, the normal rule has been that able-bodied adults between eighteen and fifty without dependent children cannot receive food stamps for more than three months during any three-year period.[57] Moreover, recipients cannot qualify unless their income and assets are below the level set by their state, and they are required to engage in work activities. Even with all these restrictions, when those in need accept that assistance, it can create suspicion that they lack a good work ethic. Although majorities of US survey respondents consistently support government "assistance to the poor," majorities also agree that "poor people have become too dependent on government assistance programs."[58]

Poverty in the United States is widely distributed but is usually temporary. One long-term study found that more than half of all Americans of working age will be part of a poor or near-poor household for at least a year at some point in their life.[59] However, in the popular imagination, poverty is assumed to be the intractable condition of a small set of Americans thought to fall outside the mainstream. US racial hierarchies contribute to this othering of the poor. At any given time, a majority of those falling below the federal poverty line are white, but the poor are often imagined as Black and brown.[60] There is a grain of truth in that image: because of discriminatory job barriers, African Americans and Latinos have high poverty rates relative to their population. Nonetheless, they are not the majority of the poor overall, nor have Americans always paid attention to their economic struggles. The political scientist Martin Gilens points out that "black poverty was ignored by white society throughout most of American history."[61] In the nineteenth and early twentieth centuries, US ethnoracial hierarchies placed northern Europeans and Protestants on top, and researchers focused on the supposed problematic work habits and low intelligence of poor Catholic and Jewish immigrants from Ireland, southern Europe, and eastern Europe.

Poverty was not popularly associated with African Americans until the mid-1960s. Gilens found that from 1950 through 1964, most images of people in poverty in three major news magazines were of white people, but from 1967 through the end of his study in 1992, the majority of those images were of Blacks, far out of proportion to their actual representation among the poor.

In the early 1990s about 60 percent of the images of poor people depicted Blacks, which was double the actual percentage of Blacks among the poor.[62] Fed by racist stereotypes and arguments that in some low-income communities of color there was a "culture of poverty" that perpetuated state dependency, this distorted representation reinforced the association of poverty with laziness.[63] These cultural models hide the true extent of white poverty and stigmatize recipients of those government programs designed to help with economic adversity.

As this history indicates, recipients of unemployment benefits are generally considered to fall on the "deserving" side of the invidious "deserving/undeserving" divide. To qualify for unemployment benefits, applicants must establish a work record in the state where they apply for benefits and then lose their job through no fault of their own, typically because their employer downsized the workforce or went out of business. Those conditions fit the cultural model of the deserving poor: someone who wants to be self-supporting but is currently unable to work. Those who left their job voluntarily, were fired, had only occasional part-time work, or are new residents of the state are ineligible. Unemployment compensation for those who qualify is not munificent, but it is more generous than that provided to the imagined undeserving poor through food stamps, TANF, or general assistance for childless adults. To illustrate the difference, in late 2019 and early 2020 before the COVID-19 pandemic began, unemployment benefits averaged $387 *a week* nationally, but the average TANF cash grant was less than half that amount at $447 *a month*.[64] In 2020, only half the states in the United States offered cash assistance to adults in need without dependent children (General Assistance or General Relief). In California, the General Relief benefit was just $221 a month.[65]

Still, even unemployment compensation is time limited. In most states it is available for up to twenty-six weeks during normal economic conditions.[66] Like other US social welfare programs, the goal is to force a return to work as soon as possible.

A deep recession is not a normal economy. As we saw during the COVID-19 pandemic, when unemployment is widespread and seen as due to causes beyond the control of the laid-off workers, there is more public sympathy, and more financial assistance is provided by the state. The larger benefit is not just a humanitarian response. It is also a pragmatic effort to put more money in circulation, lest decreased spending by the unemployed drag the economy into an even deeper recession.[67]

For these reasons, during the Great Recession certain social welfare benefits became more available. Unemployment compensation benefits were extended up to a maximum of ninety-nine weeks for eligible job seekers.[68] Although the amount of those benefits, which varied from state to state, remained skimpy by comparison with those provided by many other wealthy countries,[69] lengthening the period when job seekers could obtain this money was an enormous boon given the difficulty of obtaining a job at that time.

The American Recovery and Reinvestment Act of 2009 also expanded the food stamp program. Benefit levels were increased a little, and states were allowed to waive the three-month time limit for adults without dependent children.[70] In addition, to better help those who had little to no income, many states elected to eliminate limitations on the value of assets held by applicants.[71] These temporary rule changes made many of my participants newly eligible to receive food stamps for the many months they were out of work.

Thus, when we met in 2011 and 2012, most of my participants had received or were still receiving extended unemployment benefits, and some were also newly eligible for food stamps. Did they feel entitled to those benefits? We can discern their perceptions about which state benefits they could accept while maintaining their self-respect and which felt more problematic by examining not only what they said but also what they did not say—the types of support that seemed normal and acceptable enough to pass without comment.

The culture of poverty theory imagines that some groups have been socialized into a habit of work avoidance. Not one individual in my study fit that description. The only class difference I found in job search efforts is that the unemployed in middle- or upper-income households who had a partner or relative who could support them were typically less motivated to find another job right away than those who had fewer household resources. Some of the former said they were "taking a break" and resting before they looked for another job, as I show in chapter 5. By contrast, my low-income participants were very strongly motivated to find a job out of necessity.[72] Nor were there typical racial or ethnic differences among my participants in their willingness to work.[73] I noticed that some of my middle-aged white participants were not looking very hard for another job. One example is Mickey Muller, the engineer I described earlier who was fired in his mid-fifties and gave up his job search, which he could afford to do because his wife earned a good salary and he received financial assistance from his elderly mother. However, I would not say that whites, or members of any other racial or ethnic group, lack a good work ethic. These middle-aged participants were self-supporting for many years when they were younger but said that the difficulties they encountered finding another job, which many attributed to age discrimination, left them discouraged. The only other demographic pattern I noticed is that my first-generation immigrant participants were strikingly *less* willing to accept government benefits targeted to the poor than any other group. I discuss their views later in the chapter.

Instead of having fixed attitudes about government benefits, some of my participants even changed their views during the short period of my research. Many of those who were initially reluctant to take food stamps later accepted them as their need for financial assistance increased.

As I explained, eligibility for food stamps changed, temporarily, during the Great Recession. Previously, only those with a low income and few assets qualified. To apply for food stamps, one not only had to be quite poor but also willing to think of oneself as poor. Furthermore, one had to be willing to face possible scorn for receiving a benefit whose recipients had often been accused of taking advantage of taxpayers' generosity.[74] In the past, food stamps were coupons that, when used, were visible to other shoppers. Today, the benefit is transferred electronically to a state-issued debit card that is more discreet because it resembles other debit cards, although it may still be identifiable by another shopper looking closely or if the recipient's attempted purchases are rejected by the cashier saying something like, "You can't get a rotisserie chicken with food stamps" loudly enough to be heard by others in line.[75] When Congress and the states broadened eligibility for SNAP and made its benefit more generous, one might predict that the long-term unemployed would eagerly apply for help buying food. However, that is not what I found at first, because they interpreted the new rules with their old cognitive schemas.

A few who lacked housing applied for food stamps so they could contribute something to the households of the friends or relatives who were sheltering them, in lieu of the rent they could not afford. Some were willing to apply for food stamps but had been denied in the past because the income and asset limits had been so low; they did not reapply because they were unaware that the rules had changed. However, others were knowledgeable about the new rules but, for a long time, could not reconcile taking food stamps with their self-image.

Ann Lopez, whom I introduced at the beginning of the chapter, is a good example of someone who knew that new rules permitted her to receive food stamps but had trouble bringing herself to apply for them. Earlier in her life Ann had been married, but her husband did not have steady work as a carpenter. With no more education than an associate degree in secretarial work, she learned to download inventory data for a major telecommunications company, and her income helped provide a comfortable, middle-class life for her children. After her divorce, she became a self-taught IT worker for the telecommunications company until it began to outsource the work to third-party firms. When we first met, she had not had any work for a year. I asked Ann whether she had applied for food stamps. She replied that her adult daughter, who was a social services eligibility worker familiar with the new rules, had explained that she received a little too much from her unemployment benefits to qualify. Ann added, "Not that I want to go there." By the time we met two years later for a follow-up interview, Ann had obtained only a couple of short-term positions, and her unemployment benefits from the last job had ended. I asked her again whether she had considered applying for food stamps. Ann replied, "Funny you say that, because—no, but my daughter keeps on telling me to." She joked, "I know it's there, and it's available, but I figure the less food I eat, the better. I might get skinny." Turning more serious, she stated, "I've never had to do that, so I don't know that I want to do it."

On the surface, it makes no sense to say, "I've never had to do that, so I don't know that I want to do it." Why should the fact that she did not need food stamps in the past explain why she resisted taking them when she did need them? However, her answer is understandable if we look at her values and self-image, rather than her material needs. As I quoted earlier, Ann had been proud that "I've always been able to provide for myself." She did not like to think of herself as the sort of person who would ask for food stamps. Perhaps Ann also did not want to think of herself as the sort of person who would *need* food stamps. "I've never had to do that" could be another way of saying, "I have never been a poor person"; "so, I don't know that I want to do it" could mean, "I don't want to change my class identity."[76]

Class identity explicitly mattered to Mona Childs, who had most recently worked in marketing for retirement communities. Out of work for longer than a year and single, she still thought of herself as middle class, which she defined as "I'm not collecting food stamps yet. But, at the same time, I'm not able to afford a country club." This comment is telling: Mona viewed "collecting food stamps" as a paradigmatic symbol of being poor, and it was as distant from her middle-class identity as belonging to a country club, which to her symbolized being rich. This is a different way of understanding what it means to be middle class than the productivist and consumerist meanings we saw in chapters 2 and 3. Instead of defining being middle class in productivist ways as being hardworking or defining it solely by her consumption, Mona defined it at that moment as not being so desperate as to need a social welfare benefit for the very poor.[77]

Emily Quinn, a former executive secretary who had been unemployed for two years when we met, was similar to Ann Lopez in having a relative who was knowledgeable about the new government benefit rules. Emily's cousin reviews applicants' eligibility for food stamps and had urged Emily to apply for them. Her cousin explained that the program was open to more people like her because "'the President said he doesn't want people going hungry.'" On two occasions, Emily gave me a lengthy story about her resistance to doing so. When her cousin first raised the issue, Emily's answer was "I'm not gonna do that. I can't do that." The cousin explained that Emily would qualify for about $200 a month for groceries, but although Emily's unemployment benefits had ended and she had no other household income as a single woman, she still sat on the application.

Some of my participants never changed their mind about applying, but Emily, Mona, and Ann eventually did.[78] Emily explained that for weeks her cousin repeatedly reminded her to apply and promised that no one would know: "She would ask me, 'Have you done it?' And I said, 'I can't press Send. I just can't press Send. I just can't do it. I can't do it. I can't do it.' And finally she talked me into it, and I pressed Send." Emily's long story, emphasizing her reluctance and insisting that her cousin "talked me into it," may have been her way of performing the role of the morally deserving person who does not want to take advantage of government programs.[79] As she also explained when I asked why it was so hard for her to apply, filling out the question about her needs "was another acknowledgment of where I'm at" financially, which was difficult for her to admit to herself. Emily was soon grateful for the food stamps, saying, "It has really helped tremendously." Nonetheless, she worried that other grocery shoppers would recognize the state-issued electronic benefits card. She confided, "I still try to camouflage it in the grocery stores for those smarty-warties who may recognize the colors." She worried that others would think she did not need that benefit because she did not look poor. She imagined another shopper in line thinking, "'She's got food stamps. Look at her. She looks really nice. She's all dressed up.'"

Two years after I first met Mona, she had exhausted the maximum ninety-nine weeks of unemployment benefits. She had not found another full-time job, so she was adjusting to a lower standard of living. I asked if she was receiving any social services, and she explained that she had been telling someone about her situation, and they suggested she might be eligible for Cal-Fresh (California's food stamp program). She was happy to receive that benefit, and she showed no shame about it. In those two years, her self-image may have changed—and so, too, perhaps her perception of food stamp recipients—as that program became more widely available.

Ann also changed her mind. Only two months after she reiterated her reluctance to apply for food stamps in our follow-up interview, she sent me a happy email explaining that her fortunes had improved since we had last talked because she had just received a distribution from the retirement fund she held with her ex-husband. She added casually, "Oh, I forgot to mention that I started collecting food stamps last month also." Surprised, I wrote back to ask whether she had just learned something new about her eligibility. She answered, "I knew I was eligible but didn't feel like applying. My daughter suggested it again, and I applied two months after finishing my unemployment." Her email reveals little about her feelings about this development, but a mutual acquaintance volunteered the news: "She's just thrilled." When one has no regular income, food stamps are a blessing.

By contrast with their qualms about accepting food stamps, my participants took their unemployment benefits for granted.[80] They showed no ambivalence or shame in depending on an unemployment check. Typically, they mentioned it matter-of-factly, with their comments focusing not on whether they should accept unemployment benefits but on whether they were still receiving that benefit, how much they received, and whether it was sufficient for their needs. For example, Ichabod Jones, an unemployed social services program director, worried that his unemployment check would not go far: "Unemployment can only be so much. It's gonna be like 450 [*dollars*] a week. The house payment's gonna be 1,500 [*dollars*] for the month."

Many used the phrasing "my unemployment," wording that suggests a right to that assistance. It was not the only way they spoke of unemployment benefits; it was also common to say things like "I get unemployment." Nonetheless, "my unemployment" is telling. Contrast, for example, the reluctance to collect food stamps demonstrated by Emily, Mona, and Ann with their casual references to "my unemployment" (the underscores represent my highlighting for analysis, not the speaker's emphasis):

EMILY [*answering my question about her income last year*]: I had *my unemployment* until September, and that was $1,800 a month.

MONA: So, *my unemployment*, I'm not really certain when it runs out.

ANN: I was laid off for a year and I had unemployment for a year. I did not finish *my unemployment* [i.e., *did not take the full length of benefits available because she found work*].

I found twenty examples of my participants speaking of "my unemployment" in my interviews, but not one person said "my food stamps." This difference is unsurprising, given the history of US social welfare programs. As I explained, historically the unemployed (or, at least, some of the unemployed) have been treated as having a right to government assistance, in contrast to the desperately poor, who were the only ones eligible for food stamps but have never been considered to have a right to it.[81]

Only one participant expressed an initial reluctance to accept unemployment benefits. Charlie Mike Romero, an unemployed IT specialist at a bank, said, "I worked for almost twenty-five years there at the bank. They gave me a letter so that I could claim unemployment. At first, I didn't want to. I said, 'I don't want [it]. I'm not doing it.' But then I said, 'I still have the right to it.'" Social insurance schemes like unemployment insurance are treated both by the state and recipients as "a right." Charlie Mike is an immigrant, and his initial reluctance will make more sense when I discuss my other immigrant participants.

Yet not all native-born Americans treat unemployment benefits as a right under every circumstance. Long-term unemployment benefits fall into a gray area in public discourses about the deserving versus the undeserving poor. The normal length of unemployment benefits in the United States is twenty-six weeks. Policies extending unemployment benefits for a longer period often generate criticism, especially from political conservatives who suspect that recipients of taxpayer-funded assistance would prefer to depend on that assistance rather than work for a living. (In chapter 7, I discuss controversies about extended unemployment benefits during the COVID-19 pandemic.) Yet, as I have explained, during a deep recession, most policy makers and members of the public understand that there are many more people out of work than there are job vacancies, so that it is much more difficult than usual to find work. Under those circumstances, there are conflicting views about whether the long-term unemployed are "deserving" victims of a bad economy or "undeserving" loafers.

Although there was some public criticism of recipients of extended unemployment benefits in the aftermath of the Great Recession, my participants resisted characterizations of them and their fellow job seekers as not trying hard enough. Some scholars "associate the conservative turn in American politics with a burgeoning individualism that offers little sense of fellow-feeling or shared fate," but that is not what I found among my participants.[82] Their discourses suggest some ways that Americans can reconcile their own and others' acceptance of state social welfare benefits with their values of productivism and self-sufficiency.

I noticed that, even after my participants found another job, they remained concerned about others who remained out of work. We might have imagined that those who obtained jobs would start denigrating others who were still unemployed, but that is not what I heard. Federal extensions of unemployment benefits expired in 2013, and Congress debated whether to continue them, ultimately deciding not to do so. That debate was in the news when I conducted my follow-up interviews. Even though most of my interviewees were ineligible for any further extensions—either because they had jobs by then or had been out of work too long—they were indignant at the insulting way the unemployed were described, as if "they're collecting it and they're going to the beaches every day," as one of my participants put it. For example, by the time I reinterviewed Amber Washington in 2014, she had found a job in a social services agency. She raised the issue of the end of federal unemployment extensions before I did:

> AMBER: Now I am upset that they were not able to continue unemployment benefits for people.
> CLAUDIA: I was gonna ask about that.
> AMBER: I was, like, "What's up with that?" Thank God I wasn't getting them. But for those millions of people who—I mean, what are they doing now? I really felt for them. How are they making it? What are they doing without their benefits now?

This is a humanitarian argument, a well-recognized basis for social welfare programs in the United States.[83] However, it is not the only way my participants justified extended unemployment benefits for themselves and the other long-term unemployed.

Others accepted the distinction between the deserving and the undeserving poor but positioned themselves, and others out of work like them, on the deserving side of that divide because they were making every effort to find another job. It was not their fault that no jobs were available. If having a good work ethic makes one deserving, they reasoned that they are deserving if they want to work but are thwarted by the unwillingness of employers to hire them.[84] Although conservative commentators were the ones publicly questioning extended benefits, I heard this counter-discourse from my participants across the political spectrum. Jim Wade, a political conservative, was angry at the criticisms he had heard, such as from others in his church: "One point I want to make: people like us that are on unemployment and food stamps don't wanna be on unemployment. We don't wanna be on food stamps. We don't want government handouts. We wanna work. There's a common misconception of people who've never been through this. It's, 'Well, people who are unemployed, it's their fault because they want government handouts.' *I do not; we do not.* I wanna work." Emily Quinn, who is a political liberal, made the same point: "I know a lot of people hate people like us. [. . .] They just looked at it [*extended unemployment benefits*] as another welfare program. It wasn't. That saved my ass, and a lot of other people that I know. And all during that time, we were looking, looking, looking, sending out résumés, interviewing. Just having the door shut in our face." Jim and Emily not only positioned themselves as deserving; they also imagined a collective "we"— "We don't wanna be on food stamps. We don't want government handouts. We wanna work." "We were looking, looking, looking"—made up of their fellow long-term unemployed who were all deserving because all were trying so hard to find another job.

Many of my participants, Jim and Emily included, had gotten to know their unemployed peers in career counseling sessions and accountability/support group meetings. The smaller accountability/support groups especially offered opportunities to share personal stories over the course of multiple meetings and may have been particularly conducive to developing a collective identity. Many of the unemployed never attended such meetings, yet some of my participants who did not participate in such groups, like Carl Mathews, still developed a sense of collective identity with others in economic distress during the Great Recession. Carl traced his sense of being in the same boat as many others to a group session about mortgage modification, where he met other homeowners who could no longer pay their mortgages. That sense of shared fate was reinforced by the rhetoric of the Occupy protests, which was in the news at the time I began my fieldwork in the fall of 2011. The Occupy movement's slogan, "We are the 99%," resonated with Carl and with some of my other participants.[85]

A final way in which some described themselves as deserving is that they had been taxpayers in the past. Tom Dunn was disgusted with the politicians who questioned the motives of those receiving unemployment: "I put in thirty years before I was out of labor paying my FICA, paying my income tax, all of these things, state disability, unemployment, all of these things I've been paying my whole life. I didn't feel guilty at all getting an unemployment check."[86] He also pointed out that the amount he received in unemployment benefits was much lower than his former salary as an IT recruiter: "These yahoos in Congress that have the temerity to say that people are literally staying unemployed so they can collect $1,850 a month; they're out of their minds."[87] Tom had earned more than $6,000 a month in his last job. Several others made the point that "living on unemployment is not any picnic for anybody," as another participant put it. On average, unemployment benefits in the United States pay only 40 to 50 percent of a worker's former wages.[88]

Tom's argument that unemployment benefits are not large enough to feel guilty about applies all the more to TANF and General Relief, the cash assistance programs targeted to the very poor. To my surprise, the handful of participants who were receiving those benefits did not describe any soul-searching about it. I was surprised because recipients of those programs, popularly termed "welfare," have been the target of criticism from politicians and many members of the public. Before those programs were severely curtailed in 1996, welfare recipients were commonly accused of just "sitting around" and living off their monthly check instead of trying to work.[89] Yet, those of my participants who applied for and obtained this assistance did not express in their interviews the reluctance to do so that I heard from those receiving food stamps.[90]

One possible explanation is that recipients were less subject to public shaming for receiving the benefits than they were for food stamps, even though both forms of assistance are typically accessed through an EBT debit card. Nonetheless, food is normally purchased in public where other shoppers can see the EBT card, whereas many other expenses such as rent and utilities can be paid in private.[91]

Another explanation could be that the benefits were so difficult to obtain that the very few who qualified were desperate enough to be beyond worrying about what others would think of them. When Ginger Thi lost her job as a secretary, she became homeless. Nonetheless, the first time she applied for General Relief, she was rejected because she had $100 in her bank account. She was told that to qualify, she could not have more than $50 to her name. Every participant in my study who received TANF or General Relief was either homeless or on the verge of becoming homeless.

A final likely explanation is these benefits were so meager that they were scarcely worth feeling ashamed about. When ReNé McKnight and her daughter moved to California, she had a job lined up, but the client for whom ReNé was supposed to provide home care passed away. ReNé did not qualify for unemployment benefits because she had voluntarily left her previous job in Texas and did not have a work record in California. With no other options, she applied for TANF, which provided only $490 a month for her and her daughter. It was not even enough to cover her $500 monthly rent for the only housing she could find: a guest house that was nearly uninhabitable because it lacked a working stove, heat, and hot water. Theresa Allen, who had no dependents, qualified for just $221 a month in General Relief. It was so little that she could not pay her rent, which is why she had to move in with her mother.

My immigrant participants faced even more challenging regulations than those born in this country, accompanied by different threats to their self-identity. All but two of the sixteen first-generation immigrant participants in this study were either naturalized citizens or lawful permanent residents who had lived in the United States for at least twenty years, but that did not make them secure in their subjective citizenship—their sense of belonging to the nation.[92]

Like my native-born participants, the first-generation immigrants had no problem accepting unemployment compensation. Charlie Mike Romero, whom I quoted earlier, was the only one who mentioned any doubt or hesitation about accepting that benefit. An immigrant from El Salvador, he had been living in the United States for more than twenty-five years and had worked as an IT systems administrator for a bank. As we saw, even Charlie Mike eventually decided, "I still have the right to it." On the surface, it seems that immigrant Americans and native-born are no different in considering unemployment compensation as a right.

Strikingly, however, no first-generation immigrant in this study used an expression that translated as "my unemployment." Instead, they would say things like "I'm getting unemployment," or "I am receiving unemployment pay." Perhaps the wording "my unemployment" was not conventional in their first language. However, another possibility is that they did not feel as secure an entitlement to that benefit as the native-born do.

Saying or not saying "my unemployment" is a subtle, debatable indicator of subjective citizenship. What was not subtle at all was the vehemence with which most of my immigrant participants spurned any social welfare benefits targeted to the poor, including food stamps. With only a few exceptions, inquiries about whether they had applied for food stamps, subsidized housing, or cash welfare were met with strong denials. For example, La dama de abril, who grew up in Colombia and lived in Venezuela before coming to the United States to join her sister Lucy Guerrero, emphasized her desire to "be useful for the country": "I would never want to ask for welfare. I wouldn't like to live off the government. And it's what I avoid. I want to be useful for the country, this one or whatever country, be a useful woman." When Claudia C. asked her what she meant by "a useful woman," La dama de abril replied, "You can support yourself, without having to have someone supporting you. You yourself can have all your necessities. You are self-sufficient, to be self-sufficient. I avoid . . . I didn't come to this country to take. I didn't come into this country to be on welfare. I don't think like that. I came to be part of this country. To be useful in this country."

La dama de abril had not been able to obtain lawful permanent residency at that point, so she was ineligible for any government benefits. Undocumented immigrants do not qualify for government social welfare programs such as cash welfare, food stamps, and Medicaid (with some exceptions), and even lawful permanent residents normally need to live in the United States for five years before they can apply.[93] Still, La dama de abril found the notion of accepting those social welfare benefits abhorrent, even had she been eligible for them. Doing so was at odds with her identity as someone who had elected to come to the United States "to be useful," not "to take."

La dama's attitudes about food stamps and welfare were echoed by several immigrants who were either citizens or long-time lawful permanent residents and so were eligible for government assistance. La dama's sister Lucy, who had married an American man many years earlier, was eligible for food stamps and other assistance but turned to her church for help rather than the government. Isabel Navarro had worked for a beauty salon and then started her own cosmetology business. When Claudia C. asked Isabel whether she had "received some kind of help as Section 8 [*housing voucher*] or food stamps," Isabel replied, "No, I have never wanted to ask for it," repeating that for emphasis. Feliciano Salas had lived in the United States for twenty-five years working as a roofer, and he had become a citizen. During the Great Recession, construction jobs were scarce, but he preferred to rely on the kindness of local restaurant managers to give him a meal rather than apply for food stamps. If my native-born participants were hesitant to accept benefits targeted to the poor, most of my immigrant participants went beyond hesitancy to flat refusal.[94]

In addition to the symbolic threat posed by accepting the benefits associated with the undeserving poor, especially poor people of color, immigrants had to contend with the "public charge" laws. US immigration policy does not permit immigrants to become lawful permanent residents or citizens if they have been or are likely to become a "public charge," defined as "primarily dependent on the government for subsistence, as demonstrated by either (i) the receipt of public cash assistance for income maintenance or (ii) institutionalization for long-term care at government expense."[95] In fact, food stamps were not included in the public charge determinations at that time, but that exclusion was not widely known, making immigrants fearful of accepting them.[96] That is the explanation Jackie Gallardo gave for her reluctance to apply for food stamps during the many harrowing months when she had to choose between feeding her hungry children or putting gas in her car. She explained, "I was afraid to apply for food stamps or things like that because they say it affects your papers [*chance of obtaining citizenship*]." Jackie had become a citizen just two weeks before our interview, and she was recounting her decisions in the preceding months when she was so close to gaining citizenship and afraid of doing anything that might jeopardize it.

In sum (ironically), immigrants were more likely than the native-born to display what has been described as the typically US trait of self-sufficiency when it came to accepting government social welfare benefits for the poor. However, they were not complete rugged individualists: immigrants from Asia and Latin America were also much more likely than those who were born in the United States to give financial assistance to their parents, and they were also somewhat more likely to receive such assistance from their grown children.

Dependence or Interdependence?

At the end of Fraser and Gordon's article, "A Genealogy of Dependency," they quote the welfare rights activist Pat Gowens, "When dependence is not a dirty word, and interdependence is the norm—only then will we make a dent in poverty."[97] Is that a realistic political goal?

Based on my research, I doubt that "dependence" will soon lose its negative connotations in the United States. Most of my unemployed participants disliked having no choice but to rely on family, faith communities, or state benefits like food stamps and unemployment compensation. Earning their own income was their preference. If they had had sufficient income of their own, Theresa Allen and her husband would have been able to keep the pets that were like children to them, instead of giving them away or euthanizing them, which was a condition of living with her mother. Accepting financial help from friends without being able to reciprocate became unbearable for Della Jones; it got to the point that she felt she could no longer socialize with them and maintain her self-respect. Depending on help from his church and the state made Jim Wade feel he was being judged as not wanting to work, which was far from the truth.

However, only certain forms of assistance are considered problematic forms of "dependence" in the contemporary United States, and those forms are constantly changing. Katarina Spelling was proud to have been self-supporting since graduating from college, but having her parents pay for her college education did not seem like a problematic form of dependence to her. Others of my participants in their twenties lived with one or both of their parents without considering themselves to be improperly dependent. None of my participants felt it was shameful to accept state assistance to cover the costs of their health care. I expect that soon in the United States public provision of health insurance will be as routine as public provision of education through high school. No one is judged as improperly dependent on the state if they attend public primary or secondary schools, and it is becoming the same for government-provided health insurance.

Fraser and Gordon's more subversive move, in ending with this quote from Gowens, is to introduce "interdependence" as an alternative to the constraining dichotomy of shameful "dependence" versus proud "independence." Time and again, I noticed that the most satisfying situations for my participants were ones of mutual aid, with the unemployed giving their time and services in exchange for help with their living expenses.[98] ReNé McKnight and Marcus Walker happily described the help they received from their respective churches, to which each devoted many volunteer hours. Fred Hernandez, Daniel Horn, Stacie McCarthy, Hillary Edwards, and Mona Childs felt their aging parent or parents needed their physical assistance as much as they needed their parents' financial assistance.

Even relations with the state can be framed as reciprocal. In the early 1920s Marcel Mauss wrote that state socialism in France is "inspired by the principle that the worker gives his life and labour partly to the community and partly to his bosses [and] . . . those who benefit from his services are not square with him simply by paying him a wage. The State, representing the community, owes him and his management and fellow-workers a certain security in his life against unemployment, sickness, old age and death."[99] In other words, workers give their labor to their employers and the community, and in exchange, the state owes them financial protection when they cannot work. As my participant Tom Dunn pointed out, he had paid taxes for decades; in return, he should be able to receive government assistance when he needed it. The anthropologist Kelly McKowen observed the flip side of this reciprocity between the individual and the state in Norway. In exchange for generous state benefits, unemployed Norwegians feel a moral obligation to return to work so they can pay the taxes that support their fellow citizens.[100] It is a wonderful example of Fraser and Gordon's understanding of social citizenship, which is grounded in interdependence, not in a divide between some who are independent and others who are dependent.[101]

In this chapter I have not delved into the possible effects of gender roles on how people get by without an income. Are there the same social expectations of financial self-sufficiency for adult women as there are for adult men in the United States? How does unemployment affect men's and women's gender identities and relationships with their life partners and children? Those are the topics to which I turn in the next chapter.

CHAPTER 5

Gendered Meanings of Unemployment

The COVID-19 pandemic reignited long-standing debates about women in the paid workforce. Until recently, women were the unspoken exception to the supposed pan-human, transhistorical meanings of work. Assertions about waged work as necessary for "self-worth, community, engagement, healthy values, structure, and dignity" were really claims about work meanings during one historical period (following the Industrial Revolution) and for only half the adult population (men).[1] Women were expected to marry and find self-worth, engagement, healthy values, time structure, and dignity in caring for their partner and children.

Gradually (and unevenly) that changed. Women have long earned money in the informal workforce, but in many parts of the industrialized world today, majorities of adult women have jobs in the formal workforce.[2] In the United States the formal workforce is now almost evenly divided between women and men, and among heterosexual married couples, only 19 percent rely on the man as the sole breadwinner.[3] In 2018 the median earnings of US women working full time was 81 percent of men's median earnings. That is not parity, but it is quite a bit more than in 1979, when women's median earnings were only 62 percent of men's median earnings.[4]

Those who see such statistics as hopeful signs of progress toward equal opportunities for women were dismayed at what happened during the COVID-19 shutdowns. In the United States, women's paid work suffered more than men's did during the pandemic, for two reasons. First, women, especially women of color, are disproportionately concentrated in low-wage service jobs in retail, restaurants, and similar positions, the sorts of workplaces that were closed during the pandemic lockdowns.[5] However, that was not the only problem. Even if their job continued, many women had to leave work or reduce their hours if they had young children. Daycare centers and schools were closed, online schooling required supervision, and mothers were less likely than fathers to have a spouse or other family member able or willing to provide backup care. During the pandemic, "one-third of working mothers in two-parent households reported they were the only ones providing care for their children, compared to one-tenth of working fathers." By the summer of 2020, mothers of young children had lost more than four times as many work hours as fathers during the preceding pandemic months.[6] These sudden, conflicting demands on their time produced higher levels of distress among working mothers of young children than among women without young children or than among men, whether they had children or not.[7] Dream researchers reported that during the pandemic women's dreams (more so than men's) showed a sharp increase in expressions of "anxiety, sadness and anger."[8] Record numbers of women considered "downshifting": either working fewer hours or taking a temporary leave from their jobs.[9]

Commentary on these developments fell into two camps, depending on whether those commenting thought that mothers of young children should or should not be working full time.

Those who thought that mothers should work full time if they need or want to do so said that men should share more of the childcare responsibilities at home, the government should help make high-quality daycare more affordable, and employers should reduce the "motherhood penalty." The "motherhood penalty" refers to lower pay raises for mothers than for women who do not have children—a differential not found between male workers with and without children.[10] As a columnist for *The Washington Post* put it, "Women [*have been*] pushed out of the workforce by our family-unfriendly workplaces, lack of care-taking infrastructure and the continuing societal expectation that women—and not men—are the primary parent responsible for the well-being of children."[11]

However, other commentators looked at the same facts about working mothers' distress during the pandemic and drew a different conclusion: mothers of young children should not be trying to combine full-time work with childcare. For example, in a May 2021 article in *The Atlantic* magazine, journalist Olga Khazan reports that in recent weeks she had spoken with "half a dozen professional women who have left their full-time jobs, are now working less than full time, and are happier as a result." She does not clarify whether all are happier than they were before the pandemic when they had childcare or are happier than when they were frantically trying to work full time in challenging professional careers while also caring for young children whose daycare center or school was closed due to the pandemic.

In chapter 2 we saw examples of both men and women who formerly worked long hours deciding later that they wanted a better balance of time between their paid work and the rest of life. I agree with Khazan that not all Americans live to work.[12] However, in not discussing men's choices about work-life balance, Khazan contributes to long-standing discourses that it is natural for women, but not men, to care about their families more than about their jobs.[13]

These contemporary debates show that an unusual situation, like a public health emergency that disrupts childcare across the country, can force discussion about assumptions that are normally unsaid. My research took place during another unusual and stressful situation—a deep recession that left millions of workers unemployed for many months or years. The varying ways my unemployed participants responded to those stresses reveal their expectations about the gendered division of household responsibilities.

Until nearly the second decade of the twenty-first century, there were few qualitative studies comparing women's and men's subjective experiences of being unemployed.[14] For that reason, I recruited many women for this study. Thirty-six of my participants were women, and twenty-eight were men; about half (34) were married, engaged, or living together and half (30) were single. However, I was not the only researcher who had noticed the paucity of research on gender and unemployment. Since that time several qualitative studies have examined gender differences in unemployment experiences in the United States; most of them focused on heterosexual adults with a partner. There is an interesting divide in those studies: some found that unemployed women were more distressed by their lack of work than were unemployed men, and others observed the opposite.

An example of a study yielding the first finding is Carrie Lane's research on unemployed IT workers in the early 2000s. Several of the married male IT workers were comfortable, at least for a while, with being partly or wholly supported by their wives, who were also well-paid professionals. Lane argues that among his educated peers a male IT worker gains symbolic capital by being the kind of forward-thinking man who rejects traditional gender roles. Two of the unemployed women high-tech professionals with whom Lane spoke felt the opposite: they were distraught because they could not contribute their share to the household income, thereby placing more of a burden on their partner. Similarly, Sarah Damaske found that unemployed women in couples seemed to feel guiltier about the loss of household income due to their job loss than unemployed men did. The women generally started a job search right away and were much more likely to forego health care and take on an increased share of household work than were the unemployed men.[15]

By contrast, other recent sociological studies noticed a greater emotional toll on unemployed men. For example, Aliya Hamid Rao observed that in white middle-class families, wives put more pressure on their unemployed husbands to be ideal job seekers than husbands put on their wives. Similarly, in a thorough mixed-methods study, Gokce Basbug and Ofer Sharone found that more men than women experienced marital tensions related to their unemployment, although, as Lane's research suggests, they also noted that education made a difference.[16] According to Rao, Basbug, and Sharone, their findings show the continuing "hegemony of the male-breadwinner ideology"; that is, the expectation that men should be the primary providers for their family.[17]

My observations are closer to the second set of findings than the first, but with some critical modifications. As other researchers found, my unemployed male participants reported more tension in their relationship due to their unemployment than did my unemployed female participants. I also learned from their life stories that women left the workforce voluntarily more often than did men. These are indicators that men still have the more stringent duty to provide income for the household. That continuing expectation also explains Lane's finding: the very fact that her male interviewees saw themselves as more forward thinking than other men shows that the cultural model of the male primary breadwinner still has strong cultural standing.

Yet, my participants' breadwinning expectations also reflected the impact of current economic pressures and changing gender norms. My participants in dual-earning couples acknowledged the necessity for both incomes, and the unemployed women reported that their partners constantly pushed them to find another job.[18] Surprisingly, unemployed men who had been the sole breadwinner in a couple experienced much *less* marital tension than those whose partners worked. That may occur because dual-earning couples are the current norm, so when the man is the sole income earner, he earns a "surplus credit" of gratitude that helps sustain his relationship when he is out of work. I also found that, in general, women who had been the sole or primary breadwinners in their household reported that their partner was more supportive when they were out of work than did women whose earnings had made up a smaller share of the household income; the surplus credit explanation may apply to them as well.

Together, these findings suggest that dominant breadwinning models are shifting. In the traditional male breadwinning model, there was no expectation that wives work. In the neotraditional male breadwinning model, wives may work, but the husband's income is expected to be primary.[19] What I found to be common now could be termed a neotraditional dual-earner breadwinning model. It is a dual-earner model not only because both partners are earning income to meet household expenses but also because this is now widely accepted as typical. However, it is neotraditional in that men still have the greater obligation to be household providers than do women in heterosexual couples.

Interestingly, whether they were in a dual-earning couple or not, some unemployed men spoke of a positive transformation in their self-understanding when they took on more housework and childcare responsibilities. Some of the women in my study appreciated having more time for their children while they were out of work, but they were much less likely to say that unemployment led them to a radical new understanding of their role in the family.

Among singles, unemployed men and women alike experienced serious financial pressures. The stresses for single mothers were almost unbearable.[20] Single men and women were also alike in feeling lower self-esteem and being emotionally vulnerable while out of work, which made them reluctant to date. However, the continuing weight of male breadwinning expectations affected heterosexual single men and single women differently. Even men and women who rejected traditional gender roles still had to deal with them as they contemplated future relationships because they expected others to hold those beliefs. A few of the unemployed men said that being out of work made them feel like "less of a man," but none of the unemployed women made a comparable comment, although both women and men spoke of feeling diminished as a person. Although same-sex couples may uphold more egalitarian norms for the division of labor in their households, among my participants, sexual orientation did not affect the differing relation of gender identities to paid work.

Throughout this chapter, I speak of "women" and "men," but I do not assume that gender identities are binary or fixed. The participants in my research were cisgendered (that is, their gender identity was the same as their sex assigned at birth) when we spoke; the gender labels I use for them are the ones they used for themselves.

The History of Being the "Breadwinner" in Heterosexual American Couples

For millennia, everyone—adult men, adult women, and children—labored to sustain their families and communities. Mothers with young children tied them to their backs while they gathered water and wood or cultivated crops. If they could not bring their children with them, they left them in the care of family members. Certain tasks or specialties might be gender-typed, but women, including mothers of young children, were working, except in wealthy households.

In US farm families before the Industrial Revolution, women's labor was essential to household subsistence. Some scholars argue that the idea that an adult man should be the family breadwinner did not emerge in the United States until about the 1830s.[21] It was not until industrialization became widespread that a separation of spheres developed, with married men (along with unmarried youth, both male and female) going out to "work" for wages at factories and married women's labor around the house no longer counting as "work"—although, typically, only nonimmigrant white men were paid well enough to maintain this division of labor.[22] Even so, many women continued to earn money less visibly in the informal economy by, for example, taking in laundry or sewing, renting rooms to boarders, selling vegetables, or doing piecework at home for local industries.[23]

Between 1890 and 1930 the growth of white-collar jobs in the United States sparked an 85 percent increase in women's formal labor force participation.[24] Still, among married couples, men were expected to be the family providers. During the Great Depression, when unemployment rates rose to 25 percent by some measures,[25] the sociologist Mirra Komarovsky studied the effects of men's unemployment on their relationships with their wives and children. Her research drew on interviews with white, nonimmigrant families in which the man had been the sole formal wage earner before he lost his job. Most had worked in skilled blue-collar jobs. Even though all the men in her study had been out of work for at least a year, some resisted their wife taking a paying job. Those husbands made statements like "I would rather starve than let my wife work," or "I would rather turn on the gas and put an end to the whole family than let my wife support me."[26]

Why was it so important to these men that they be the sole breadwinner? Komarovsky assumes that controlling money gave a man authority over his wife and children. When he could no longer provide for them, they had no reason to defer to him. As Komarovsky puts it, some of the wives felt freer to express their grievances "now that the man holds no economic whip over her." One of the husbands said, "Love flies out of the window when money goes." However, beyond this power struggle, Komarovsky believes that men's gender identities rest on providing for their family. She concludes that the unemployed family man "experiences a sense of deep frustration because in his own estimation he fails to fulfill what is the central duty of his life, the very touchstone of his manhood—the role of family provider."[27]

I question whether Komarovsky's sweeping conclusions are supported by her evidence. She acknowledges that her team recorded examples of the husband losing status in only thirteen of the fifty-nine families studied.[28] Still, it is interesting that several of the unemployed Depression-era men made exaggerated statements of suicidal or murderous intent like "I would rather turn on the gas and put an end to the whole family than let my wife support me.'" That kind of hyperbolic wording, I have observed, marks statements that the speaker thinks are the common opinion in their opinion community.[29] It seems that these Depression-era men not only accepted their duty to be the sole family provider (not counting any informal income generated by their wives) but they also spoke as if they expected social support for feeling so strongly about this role. Yet, the very fact that they felt they had to resist their wife working outside the home indicates they were aware it was a real possibility.[30]

Komarovsky conducted her research in 1935 and 1936. By 1940 one-quarter of working-age women were in the labor force.[31] By the mid-1960s, dual-earner couples were more common in the United States than ones in which the husband was the only one earning an income.[32] But just because both partners are working does not mean that each partner's earnings are considered equally important. The sociologist Jean Potuchek draws an important distinction between *working* (having paid employment) and being the family *breadwinner*.

Relative earnings can affect who is considered the family breadwinner. In 1970 working wives contributed approximately 27 percent of their family's income. At the time I conducted my research in 2011, wives' earnings averaged 37 percent of the family's income, which was still less than half.[33] However, Potuchek argues that the size of a paycheck is not what matters the most. Instead, she emphasizes two key criteria: (1) earning money to provide for the family rather than for personal spending, and (2) "the day-to-day obligation to earn money . . . a duty to work" so that "leaving the labor force (even temporarily) is not an option."[34] Hers is an important analysis because it goes beyond the amount of men's and women's earnings to consider their meanings.

In study after study of US dual-income households in the 1970s and 1980s, Potuchek notices the same pattern: in most families, both the husband and the wife depicted the husband as the primary breadwinner, regardless of the relative size of their earnings. For example, in the late 1980s and early 1990s, Nicholas Townsend interviewed married men whose wives' income was needed to help pay the bills. Nonetheless, he found that the men often downgraded their wives' monetary contribution, saying that their wives worked for "extras" or "to add variety to their lives, for social contacts, or 'to get away from the kids.'"[35] In other words, as the men described it, their wive's work did not fit either of Potuchek's two criteria for being a breadwinner because the wives were working for their own spending money and they did not have an obligation to work.

However, it was not just men who saw it that way. Potuchek cites studies of working women in dual-earner households who also did not consider themselves the family breadwinner. For example, in Ellen Rosen's study of New England factory women, whose wages contributed 45 percent of their family's income on average, women often offered "a strong assertion that it was her husband who really supported the family." Many of the women said their husband was the breadwinner because his earnings covered the mortgage and monthly utility bills. In contrast, the women were only "helping" or working for "extras"—even though those "extras" turned out to be "gas, groceries, things for the children, or savings."[36] Rosen's findings show that for women to be considered breadwinners, it is not enough for their earnings to help support the household; they also have to be directed to the most highly valued family expenditures, which is often housing.

Potuchek also found that her second component of breadwinning—"the day-to-day obligation to earn money . . . a duty to work"—was commonly assumed to apply to men more than to women in the early 1980s. She cites a survey her students conducted of their peers at that time. In response to the question, "Assuming your spouse has a sufficient income, would you expect to work?" there was almost no difference between men and women. Nearly all the students expected to work in the future. However, in response to the question, "Assuming that you earn a sufficient income, would you expect your spouse to work?" there was a stark gender divide. Two-thirds of the male students said they would leave that choice to their spouse, but more than 80 percent of the female students said they would still expect their spouse to work.[37] At that time, same-sex marriage was not legal so the survey assumed heterosexual couples. In other words, the female students imagined a future in which their husband would work, but the male students were less likely to care whether their future wife was employed.

This breadwinning role for men had additional expectations. The men whom Townsend interviewed "measured their success, in terms of a *package deal*" that required being married, having children, holding a steady job, and owning a home.[38] Men had to achieve all four goals to live up to the hegemonic model of masculinity. Drawing on his own research and that of others, Townsend states, "Men who do not have jobs are frequently branded as unworthy, morally inferior, and failures as men," a conclusion much like Komarovsky's Depression-era study.[39] The difference between those eras is that Townsend's interviewees were neotraditional primary breadwinners, not traditional sole breadwinners. They were not saying, "I would rather starve than let my wife work." Still, they were defensively "doing cultural work" to interpret the division of labor in the household as conforming to the model of the male primary breadwinner.[40]

Potuchek's literature review and Townsend's study give us a glimpse into the gendering of breadwinning in the 1970s through the early 1990s. Does that differ in the first few decades of the twenty-first century?

Beginning in the early 1990s, the United States has shifted to a post-Fordist economy. Automation, global competition, and attacks on unions have sharply reduced the number of factory jobs with good wages and benefits. In 2012, when I was finishing my first round of interviews, the real (inflation-adjusted) median household income in the United States was lower than it was seventeen years earlier.[41] Given stagnating wages for most workers along with increasing consumption norms (see chapter 3), it is no longer possible for most men to earn enough to be the sole support for their family.[42] Increasingly, a college degree is necessary for a good job, and women now outnumber men both as college graduates and as holders of postgraduate degrees.[43] Even though, on average, men's wages are still higher than women's at every educational level, wage trends have moved in different directions.[44] From 1979 to 2010 the inflation-adjusted wages of men without a college education fell, but the average wages of women, even those with only a high school education, rose.[45] Many men no longer anticipate being able to support a family with their income alone, and many young women are capable of supporting themselves alone or of contributing at least half of a household's income.

To examine the impact of these social changes, I consider, in turn, dual-earner heterosexual couples, heterosexual couples in which the man was the sole provider, heterosexual couples in which the woman was the sole or primary provider, same-sex couples, and singles.[46] Finally, I discuss whether my unemployed participants felt they were living up to gender norms. Throughout, I indicate the distribution of the trends I describe among my interviewees. My participants are not a random sample of the unemployed, and I would never claim that the same percentages would be found in a larger, representative sample. Nonetheless, some of the patterns are intriguing.

Dual-Earner Couples

When I interviewed Fred Hernandez, he was in his early fifties, and he had had a hard life, including time in prison and a period of homelessness. One thing he was proud of, however, was having earned enough as a truck driver when he was in his mid-twenties to afford a large home with a pool. However, Fred did not take sole credit for earning the money needed to buy his home. Instead, he fully acknowledged, "I could have never done it without the help of my ex-wife," who worked at a post office. He added, "She couldn't have done it without my help either." Fred's recognition of the need for both incomes was typical among my participants.

Men who recognized the importance of a second income for meeting household expenses put pressure on their unemployed female partner to return to work, just as women expected their unemployed male partner to find another job. My participants' living expenses, including some that could not be easily reduced such as their mortgage payments, had been undertaken with the expectation of two incomes. Their household budgets were fragile structures that would topple under pressure. Each member of the couple did not have to contribute equally—that was rare—but both incomes were needed. Whether it was the woman or the man who was unemployed in a couple, the still-employed partner seemed to be thinking, "I'm doing my part. You need to do yours."

For example, Mary Brown had worked in an outreach program for disadvantaged youth until its funding was cut. On two occasions, Mary mentioned that she liked having more time with her twelve-year-old son while she was out of work. However, both times she quickly added that she could not just relax and enjoy that time, because she had to find another job as soon as possible. The pressure on her to find another job was clear when I asked how her husband was reacting to her being out of work. Mary replied,

> Umm . . . He's a little stressed, you know, because like I said, we just bought a house, and most of the burden is on him. [. . .] He's kind of a little stressed like, "Okay, have you found anything? What are you doing?" (*laughs*) You know. Because he's kind of like feeling—you know he just tells me what's going on in his job. There's changes. There's always changes at his job. So, he's just, like, having—just making me cognizant of that so that I can kind of put a little fire under my buns.

Mary's husband was a computer programmer working on grant-funded research projects at a university. Future grant funding was not assured, and he was nervous about their ability to continue paying all the bills without Mary's income.

Pressure on the unemployed wife in a dual-earner couple was also clear when I interviewed Maria Carrera, a quality assurance supervisor for a consumer goods company. When her company began downsizing and let her go, she took a class on how to search for another job. She was happily occupied with learning how to write her resume and give the best response to typical job interview questions when her husband, an operations manager who continued to work for the same company, became impatient: it seemed to him that Maria was spending more time on learning how to search for a job than on finding another position. Maria reported, "He goes, 'You have to find a job. You know that?'" He showed her the bills and how little money was left at the end of the month without her income. Maria was in her mid-fifties, and she had considered retiring. She did not mind working in quality assurance, but her job satisfaction lessened after she got a promotion that gave her new responsibilities, and she would have preferred to do something of service to the community. However, Maria's husband brushed aside any talk of her retiring. Although Maria described her husband as "very supportive," he did not see how she could stop working because they still needed her income, and she agreed. Rejuvenated after a year out of work, Maria found another job in quality assurance.

I noticed the same expectations among some younger dual-earner couples. When I first met Katarina Spelling, she was in her late twenties, and she had not held a full-time job in nearly a year after being laid off from her last position as a branch manager of a social services agency. She had a bachelor's degree in communications, but her real passion was singing. However, she could not make a living as a singer. One month after being laid off, she married a man who had nearly $100,000 in student debt. Katarina added to their student debt when she took out more loans to pay for her master's program. He had a job as a web programmer, but his income alone was not enough to pay their rent, student loan repayments, and other expenses. He convinced Katarina that she could be a singer during her off-hours while she worked at an unexciting but dependable job to help pay the bills, like the one she took as an assistant in an accounting office.

This expectation that both will work is, of course, completely unlike what Komarovsky described during the Depression. None of the unemployed men I interviewed said anything like, "I would rather starve than let my wife work." Nor did any of the women report that their male partner resisted their working. More subtly, however, these findings also differ from those of researchers like Potuchek, Townsend, and Rosen who explored meanings of breadwinning from the late 1970s through the early 1990s: they found that both men and women portrayed the man's income as essential for the family and the woman's as inessential. By contrast, only a few of my participants (both male and female) represented their income as sufficient for their household and any earnings from their partner as paying only for unnecessary "extras."

Before they lost their jobs, the women's earnings might have been used for some personal spending as well. For example, Maria Carrera was raised by a mother who was an accountant and a feminist, so being independent was important to her: "I'm going to be independent again, because my mom's like that." Maria missed her independence because she felt that, without a paycheck, she should ask her husband for permission to shop for herself or her daughter or buy presents for relatives, even though he never demanded control over her spending. Maria was not extravagant, but she always looked fashionable when we got together. Yet, if she was not contributing an income, she did not feel right spending money on nonessential items.[47] Moreover, Maria had additional reasons for wanting to work again. She had convinced her husband that they should pay for their daughter's college and graduate school education, which added to the pressure on her to find another job.

Although Potuchek's first breadwinning criterion—earning money to provide for the family, rather than just for personal spending—was largely satisfied by the unemployed women in dual-earner couples, was the second one—"the day-to-day obligation to earn money . . . a duty to work" so that "leaving the labor force (even temporarily) is not an option"—fulfilled as well? Maria had considered retiring while her husband continued at his job. What about other unemployed women? I noticed in my participants' life histories and in the decisions they made over the years I knew them that some women assumed that their male partner had a stronger obligation to keep working.[48]

That assumption was clear when Linda McDaniel decided not to look for another job. Then in her fifties, Linda had been working as an executive assistant in the same construction company as her husband, who was second in command. Construction companies struggled during the Great Recession. When that business closed, both Linda and her husband lost their jobs. She said that was particularly difficult for him because "he's concerned about being the breadwinner." Nonetheless, Linda diligently searched for work and obtained a position as an executive assistant and then program manager for a local nonprofit organization. When I reinterviewed her two years later, she had completed a fulfilling year and a half of work before being laid off again because the organization's grant funding ended. By that time, her husband's income in his new job was more secure, but then their son's wife left him. When we spoke, their son and his young children were about to move in with Linda and her husband. Even though Linda's household income was not back to the level she and her husband had previously earned when they both worked for the construction company, Linda decided, with the agreement of her husband, to suspend her search for another job so she could be on hand to care for their grandchildren. She was also the one who assisted her elderly mother and her husband's father, both of whom required increasing care. She commented, "My husband has always known that my priorities have always been the family versus the breadwinner. He gets to be the breadwinner." She quickly added, "Not that we're a traditional family, but I've always been really upfront with him, 'Honey, I need to go do this.'"

Linda's defensive comment, "Not that we're a traditional family," is interesting. She is college educated, and she knows that I am as well. She may suspect that college-educated professionals like me would look down on a "traditional" household in which the man is the sole income earner. Still, it seemed obvious to her that her husband should keep working while she stopped trying to find another job and looked after their grandchildren and aging parents. Why? Men can do family care work too—in fact, one of my male participants was happy to care for his granddaughter while he was unemployed. However, financially, it made more sense for Linda's husband to keep working because his income had always been much higher than hers. Both Linda and her husband had been breadwinners by Potuchek's first criterion, with both of their incomes supporting their household. However, when someone was needed for family care, he had the greater obligation to keep working, and she took on the tasks of supporting the older and younger generations. Furthermore, being the family breadwinner mattered more to Linda's husband than to Linda, by her account.

Gender asymmetry in the obligation to keep working was also evident in the case of Lucy Guerrero. Lucy had worked for a courier company, first as a driver, which she enjoyed, and then in their HR department, which she found stressful. With the money she saved from her job, she was able to give her second husband money to open an auto repair shop. Then Lucy was dismissed from her job. Initially, her reaction was, "I was married and said, 'Well, I guess I'll take a well-deserved vacation.'" Her husband supported them for a while, but his auto repair shop failed to make money during the Great Recession, and they were no longer able to make payments on their condo. After two years of struggling, Lucy asked her husband to leave. He did not want to end the marriage, but she decided on New Year's Eve, "I am not starting this year with this man." Lucy gathered all his clothes and put them outside, and he had to leave. Claudia C., who interviewed Lucy, clarified that the problem in their relationship had not been Lucy's job loss but rather her husband's economic failure because "he doesn't know how to do business." There were other issues, including the fact that his mother was living with them and that he did not communicate well, but for Lucy, the main problem was his failure to support them:

LUCY: They were issues, but yes, the economy had a great effect because he never contributed, never gave—
CLAUDIA C.: [*completing the thought*] He never took responsibility.

Lucy: [. . .] If we had maintained that economic income, nothing would have been lost. Nothing, nothing would have been lost.

Claudia C.: You were the giver.

Both Claudia C. and Lucy assumed that it was acceptable for Lucy to take a "take a well-deserved vacation" from working and that her husband should have continued to provide for them. Lucy should not have had to be "the giver."

It is also significant that Lucy's husband did not decide to leave her because she was not earning an income; instead, she decided he needed to leave because he was not earning enough. As I explained earlier, some previous research has found that divorce rates are more strongly related to a man's unemployment than to a woman's being out of work.[49] It could be that the woman's unemployment does not create as much financial hardship, assuming her earnings had been lower. Another possibility is that expectations about whether the man or the woman has the greater duty to provide for the household shape each partner's response to the other's reduced income. If there is a stronger social expectation that the man should keep working to provide for the family, then his unemployment is more disruptive of their identities and mutual expectations than is hers.

Consistent with the previous research, among the heterosexual couples in this study, the man's unemployment or underemployment led to much more relationship strain than did the woman's unemployment or underemployment. In seven of the twelve dual-earning couples in which the man was unemployed, he reported some strain or serious problems in their relationship caused by his reduced earnings. By contrast, only one of the eight women in a dual-earner couple (Jackie Gallardo) attributed relationship strain to her loss of work hours. That was a special case because her husband worked at the same company, and he had lost work hours as well. With both of their incomes drastically reduced, they could no longer afford their house payments, and the bank foreclosed on their mortgage. His frustration and anger, which led to him beating her on one occasion, could have been as much a reaction to his own reduced income as it was a reaction to hers. As she put it, "Once, he beat me—the stress of not being able to make the house payments, we were losing it." That atypical case aside, the women did not report problems in their relationship because they were out of work. For example, although Maria Carrera's husband urged her to find another job, she also observed, "He's very supportive, I don't have problems with him or anything." By contrast, several of the unemployed men reported recriminations from their wife or other tensions in their relationship.

Charles Toppes, who had been a director of manufacturing for a furniture company with a salary of about $160,000, is an example of a man who reported relationship strain. His wife had not been working for many years, but when it looked likely that he would be laid off, she trained to become a medical technician and found a job in that field. When I met Charles, he had been out of work for a year and a half, and he and his wife had two teenagers. His wife was the money manager in their household, and she was all too aware that their expenses exceeded their income. In response to my question, "How has your wife been about all of this?" Charles replied, "It's been very stressful. There's a lot of stress in the family. She was going through some stress when she first went to work simply because of the new job, new career, and everything, although it's what she wants to do." He concluded, "It's been a strain on all of us. It's been a strain on the marriage; it's been a strain on family life." Charles also worried about the effect of his unemployment on his "legacy" as a father; that is, the kind of memories his teenage children would have of this period in their lives. Thinking especially of his fifteen-year-old daughter, he said, "It bothers me not being able to do these kinds of things because then my legacy is affected as her dad. You know, [*imagining her thoughts*] 'When Dad had money, we were able to do this, but then Dad didn't have money, so we had to stop. And we didn't have the fun that we had.'"

The strain was even greater in households in which the husband was unemployed and the wife earned enough to be self-supporting.[50] Stephen Smith and his wife had both held high-level management positions in large companies; in fact, she had interviewed him for a job he held early in his career. Later, he moved to a different company so that they would not be vying for the same promotions. She stayed with the company where they met, and several career moves later, he became a senior director at a division of a Fortune 500 company in the leisure industry. Together, they earned more than $300,000 a year. In my first interview with Stephen, he stated that he was grateful that his wife's income "gave me added breathing room. I didn't have necessarily the same stresses that would be there had I been the only wage earner in the family." In the next interview, however, he revealed his wife's fury with him. Although they had saved enough money to complete $80,000 worth of home improvements after he lost his job, she berated him for the loss of the stock options that were supposed to pay for their children's college education. When Stephen was let go during the Great Recession, he was forced to sell the stock options just as the market was tanking and after the stock had lost most of its value:

There isn't more than probably a month or two that doesn't go by especially in our current circumstances with paying tuition that [*his wife*] doesn't remind me of that and tell me how aggravated she is. [*recounting his wife's comments*] "How could you have possibly done it? I still

don't understand. It was your fault and you ruined [*their son's*] education. You were supposed to do this. You were supposed to have that taken
care of. You fell down. You didn't accomplish it, and now we're paying
dearly by either using my retirement or our life savings that was never
intended for that."[51]

Moving to a less expensive home was not an option; that, he was certain, would
lead to a divorce.

When I first met Stephen, it was three years after he had been let go. In his
previous job, he was a senior director of a division with more than 10,000 employees and more than one billion dollars a year in sales. He had not been able to
find another job at the same level. During the several years he was out of work,
his wife asked that he not tell their friends that he was unemployed. She also
punished him by not giving him spending money. He wanted to stay active and
useful by working on the yard and pool, but she did not give him money for
tools and supplies: "Since I'm no longer a wage earner, no longer contributing
financially to our ongoing existence, I have a very difficult time trying to justify
anything from an expense standpoint with my wife." She would say, "'Well, if
you think that's such a good idea, then you go spend money on it. You go get
your own money.'" Stephen was worried about how her obvious disdain would
affect his standing in the eyes of their teenage son, whom he imagined thinking,
"Do I listen to what Dad says or what Mom says? [. . .] Mom is the one who
bought me my new shoes. Mom is the one who said I could go skating."

Stephen eventually found another job after he lowered his salary expectations and took a lower-paying position with a smaller company. When I met
with him again, he reported that his wife was still not satisfied. His frustration was evident: "How do I turn around and answer the question, 'Well, you
didn't hold up your end of the bargain?' What end was that? My end of the
bargain was to, come hell or high water, death, taxes, whatever, I was gonna
write a check and hand you $200,000 a year every year between now and when
I'm dead? Was that the bargain I didn't hold up? I didn't know I had a contract
that said this was what I had to do." Stephen was sure his wife would have left
him but for the fact that California is a community property state and she did
not want to be forced to share her pension, which was larger than his. Another
unemployed interviewee's wife, who earned a middle-class salary, told me she
had the same reason for hesitating to divorce her unemployed husband, although she did eventually leave him.

In contrast, in five of the twelve dual-earning couples in which the man
was unemployed, he reported no relationship problems as a result of his reduced income. Some men even described a stronger bond with their partner

and children, as did some of the men who had been the sole income earners when they were employed.[52]

Jorge Paiz, an immigrant from Guatemala, had been a well-paid construction worker before he was laid off in his early forties. He explained that when he was working all the time, he used to come home late. After losing his job, he was able to go for walks with his baby and to take his older children to sports practice while his wife Isela worked at her clerical job. Isela translated his comments: "He said that now he feels love. (*laughs*) Before, he said that working and bringing home food and whatever they need, that's all I'm supposed to provide. And now he knows that the love of the kids is the best thing." She added that he also helps with cleaning. Jorge interrupted to add proudly, "And cooking too. I cook." Isela put him in his place, retorting, "Sometimes." Still, it was clear that she was grateful for his help, and he felt that his role in the family had become deeper and richer.[53]

Similarly, an unemployed IT worker who had worked the night shift was glad that losing his job gave him more time with his partner. Although more time together led to more arguments, he commented, "We are understanding each other better day by day." Overall, he said, "It had brought us closer."[54] Some of the unemployed women in dual-earning couples, like Mary Brown, also mentioned that a benefit of being out of work was having more time with their family. Interestingly, however, the women did not report this change in the same way as did Jorge Paiz did—as a major shift in their self-understanding. Quite likely, even when they were working, their roles in their families had never been limited to providing money.[55]

Overall, a little more than half of my male participants in dual-earner couples experienced relationship troubles because they were unemployed. Strikingly, however, when the man was the sole income earner before he lost his job, the female life partner reacted very differently: all but one sole breadwinner reported strong support from their female life partner while they were out of work. In their stories we can see how the new dual-earner norm even shaped the relationships that on the outside looked like they followed older patterns of male breadwinning. My examples of women who were the primary breadwinners show even greater changes.

Sole Breadwinning Men and Primary Breadwinning Women

There were seven heterosexual men in my study who had been the sole breadwinner in their family before they were unemployed. Six of those seven reported that being out of work had not created much tension in their relationship and that their wife was sympathetic and encouraging. In addition, two women had been full-time homemakers and were just starting to look for a job because their husband was out of work. Neither disparaged her husband. Their examples raise the intriguing question of why these wives were so much more emotionally supportive than their counterparts in dual-earner couples.

Robert Milner, an unemployed supply chain strategist for a midsize company, did not report tensions in his relationship with his wife during the eighteen months he was out of work preceding our interviews. Without any prompting from me, he exclaimed, "She's been amazing. [. . .] My wife has been amazing through this whole thing." He added, "I look at my wife every day and feel so blessed that I have her in my life." Robert's wife used to bring in a little income by working in a family member's business, but about four years before I met him, that business closed, and nerve damage made it hard for her to take another job. Two years after that, Robert lost his job.

Robert, who was in his early fifties, completely accepted the "package deal" of male responsibilities that Townsend described: holding a steady job, marrying, having children, and owning a home. When I asked him what he was proud of in his life, he replied: "I'm proud of my family. I'm proud that I was able to marry a wonderful woman. Produced two beautiful kids. [. . .] We're coming up on our thirtieth year of marriage. We've been through some tough times economically. But I guess I've always hung in there. [. . .] We got married. We bought the home. [. . .] We have two kids. That whole—you know?" Yet Robert could not exactly boast of being able to hold a steady job. His current lengthy stint of unemployment was not his first. He used to work in aerospace, but after those companies downsized, he switched to health and beauty products. However, he could say that, despite the "tough times," he had "always hung in there," and he had been able to check off the rest of the boxes (successful marriage, children, home ownership) in what he framed as a culturally recognizable package: "That whole—you know?"

Robert was especially proud of his achievements as a husband and father because his own father had failed in those respects. His father had been a bartender, and his mother worked in bars as well, when she worked at all. Often, she did not work because she had an alcohol problem. His parents separated when he was young, and for a while, Robert and his brother were in foster care. Robert did not want to talk about his childhood, but after detailing his success in staying married, buying a home, and raising two beautiful children, he imagined himself saying to his father, "I did it the right way, Dad."

Yet, as proud as Robert was of fulfilling his responsibilities as a father and husband, he sometimes wished his wife was still working. I always followed the "What things are you proud of in your life" question with "Is there anything you're not so proud of?" At this point, Robert stopped sounding like Townsend's interviewees who in the late 1980s and early 1990s denigrated their wife's financial contributions. It was quite different with Robert Milner. Even though his income had been much greater than hers, he missed her earnings once she had to stop working. Although Robert wanted to be good provider, he resented being the *sole* income earner:

> I got to a point where I was working so many hours, and coming home every weekend and doing the normal stuff—mowing the lawn. And after doing all the duties around the house and realizing that my weekend was gone—there was no time. There was no money for me to go do what I wanted to do [*e.g., go fishing*]. And for a while, I became very bitter. [. . .] I guess, in some way, I blamed my wife. You know? Because she wasn't working. I never told her that. But you know subconsciously, in some way, you think about that.

Robert berated himself for blaming his wife because he knew that her nerve damage prevented her from working; he concluded, "It's probably the biggest thing I was not very proud of." He portrayed his wife as his financial partner in other respects because "she makes dollars stretch." She seemed to be the main money manager in the family. When I asked Robert what was the interest rate on their mortgage, he replied that his wife would know. It was immediately after that exchange that he volunteered the comments, "She's been amazing. [. . .] My wife has been amazing through this whole thing."

Tony DeLuca, an unemployed vice president of HR for a large company, also spoke of his wife's strong emotional support and money-management skills. When they were younger, she was a teacher, and in the early years of their marriage, they relied on her fringe benefits. However, by the time their children were born, his job provided a higher salary and better benefits than hers, and she quit her teaching job to stay home and raise their children—a decision, he made a point of stating, that was her choice, although he was happy to support it. Still, they figured that, if he were ever unemployed, she could easily find another job. That supposition was wrong. While he was out of work, she started looking for another teaching job, but because she had not worked for fifteen years, she found it nearly impossible to enter the teaching field. Still, like Robert Milner, Tony framed her as his financial partner: "She has saved more money in coupons—I'm not kidding. I think we bought a third of this house under coupon savings." That is likely an exaggeration, but he seemed genuinely grateful for her skills in managing the household budget. He concluded, "Between the two of us we make a good combo" financially.

Tony was also grateful for his wife's emotional support. When I asked how she had reacted to his unemployment, he replied, "Oh, she's such a trooper. She is wonderful. And she's the one who kinda keeps me up. She's the one who has to remind me it's like, 'Honey, you know we're gonna be fine. Don't worry. Don't panic.'"

Robert's exclamation, "My wife has been amazing through this whole thing," and Tony's grateful comment, "Oh, she's such a trooper. She is wonderful," reveal a different emotional dynamic than we saw among many of the dual-earner couples. I was particularly struck by Robert and Tony's representation of their currently not-working wives as their financial partners because it differs from other male breadwinning models. For example, a description of unemployed working-class men in an economically depressed part of the United Kingdom in the 1990s said they were torn between their duty to support the needs of their family and their desire to spend their job seekers' allowance socializing with other men at the pub. Several of those men said they provided money for the household only to appease "the missus" and avoid tension.[56] By contrast, most of my American participants, whether male or female, described consumption projects they shared with their partner, including the major expense of paying for a single-family home. Only one of the sole breadwinning men commented that his wife's spending goals and his had been at odds, blaming her unreasonable desires ("my wife always wanted this, this, and that"), rather than his stints of unemployment, for their shaky finances and poor credit.

Although we might expect the sole breadwinning men to have the most rigid, traditional gender constructs, that was not the case. In each of those couples, their partner had either worked after they began their lives together or he had no problem with her working in the future. As we can see in Robert's case, he even resented that she was no longer able to bring in an income. He partly excused himself for those ungenerous thoughts by saying, "You know, subconsciously, in some way, you think about that." That wording suggests that Robert believed that his resentment at being the sole provider was normal: it was what anyone in his position would think.

Although I was not able to interview all my participants' partners, I do have the perspectives of two women whose husbands had been the sole breadwinner before losing their job. Because I recruited anyone who was either unemployed or looking for work, a few participants had not been in the workforce recently but began looking for a job when their spouse was out of work. That was the situation of Theresa Allen and Paula Jackson, who had worked in the past but who in recent years had been full-time homemakers until each of their husbands lost his job. Although these women did not say much about what it meant for them to be out of the workforce, they had a lot to say about what it meant for their spouse to be unemployed.

Even in the privacy of the one-on-one interview, neither blamed nor disparaged her husband, although both were distressed by the downward mobility they experienced as a result of his job struggles. As we saw in the last chapter, Theresa Allen and her husband had to leave the home they owned and rent an apartment; then they had to move in with her mother and give away or euthanize their beloved pets. Still, Theresa was very understanding about her husband's difficulty finding another job in his fifties: "He's sending out resume after resume. He's joined the folks out there in no-man's-land that are sending out resumes and barely getting acknowledged." Theresa knew how bad the job market was; she was unable to find a job as a waitress, her former occupation, because restaurants had cut their staff during the recession.

Similarly, although Paula Jackson had to move to a smaller house and give up her beloved Mercedes when her husband lost his high-level job in a financial services company (see chapter 3), I never heard her voice any resentment toward him. She was shocked when I said that some wives were angry that their husband was out of work. She declared, "I would never downgrade my husband because he lost a job," adding, "If you make the money, you're gonna get that back. But how are you gonna get love?"

Yet it was not smooth sailing for the relationships of all the sole breadwinning men. Jagat Bodhi, an unemployed telecommunications technician, was the one exception in experiencing some relationship strain. Like Robert Milner, he had not wanted to be the sole income earner for his family. In our first interview, he stated, "When I got married, I was counting on my wife to be working at the same time so we could both contribute." His wife had been a manager in a financial institution until she had to leave work to care full-time for their daughter, who had serious medical problems. Jagat's subsequent unemployment created additional stress in a situation that was already difficult for his wife. When we met later for a follow-up interview, after he had found another position, I asked how his being out of work had affected their relationship. He said, "Bills started mounting up. So, that creates extra stress. It's very stressful. And the unemployment [*benefit*] only covers so much. And we have a pile of debt, so . . ." He added, "Especially when you have only one spouse working, the other spouse cannot contribute anything." When I pressed him about how his wife had reacted to those stresses, he said, "She does have a temper, so, (*laughs*) so, it makes it very challenging for me."

Jagat understood that his wife had to leave work to care for their special-needs daughter, but clearly the financial strain was greater than he had anticipated. Unlike the sole breadwinning husbands in Komarovsky's study conducted during the Depression, Jagat and his wife began their marriage with the expectation that both would bring in salaries from managerial/professional jobs. The loss of his income combined with her need to leave work was a double load of financial setbacks. Those financial challenges, along with his wife's sacrifice of her career aspirations to stay home with their daughter, probably all contributed to his wife's unhappiness, as Jagat acknowledged, adding that he understood her occasional outbursts: "You're under stress, you know, so that is expected."

In sum, more than half of the dual-earner couples experienced some relationship strain or severe problems when the husband lost his job, but that was the case for only one of the nine households in which the man had been the primary breadwinner and then became unemployed (including the households of Theresa Allen and Paula Jackson). Nor did these male sole breadwinner couples in my research sound like the male sole breadwinners Komarovsky studied during the Depression who said, "Love flies out of the window when money goes."[57] Why?

There are significant differences between American families in the 1930s and the 2010s. Although Komarovsky found some happy marriages, she also described some wives who had contempt for their husband and others who were "subordinate and resentful."[58] They stayed in those relationships only because there were few jobs for women in which they could earn a living wage, and divorce and single motherhood were stigmatized. If women wanted children and if they also wanted to stay out of poverty, they had little choice but to marry and depend mostly or completely on their husband's income. That did not mean, however, that they were happy about their limited possibilities, and their frustration could boil over when he stopped providing for the family.

By contrast, US women in the twenty-first century have more choices. Most of my male participants who were the sole breadwinners had wives who had worked in the past and who knew paid work was an option for them in the future. Until their husband's recent unemployment, working outside the home was not necessary because he had earned a salary sufficient to support them and, in some cases, to support them very well. Among the heterosexual participants who had been in male sole-breadwinner households, the husbands' highest income in the past had been between $50,000 and $80,000 a year for the bottom third to more than $250,000 a year for the top third. With greater options—and husbands whose average earnings had been much higher than those of the skilled working-class men who dominated Komarovsky's earlier study, even accounting for inflation—perhaps the spouses in these households had fewer pent-up frustrations when the man lost his job. John Davis, one of the unemployed men in the top tier of earners, explained his wife's reaction to his being out of work this way: "She's waiting on me to turn from a frog into a prince again, I suppose." When he was working in upper management, his annual income had been more than $500,000.

As mentioned earlier, I propose that because dual-income couples are the norm now, these sole income-earning men reap a "surplus credit" of gratitude from their partners for exceeding the norm by taking on the whole burden of providing income for the household. The men then have a gratitude credit reserve, of sorts, to draw on when they are out of work.

Couples did not have to adhere to a neotraditional division of household labor to be happy. The relationships in which the woman was the sole or primary breadwinner also seemed to hold up well after she lost her job, with one sad exception.

In 2011, wives were the sole breadwinner in just under 7 percent of US heterosexual married couple families.[59] Given the rarity of this arrangement, both nationally and among my participants, I broadened this category to look at the effects of unemployment on the relationships of women who were the primary, not only the sole, breadwinners: they not only earned most of the household income but also were acknowledged by both partners as the main pillar of household support, even if their spouse or partner also earned an income. Five women in my study had been the primary income earners before they lost their jobs. In addition, one of the men I interviewed was in a household in which his wife was the primary income earner even before he lost his job.[60]

Most of the women who had been the primary breadwinners in the couple reported that their spouse was very emotionally supportive while they were unemployed. The appreciative manner in which each talked about her husband echoed the comments of the sole breadwinning men who described their wife being "a trooper" or "amazing."

Caroline James and her husband met in an acting class. But while he continued with acting, script writing, artwork, and various business ventures in the arts, she took office jobs, learned about the HR field, and then moved up in the HR ranks at a multinational company. By the time she was in her forties, she was that company's senior vice president of HR with a six-figure salary that let her husband continue the artistic work he loved, even though it did not produce a reliable income. Because he worked for himself, he was free to accompany Caroline when her promotion required a move out of state. I asked Caroline if they had considered him taking over as the primary breadwinner while she was out of work. Caroline said, "We debated it. We really debated it. It's just, we, you know, if we're honest with our skill sets and what we do and what we like to do, our temperaments, it just made more sense to continue this way." When I asked how he had reacted to her unemployment, Caroline replied warmly, "He's been super supportive. He's been really great. I've had moments of freaking out, like, 'How am I going to afford this?' [. . .] He's really good at budgeting it out and just being really logical about it, and if he's been worried or if he's had moments, he's hidden it from me, because he's really been really, really good." Caroline's high-pressure job used to require extremely long workdays with few vacations. She took her time finding another job because "I was enjoying spending time with my husband and the dog and the cat." Her year-long severance package and savings from her high salary helped a great deal, and they had no children. Four months after we met, she found another job, but then there was talk of possible layoffs at her new company. When we met again two years later, Caroline's husband continued to help her cope. She commented gratefully, "He's on my team, and he's supportive, and [he] said, 'We'll make it work.'"

Unlike Caroline James, Lisa Rose's husband had a steady income, but it was much lower than hers. Lisa Rose shared that when she was growing up in a traditional household in the 1960s and 1970s, "I never imagined that I would be working my entire life." Instead, she imagined a life like her mother's: "The way I was socialized, I thought I was going to get married, you know, probably out of high school or early in my twenties. I didn't get married until I was thirty-five. I thought I was going to be driving the station wagon with four kids, but that didn't happen." By the time she and her husband married, they felt it was too late to have children. Lisa earned a master's degree in public health, and she started working her way up into management-level positions in nonprofit organizations. Before Lisa was laid off, her salary was approximately twice her husband's as a teacher in the public schools. As Lisa explained, "We relied on my income to make our lifestyle work." So, with Lisa out of work for more than two years except for short-term, contract positions, she told me, "It got pretty scary pretty fast, like 'Okay, do we have to sell the house? What are we gonna do?'" Still, when I asked how her husband was dealing with her unemployment, she laughed and said, "He's been great. I feel badly for him because this has not been easy, I'm sure. And he's kinda my defender in the sense that he always reminds me that it's not entirely my fault." Lisa appreciated him "making sure I'm okay and sometimes just letting me know when I'm being too overwrought. And he's very funny, and so he helps make me laugh." In my follow-up interview with Lisa, held after she began working at a new job, I asked how her unemployment had affected their relationship. Lisa replied, "Like most things that are very stressful or challenging, it can bring you closer. It definitely kind of does that for us." Lisa explained that one of the things that had been challenging had been their role reversal. It had been easier for her during an earlier period in their relationship when he was having work problems and she was the emotionally supportive partner. It was harder for her to have the roles reversed, when she "wasn't feeling as successful." Still, she thought that working through that challenge, along with helping care for his mother while she was out of work, ultimately made their marriage stronger.

Thus, the general pattern I found is that, at present, when American couples agree on a division of labor by which one of them will bear the primary financial responsibility for the household, the more financially dependent spouse remains loving and supportive during the primary breadwinner's unemployment. Unemployed primary breadwinning wives, like unemployed sole breadwinning husbands, may earn a surplus credit for exceeding the customary dual-earner arrangement. Like their male counterparts, these wives can draw on that credit when they are out of work.

However, unemployed sole breadwinners do not always have grateful partners, as we can see from the unusual example of Anastasia Tang. Her situation made me question some of the basic assumptions other researchers and I held about earning money and having power in relationships. Anastasia and her husband were both immigrants—he from northern India, she from Southeast Asia. Shortly after the birth of her second son, Anastasia lost her job as an HR manager in a midsize company. Then her husband declared that he was burnt out from working his demanding job as an accounting manager, so he quit, stayed home, and talked about starting his own business. His reasoning was like that of many women, such as Linda McDaniel, whose partner earned an income sufficient to support the family and who wanted to put more time into childcare. He pointed out that Anastasia had a master's degree, while he did not have an advanced degree. He figured that she would find another job soon, and her earning potential was greater. Both Anastasia and her husband devoted time and money to their two little boys, who were three and four years old when I checked back in with Anastasia two years after we first met. The boys were in an expensive preschool that expected parent involvement, and they had many enriching activities outside of school. Because he did not have a job, Anastasia's husband was available to help with those activities.

However, Anastasia's husband was hardly egalitarian. It did not sound as if he had consulted Anastasia before he stopped working. As she put it, "He decided, 'I don't want to go back to work.'" When I first met Anastasia, she told me her husband was taking care of their toddlers. However, she also said that he should not be expected to take full charge of two energetic little boys because it is too "hectic" and "he doesn't really have the patience": that is why they kept their nanny. He criticized her for failing to find steady work, but

HR management jobs are increasingly likely to be temporary contract positions rather than permanent employment as companies outsource those functions to save money.[61] It was seven months before Anastasia found any job, and for three years her only jobs were short-term contracts lasting a few months. Her husband would also criticize her for not asking for a higher salary, but during the recession and slack labor market several years afterward, salary offers had dropped considerably.

When I asked Anastasia, "How would you say your husband's been? Do you consider him supportive or helpful?" Anastasia replied, "Not been very supportive; that's my feeling." She added, "I feel like he is criticizing a lot. He's very hard on me." The lack of appreciation she received at home made her miss working more. She said that, even though she had not considered her job as central to her identity, "Now it's like you don't feel sometimes you're needed or you're interesting."[62] She worried about her marriage: "We're supposed to celebrate our five-year anniversary this year. We've been together for a long time, but I don't know how this is going to survive this whole thing—whether, you know, our marriage can survive." She implied that ending the marriage would be his choice, not hers: "Economically, I know he'll do very well regardless of whether I'm there or not."

This was not the first time her husband had been critical or domineering. One of Anastasia's New Year's resolutions, before she had lost her job, had been to "find inner voice." When I asked her to explain what she meant, she replied,

> Being married to an Asian also sometimes is difficult because my husband is very traditional and wants me to do a lot of things. It's sometimes hard to feel I was being heard. I have to be sometimes very subservient. I do all the cooking in the house. He does a lot more of the cleaning, which I hate. But sometimes he's very dominant; he wants things to be done a certain way with the kids and all that. I feel like we both can have our own voices without canceling each other out or making each other feel we're not worthy of each other. That's been hard.

Two years later, Anastasia was out of work again after finishing another temporary job, and her husband was still not employed. When I asked whether she had found her inner voice, she said she had not—either in her jobs or with her husband. Even when she could find work, she was only on temporary contracts, and she could not make waves in the company. She told me that, at home, "When you don't have a job, you really don't have a say." However, that only seemed to apply to her, not to her husband, who still had his dominant voice even though he was unemployed. During our interview, her husband called her at 1:00 P.M. because he had expected her home at noon. Anastasia said she had "learned to control her tongue" to "keep peace."

Anastasia's situation as a sole breadwinner with an unsupportive spouse, although rare among my participants, is important because it raises a fundamental question: What is the relation between income earning and exerting authority in intimate relationships? Komarovsky assumed earning income is essential for decision-making power within the household when she argued that the wife of an unemployed man would feel freer to express her grievances and get her way "now that the man holds no economic whip over her."[63] My surplus credit explanation for supportive spouses of unemployed primary breadwinners, although different, is also transactional: unusual past financial support is repaid in present emotional support. Cultural variation helps us see that this transactional reasoning may apply to most couples in the United States, but it is not universal. Cultural norms about family roles matter as well. Anastasia's husband had grown up in northern India, known for its classic patriarchal family structures.[64] Perhaps his temperament or experiences also contributed to his assumption that he should have the dominant voice in the household, whether he was contributing economically or not.

Studies of other immigrant groups reveal cultural variation in family dynamics. Rosen's study of New England factory women found that among the Portuguese immigrants she spoke with, the men assumed that their authority rested on their traditional prerogatives. Like Anastasia Tang's husband, they did not need to be the sole or primary family provider to have the dominant voice.[65] Victor Tan Chen's study of the effects of unemployment on the relationships of well-paid blue-collar workers found that it was common for unemployment to precipitate the end of marriages in the United States, but that was much less common for the unemployed Canadians he interviewed. Chen gives several possible explanations, including the greater materialism of his US interviewees.[66] Cultural assumptions about relationships also affect their dynamics. In other words, people who share the cultural model that it is natural that "love flies out of the window when money goes" will act on that basis, but people with other assumptions may not, as we see next for same-sex couples.

Same-Sex Couples

Some neoclassical economists have theorized that relationships are strongest when they are specialized, with the member having the better labor market prospects being the sole or primary income earner while the other member focuses on care of the home and any children.[67] One sociologist tested this neoclassical economic theory by comparing same-sex couples and heterosexual couples, given previous findings that lesbian and gay couples "value equality in both earnings and housework."[68] As she hypothesized, she found that among heterosexual couples, nearly equal earnings were correlated with a higher risk of a breakup, but the exact opposite occurred among same-sex couples: nearly equal earnings were correlated with a lower probability of breakups. She concluded that an efficient division of labor in the household does not entirely explain the strength of relationships; the values of the couple are also significant. Same-sex couples, who tend to value equal earnings, had stronger relationships when they achieved that goal.[69]

Katherine Newman's study of unemployed Americans in the mid-1980s also found that unemployment had different effects on households in the LGBTQ community: the unemployed gay professional men with whom she spoke were under less psychological and financial stress than those who were straight, in part because at that time they were less likely to have a dependent partner and because their "community does not pass judgment on its members by reference to occupational success."[70] It would be interesting to see whether those generalizations still hold true today.

Only one of my participants was in a same-sex relationship when I conducted my research, but he presented an interesting variation on findings from previous research. Terrance West came from a working-class family, had an associate degree, and most recently had been a shipping and receiving clerk. At his last job, he had been harassed for his sexual orientation, and his irritation at the way he was treated probably led to him being fired. He was in his early forties and had been without work for more than two years when we met. His boyfriend "Sebastián" was in his mid-twenties at the time; he was also from a working-class family and also lacked a four-year college degree. When I first met Terrance, Sebastián was looking for work and hoping to take some college courses. With neither working, they could not afford their rent and lived with relatives.

Given their age difference, Terrance took primary responsibility to provide for their household: "I want to be able to take care of my family, even if it's just me and [Sebastián] and our dog; I just want to be able to maintain my family unit." Terrance was worried that his boyfriend would leave him for someone with more money: "There's times where I'm, like, wondering why he's even staying with me, 'cause he's struggling right alongside me. And then it scares me, too, because my cousin has this friend [. . .] and he drives a real fancy Audi, and he's living the fabulous life. And my guy sees that, and he's like, 'Wow, look at his car,' 'Wow, look at this, look at that.'" I asked Terrance whether he was scared that Sebastián would leave him for someone like that.

Terrance replied, "Sometimes I think that. That, oh, yeah, he's just gonna jump up one day and say, 'You know what? I'm tired, and I have no fun. I'm gonna go have fun with this guy or that guy.' And that worries me."

Years later, Terrance finally obtained steady work, and his expectations about the division of responsibilities in their household changed. As Sebastián grew older, and with Terrance's place in the relationship more secure because he was working, he became increasingly critical of his boyfriend's disinclination to contribute to their household income. When I met Terrance, his income had never exceeded $46,000 a year. His income may be higher now that he has acquired more certifications and been promoted, but he is still struggling. Sebastián studied in a cooking school and took a job as a cook, but it did not last long. Terrance and I exchanged Facebook messages in which he complained that his guy still was not working. Terrance phrased that not in terms of an ideology of equality but rather of stark financial need: "Maybe he enjoys watching me work like crazy just to continue to fall behind on everything?" Terrance did not need Sebastián to contribute equally, but he wanted him to try to help out.

Further research is needed on the effects of unemployment on members of same-sex couples. Being the target of harassment at work may help explain the fact that men (and, to a lesser extent, women) in same-sex relationships have somewhat higher rates of unemployment than do married men and women in heterosexual couples.[71] Further research is also needed to explore how socioeconomic class and relative ages affect breadwinning expectations in same-sex couples. Terrance's felt responsibility to be a sole support for Sebastián when he was younger and the primary support for him later contradicts some scholars' generalization, "Homosexual men do not feel an obligation to support their partners financially."[72] Still, Terrance West's complaints about his partner's unwillingness to contribute at all suggest that current economic pressures shape the relationships of both straight and gay couples.

Singles

The mix of continuity and change in gender norms that I found in couples affected the ways those who were single thought about the division of labor they wanted in a future relationship.

Most single women and men were alike in saying they had little interest in dating while they were out of work. There were several reasons why their long-term unemployment dampened their desire to seek a relationship. Chipper Goodman, the college graduate in his mid-twenties described in chapter 4 who had been unable to find a meaningful career, said he felt too unsettled to consider a serious relationship: "I don't think I'm really in the spot to have a girlfriend, because I'm not financially stable, and I need to concentrate on my career and my life and finding out who I am or what I'm gonna do before I can share it with somebody else." Others who were older and had been in an established career said that all the rejections they received while looking for another job for many months or years had hurt their self-confidence. Amber Washington, a professional woman in her early sixties, explained, "I'm not interested in *love* right now. No. I want a job. I want a job. That is what I want. Everything else I feel will fall in place once I have a job. I'll feel better about myself, and I can start thinking about other things." Pepper Hill, a professional woman in her late fifties, explained that the problem with looking for a romantic partner while you are job hunting is that it creates more occasions for others to reject you. She observed, "Mate hunting and job hunting are very similar." In both cases, there is an initial interview where "they have to like you." She found "it was too many places to put myself out vulnerably, to expose myself."[73]

In a sign of contemporary women's potential for economic self-sufficiency, only one of the twenty-two single women we interviewed, Isabel Navarro, was letting a man support her out of economic necessity. Isabel was in her late fifties, a former worker in a health maintenance organization, and an esthetician (cosmetologist specializing in skin care). She had always been ambitious and hardworking, but discrimination against immigrants from Latin America, her parents' recent deaths, and breaking her foot had taken away some of her options and energy. When Claudia C. asked her how she felt about no longer being financially independent, Isabel spoke of having to "swallow her pride" because "I'm not a hundred percent comfortable with it." What made her uncomfortable was that her new relationship was far from ideal; she had compromised on what she wanted from a partner to receive greater financial security.

Most of the other single women rejected being financially supported by a man while they were unemployed. Some framed this as not wanting to be a "financial burden" or as wanting to be a "giver" in the relationship.

ReNé McKnight, in her thirties, faced overwhelming financial pressures as an unemployed single parent. Nonetheless, she was not looking for a man to support her daughter and her: "I don't want a man to take care of me. I want to be able to give to a relationship [*but*] I can't contribute anything right now." I wondered why she said she could not contribute anything to a relationship, pointing out, "I mean, you've got yourself. You know?" She thought about it and replied, "I would hate for someone to think that I'm there for money. I guess that's probably what it is. I don't want them to think I'm trying to use them." ReNé said she saw herself as a "giver," not a user. Similarly, Celeste Rue ruled out looking for a relationship while she was out of work because "I would feel like someone's burden."

Still, the persistence of a cultural model in which a woman can be economically supported by her life partner without social stigma was always present in the background, coloring the women's choices of future partners—although it also depended on the partners available in their socioeconomic class.

Currently, marriage rates are dropping steeply among all income levels, except the top 20 percent of income earners. One sociologist described marriage as "almost like a luxury good that's attainable only by the people who have the highest resources in society."[74] Among those who live with a partner but are not married, the most common explanation given for not marrying is that they are not yet financially ready.[75] Class differences are magnified in dating, given the current tendency in the United States toward "educational assortative mating": marriage between those with similar educational backgrounds.[76] My college-educated, single-women participants likely only considered entering into a romantic relationship with someone who was also college educated, which would increase the odds that their partner could earn a good income. However, given their own college education, they could support themselves, which gave them options. By contrast, women who had not completed college typically considered a pool of potential partners who also had not finished college and often could not earn a good income. I found striking class differences among the unemployed single women participants when they discussed dating.

Many of the single women who had not completed college were reluctant to become romantically involved with a man. Several were divorced or separated and had psychological scars from previous relationships. For example, Ann Lopez did not want to remarry if the man was going to depend on her earnings again. Ann came from a working-class background, but she had built a financially secure life through her own efforts and with little help from her ex-husband. He had been a carpenter who "went up and down with jobs," so she went to work to help support the family. As I explained in the last chapter, although she had only an associate degree and no special training, she learned to download inventory information from the computers of a large telecommunications company and later became a self-taught IT worker for them until they replaced their employees with workers from an outside contract firm. Nine years before she lost her job, her husband had left the family and refused to pay the child support he owed. On her own, Ann put her daughter through college, paid the mortgage on her home, and built a pension for her retirement, which she was required by California law to share with her ex-husband. She explained her wariness about getting involved with another man:

ANN: I'd love to meet Prince Charming. But that isn't happening. And sometimes I figure I may end up alone forever. Which—I'd love to have the company. But it's very difficult to find a man that can hold his [own]. Put it that way. I have a lot to offer. But I'm not gonna offer it without them meeting me halfway.

CLAUDIA: Do you mean financially or what?

ANN: Financially. I have a home that's almost paid off. You know, I'll be darned if I'm gonna have someone come live with me, and I'm gonna support them. I'm not gonna do that again. I'm not gonna do that.

When we returned to the subject in a later interview, Ann explained that the financial split with a future partner did not have to be equal, but she did not want to be a "sugar mama." Ann felt that her ex-husband had taken advantage of her financially, and she was not interested in another relationship like that. Given the current difficulties that many men without a college education have in earning a good living, it was unlikely she would find a man with a background like hers who could earn as much as she had.

Krystal Murphy and Summer Carrington, sisters in their late fifties and early sixties, were also wary about romantic relationships. Their stories show the forces that have changed working-class families like theirs. Their father was one of those midcentury men who had stayed in an unfulfilling factory job because it was the best way he could provide for his family. As an adult, Krystal had put up with an ill-tempered husband who earned excellent wages working at the same steel mill as her father until it laid off most of its workforce during the wave of deindustrialization in the United States in the early 1980s. He refused to look for that kind of work again, which infuriated Krystal. Remembering their arguments about it upset her so much that she became teary:

When we were kids, my dad had three girls. He knew that there was nowhere else he was gonna get a job that supported us, kept a roof over our head, had hospitalization, had dental, had everything to cover the family. He hated that job every day he had to go there. He hated it. But he knew that that's the best he could do for our family. I'm gonna cry. I'm sorry. I said to my husband once, cause he—it was right when Kaiser [the steel mill] was getting ready to close, and my dad knew people, and he said [to Krystal's husband], "I can keep you on longer. You won't be doing the same job, but we'll get you another. You know there's another way you can stay." He [Krystal's husband] said, "I don't want to do it." I got so angry. I rarely raised my voice around him because it incited him more. And I said, "Do you think this is what my father planned for his life? Do you think that this is what he wanted to do? The answer to that is no."

Krystal's husband never found another job that could support the family. Both he and Krystal had learning disabilities. She worked as a medical lab technician and later in clerical/administrative support positions, all of which paid poorly. They separated, and she was not interested in another relationship. She commented, "I've never felt the need to have a man in my life to be a person."

Her sister Summer had an even more traumatic marital history. Her ex-husband had been a musician and drug dealer. After they divorced, he lived with a woman who stole Summer's Social Security number, with the result that Summer lost her home and vehicles. Summer asked a friend of hers who was dating, "I gotta ask you a question. When you don't really know anybody, how do you put your purse down and lay down next to him and go to sleep? I don't trust anybody enough."

By contrast, the professional and managerial single women I interviewed spoke as if they had many options. Given their own education and that of the men in their socioeconomic class, they had the choice of marrying someone who could support them both with his income, being part of a dual-earning couple with someone who had a similar income, being part of a dual-earning couple with a partner who earned less than they did, or remaining single and continuing to support themselves fairly comfortably once they found another job. They imagined multiple life choices for women like them and defined themselves in relation to that range of possibilities.

Elizabeth Montgomery had been a highly paid business-to-business furniture salesperson, but she had to buck traditional ideas of women's roles, both in her marriage and at her last job. She believes her ex-husband divorced her because "I think he wanted, deep down inside [. . .] someone who would stay home." She commented, "So what he thought he wanted and what he wanted, I think, were two different things." In other words, he thought he was happy to have a wife who had a successful career, but perhaps her business success was threatening to him. Shortly after leaving Elizabeth, he married a woman who did not work. When Elizabeth informed her boss that she was going through a divorce, she was forced to resign. To me and to a lawyer she consulted, this was a shocking example of gender discrimination. Would a man have been pushed out because he might be distracted by an impending divorce? Elizabeth decided not to fight her termination, and fortunately, she had substantial savings. As she looked to the future, she wanted another relationship and expected that possibly she would be the higher earner again. She explained, "I'm not expecting the guy to do well. I'm expecting me to do well. If he does well, that's frosting on the cake." She was proud that this made her "different" and "oddball" when it came to romantic relationships.

Unlike Elizabeth, Pepper Hill, who had held a high-level professional job at a nonprofit organization and had never married, was not looking for a romantic partner while she was out of work, even though she wanted one eventually. Right after making the comment I quoted earlier about her reluctance to be job hunting and mate hunting at the same time, she added, "Now, some people, when they weren't working, that's [*marriage*] what they go for; that's their security." Pepper recognized that getting married for greater economic security was an option for women in her class, but it was one that she rejected.

By contrast, two college-educated women entertained the idea of finding a romantic partner who would support them financially. Mona Childs had worked in marketing before she lost her job. She was in her mid-fifties but looked younger. I asked Mona, "Do you ever think to yourself, 'Well, if I had some guy supporting me, then my money problems would be over'"? She thanked me for the question because it had been on her mind. Her money problems were not too severe because she had paid off her mortgage and had considerable savings. But the possibility appealed to her: "If I were to, let's just say, find a man that I'm attracted to who has not been in a relationship for a long time [*unlike two men who were interested in her but were in other relationships*]— he's not looking for another income, he would love to have someone take care of the house, to be there for him in the evening—that would be me." Mona had been talking about such a scenario with a friend who was also having trouble making ends meet. She explained, "She'd like that, too. Because she's in the same kind of boat for the most part, too. We wouldn't mind being 'the little missus' and supporting somebody [*in nonfinancial ways*]. Do I think that if I were in that situation and not have to worry about money and everything like that, would I flourish again? Yeah." Mona said that under those circumstances, she would still want to work, but not full time. The problem with dating while she was out of work, however, was that she did not feel good about herself: "I've had two guys tell me that they find me interesting. They like me; they're attracted to me. But I'm not attracted to myself, and it's because I've always been wrapped up with how I feel about myself based upon my job." In this interesting blend of different gender models, Mona would be happy to be financially supported, but to feel attractive to a potential partner, she needed the self-esteem that she used to get from being successful at her job.[77]

The other woman who considered being supported by a partner was Amber Washington. Amber is bisexual. She said she was not looking for *love* "unless it's a sugar momma or a sugar daddy." (I believe she meant a real romantic relationship with someone who could support her, not purely transactional "sugar dating.")[78] In her last relationship, her female partner did support her until Amber became bored and looked for work. Amber's sexual orientation did not alter the gender roles she had imbibed from popular culture and that she blamed for her "princess syndrome." When I asked how she had imagined her life would go after she left college, she replied, "When I moved to California . . . I saw myself getting involved with the glamour life. I was gonna meet somebody who was gonna sweep myself off my feet, man or woman, and that I was just gonna have the life of a princess. That's really what I was thinking." She realized, however, that this was unrealistic: "The knight in shining armor—I have *anger* with the movies and the books that just kinda promote this. Every movie that you see that's a romantic comedy, the guy always gets the girl, the girl always gets the guy. [. . .] You know, and it's like this is what girls are seeing and looking at and even in the books and it's so . . . it's a fantasy." Amber said she still would enjoy being a princess, but she knew she could not pin her hopes on a Hollywood fairytale ending. Furthermore, like Mona, she could not think about dating until she had a job, which she needed to "feel better about myself."

In sum, there was considerable variety in the way single women thought about potential relationships. Notice, however, that often their choices were still inflected by a neotraditional male primary breadwinner model. Even if they defined themselves in opposition to that model, it colored their decisions about relationships. For example, the cultural standing of that model kept ReNé from dating because she did not want a potential partner to think that "I'm there for money." Others (such as Ann Lopez) believed that men should at least meet them "halfway" as breadwinners but did not see that as likely, given their marriage prospects. For still others—Mona Childs and Amber Washington—being financially supported was appealing, but they did not want to date when they lacked self-confidence because they were unemployed.

There were some exceptions. For example, Magenta Love, a hairdresser who had a bachelor's degree, owned her own salon, and had taught college courses in cosmetology, wanted to find a "soulmate, love of my life." She did not mention any financial threshold her soulmate would have to pass, nor did she proudly reject taking that into consideration. Single women like her, however, were less common among those we interviewed than those who spoke as if being financially supported was a live option, either as a trap or a haven. To reject the choice of depending on one's partner presupposes that one has that option to reject.

Romantic options for the unemployed single male participants were much more limited. All the single men we interviewed had few financial reserves. To put it plainly, they were broke. By contrast, the unemployed men who had corporate severance packages and substantial savings to help tide them over while they were out of work were all married, further evidence of how marriage in the contemporary United States is shaped by class position.[79]

None of the single men we interviewed said they considered finding a partner who would support them while they worked part time or pursued their avocations. Nor did any of them proudly reject that option, as did several of the women I interviewed, or require that a potential partner contribute at least half the household income, as Ann Lopez expected. To the extent that they mused about their romantic options—which was rare—they did not mention their potential mate's paycheck at all.

To be fair, we did not raise the possibility of finding a partner who could pay the bills in our interviews with the single men, which reflects my own cultural assumption that this was not realistic. In retrospect, I wish we had asked them about this option; their answers would have been revealing. Still, I only asked a few of the women how they would feel about being supported by a partner; it was not a standard question. Most of the women's commentary on this topic was offered spontaneously.

The men who were not already in an exclusive relationship and who discussed dating raised two problems: being expected to pay for expenses incurred on those dates and being rejected because they were unemployed. Chipper Goodman, who was in his mid-twenties, and Bob Roberts, a middle-aged man who was one of my pilot interviewees, both worried about being expected to pay for dates. Both are college educated. When Chipper responded to my question about how being unemployed had affected his social life, he said it meant not going out with his friends. He added that it was also a problem for dating, because dating normally means "you go have something to eat and a few drinks." I do not know whether he could not afford to pick up the entire tab for the food and drinks, or he could not even afford to split the bill. Whichever scenario he imagined, he saw dating as unaffordable without a steady job.

Bob, who was older than Chipper, commented, "Honestly, I've kind of put dating on hold because dating takes money. I'm sure there's plenty of things you could do for free, but even if you want to go to a park, you're going to want to eat afterwards, and you know, as the guy, I kind of feel pressured to pay, so that's $20 that I don't have." Even an inexpensive meal was beyond his means.

No single woman spoke of a cultural expectation that she should pay the entire bill for a date. When I searched for information on current dating etiquette, I found a dating website for single professionals that had surveyed 300,000 of its users about who should pay for the first date. Two-thirds of the men expected to pay for a first date, although just under half of the women thought the man should have to do so. However, even in that 2019 survey, only

5 percent of the women and 2 percent of the men thought that the woman should pick up the whole tab.[80]

Social pressure to pay for the costs of a date are minor, however, compared to the larger problem some of the men faced of being rejected outright by women because they were out of work. Bob spoke about this at length: "I've actually had some women reject me because I'm unemployed. [. . .] It's difficult. It's a big shot to my ego."

An unemployed welder and burner who was another one of my pilot interviewees, Earl Apache Longwolf, bluntly assessed his dim prospects for finding a romantic partner. We were talking about his health, when, seemingly out of nowhere, he said, "One of my [work] partners, him and his wife asked me, 'When you gonna get married?' I said, 'How can I get married? I can't find a job. Ain't no woman want no broke-ass man.'"[81]

Someone might look at Bob or Earl's comments and see them as a way of blaming women for problems in their relationships. In fact, some of the single unemployed men we talked to were dating. Yet, Bob and Earl's belief that no woman would be interested in a "broke-ass man" makes sense, given the continuing weight of the neotraditional male primary breadwinner model. That model also explains why not one of the single women we interviewed said that no man would be interested in her because she was unemployed.

Are my participants' views typical? A 2014 Pew survey of never-married adults found that 46 percent of the men said that "a steady job" would be "very important" to them in choosing a spouse or partner. A potential mate's earnings may be more important for a random sample of American men than this factor was for the unemployed single men in my study, who were too preoccupied with their own poor prospects in the marriage market to be picky about the job status of a potential partner. Still, it is striking that in the same survey 78 percent of the female respondents said that whether a potential spouse or partner holds a steady job would be "very important" for them, far more than the percentage of men for whom that mattered.[82] The Pew survey results reinforce my finding that long-term unemployment makes it harder for both women and men to establish a committed relationship, but more so for heterosexual men, given the still-present gender asymmetry in Americans' breadwinning expectations.

So far, I have focused on the way gender and class affect unemployed single women and men's relationships with a potential partner. What about those who were parents? The single mothers in my study were under far more stress than anyone else, to the point that some contemplated ending their lives. Among unemployed single parents, women face a huge disadvantage because typically their prior earnings had been lower than those of men, and there is little state financial assistance for them.[83]

ReNé McKnight, a single mother whose daughter was fourteen when we first met, described the challenge of having few emotional reserves left for her daughter, given her daily struggles to provide the bare necessities for them. ReNé had moved to California, where her daughter's father was living, in the hope he would become more involved in her daughter's life, but after she arrived, the job she had lined up fell through. She was willing to take any job but could find nothing—a common experience at that time. Because ReNé had voluntarily left her job in Texas and moved to another state, she was ineligible for unemployment compensation. As I explained in chapter 4, she had to provide for her daughter and herself on food stamps and a $492 monthly allotment from Temporary Assistance for Needy Families, an amount so little it did not even cover the rent for the nearly uninhabitable guest house where they were living when I met her.

Two of the questions I asked everybody were, "What makes you feel proud about your life? Or, what would make you feel proud?" I followed up with, "Is there anything you don't feel so proud about?" ReNé was proud of having earned her associate degree, which took a long time because she had to pay for it herself and complete it while working. When we met, she was nearly finished with her online bachelor's degree, another source of pride. When I asked what she was not so proud of, she replied, "Not being able to financially support the way I think I should be supporting." She said, "I had to ask my daughter, like, 'Am I a good mom?'" I asked ReNé to explain how being out of work had affected her relationship with her daughter:

> RENÉ: Being all sad and thinking about what's due, what you don't have, what you need, I'm not showing the love. Like I used to hug her and kiss her and [*say*] "I love you." I haven't been doing that lately.
> CLAUDIA: You haven't?
> RENÉ: No.
> CLAUDIA: Why?
> RENÉ: I guess I'm caught up in all of the worries and stress. So yesterday after school I picked her up. I said, "Can I have a hug?" (*small laugh*) She's like, "Of course." So now I'm trying to actually tell myself to hug her 'cause it doesn't come naturally anymore.

ReNé's financial struggles were so severe that she battled suicidal thoughts. Knowing she is responsible for her daughter kept her going: "Thoughts [*of suicide*] have come, but it's like I've come too far to let go. And my daughter, she's my only child. She's my reason for living."

Another single mother, Miriam Ramos, felt she could not be a good parent without the income she had received from her work as a hairdresser. Miriam had divorced her husband after she discovered he was cheating on her. She had two boys in elementary school when her work hours were cut drastically at her salon. Her van was constantly breaking down, so she started seeing clients at a salon closer to home. However, her new shop was a long distance from her old salon, so only some of her clients followed her to the new location. For several years, her income barely exceeded her expenses. She was overwhelmed with anxiety about money, along with other issues in her life. Two years after we had first met, her older son was about to go into eighth grade. He had some digestive problems, and Miriam wished she could seek treatment for him. Her worries, large and small, made her feel that any small thing would push her over the edge and make her want to end it all:

> What all this is starting to feel like is something as tiny as, like, my nail would have broken at the wrong time, that I was just going to lose it. And that's a scary feeling to have. So, I have children, and the guilt of even thinking something like that when you have children, people saying you're so selfish when mothers do this, and they do that, how selfish of them. Sometimes you're thinking it's the best thing for your kids because you don't want to burden them with you and how you're feeling and everything you're going through because you want so much for them. *(crying)* Yeah. At that moment, that's what I was feeling. I want so much for my kids, and I'm not doing it for them.

Fortunately, Miriam, too, found the strength to go on.

Women's disproportionate responsibility for childcare, which we saw during the pandemic, has meant that there are fewer men taking the major responsibility for raising their children. I interviewed only one male single parent, a divorced father of three boys. Tom Dunn said for many years he had worked nights in any low-level computer operator job he could find, so he could be home with his boys during the day. However, eventually he became an IT recruiter, earning over $70,000 a year until he got into a dispute with his boss and was laid off. The unemployment compensation Tom received for nearly two years was quite a bit less than he used to earn, but it was approximately four times the amount ReNé received in welfare. Thus, he had fewer financial worries than ReNé or Miriam had—at least, until his unemployment compensation ended and firms still were not hiring. Fortunately, by then, his three sons were in their late teens or early twenties, and Tom did not need to support them financially, although he continued to be very involved in their lives.

In sum, neotraditional gender roles disadvantage unemployed single men in the marriage market but help them as single parents, with the reverse for unemployed single women, who face crushing burdens if they are also trying to care for children.

Gender Identities and Work

A qualitative study like this one cannot offer a representative sample. What it can do, however, is reveal the complexities of people's experiences, thoughts, and feelings. One such complexity concerns the way that not working is related to gender identities. The continuing obligation of men to be in the workforce affected the gender identities of some of the unemployed men we interviewed. Interestingly, even those who did not adhere to traditional gender ideologies or practice traditional gendered behaviors still connected work to masculinity.

Earlier I described Jorge Paiz, the construction worker who was proud of helping his wife with cleaning, cooking, and childcare while he was out of work. Jorge struck a different note when I asked whether he ever looked down on himself for not working. Without waiting for Isela to translate, Jorge replied, "Yes. All the time." He continued in Spanish to explain his thoughts at greater length, and Isela translated: "When he sees the neighbors getting home in the afternoon coming from work. Sometimes he's outside with the kids or doing something. And then they see him. When he sees them, like, for example on a Friday, you know they get paid on Friday. And he's thinking, 'Oh, he has his paycheck today.'"

In Jorge's example there is a lot of male gazing, but it is men looking at other men. Jorge is imagining his male neighbors coming home and observing him outside with his children. Meanwhile, he is looking at his male neighbors, wishing that, like them, he was arriving home with a paycheck. He gives this example in response to my question of whether he ever looked down on himself for not working; it seems that, as much as he enjoyed spending more time with his children, his self-esteem is lower because he is not working. Although he does not say so, he may also imagine his male neighbor judging him to be less of a man.

Marcus Walker was clearer in connecting not working to being less of a man. When I met Marcus, he had turned his life around after periods of drug dependence and being in and out of prison for drug dealing. He said, "Since 2005, God has given me a car. He's given me a beautiful wife." His wife had a steady office job as an administrative assistant, while Marcus took a variety of manual labor jobs. Although they did not pay as well as his wife's job, he had contributed financially to their household, and the arrangement seems to have been satisfactory to both. However, for more than a year during the slack labor market following the Great Recession, he had not been able to find any work. One problem was his prior felony conviction: as soon as he entered that information in an online job application, the computer ended his application. When I asked him in the first interview about the meaning or importance of work for him, he responded, "My wife would know she got a helpmate. (*laughs*) Helping bring in some cash to take care of some of these bills. That would be the most peacefulest thing. Then being able to take her out to dinner or—we don't have the money like this. So now I have to cook at home in order—to make it romantically at home in order to keep some spice in our life, you know what I mean? Instead of being able to take her to a restaurant or take her to the movies." Marcus agreed with the statement "Work is central to my identity" because "I need work in order to have money, in order to be able to pay bills, in order to be able to be the man that I'm supposed to be." For Marcus, being "the man that I'm supposed to be" would mean contributing some income to the household to help pay the bills, even if he was not the primary breadwinner.

Jake Taylor also saw being unemployed as a potential threat to his masculinity. Jake was a twenty-two-year-old Air Force veteran who struggled to find work after he completed his tours in Afghanistan and Iraq and returned to the United States. Jake was engaged, and he said, "If my fiancée got pregnant or something, and it happened like that to where I had to take care of both of them, then I would feel pretty emasculated about it." Jake also recounted the time he almost left his great-aunt's home where he and his dad were living because she said to him, "'Men have work, and you can't even support yourself.'" Jake was incensed, seeing her remark as an insult to his manhood: "She basically told me the one thing anybody should not ever tell me [*which*] is that I'm not a man." Interestingly, Jake eventually studied to become a nurse—a career that he worried his working-class father would denigrate ("I'm surprised he didn't call me a wuss when I told him I was going to do nursing"). Apparently, Jake had no need to enact traditional gender roles entirely—except when it came to providing economically for a family.

Gay men could also connect being a provider to masculinity. Terrance West told me, "I feel less of a person and less of a man because I'm not working." He continued, "Right now I don't really feel very important to anything or anyone because of the fact I feel like I'm not contributing. It emasculates you." Note he said he felt both "less of a person" and "less of a man." Those are different ways of feeling diminished.

The four men who explicitly (Jake, Marcus, and Terrance) or implicitly (Jorge) felt diminished as men while unemployed did not have narrow constructs of masculinity. Terrance is gay; when we first met, he had a long, man-icured nail on his index finger. Marcus did not mind earning less than his wife; he just wanted to contribute some income to the household. Jake chose a career in nursing, which is a stereotypically feminine occupation. Jorge en-joyed expanding his role as father and husband beyond being an income pro-vider. Yet, however flexible their notions of masculinity, their gendered self-understandings could not easily accommodate being out of work.

Of the twenty-eight unemployed men we interviewed, only these four men indicated that not working was a challenge to their masculinity; it was not a typical comment.[84] However, that is four more than the number of women who suggested that not working was a challenge to their identity as women.

None of the women said or implied that their gender identity was affected by their unemployment. Instead, they talked about their diminished self-esteem. We saw that, for example, in Mona Child's statement: "I've always been wrapped up with how I feel about myself based upon my job." Even among the women who said that working either was, or had been, central to their identity, none added Terrance's phrase and said she felt like less of a woman because she was not working. At present, US cultural models of wom-anhood are still not as closely associated with the duty to provide financially for the household as are cultural models of manhood. One small benefit of women's typically lower wages and greater childcare burdens is that unem-ployment is less destabilizing to their gender identity and committed relationships—although it is harmful in all the other ways that affect women and men alike, as I explain in the rest of this book.

The Gendering of Work and Breadwinning in the Future

As we have seen, adults in the United States today do not face a choice be-tween two options—either a "traditional" or an "equal" division of labor in the household. Instead, there have been many shifts over time in the division of household labor. On family farms until the mid-nineteenth century, every member helped support the family, although often at different tasks. After the Industrial Revolution, there arose a division of spheres among native-born whites, with married men more likely to leave the home to earn an income while women's earnings were limited to informal jobs they could do at home. Some of these men opposed their wife working outside the home. In the mid- to late twentieth century, many married women worked outside the home, although often earning less than their husbands and not being acknowledged as providing income essential for the household. At the time of my study, in the second decade of the twenty-first century, married women commonly work outside the home, and among my participants their earnings were usually seen by their partner as important contributions to the household. Some of the married men I spoke with were unhappy when their wife was unable to contribute financially. Still, women continue to have greater childcare, eldercare, and housework responsibilities and a lesser obligation to work full time. This is a neotraditional dual-earner breadwinning model. With this history in mind, we can imagine a variety of possible future arrangements.

In the final chapter, I will discuss the implications of my research for work policies and the future of work. The experiences and self-understandings of the men and women who participated in this research suggest that both men and women want more flexibility. Many men want to share breadwinning responsibilities and want more time with their family or for their leisure activities. Many women, too, want options that will allow them to combine engaging in paid work, with time for self-care, care for others, and other interests.

These desires of many of my participants fit what the feminist scholar Nancy Fraser calls a "universal caregiver model." She critiques the "universal-breadwinner model"—one in which women are encouraged and institutionally supported to work full time—because it gives too little attention and respect to care work. Instead, she proposes a model in which both men and women share breadwinning and caregiving, and jobs are designed to better accommodate that combination.[85]

Before the pandemic, some scholars proposed that if companies permitted workers to have more flexible schedules and to work from home, that could help both women and men combine work responsibilities with family care. Indeed, those provisions have allowed more parents of young children to work when that would have been difficult otherwise. However, pre-pandemic research in Europe and the United States found that flexible work schedules and working from home did not have the same outcomes for women and men. Although gender ideologies, as well as an organization's own values and policies, make a difference, in general women's continuing greater childcare obligations have meant that either women were using flexible work time to increase their childcare responsibilities or that is what their employers expected them to do. Although the mothers were able to continue working along with caring for young children, their work was sometimes taken less seriously by their employers than that of fathers who asked to work from home or on a flexible schedule.[86] Flexible schedules and remote work need to be combined with a universal caregiving model.

As I discuss in the last chapter, a different shift is underway toward more nonstandard employment and self-employment for men and women alike—patterns that were more typical of US women's work a century ago. Over time, it will be interesting to see whether these postindustrial changes lead to a more sustainable and equitable division of childcare and income-earning responsibilities in heterosexual couples and in what counts as breadwinning, including opportunities for both men and women to take breaks from working. Same-sex couples may also provide new examples for the future.

Still, work is not just an onerous responsibility or a way to earn money. Many of those with whom we spoke, both women and men, said at least one of their jobs had been an important source of meaning or was "fun." In the next chapter I present what mattered to them in a specific occupation or job, as opposed to how they felt about working in general.

CHAPTER 6

Good-Enough Occupations and "Fun" Jobs

The work meanings described in the preceding chapters—working driven by a productivist work ethic, working to realize the American dream of prosperity or at least middle-class consumption, working for self-sufficiency, and the gendering of work—are about abstract labor; that is, they are about *working*, as if one's particular job does not matter. But, of course, it does matter. Work always occurs in specific occupations, with typical tasks, in particular physical environments, and with agreeable or disagreeable individuals. The meaning of work for my participants was not just about what it meant to work at something somewhere; it was also about the meaning that their specific jobs had for them. Unfortunately, there is a common assumption in the United States that some people want to work for a living and others do not, without recognizing that specific past work experiences and future opportunities shape feelings about working and not working, as well as approaches to choosing a job.[1]

It took me a long time to fully appreciate that my participants' experiences in the jobs they held in the past shaped the meanings of working and unemployment for them as much as or more than their attitudes about work considered abstractly. That seems obvious now, but it was not always so. When I look back at my interview guide, I realize that I, like many other commentators, treated work as an abstraction when I asked, "What is the meaning or importance of work for you?" or asked for reactions to this statement, "Work is central to my identity." Fortunately, those questions were only a small part of the interviews. I obtained more specific information when they shared what they had liked or disliked in previous jobs and as they discussed what kind of job they wanted next. Even their responses to my abstract questions about the meaning or importance of work were often colored by their specific job experiences.

In my defense and in defense of others who have written about work meanings abstractly, that is a dominant way of talking about work meanings in this society, so it is an easy habit to fall into. Alexis de Tocqueville proposes that Americans tend to reduce work to an exchange of labor for money, a commonality that makes all jobs similar.[2] Karl Marx states that economists' treatment of labor as an abstraction is a product of societies with many different forms of labor, none of which is dominant.[3] Both recognize that treating all labor as essentially alike is an odd social construct.

That raises the question: In addition to a paycheck, what do job seekers look for or appreciate in a job?

Some organizational researchers have written about a "meaningful job" as the ideal. According to one definition, that means believing that one's work "contributes to one's life purpose, perceiving one's work as contributing to personal growth and one's understanding of the world, and believing that one's work serves a greater purpose."[4] Some of my participants had held jobs that were meaningful for them in those lofty ways. However, not everyone seeks a job that meets those high-minded goals, and even fewer succeed in finding such positions. What I found is that most of my participants did not need to find their job deeply meaningful to like it. Using a common American term, many said one or more of their jobs had been "fun."

Finding "Fun" on the Job

The word "fun" came up over and over in my participants' descriptions of some of their former jobs. Here are examples from among the many such comments I heard:

> CELESTE RUE: [*On bringing data files into an Excel spreadsheet as an administrative assistant*] That was just fun, and I could sit there at my desk all day and do that.
>
> CHIPPER GOODMAN: I got a seasonal job at UPS as a truck driver down the airport runway. It was a temporary job, though, just Christmas help, but that was probably one of my most fun jobs I ever had.

SAM LENNON: I really liked working in that dress place. That was fun.

ELIZABETH MONTGOMERY: [*On being a buyer for a department store chain*] So that was really, really fun.

ROBERT MILNER: [*On the cosmetics industry, where he was a supply chain strategist*] I'd love to stay in the cosmetic industry. It's a fun industry.

MONA CHILDS: [*On marketing for a retirement community*] He hired me 'cause he knew that I was really good in sales [. . .] in the fifteen months he was the manager he had never been able to get it above the red, but within a five-month period, we had it completely filled. It was fun working with him.

TOM DUNN: [*On being an IT recruiter and consultant*] It was really fun. It was really fun. [. . .] It was just a thrill. It was really a thrill.

TONY DELUCA: [*On heading up the international HR function for a large company*] It was a lot of fun. It was something I'd always wanted to do.

LINDA MCDANIEL: [*On being an executive assistant for a nonprofit*] It was a lot of hard work, but it was fun.

EMILY QUINN: [*On being the assistant to the top executive in a law firm*] That was fun, 'cause I was in that position. I always loved working at the top because you were where all the decisions were made and where everything happened first. I loved that.

As these examples illustrate, any manner of work or workplaces can be fun. About 30 percent of my participants (nineteen of the sixty-four) said that one or more of their jobs had been fun or that they had had fun on a job.

Why "fun" of all words? I would guess most of us think of fun as associated with leisure activities, not paid work.[5] When I searched "fun activities" online I found articles recommending board games, wine tastings, dance classes, and going to the park ("Swing on the swings like when you were a kid").[6] Bringing data files into an Excel spreadsheet and driving a truck at the airport were not on the list.

The Dutch cultural historian and comparative linguist Johan Huizinga claims, "No other modern language known to me has the exact equivalent of the English 'fun.'"[7] Yet, given that no one is fluent in all seven thousand or so languages of the world, he may have missed some that do have this concept. A professor of Spanish whom I consulted said that *divertido* is an acceptable translation of "fun" in Spanish, although she did not think it would be common for Spanish speakers in the South American country she came from to describe a job as *divertido*.[8]

Robert Myers offers a short, clever analysis of the importance of fun in the United States. In the parodic tradition of Horace Miner's "Body Ritual among the Nacirema," he describes the striking keyword in Nacirema culture "nuf": "When someone departs, whether for a casual outing or for a more important activity, they say 'Have nuf!' Upon a person's return, he or she will be asked, 'Did you have nuf?' They write songs about nuf, use it liberally in advertising, and even seem to make a religion of it."[9] Almost anyone who has taken an introduction to sociocultural anthropology course in the United States knows that the "Nacirema" are Americans, and, using the same estrangement-producing device of spelling words backward, "nuf" is, of course, fun.

To the limited extent that the construct of fun has been described by ethnographers of the United States, it is usually posed as an alternative to work. For example, an ethnography of student culture at Rutgers University in the late 1970s describes students' desire to balance doing well in their classes with having fun socializing. The students compartmentalize these pursuits: their academic studies are work, and nonacademic social interaction is fun.[10] The famous anthropologist Clyde Kluckhohn observed in a 1949 publication that "'having a good time is an important part of life'" in the United States, especially in youth culture, but "this emphasis is restrained or even guilt-producing by the Puritan tradition of 'work for work's sake.'"[11] That Americans would have fun at work does not fit these descriptions of American culture. Intriguingly, Myers suggests there may be a new blurring of the boundaries between work and play in the United States. Yet, although he talks about working hard at play, he does not give examples of Americans having fun at work, except that "occasionally scientists will describe their work as nuf."[12]

The comments I quoted from my participants about having fun on the job may seem an oddly rosy image of work. Did my participants' long-term unemployment lead them to see their former jobs through a nostalgic, hazy lens?

Perhaps, but the often-positive tone of my participants' descriptions jibes with findings drawn from surveys of working Americans—although survey responses depend on whether you are looking at work "engagement" or "satisfaction." Engagement levels tend to fall below job satisfaction levels, producing conflicting headlines like "Why So Many Americans Hate Their Jobs" and "85% of American Workers Are Happy with Their Jobs, National Survey Shows."[13]

The low engagement/high satisfaction paradox is understandable when we see how these constructs are measured. One common measure of engagement is a Gallup workplace survey that asks how strongly employees agree or disagree with twelve statements such as the following: "At work, I have the opportunity to do what I do best every day"; "In the last seven days, I have received recognition or praise for doing good work"; "The mission or purpose of my company makes me feel my job is important"; "My associates or fellow employees are committed to doing quality work"; and "I have a best friend at work." The Gallup survey has the laudable goal of giving managers advice on how to improve their workplace culture. As a result, its engagement questions set a high bar: "At work, I have the opportunity to do what I do best *every day*"; "My associates or fellow employees (*all?*) are committed to doing quality work," and "I have a *best* friend at work." No wonder only approximately one-third of the thousands of US workers polled in recent years agreed that most of those superlatives applied to their job. Half or more of respondents were neither highly engaged nor in the lowest category of the "actively disengaged." They did not hate their jobs; instead, they had a middling level of engagement.[14] It is inaccurate to construe these figures as evidence of a predominantly disengaged and unhappy workforce, a mistake often made by commentators when the annual Gallup engagement survey results are published.

By contrast, another annual Gallup national survey asks, "How satisfied or dissatisfied are you with your job? Would you say you are completely satisfied, somewhat satisfied, somewhat dissatisfied or completely dissatisfied with your job?" Between 2012 and 2022, on average only 11 percent of US respondents were somewhat or completely dissatisfied. Similarly, in response to a different survey that asked, "Aside from the money it pays you, does your job provide you with great personal satisfaction, moderate personal satisfaction, very little personal satisfaction, or no personal satisfaction at all?" just 12 percent of a national sample said their jobs provided little or no personal satisfaction.[15] Most Americans like their jobs, on the whole.

Eleven or 12 percent of US workers who are dissatisfied is still a lot of people: that means between seventeen and nineteen million workers do not like their jobs. Some of my participants could have been among them because they did not like every job they had held. Some of the disagreeable conditions they described ranged from the unpleasant (boring work, not enough to do, lack of recognition for their contributions) to the truly dreadful (harassment from coworkers or bosses, grueling tasks that left them physically injured or created unbearable stress, morally repugnant tasks such as selling goods or services they felt their clients did not need or discovering that their organization was defrauding its customers). Those whose previous jobs included any of those conditions either left voluntarily or were happy to have been laid off because it forced them to look for something better.

My participants' stories of bad jobs, some of which I recount later in the chapter, show that they were not indiscriminately nostalgic about their previous employment. They had enjoyed some jobs but disliked others, or they had enjoyed some features of their past jobs but not other aspects. Still, they maintained an overall level of satisfaction with their previous jobs in line with national statistics: most had held one or more jobs that provided nonfinancial rewards that made the jobs more satisfying than not.

What I find intriguing is not just American workers' positive views of their jobs but also that so many use a word usually associated with play and leisure to talk about their work. Who used the word "fun," and who did not? Are there different types of fun on the job? Did my participants use "fun" to describe all the nonfinancial rewards they gained from their jobs or only some of those? "Fun" should always be imagined in quotation marks in the rest of this discussion.

Some of my participants never described their jobs as fun, but it was not because they disliked those jobs. Among my participants, there were two groups who never (or almost never) said their jobs were fun: first-generation immigrants and those with an occupational passion.

As I explained in the preface, my research assistant Claudia Castañeda interviewed ten unemployed or underemployed first-generation immigrants from Latin America. Among those I interviewed, there were an additional six first-generation immigrants from Latin America, southeast Asia, and Europe.[16] Her interviews were conducted in Spanish. One of mine was in Spanish and another in Lao (both with the help of interpreters); the rest were conducted in English. With one possible exception, none of those sixteen immigrants used fun or a word that was translated as fun to talk about their jobs, even though several had greatly enjoyed their work.[17] Instead, they said, for example, "I liked everything about it, I enjoyed working with people" (Monserrat León on waitressing); "That job made me happy. I liked it a lot" (Isabel Navarro on her first secretarial/clerical job at a health maintenance organization); "So you get yourself deeper into work, and you feel fulfilled by work" (Abel Jimenez on his produce business). If my colleague is right, those with Spanish as a first language may not be in the habit of referring to a job as fun.

Nor did all my American-born participants characterize their jobs or anything else they did as fun. Again, it was not for want of enjoyable activities in their life. One anthropologist reader of this manuscript who grew up in the metropolitan New York City area said fun is not a word she uses readily; she wondered whether there were regional differences in its usage.

I do not have enough information about possible regional differences to verify her impression that New Yorkers are disinclined to use the word fun, but I did notice differences among my participants depending on their approach to finding an occupation.[18] The differing mindsets with which job seekers set about entering an occupation and finding a job help explain what they liked or disliked about their jobs when they were working, what type of enjoyment (if any) they found in their jobs, and how this affected their reactions to being unemployed.

It is important to keep in mind that "work" can refer to one's occupation or one's job. Attitudes about occupations (the type of work one does) differ from attitudes about specific jobs in an occupation. It is possible to feel drawn to an occupation but to dislike a job in that field or to feel indifferent about one's occupation but to really enjoy one's job. I speak of "entering" an occupation rather than "choosing" one; as we see shortly, some of my participants did not feel they had much choice.

Entering an Occupation

In their classic analysis of American culture, *Habits of the Heart*, Robert Bellah and his coauthors propose that Americans can think about work as (just) a job, as a career, or as a calling. These categories were fruitfully operationalized and investigated by the psychologist Amy Wrzesniewski.[19] To these three culturally salient categories, I add a fourth that has been less recognized but may be the most common approach: a "good-enough occupation."

To get an intuitive feel for the differences among these, consider the outlook of students graduating from high school or college and getting ready to enter the job market. Growing up, they may have noticed conflicting messages about what should matter to them in looking for work.

One widespread ideology proclaims that work should be more than a paycheck: it should be an opportunity to use your unique talents in personally meaningful and satisfying ways. Graduating seniors are routinely exhorted to "follow your passion." From this perspective, finding the right occupation is like finding your life partner. Somewhere out there is the perfect match, and you should no more settle for an occupation you do not love than marry someone you do not love.

"Follow your passion" is commonly intoned at graduations because speakers are trying to counter another common cultural model: the graduate should enter a lucrative or high-status career, one with opportunities for advancement in pay and positions. This careerist ambition is well represented in popular culture and in advice from parents, peers, and many others.

However, not everyone has the option of deciding between a fulfilling career and one that is lucrative. For millennia, humans did not "choose an occupation." Instead, the work they did was largely determined by their age, gender, and setting. In the United States today, many people do not start their occupational search by thinking, "Hmm, do I want a high-paying career, or do I care more about personal fulfillment? Could I have both?" Many Americans—those who cannot afford higher education, job seekers with considerable debt, those with family responsibilities, and undocumented immigrants—are more constrained in their job searches. Occupational possibilities are also restricted for middle-aged and older job seekers, like many of the unemployed workers in my project, who have well-honed skills in one field and are unlikely to be hired to do anything else at their age. For those looking for work in that situation, there are other American discourses. Such job seekers may receive many clichés by way of advice: "All work is dignified." "Being an adult is learning to compromise." "Life doesn't always give you what you want." "Shoulder your responsibilities and earn a living—you can pursue your avocations on the side." As some of my participants put it, "Work is work"—it does not matter what you do, so choose any occupation in which you can find a paying job.

Suppose, however, that the graduating students do not have any occupational passions and do not care about advancing in a career. They want to make enough money to have a good life, but they do not want to hate their work either. They consider what marketable skills they have and what they might enjoy doing. If they cannot find a job that meets their criteria or if their first jobs are unsatisfying, they try another field until they fall into a good-enough occupation.

Because I studied people who had been employed and then lost their jobs, my participants were not looking for work for the first time. Nonetheless, I noticed examples of each of these four approaches in the ways they looked for work—as a job, a good-enough occupation, a career, or a calling—and in the type of satisfactions they found from their jobs.

Work-Is-Work

Ginger Thi's parents stopped supporting her in her mid-teen years. She had to make a living as best she could, and she became a secretary. When I asked the meaning of work for her, she began by questioning my implicit equation of "work" with paid work. Instead, she considered work to be "doing things in life." There were many things she liked to do, including reading, learning about current events, cooking, gardening, doing creative projects, and communicating with friends through social media. However, she told me, "If you're talking about going to a job from 8:30 in the morning 'til 5:00 in the afternoon, that's doing death for nine and a half hours so I can get money so I can live." However, that did not mean she resigned herself to long, dull hours. She added, "But within that death I'll find something creative and fun for me to do and believe me, I'll make it an enjoyable day."

For Ginger paid work is "doing death for nine and a half hours so I can get money so I can live." That is a memorable way of expressing what Bellah, Wrzesniewski, and their colleagues call a "Job" approach to work. They describe this approach as follows: "People who have Jobs are only interested in the material benefits from work and do not seek or receive any other type of reward from it."[20] The problem with this definition is that although those like Ginger may not *seek* any nonfinancial rewards from the work they do, they can still *receive*, or *create*, such rewards at their job. Ginger can "find something creative and fun for me to do" at her office and "make it an enjoyable day."

I prefer the term "work-is-work" to label this approach, because that is a phrase several of my participants used. When I asked Carl Mathews, an unemployed security guard, whether work was central to his identity, he replied, "Not necessarily. Work is work. It's a source of income. It's not my life, it doesn't define me." A *work-is-work approach* holds that one should not expect work to have a meaning beyond providing an income. Thus, it does not matter what occupation or job one chooses, so long as one is qualified for it and the pay is sufficient.[21]

Carl's statement "work is work" considers but dismisses the view that one's job should be meaningful. Some of my participants were instead resigned to a work-is-work approach as their only option because they could not obtain more fulfilling jobs. La dama de abril had been a successful esthetician in Venezuela with celebrity clients before she came to the United States in her early thirties to help her sister, who had just had a baby. As is common, she came legally on a tourist visa and then stayed. When she spoke with my research assistant, Claudia C., La dama de abril had not yet regularized her status. (A year later, she finally succeeded.) Her training and license from Venezuela were not accepted in the United States, and without a green card, she could not obtain any job in the beauty industry. Nor could she pursue her other passion of being an actress, which she had done in Venezuela. She had to fall back on the limited occupations open to immigrant women without papers in the United States: she was a nanny and then began a housecleaning business.[22] She did not particularly like that work or the way she was treated in those jobs, but she was able to earn a living for nearly twenty years until the Great Recession forced her clients to let her go. When Claudia C. interviewed her, she was in her early fifties and despondent: "I have been doing this for years, and I feel frustrated because I have been doing something for years that I don't like." La dama de abril blamed herself for listening to the standard advice she had heard from other immigrants: "What they taught me, 'Make credit, use cards, and what's important is having job. It doesn't matter that you don't like it.' That is the first thing that people you meet here tell you. And it turns out it's not like that." She felt that to work as a housecleaner is "to enslave myself." Claudia C. asked how she would feel if she were an esthetician. La dama replied, "Then it wouldn't be a job. Then it would be something that you are doing because you like it." For La dama de abril, a work-is-work approach was a fallback option. She had an occupational passion, but she was not able to obtain a job doing it in the United States.

In another version of a work-is-work approach, some of my participants never entertained the notion that they could choose the kind of work they did. Their assumptions were so out of sync with the way Claudia C. and I thought about finding an occupation that they led to exchanges that were almost comically misaligned. One such example was Claudia C.'s conversation with Luis Segura, who had grown up on a farm in Michoacán, Mexico. After he came to the United States in his teens, he worked as a gardener for more than thirty years. The mismatch between their ideas about entering an occupation emerged when Claudia asked Luis, "What would have been your ideal job?"

> LUIS: Cutting grass, trees, all that, that's what I know how to do. My
>   whole life.
> CLAUDIA C.: And what did you do in Mexico?
> LUIS: In Mexico, in the field, cultivating corn and all that, beans,
>   garbanzo.
> CLAUDIA C.: You've always liked it.
> LUIS: Well, there was nothing else to work in; I was living on a farm.

Claudia C. assumed that if Luis had been working on the land his whole life, then he must like doing that. She and I began with the assumption that one *chooses* an occupation the same way one might choose a favorite leisure pursuit. For Luis, however, you do not become a farmer because you like farming: it is just what you do if you live on a farm. Her very question, "What would have been your ideal job?" was at odds with the way Luis thought about entering an occupation.

Still, Luis was the only immigrant who used fun to talk about work, although his comment is ambiguous. In a later part of her interview, Claudia C. began asking in Spanish, "What is 'work' to you? What part of your life is—there are people who view work as . . ." At that point Luis interrupted to say, *diversión* (fun). It is not clear whether he meant whether working the land is fun for him, or that is how some other people view it, but in either case, he imagined that work could be fun.

Carl Mathews, the security guard who said, "Work is work," could find fun on the job as well. He described a custodial job at the airport when he was young where the workers whiled away time with cards, dice, and dominoes: "I had so much fun because we did so much stuff that we wasn't supposed to do, you know what I'm saying? It was like fun going to work." Carl did not care about choosing an occupation that was personally meaningful, but he could still have fun on the job. In fact, it was because he did not view the job as relevant to his identity that he felt free to do other things to ensure that it was "fun going to work."[23]

Ginger and Carl's ways of making their workday enjoyable are examples of one type of fun on the job, a type we could call having fun *at work,* rather than having fun *from work.* Ethnographers of work have observed creative examples of workers making fun at work to cope with boring jobs, such as routine factory work. They have described workers playing games, pulling pranks, singing to themselves, or daydreaming. One sociological observer who was also a full-time worker in a beer-bottling factory in the late 1970s and early 1980s observed a bored worker making a hand sculpture by filling a work glove with glue from his glue gun, and another coworker listening to a transistor radio hidden under his shirt against company rules.[24]

These subversive forms of workplace fun are far from the management fad of creating a "fun culture" at work. The premise behind fun culture is simple: if managers introduce opportunities for play, then employees will be happier, and if employees are happier, they will be more productive.[25] How do managers make work fun? In one survey of HR managers, some of the frequently listed fun activities were recognition of birthdays and hiring anniversaries, social events like picnics and parties (Halloween parties were popular), awards banquets, games, jokes in emails and company newsletters, and friendly competitions (like, attendance and sales contests).[26] In the sardonically titled special journal issue, *Are We Having Fun Yet?* the European management theorists Bolton and Houlihan question the motives behind this North American import of "packaged fun," which researchers have characterized as ways to distract "attention from the boring work by injecting 'non-work' themes into the labour process" for workers whose jobs are routinized and highly controlled. At the other end of the pay scale, packaged fun can be a tool to recruit educated workers accustomed to the wraparound services and enjoyable activities on college campuses.[27] Silicon Valley offices are known (or were known before the rise of teleworking and cost-cutting measures) for their ping-pong tables and fitness rooms so workers "can have their break in the office and not be that far away from their desk."[28]

Few of my participants said management-led amusements had made their job enjoyable. Terrance West cited company picnics and barbeques as one of the reasons he had liked working as a shipping and receiving clerk for "H Company," a snack manufacturer, but he was an outlier. No one else brought up parties and other such social events as a factor in their work enjoyment; in fact, Anastasia Tang, an HR manager, resented compulsory after-hours office social events because they intruded on her family time. She was fired after she declined to attend a company picnic and the annual company awards dinner. Anastasia's story illustrates the way such compulsory fun can become exclusionary.[29]

Bolton and Houlihan distinguish management-led "packaged fun" from the "organic" ways in which workers have fun at work.[30] As we saw with Ginger Thi and Carl Mathews, and as we see in other examples later, organic fun at work is created by the workers.

Job seekers with a work-is-work approach are not very fussy about their next job; this attitude helps them land another position more quickly than those who have ambitions to advance in their career or who try to follow their passions. However, the downside of a work-is-work approach, as some of my participants saw it, is that they will take jobs for which they are not well suited, leading them to later quit or be fired.

Katarina Spelling adopted a work-is-work approach shortly after she married. Her husband had $98,000 in student debt, and Katarina added to that total by getting a master's degree in public administration. She and her husband decided she should put aside her dream of trying to make a living as a singer. It was not working out, and they needed to focus on making money to pay off their loans. She saw the wisdom of that approach, recounting her conversations with her husband about it: "He's helped me to see it. Work is work, and you are who you are, no matter (*small laugh*) where you work. You know, it doesn't change. If you are a musician, you don't stop being a musician if you work in accounting, or if you're a painter or whatever it is, you can still be that person." In other words, your occupation can be disconnected from the pursuits central to your identity. Katarina resolutely put aside her own preferences and applied for various office jobs, even though in her previous office jobs she had felt like "I was a flower in a closet." When I first met Katarina, her work-is-work approach had led her to apply for a data analysis position. Although she got to the third round of interviews for that position, she wondered whether she could last in a job like that, which did not interest her at all: "Do I really want this job? And—I don't know. I don't know if I can answer that, because then I look at other job descriptions and I'm like, 'Oh, I'd love to do that. I feel the passion for it,' whereas this would be a job to pay the bills. So, hopefully I don't get burned out in six months and hate life."

Katarina never had the chance to find out whether this job would make her "hate life" because they offered the position to someone else. As I describe shortly, her journey took her from a work-is-work approach to a good-enough occupation.

I term "work-is-work" and the other three ways of finding an occupation as *approaches*, rather than orientations. *Orientation* may suggest a permanent disposition,[31] but with some of my participants, the approach they took to finding an occupation changed depending on their opportunities and experiences.

For example, when I first met Jake Taylor, he was twenty-two and had been discharged from the Air Force with wounds that kept him from reenlisting. I asked him what kind of work he wanted to do, and he responded that he had acquired hydraulic expertise in the Air Force, so he figured he should start by looking for jobs in that field even though he did not particularly like it. I really enjoy my work, so it was hard for me to hear someone who was just starting out in life making plans to enter an occupation that he did not like. Instead of moving on in the interview, I asked, "Is there something else that would excite you more?" Jake replied, "I never really figured that out. I don't know. I'd have to think about that question more." He added, "I was never super excited about doing anything that was work. Work is work."

Initially I thought that Jake was following the example set by his father, a mechanic who did not like his job, but Jake's work attitudes had a more complicated explanation. Another part of the reason he had a hard time getting excited about work is that the civilian jobs he had found did not seem worthwhile compared to being in the military, where he had volunteered for search-and-rescue missions and became the leader of his squad. He explained, "After the military I would go job to job, and I was depressed about not being in the military anymore 'cause I really liked it. So just kinda, like, after going from being something important to something that to me was meaningless, I don't know, it's hard to take jobs seriously like that." He added that his civilian jobs were not ones "I was proud to be doing or anything."

In one of Jake's jobs, he had been a "lumper," unloading delivery trucks at warehouses. He did not enjoy it: "They used to call us 'lumpers' because every time we'd be pulling a cart with about 600 pounds worth of merchandise on it, and the wheels would be all gunked up with all kinds of dirt and grime and stuff. So, you're basically pulling this thing and the wheels are barely turning. And, when you're pulling it from behind you [. . .] and the cart will sometimes hit the back of your Achilles and you'd get a big old welt or lump. So, they called us lumpers, and it hurt like a son of a bitch." Jake knew that a college degree would give him more options, but he could not afford it.

When I talked to Jake again two years later, he was completely transformed. He had learned that the GI Bill would pay for his college tuition and give him a living stipend. He was studying to be a nurse, which was the specialty he had initially wanted to pursue in the military instead of hydraulics and which required science courses that he enjoyed. He was excited about this future career: "I'll be able to provide for my family, and I'll be helping others. So, when it comes to how I feel about it, it's all around the perfect job for me." Jake wanted to be a pediatric nurse because he loves children. When he learned he could afford college, Jake went from a disengaged work-is-work approach to being excited to prepare for "the perfect job for me."

In sum, my participants acted on a work-is-work approach to choosing a line of work for a variety of reasons and accompanied by a variety of feelings, including unquestioning acceptance, pragmatic accommodation, contemptuous dismissal, and sad resignation. In every case, however, their attitudes about work were more complex than the minimal meanings suggested by saying that they see work as "just a job."[32]

The Good-Enough Occupation

Unlike those with a work-is-work approach, most of my participants were at least somewhat selective in choosing an occupation. That does not mean that all had an occupational passion or a definite career plan. Instead, they looked for a job that they thought would be a reasonable fit for their talents, skills, values, and interests. This middle ground between the follow-your-passion and work-is-work extremes is a *good-enough-occupation approach.*

Luis Segura, the gardener who grew up on a farm in Mexico, participated in the interviews with another Mexican immigrant Feliciano Salas. Both were working as day laborers while they waited for the economy to recover so they could return to steady jobs. Feliciano grew up in a more urban environment than Luis, in Ciudad Guzmán in the state of Jalisco, which exposed him to a greater variety of jobs than Luis had had the opportunity to pursue. When Feliciano was young, he worked in a hardware store, but he grew to dislike being cooped up indoors. He decided, "I wanted any job other than being closed in." Therefore, when he came to the United States, he looked for work in construction and became a roofer. For him, work was still primarily a way to earn money, but he wanted it to be enjoyable too. That was typical of those who took a good-enough occupation approach.

Natalie Harper, a grant writer, exemplifies the good-enough-occupation approach. Her work history was one she described as "stumbling along" instead of a linear career. After she obtained a master's degree in English, she sold college textbooks for a while, but that job did not leave her enough time with the man with whom she had fallen in love. She parlayed her sales experience into a job recruiting members for a philanthropic organization. When her husband moved to a college town, she had to find a different job if they wanted to stay together. Natalie described how she ended up in grant writing: "I said, 'What can I do?' Well, I was an English major. I know how to write. I'm comfortable with the academic world." Drawing on her skills as a writer, her undergraduate and graduate school jobs working for college administrators, and her previous job in philanthropy, Natalie moved into grant writing for the local college. As she put it, "So I kind of stumble along and find something." At that time, she and her husband were living on the East Coast; when he took a job in California, she found a temporary position as a grant writer and then was offered three full-time jobs: two in higher education and one obtaining funding for children's programs for the county. She chose the county job as most aligned with her values because it let her "better the community" by helping at-risk children. Natalie is proud of her success at that job ("we brought in over forty million dollars to various projects"), the reputation she developed as a grant expert, and the staff development programs she initiated. Yet, despite her pride in the good she was able to do at her jobs and the recognition she had received, when I asked her whether work was central to her identity, she replied, "No, it's just that—I mean I do a good job. I'm professional. I leave it at the end of the day." Nor did she care about her job title. After her bout of unemployment, she took a lower position at a state school so she could become vested in the state pension plan. She said, "I don't care what you call me, as long as you pay me."

Those with a good-enough-occupation approach weathered their job search fairly well. Unlike those with an occupational passion, these job seekers considered other occupations if they could not find work in the field of their last job. For example, one man had been a successful general contractor, but during the Great Recession there was no money for construction, so he returned to bartending, which he had done earlier in his life. Unlike those who wanted to move up in a career, these job seekers were willing to take a lower-level position if necessary, like the grant writer Natalie Harper, who did not care about her job title. Still, unlike those with a work-is-work approach, they had enjoyed their jobs and looked forward to working again, both for the paycheck and for the nonfinancial rewards.

Katarina Spelling eventually fell into a good-enough occupation. At the end of our initial interview, she mentioned in an offhand way that later that day she was going to start a part-time job as an assistant in an accounting firm. She did not have high expectations for it. As an undergraduate she had taken a job as a bank teller and frankly admitted, "I was a terrible teller." She did not think she was good at detailed work like that. Still, she decided that a part-time job was better than nothing, so she planned to work there while she continued to apply for full-time jobs.

To Katarina's surprise, she liked working at that accounting office. When I spoke with her again two years later, she had a toddler and was still working there. They let her do some work from home and some at the office, which was perfect for her as a new mother, and she had learned how to make data entry enjoyable by thinking of it as like playing a computer game: "I really like puzzles and Tetris, so when I'm at the accounting firm, for example, I just feel like that's what I'm doing. I'm playing solitaire, which is one of my favorite games. I just feel like that's what I'm doing all day."

There were many other things Katarina found she liked about working at that accounting firm. For one, she appreciated getting out of the house and socializing with adults. The day before our follow-up interview, she had spent six hours at the office where she chatted with her coworkers and joked with one of her bosses. Even though she is Republican and they are Democrats, they got along well. Katarina discovered that that job provided satisfactions she did not get as a stay-at-home mother; she had expected to miss her baby, but she did not. As much as she loved her daughter, caring for a toddler was not as mentally stimulating as her job, and it did not give her the same sense of contributing to an enterprise and being valued.

We held this interview in the children's section of the local library, where Katarina's daughter ran around while we talked. As Katarina kept one eye on her daughter, she commented on what her work at the accounting firm had come to mean to her:

> I think that's probably the main reason I don't have any postpartum depression or anything is because I had a little bit of work to do. And it wasn't just church stuff. [*Katarina did extensive volunteer work for her church.*] It was like, no, you have actual work. Like numbers to crunch and reports to make and emails to answer. And having all these little favors, or whatever you want to call it, asked of me to—like run these events and stuff—has been really nice for me mentally because as much as I love this work [*of caring for a child*], it's not as rewarding as having somebody need you as an adult. "I need you to do this thing for me." And that's what I've noticed. The difference between working for yourself like this [*said while looking at her daughter*] and working for someone else. And that makes me happy.

At that point Katarina categorized her accounting office work as a "job" rather than a long-term "career," but two years later, Katarina became an accountant at that firm.

If Katarina had stuck to the advice to "follow your passion," she would have been single-minded in her pursuit of a career as a singer, and she would not have invested time in any occupation that could deter her from that path. She did continue to take singing gigs on the side, but she also made the pragmatic choice to look for something else that would provide a more reliable paycheck. Although she began with a work-is-work attitude and without any commitment to remaining at the accounting firm, she discovered that she liked it. Accounting eventually became her good-enough occupation. It is not a passion, but it still provides nonfinancial satisfactions.

Many of my participants had stories of ending up in a good-enough occupation. When they needed a job, they considered their options and chose the one that was of greatest interest; fit their values, skills, and experience; had the kind of working conditions they wanted; and paid enough to meet their needs. By repeating this process, they gradually developed expertise and interest in one field, which became their good-enough occupation.

If those with a good-enough occupational approach enjoyed their job, what they appreciated are small work pleasures. These are not the deep meanings of believing that one's job contributes to one's life purpose or a better world. Instead, small pleasures could consist of enjoyment of the tasks and feeling competent at them, enjoyment of the physical work environment, and enjoyment of socializing on the job.[33] Those ways of enjoying work were not limited to those with a good-enough occupational approach, but they were common among them.

My participants varied in the kinds of tasks they liked. There has been interesting speculation among critical theorists about the possible adverse effects of postindustrial "immaterial labor"; that is, "labor that produces an immaterial good, such as a service, knowledge, or communication," as Michael Hardt defines it.[34] A potential problem with producing immaterial goods is that the results of one's work are (by definition) intangible, which may be unsatisfying. Some of my participants agreed. Chipper Goodman, a former high school football player who was in his mid-twenties when we met, said office jobs put him to sleep. He preferred being outside doing hard physical work connected to sports and fitness, like his temporary job setting up the courses for outdoor sporting events such as mud runs and triathlons. He said, "It's fun; I enjoy fitness and outdoors." He also liked his work to have tangible results: "I enjoy work that I can see productivity, that I can see it happening, such as like these events. Building an eight-foot wall that's ninety-seven feet long." He preferred that to "doing work that I don't see the end result."

Others, however, found fun from immaterial labor, especially jobs that presented novel challenges.[35] Robert Milner, a former supply chain strategist in a cosmetics company, described what he enjoyed about his work: "One day, you're thinking about formulas, and you're dealing with laboratories and engineers and biochemists. And the next day, you're dealing with the marketing department and the creative department to try to come up with a design. Real fun. I liked that." The intellectual challenge of wrangling office software was what Celeste Rue enjoyed so much as an administrative assistant. She told me that in one of her jobs, "I would have to do a really complex sort to bring the data into an Excel spreadsheet from a different type of file, and that was fun. That was just fun, and I could sit there at my desk all day and do that." The fact that Celeste was good at this kind of work also greatly contributed to her enjoyment of it.

Even without novel intellectual challenges, immaterial work can be satisfying. When the anthropologist David Graeber posted an online essay about "bullshit jobs" ("paid employment that is so completely pointless, unnecessary, or pernicious that even the employee cannot justify its existence"), workers doing immaterial labor were a large share of those who wrote him saying that was a sadly accurate description of their job.[36] However, even if it is true that a majority of those who have "bullshit jobs" are doing immaterial labor, it does not follow that the majority of those doing immaterial labor feel they have pointless or pernicious "bullshit jobs." Katarina Spelling did not believe that having "numbers to crunch and reports to make and emails to answer" was pointless; that work helped the firm, and it made her happy to do work that was needed.

The sensory qualities of their workplace mattered to many of my participants as well, although they differed in what environments they enjoyed. Terrance West had appreciated the occasional company picnics and barbeques when he worked as a shipping and receiving clerk for "H Company," a candy company, but they were not the main attractions of the job. The first thing he mentioned was that he was happy to begin working there in his mid-thirties because his previous jobs had familiarized him with the tasks, such as printing bills of lading and dealing with delivery truck drivers, and he felt competent at them. The next thing he said was, "I would go to work in the morning, and the building smelled like chocolate. (*laughs*) [. . .] it was nice." He also mentioned that the building was kept air conditioned and dim to preserve the candy, making a very comfortable working environment for him. He had more profound reasons for "really loving that place": he also valued the charitable work of the company's founder, and he was proud that his bosses appreciated his many talents and dedication to the job. Yet, the small pleasure of a comfortable working environment contributed significantly to why he "would get up in the morning happy to go to work."

By contrast, Chipper Goodman and Feliciano Salas would have hated being cooped up in Terrance's dim candy warehouse. Feliciano said that he was completely "comfortable" only when he was working outdoors as a roofer.

Regardless of their approach to an occupation, many of my participants enjoyed socializing with workmates. It was everyday socializing that they appreciated, not management-led special events. Katarina Spelling enjoyed talking to coworkers and joking with her boss. Similarly, José Navarro liked the congenial interactions with his coworkers at food concession stands at Dodgers Stadium. He explained, "I like to work at Dodgers because even though there may be some work conflicts, when I get there, I greet a lot of people, and a lot of people know me, and most of them like me. I think that 80 percent of the people I greet, like me. I can feel that vibe. [. . .] I can joke with them, and we laugh together."

Emily Quinn used the striking metaphor of "play" to talk about the enjoyment she had derived from casual social interaction at the office. She was never able to obtain another job after she lost hers during the Great Recession:

> I wanna play and they won't let me play. They won't let me in. They won't let me in the door. I can't get in. I can't get back. I miss being in the office. It's fun. With work I connect being—I first of all think of connecting, being with people, being friendly, feeling human. I have an opportunity to care. I have an opportunity to ask somebody "How are you doing? How did your daughter do in that water polo meet?" and have them ask about me, have somebody make a joke—you know how you're always kidding with each other.

While she was out of work, Emily felt, "There is no connection. There's no human interaction and I miss that." When I asked her to draw her place in society, she drew herself alone, behind a fence. On the other side were people she described as "working, living, earning, laughing, talking, contributing" (chapter 2, figure 2.1).

Sam Lennon, who had worked mostly in service-sector jobs (sales associate, cashier, food preparation, stockroom) until she was permanently disabled with injuries, similarly commented on social interactions with coworkers as making work fun: "If you've got a job, and you go to work, that's like your family there. It's like another little world." When I asked if she would want to work again if she could, she said, "I would. Yeah, I'm really tired of the cats. It's fun to work."

Social interactions have long been recognized as a source of job satisfaction,[37] although some worry that may be changing. Those concerns were voiced well before teleworking became common during the COVID-19 pandemic. For example, Aronowitz and DiFazio conclude that "the main value of having a job (besides its economic function for individuals and households), is that it once provided a 'community.'" They believe, however, that "the culture of the factory and the large office is dying."[38] Some cultural theorists speculate that wanting to belong to a workplace community is a futile "melancholic longing" for a de-parted Fordist past.[39]

Other researchers would agree. One research summary reports, "In 1985, about half of Americans said they had a close friend at work; by 2004, this was true for only 30 percent." The author concludes, "Now, work is a more trans-actional place. We go to the office to be efficient, not to form bonds."[40] That conclusion overlooks the value of casual friendships. Workers do not need to have a close friend at work; what they want is people with whom they are friendly, a feeling of belonging somewhere, of human connection.[41]

During the COVID-19 pandemic, when many office workers had to work from home, one technology writer began his lengthy analysis of remote work on an upbeat note about the great productivity gains that companies were observing. His article ends, however, this way: "As much as our offices can be inefficient, productivity-killing spreaders of infectious disease, a lot of people are desperate to get back to them." He quotes one teleworking em-ployee "who longs to hang out with her 'peeps. 'You know—we're drinking coffee, or maybe, *Hey, want to take a walk?* I miss that.'"[42] What many (al-though not all) office workers want now is a mix: some days working from home, so they do not have to spend so much time commuting, and at least occasional days working at an office to feel more connected to others.[43]

So far in this section I relayed positive stories about work, but there are neg-ative ones as well. If interesting tasks make work fun, spirit-dulling and back-breaking tasks make it drudgery. If a comfortable workplace and pleasant social interactions with coworkers make work enjoyable, an uncomfortable work-place and unpleasant interactions can be unbearable. The kinds of jobs that are available will have an enormous effect on how one thinks about the place of work in a good life.[44]

Some of my participants' least favorite jobs were in warehouse work, which is the only job sector that was booming in the Inland Empire region of south-ern California in the 2010s. Amazon and many other retailers have large ware-houses and fulfillment centers in that area because it has lot of undeveloped land and many workers desperate for a job.[45] I already shared Jake Taylor's description of the miseries of being a warehouse "lumper." Summer Car-rington's feet were injured after a temporary holiday-season job working as a picker in an Amazon warehouse. When a customer places an order, the picker is responsible for pulling the items from the shelves of the enormous ware-house. Summer said she was timed in her work, and no one was allowed to sit down except for short breaks. When I talked to her after it ended, Summer did not have anything good to say about that warehouse job other than that it provided a paycheck she needed.[46]

Toxic interpersonal relations forced at least two of my participants out of jobs. In both cases, they faced racism or xenophobia. José's sister, Isabel Navarro, also participated in this study. She was more ambitious than her brother and had worked very hard to advance in her career; however, in two jobs she was blocked by a supervisor or harassed by coworkers who were prejudiced against her because she was an immigrant from Mexico, as I explained in chapter 1. Terrance West, who is Black and gay, never obtained any support or redress when he was harassed by racist or homophobic coworkers or supervisors. He usually liked working with others, but after being goaded into leaving a job by a racist coworker, he applied to be a truck driver so he could work alone. The option for remote work during the pandemic has been a boon for those who felt they were outside the dominant social groups at work. One survey found that Black knowledge workers were more likely than white knowledge workers to prefer hybrid or remote work, a difference that could be due to a less welcoming social environment for workers of color in those positions.[47]

Less visible were the ways that some of my participants' paths into good-enough occupations were smoothed by privileges not commented on by those who had them but noticed by those who did not. For example, when Daniel Horn—a white man born in the United States—was still in college, he was invited to move into management at the restaurant chain where he was working. José Navarro, by contrast, noticed that, at one of the sports venues where he worked, Latino/a employees in food services were not offered management positions. As other researchers have found, when employers look for someone with a good "fit" to an organization's culture, they can exhibit gender, racial, ethnic, and national origin biases.[48]

There was also some assumed gender sorting in the kinds of good-enough occupations my participants fell into. After Daniel Horn worked in restaurants, he became a successful general contractor even though he had no experience in construction other than having built a tree fort as a child. I suspect that a woman with no prior experience would not have been so readily accepted as general contractor, nor did any woman we interviewed mention considering that as an occupation.

In sum, the paths to good-enough occupations were shaped not only by the job seekers' values, interests, experience, and skills but also by the learned assumptions that led them to consider certain kinds of occupations over others, their class background and education, and the opportunities that were offered to some and withheld from others depending on their gender, race, and national origin. Still, the high fences or open gates guiding job seekers into some occupations and away from others were not limited to those with a good-enough occupational approach. They also hindered or helped those with the two occupational approaches I describe next: seeing one's occupation as a career and seeing it as a passion.

Moving up in a Career

The opportunity to move up a career ladder presented by a job is a culturally recognized basis for choosing it. The metaphors of "moving up" and of a career "ladder" stand for advancement in title, salary, responsibilities, recognition, or other markers of status and achievement.

Titles can be an important indicator of career advancement; one interviewee was disappointed that he had only achieved the level of director or vice president in his jobs and never senior vice president. So are moves to a bigger or better-known organization. The self-employed have their own indicators of career progress, such as increases in the number of sales, customers or clients, online "followers," subscribers, page views, and so on.

As Wrzesniewski and her coauthors explain, when someone cares about career advancement, they "mark their achievements not only through monetary gain, but through advancement within the occupational structure. This advancement often brings higher social standing, increased power within the scope of one's occupation, and higher self-esteem."[49] This definition was useful for my study, particularly its emphasis on self-esteem. Those with this *moving-up-in-a-career approach* judged themselves and felt they were judged by others by advancements in their career.

What this definition underplays is that career success can also be enjoyable. As I discussed in chapter 2, many of those who had thrown themselves into their careers did so because they found their measurable accomplishments gratifying. Some described achieving challenging goals at work as fun.

Elizabeth Montgomery, a business-to-business saleswoman who before we met had hopped from one job to another for better opportunities in her nearly thirty-year career, used the word fun so often in recounting her achievements that I had a hard time picking just one example for the list at the beginning of this chapter. Early in her career, she was a buyer for a department-store chain. She commented, "I was responsible for forty stores. And I'd never really understood the clout we had until you'd walk into a tradeshow because there were very few retailers at the time that had forty stores. So that was really, really fun." In the early 2000s, she had the idea of venturing into internet sales when working for another company, which had never done it before: "We went from zero; we grew it five times over." She said it was "a blast," which is another way of saying it was fun. In her last job before I met her, she was working for a large organization and was responsible for one of its biggest territories. Although there were problems with that company, she liked the autonomy: "It was like having my own company out here. They gave you all the P & L [*profit and loss statements*] and just basically said, 'Here's what we need you to do. Here's your expenses and go for it.'" She concluded, "So that was a lot of fun."

In Elizabeth's examples, we see three aspects of jobs that can make them fun. These three features matter not only for those who care about advancing in a career but also for others: having "clout" (influence because of one's position or accomplishments), achieving challenging goals (such as her success when taking her company's sales online), and having autonomy/decision-making power.

Charles Toppes, director of manufacturing at a furniture factory, was proud when he achieved a very challenging goal:

> The company had a program wherein all the facilities competed for several different recognition awards, the crowning jewel of which was the factory of the year, the quality factory of the year. One of the first tasks assigned to me by the president was that this facility in all of its existence of forty something years had never even been in the top three, getting close to getting that award. Well, he didn't want to be in the top three; he wanted to win that award. Basically, he gave me that task. He said, "Your primary task is to win this award for this company for this facility the next time around."

It sounded impossible, like a knight's quest in a medieval tale. I felt his excitement as Charles explained how he devised metrics to set goals and built teams to achieve them. And the outcome? "By the end of the year we pulled it off. We got factory of the year for that facility. Then not only did we get factory of the year for that facility, but we also got it the following year." Clearly, Charles's success at meeting this difficult challenge was very gratifying to him.

Emily Quinn, the executive secretary quoted earlier who said she wanted to "play" again, enjoyed both the clout and the decision-making power she had when she was an assistant to the head of her company: "I was always in charge of arranging everything, whatever the celebrations, the parties, the golf tournaments, all the "rah-rah" stuff, news releases, luncheons. People came to me, and it was wonderful. It was a lot of fun. It was very enjoyable."

When I asked Elizabeth about the meaning or importance of work for her, she compared it to winning sports events. She had been a standout high school and college athlete, and she saw career successes as like athletic trophies. In both cases, "You set the goal. You go out and achieve it." Your salary, and what you can buy with it, reflects your achievements: "The money is secondary, but yet it isn't, 'cause I like nice things. [. . .] Where that [*money earned*] comes into play is how much do you make, to buy those things." Money matters not only for consumption but also as a visible sign of one's accomplishments. Max Weber observed that wealth played a similar role for early Protestants, but he thought for them it was an outward sign that they were among those destined to achieve eternal salvation. Weber observed that, by the beginning of the twentieth century, "In the United States, the pursuit of wealth, stripped of its religious and ethical meaning, tends to become associated with purely mundane passions, which often actually give it the character of sport."[50]

Unemployment during a lengthy recession was especially difficult for those who had a moving-up-in-a-career approach. These job seekers were reluctant to take a salary cut or a lower position because they were signs of failure to progress in their career. Also, if they set their expected salary too low, it could signal they were not the kind of ambitious high achiever that the organization was seeking. Yet, if they held out for the salary or position that was the next step up in their career, they could be passed over by employers who had no shortage of qualified applicants willing to work for less. As their months of unemployment turned into years, their long-term unemployment became an additional liability because it suggested hidden weaknesses or that their skills were out of date. Many employers do not even consider applications from the long-term unemployed.[51]

Stephen Smith experienced this dilemma. He had been a regional finance director for a division of a Fortune 500 company that was hard hit by the Great Recession. Although he interviewed for many jobs, he was out of work for three years because employers thought, correctly, that he would be reluctant to take a salary cut. When we first met, Stephen spoke of compensation as "a measure of your net worth to society." He was forced to reconsider what his compensation said about his social value because when he eventually found another job, he had to take a 25 percent cut in his base salary. He told me that he was aware that such cuts were typical after the Great Recession, but as we saw in chapter 5, his wife was not pleased with his lower salary.

Hillary Edwards erred in the opposite direction by asking for too low a salary. She had held a senior position in a bank that failed. After being out of work for three years, she was approached by an executive recruiter. He kept pressing her to state her salary requirement. She was reluctant to give a figure, but eventually she said, "Seventy-five thousand maybe. I'm looking in that area." His response was, "That's too low. I was really expecting for you to tell me something higher." She did not get the job.

Those who cared about career advancement had to adjust the way they viewed themselves, and were viewed by others, after they ended a long bout of unemployment by taking a job that was a step—or several steps—below their previous position. Lisa Rose had a painful adjustment after she was laid off from her leadership position in a well-known local nonprofit organization. When we first talked, it was a year and a half after her layoff, and she had obtained only occasional short-term contract work in the interim. She was ready to lower her expectations about the kind of job she could get next, but she also had to deal with reactions from others. She said, "I told people about two positions that I was applying for, which are clearly positions that people would see as a step down or a step back, right? Not even lateral moves. And the immediate reaction"—from peers who had jobs—was, "Well, how is that possibly the next step in your career?"

Two-and-a-half years after Lisa was laid off, she settled for a much lower-status, nonexempt position, which I described in chapter 2. It was still in philanthropy, the sector she wanted to be in and where she felt she was contributing to the world with her work, but it was at an entry level position. The hardest adjustment was the way others treated her because of her lower status. She commented, "We tend to treat people like their jobs or their job titles, right?" Despite her many years of experience, she said, "I'm definitely not one of the most important people in the meeting. Like, if I'm there, sometimes it's almost like we're invisible." If having clout is fun, having so little influence that one feels invisible is the opposite. Fortunately for Lisa, a few years after she was hired, the organization promoted her to an exempt position that was more commensurate with her skills and experience.

Pepper Hill had a similar experience of settling for a new job that was a rung down her career ladder after she was let go from a management-level position for a large nonprofit organization. Following a job search that lasted more than five years, during which she could find only part-time work, Pepper landed a full-time job working for a smaller nonprofit organization where she had been volunteering and working part-time. Her previous job had been with a national nonprofit organization with revenues of more than $200 million a year; her new job was with a local nonprofit with revenues of just over $1 million annually.[52] In her previous job, she had been a director; in her new job, she had no decision-making power. In addition, her salary was much lower and (like Lisa), she had to work in a cubicle rather than an office with a window. Pepper realized that when she was younger, she used to look with disdain on someone if "they kind of went down to a different position." She had assumed, "They're not so good," but "I'm now realizing that's me. (*laughs*) And I'm feeling guilty for the people that I was—not *mean* to, but I didn't always accept their knowledge." Taking this lower position required redefining what mattered to her: "I have challenges with it, and I knew I would, and I'm working on it." Still, Pepper enjoyed her new job because she shared the organization's mission, and "I feel that my work is my way of contributing to society."

Pepper Hill and Lisa Rose wanted to advance in their careers and also contribute to society with their work. This mixture of motives is not always recognized, either by scholars or in American society.[53] Caring about career advancement can carry a whiff of moral expediency, as if those who care about getting ahead in their career have no interest in doing good. Indeed, one dictionary definition of "careerism" is "the policy or practice of advancing one's career often at the cost of one's integrity."[54]

One of my participants implied he may have been careerist in this negative sense, and he paid for it. John Davis was a vice president of HR at a multinational corporation when, early in 2006, he was offered a higher-level position in a company that specialized in subprime mortgages. He was attracted by the opportunity to do more innovative HR work, as well as by "a substantial raise and a lofty title." His wife did not like the values of the men he would be working for, especially after she read an interview in which the CEO bragged about encouraging his employees to spy on each other, but John wanted to give it a try. Within a few months he recognized that the company was in financial trouble, and he left before the year was out, long before its leaders were charged with fraud that helped bring about the global financial crisis in late 2007. Even though he got out quickly, John never obtained another full-time position. Although he did not say so, he may have been tainted by his association with that company. He commented, "It's all been downhill since," and he implied that his fate was a punishment for that bad decision, which his wife had warned him against. Toward the end of our first interview, he commented, "Things don't just happen. They happen justly."

Yet, even though advancing in one's career can be in tension with wanting to make the world a better place through one's work, the same person can care about both, as we saw with Lisa and Pepper. John, too, has strong ethical concerns, leading him to see his unemployment as a just punishment. John is Black, and in his previous jobs he had used his high-level HR positions to advocate for greater inclusion of minorities and women in the management of the companies where he worked. The world is not divided between people who have base motives for working and those with noble motives. Most people have a mix of these motivations.

Occupational Passion

Miriam Ramos is passionate about hairdressing. In telling her life story, she described her excitement as she took the classes ("I was really passionate about cosmetology and going to school"), and when we talked about the meaning of work for her, she said, "I'm fortunate that's my passion, but for a lot of people, it's their money. I get to have both." Yet, after her first salon reduced her hours and then went out of business, Miriam went several years without being able to make a living from her passion. To make ends meet, she had to work as a sales associate in a discount clothing store, where she frequently clashed with one of her managers. Miriam still saw a few hairdressing clients at a different salon closer to home, and she became my hairdresser. One time when I asked her how that sales associate job was going, she simply replied, "Work is work." End of conversation. By contrast, she never considered it "work" to cut, color, and style hair. Finally, nearly two years after she had taken the clothing store job out of desperation and about five years after she lost full-time work at her beloved first salon, she was offered a full-time position as a master stylist in a salon that she respected. Money was still tight, her father's dementia worsened, and her relationship with her on-again, off-again boyfriend was still full of drama, but for several years Miriam was more contented than I had ever seen her. One day at her new salon, I noticed that she had a tote bag with the message, "I've been a hairdresser all my life. It's what I do. It's what I love." It was a quote from a famous hairdresser that perfectly described Miriam.

Earl Apache Longwolf did not use the word "passion" to describe his occupation of being a welder and burner, but he too loved his field and could not imagine doing any other kind of work. The first time I met Earl, he was wearing a United Steelworkers baseball cap with a button that said, "I ♥ my fucking job." When we entered his neighborhood convenience store, where we sat for the first interview, he was proud that the proprietor greeted him by his nickname "Steelman," and before we settled into our interview, he showed me a photo of himself in a welder's suit. Earl was particularly proud of his service to the country when he was hired to cut away the wreckage of the Twin Towers in New York City after 9/11.

Earl's passion for his occupation preceded and followed that Twin Towers job and had an origin story. When Earl was six years old, his mother, father, two sisters, and brother were killed in a car crash. When he was fourteen and in foster care, his social worker asked him what he wanted to do for a living. Earl said, "'If you could tell me what my father did, I would be the best at it.' He [*the social worker*] said my father was a welder, burner, bender, melter, iron-worker, steelworker." Earl went on to do the same. Two years after we first met, when he was in his mid-fifties, he said he had no plans to retire soon: "I've got a 401(k) I haven't touched. I'm going to stay until the thrill is gone, Claudia, because I love what I do. When you love what you do, it's really hard to picture me retired watching TV."

Miriam and Earl see their occupation as a passion. I define an *occupational passion* as having a deep attachment to one's occupation based on the belief that it is what one is meant to do, given one's talents or life experiences. It is close to the way some researchers describe seeing one's occupation as a calling, which is another term some of my participants used.[55] For example, Rebecca Robinson, an administrative assistant, prided herself on setting up good systems to keep things organized and functioning smoothly in an office. When I observed, "Well, it does seem like you're awfully good at what you do," she agreed: "Yes, I think I'm very good at what I do. And I enjoy what I do. [. . .] I think that is my calling." However, "passion" was the more commonly used term.

Many critical theorists see social discourses of work as a "passion" or a "calling" as ideologies that serve to extract more labor from employees. Kathi Weeks is an influential theorist in this vein. Weeks would not be surprised that there are workers who love what they do, but she proposes that such work attachments are the product of socialization in a postindustrial capitalist society. She argues that "the new postindustrial work ethic . . . that characterized work as a path to individual self-expression, self-development, and creativity" is in the end like the old Protestant work ethic, promulgated to inculcate "systematic devotion to waged work." She repeats Weber's description of the Protestant work ethic, according to which workers are enjoined to treat their job "as if it were an absolute end in itself, a calling."[56] To perform labor *as if* it were a calling means one does not really feel called to one's occupation, but one should work with enthusiasm anyway.

Ilana Gershon is also critical of discourses of passion about work, but unlike Weeks, her account is grounded in ethnographic research. When investigating contemporary advice given to American job seekers, Gershon noticed that "passion has become such a frequently repeated word that everyone involved in hiring seems to agree that one of the most important qualifications for someone to show in an interview is an overwhelming enthusiasm for the job." For example, one manager told her that "he would much prefer choosing the not-so-talented person to work on his project as long as he or she was passionate about the work." When Gershon asked him why, "He laughed and said that this is what guarantees that the employee will work the long hours necessary to get the job done. He could teach the skills to someone who didn't already know how to do a task, but he couldn't make someone deeply committed to tasks if they didn't feel committed from the outset."[57] Gershon makes the insightful point that an ideology of occupational passion can supersede company loyalty, because employees who follow their passions may leave if their job no longer excites them. Still, like Weeks, Gershon emphasizes that the language of passion can be used to extract additional labor from workers who are expected to display zealous devotion. This discourse can also deflect job seekers' attention from barriers to employment created by structural inequities: if they are having trouble finding work, it must be their own fault for not being passionate enough.[58]

I share these critics' concern with the use of productivist discourses to force people to labor in unsatisfying jobs.[59] I also share their concern with overwork. However, their criticisms do not target what my participants meant. A productivist (Protestant) work ethic and a follow-your-passion approach to an occupation are not the same. As I explained in chapter 2, a productivist work ethic calls for dedication to working, regardless of the job. It makes abstract labor an end in itself. By contrast, the follow-your-passion approach is about being drawn to a specific occupation. Miriam was a conscientious sales associate, but she had no passion for that job. It was only hairdressing that she described as her passion. Similarly, Earl took a job for a while as a forklift operator, but when the shipments stopped and he was laid off, his attitude was, "Good riddance." Only steel work was his passion.

Furthermore, Miriam's and Earl's occupational passion did not blind them to exploitive work conditions. Miriam was shocked when another hairdresser reported that her boss gave her only one day off a week. Miriam commented, "The whole point of working is not just to work. It's to have a balanced life." She often spoke out on behalf of workers' rights at her jobs. Earl criticized his last employer: "They want you to work to death but they treat you like dog doodoo. It was about, 'The hell with how you feel. Do it or get out.'" Miriam's and Earl's love of their occupation was separate from their attitudes about specific employers and jobs.

Gershon's concern is about job seekers' requisite displays of enthusiasm and employers' eagerness to take advantage of them. Some of my participants agreed that it was necessary to show enthusiasm if they wanted to be hired, but that was quite different from feeling they were meant to do a certain kind of work in life.

Some participants, like Earl, had occupational passions that originated in hardship and loss. Their traumatic experiences made them feel they needed to enter a certain line of work to turn their suffering into something positive. For example, Alice Joyner's persistent effort to become a family counselor was driven by a tragedy that I cannot imagine bearing as a parent. Long before I met her, her mentally ill son killed one of his siblings. Following this horrific event—one of her children murdered by another who would then spend the rest of his life in prison—she decided to dedicate the rest of her life to helping troubled families. She got her bachelor's and master's degrees when she was in her seventies.

Fred Hernandez felt he had a calling from God to redeem his life by becoming a substance abuse counselor. When he was in his twenties, Fred had earned a good living as a truck driver, but his license was revoked for drunk driving. He nearly lost his life in a drunk-driving accident. The doctors and his family thought he had died, but when his brother-in-law grabbed his hand, Fred squeezed back. The doctors realized he was not dead yet and resumed their efforts to save him. Fred is sure God kept him alive "to do what I'm doing now. To help other alcoholics." Helping others who have been driving under the influence is Fred's way to find redemption for the many mistakes he has made in his life.

In these stories we see that an occupational passion is not a neoliberal ploy to extract work. Instead, it is driven by meaningful life experiences and skills. When I asked Alice Joyner whether her work was central to her identity, she objected to that wording: "What I do doesn't make me who I am. Because of who I am, what I do is what I do." In other words, she did not think that first you find work, and then it defines who you are. Instead, she saw who she was as paramount in the occupation she was determined to pursue.

Whether they saw their occupation as God's purpose for their life, as their destiny, or simply as what they loved to do, those who had previously obtained work in the field they were passionate about persisted, often for many years, in their attempts to return to that occupation when they were out of work. They knew they could make a living doing what they felt they were meant to do in life, and they were determined to go back to it. Phoenix Rises, a special education teacher, described herself as "passionate about what I do." When she could not find a job after being out of work for three years, she knew she should consider another field, but "I wouldn't be happy. I could just see it—just dragging in, dragging out. It'd be like a death sentence almost." Unlike my participants with a work-is-work, a good-enough occupation, or a moving-up-in-a career approach, those who were passionate about their field resisted changing it.

Those with an occupational passion differed from the rest of my participants in another way: surprisingly, they rarely spoke of their work as fun. It was as if that word failed to convey just how meaningful their work was for them. Having fun is only one kind of nonfinancial reward.

For example, compare the way Tom Dunn talked about a job he enjoyed in a good-enough occupation with one that became more of a passion for him. For eight years Tom was an IT personnel recruiter and consultant for health care organizations. It was challenging, well paid, and required travel to the San Francisco Bay area, which he liked. He said of that job, "It was really fun. It was really fun." For emphasis, he added, "It was just a thrill. It was really a thrill." After he lost his job due to a dispute with his boss, he could not find another position during the Great Recession. He was divorced, with no other source of income, and his younger sons were still at home. Bills started mounting; he stopped paying his mortgage and ignored dunning calls about his credit cards. He prayed to God, "Just show me what I need to do, and I'll do it." Tom got the idea of starting his own business delivering medical marijuana, and it took off. The business was not only lucrative but also deeply fulfilling because he took time to talk to his customers about their troubles. Tom was proud that "they count on me. Not just for the weed but to be their friend. To be their kind of sounding board. Maybe their counselor." Tom did not describe that job as fun. Instead he said that job enabled him to put into practice the values he cared about: "Peace within me and my opportunities and ability to help other people."

Similarly, before Miriam Ramos was a hairdresser, she was a visual merchandiser responsible for dressing mannequins and creating displays in a clothing store, which she described as "a really, really fun job." By contrast, Miriam did not use the word fun when talking about hairdressing. Instead, she had statements like "For me, it truly makes me happy" and "I really find love in my work. I get love from making clients happy through customer service."

In fact, only one of my twelve participants who had an occupational passion described a job in that field as fun. In my first interview with Tony De-Luca, he talked about his dedication to the HR field, which at that time he saw as fulfilling his "calling to touch people's lives." In one of his HR positions, he was director of international HR for his firm, which he described as "a lot of fun." That international job may have been especially enjoyable because it offered opportunities to see other parts of the world. Tony also cared about advancing in his career, and rising to that level may have been fun for him because it was a high-level position. As that example illustrates, it is possible for a fun job to be in a field that people consider to be their calling or passion.[60] Nonetheless, the rest of my participants implicitly distinguished fun jobs from the deep fulfillment they felt from working in the field they loved.

As one of my participants Ralph Edwards put it, "If you ever do make a living from your passion, you're truly blessed." However, an occupational passion approach could be a curse for those unable to make a living from what they felt drawn to do. I have read sad examples of people who made midlife career changes to follow their passion and were subsequently unable to support themselves.[61] Those lofty graduation speeches exhorting new graduates to follow their passion can lead people astray, raising unrealistic hopes that anyone can make a good living from a field about which they are passionate. "Follow your passion" downplays other ways of finding work that can pay the bills and be enjoyable or fulfilling.

Pleasures beyond Fun

Whether they viewed their occupation as a passion or not, my participants described some job pleasures that went beyond fun. Recognition for their contributions from coworkers and supervisors made jobs satisfying for many of my participants, and its absence while they were unemployed left them feeling empty. Terrance West did not have an occupational passion, but whatever he did, he wanted to do well: "Once I'm working somewhere, I wanna be the best at it." He was proud that, at most of his jobs in the past, he was the one put in charge when the boss stepped out and "the one that they'll call in the middle of the night and ask, 'Well, how do you reboot the system?' or 'How do you cash out for the night?' or whatever. I've always been that guy." That recognition mattered a lot to him: "I want to be important to somebody or to some organization or to something. And right now, I don't really feel that very important to anything or anyone" because he was not working.

Similarly, Rebecca Robinson, the administrative assistant who felt she had found her calling in bringing order to offices, commented, "We all need that—the affirmation that what we're doing is doing something for somebody." During our interviews, she recited the commendations she had received, such as the supervisor who wrote that Rebecca "walks on water." While she was out of work, she felt no purpose in living. All the job application rejections Rebecca received during the seven years she could find only occasional temp jobs raised a basic existential question: "What am I still here for? Nobody needs me. In other words, is there a purpose? I feel purposeless." Rebecca's sister, exhausted from her job as a teacher, commented enviously, "Well, you're lucky you don't have to go to work the next day." Rebecca's response was, "No. You don't get it. I would enjoy going to work."

Many of my participants did not want to be appreciated only for their individual achievements. They also took pleasure in working closely with others to achieve common goals. Descriptions of American culture that emphasize individualism overlook the value that many people place on contributing to a larger whole—a feeling that several participants expressed, regardless of their occupational approach.[62] As we saw, when Katarina Spelling felt her work was needed at the accounting firm, she told me, "That makes me happy." Stephen Smith, the former regional finance director for a division of a Fortune 500 company whose moving-up-in-a-career approach I described earlier, also spoke of "that sense of gratitude and fulfillment" that comes from "being involved with a group of other people where you've got a common cause and you're able to have a meaningful contribution." He saw contributing to a common cause at work as being like an Olympic athlete because the athlete's achievements contribute to a national team's success. Similarly, Lisa Rose spoke of a non-profit job she had enjoyed because "it was a very diverse group of people, intentionally diverse and inclusive. And it was just great to feel like you're part of a really smart team of people who really cared." Pepper Hill had started a consulting business to fill the unemployment gap on her resume, but she did not like working for herself in part because "at the end of the day your job really is to get yourself more business." She said, "I'd rather be waking up thinking about the mission of the organization." Terrance West said, "It gives me a sense of pride that I was able to do something that is beneficial not only to myself, but to a group, to the team."

I had no examples of participants using fun to describe the fulfillment they felt when they worked together in their job for a common mission. It felt rewarding to them in a way that fun apparently does not capture. Celeste Rue differentiated between the fun she derived from the personal challenge of figuring out office software, on the one hand, and her contributions to the group, on the other. When asked to explain the meaning or importance of work for her, she replied, "The first thing that comes to my head is having fun—having fun and doing a good job. I could get lost in a spreadsheet—in a complex spreadsheet (*small laugh*). I could get lost creating a PowerPoint. I could get lost formatting a document." Listening to herself, she added, "I guess all of that is an individual thing. It's not a team kind of thing. It's personal satisfaction." However, she went on to explain that because she was willing to take assignments that others avoided, and she performed them well, she contributed to the group: "I think we are there, even as an individual, pulling together to get to a common point successfully." "Pulling together to get to a common point successfully" may not be fun, but it mattered to her. It is a classic sociological and anthropological observation: it is fulfilling to be a valued member of a group.

Nor do I have any clear examples of my participants using the word fun to talk about contributing to society through their paid work, even though that too could make them feel good about their job.[63] I counted at least twenty-five participants who spoke of finding fulfillment from helping others through their job, taking pride when their organization did something valuable for society, or wishing that they had a job that contributed more to society. This count requires sensitivity to what other people see as contributing social value and not imposing one's own ideas. For example, Mickey Muller, an electrical engineer and military history buff, made a point of mentioning that in his first job he worked on circuit boards for nuclear submarines. He added proudly, "The ones that launched the missiles." A pacifist would disagree, but as Mickey saw it, that job contributed to society. As Michael Pratt, a professor of management, points out, people have differing views about what kind of work contributes to society.[64] My grandmother used to describe PhDs as "the kind of doctor who doesn't do anybody any good." I disagreed, of course.

Yet, just as those whose occupation was not a calling could still care about their social contributions, those with an occupational calling were not necessarily drawn to it because their work made the world better. Earl was proud of his work clearing the wreckage of the Twin Towers following the 9/11 attacks in New York City, but that is not why he became a welder and loves that occupation. Rebecca Robinson felt she had a calling to be "the person that brings order out of chaos" at the office. If the organization for which she worked did good in the world, she took pride in that, but that was secondary. She became disenchanted with her job at a cancer treatment center when it became clear that her boss did not share Rebecca's zeal for well-organized files; it did not matter that she worked for doctors treating cancer.

I point this out because in Bellah and his colleagues' delineation of work orientations (job-career-calling), they describe a calling as the "strongest sense" of work, one in which work is valued in itself and is "a contribution to the good of all." Building on their work, Wrzesniewski and her coauthors comment, "Work that people feel called to do is usually seen as socially valuable— an end in itself."[65] My participants often did find fulfillment in making a social contribution through their work, but the occupations they described as their passion or calling were not always chosen for that reason. Bellah's and Wrzensniewski's definitions seem to impose a value judgment that people *should* choose work that contributes to the social good. My participants found pleasure not just in work that they saw as socially valuable in some larger sense but also in work that was valuable to their employer or work team. The larger social entity to which they contributed might be nothing more than their accounting firm.

All in all, it seemed that the features of jobs that my participants called fun made the job enjoyable without being deeply meaningful. That makes sense, given the Merriam Webster dictionary's definition of fun (adjective: "providing entertainment, amusement, or enjoyment"). There is a sense in which calling a job fun both elevates it and denigrates it. Other nonfinancial rewards were described with different terms, such as "fulfilling" or "makes me happy."

Is It Bad to Mix Work with Play?

I believe that the enjoyment that many of my participants found in their jobs is further evidence that it is misleading to characterize most Americans as motivated by a grim Puritan work ethic. Others, however, see a deeper compatibility between fun jobs and a Puritan suspicion of pleasure.

One connection we have already discussed is managers' use of "packaged fun" to get employees to put in long days at the office or stick with jobs that are boring. However, another author sees a subtler connection. Writing in the mid-1950s, Martha Wolfenstein proposes that over the twentieth century there had arisen in the United States what she described as a new "fun morality": a duty to have fun. Thus, having fun is obligatory; we are expected to enjoy not only leisure activities but also daily chores and paid work.[66] Although the new value placed on fun seems at odds with the earlier Puritanical suspicion of pleasure, Wolfenstein argues that "fun morality" is a new form of Puritanism, insofar as it diffuses gratifications. Instead of pleasures being "deep, intense, and isolated," they are reduced to lighter, permissible amusements that are allowed "to permeate thinly through all activities": they are diluted. She comments, as does anthropologist Robert Myers several decades later, "Boundaries formerly maintained between play and work break down."[67] In her opinion, those boundaries should be maintained, so that play is a greater contrast to work.

Wolfenstein seems quite right about the lighter quality of fun, compared to more intense pleasures, and the way fun can "permeate thinly through all activities." For some of my participants, any area of life could be "fun." Elizabeth Montgomery, the business-to-business salesperson, not only had fun in many of her jobs but she also was able to find fun when she was out of work. She said about being unemployed, "This whole transition's been really fun. I've done things I never would do." Ann Lopez used "fun" to describe her side hustle of driving a limo, volunteering at a local school, her hobby of tole painting, and being with her grandchildren.

In support of Wolfenstein's claim that it is obligatory for Americans to have fun—or, at least, say they are having fun—at work, as well as in all other realms of life, we could point to the positive thinking ideology in the United States, which I described in chapter 1. The chipper affect of "Fun!" is appropriate for the positive thinking that leads Americans to highlight the good side of a negative experience.[68]

Still, I question Wolfenstein's thesis that Americans feel a duty to see everything as fun. My participants made distinctions: some jobs, and some aspects of their jobs, were fun, but others made them miserable. Summer Carrington loved her challenging work as an asset manager at a bank, but she disliked her job pulling items from the shelves of an Amazon fulfillment center. Emily Quinn had great fun as an executive secretary, but she had not enjoyed the jobs she took as a lowly, poorly paid temporary agency worker. Robert

Milner found the constant learning required to be a supply chain strategist for a cosmetics company great fun, but he felt "bitter" about the long hours required for the job. In this chapter I focused on my participants' comments about having fun at work because it is an important and overlooked part of many Americans' work meanings—but fun was only one facet of their work meanings. Some aspects of their jobs were fun, but others most definitely were not.

I also question Wolfenstein's implicit assumption that there should be a strong boundary between paid work and time outside work, with all pain on one side and all pleasure on the other. Why is that better than finding some pleasures in each?[69]

Missing Meanings of Work

This chapter focused on the meanings of specific occupations and jobs for my participants, including meanings that are easy to miss in descriptions of how Americans think about work.

One reason it is easy to miss these meanings is that some are unshowy. Settling for a "good-enough" occupation and a "fun job" is not as dramatic as either hating or loving one's work. It is a moderate way of thinking and feeling, a way of finding small pleasures from work. As I explained, these are not the only ways my participants thought about their occupations and jobs, but they are aspects that have not been much discussed in previous research.

Another reason it is easy for researchers to miss these meanings has to do with weaknesses of both etic and emic analysis in the social sciences. Etic constructs are ones devised by researchers, drawing on theories they assume apply universally; emic constructs are locally meaningful and described using terms from that community's ways of speaking.[70]

The weakness of the universalizing etic approach is that it overlooks or homogenizes culturally specific meanings, like the connotations of fun for Americans talking about their jobs. My aim as a cultural anthropologist is to understand local meanings.

Yet, there are ways in which an emic analysis can overlook important meanings as well. Typically, an emic analysis begins with keywords in the local language, but that method omits the covert categories, like good-enough occupations, that have no simple, widely used cultural label.[71] Keyword analysis, of the sort I did in exploring the meanings of fun, can be misleading. As I explained, the word fun was rarely used when my participants talked about their occupational passion, if they had one, or the fulfillment they felt contributing to their organization or society, even though those contributions mattered greatly

to many of them. Nor, of course, did fun convey any complaints my participants had about their jobs. It is easy to be seduced by the cultural distinctiveness
and oddity of applying fun to work, as if this keyword alone unlocks the mys-
tery of Americans' work meanings. Although it is important, it is only one aspect of how Americans think about work—and not all Americans at that.

A final reason the meanings discussed in this chapter are easy to miss is that
they do not conform to standard cultural descriptions of how Americans think
about work meanings.[72] Those cultural descriptions are about Americans'
Puritan work ethic, Americans' consumerism, Americans' self-reliance, and
American men's gender identities, the topics of the last four chapters. Work
meanings in those senses are about *working*; that is, about work as abstract
labor. Many of those meanings are important to my participants, but their
meanings of working are not just generic work meanings: they are also feelings about specific occupations and jobs. The standard cultural descriptions
omit the meanings of concrete labor, but we cannot understand Americans'
work meanings without them. Nor do the laborist or post-work theories I describe in the next chapter pay sufficient attention to concrete labor. In the
concluding chapter, I explain why we need a better understanding of meanings of working in specific kinds of jobs for more productive debates about
work policies and for thinking about the future of work.

CHAPTER 7

A Post-Pandemic Update and the Future of Work

Americans have been characterized as workaholics "addicted to their work, who think constantly about their jobs and who are frustrated if they are kept away from them, even during their evening hours and weekends," as one source put it.[1] It should be clear by now that I disagree. Only a minority of Americans are workaholics; most of the rest have what I term a diligent 9-to-5 work ethic. They take pride in being a good worker and find many nonfinancial satisfactions in their job, but they are happy to leave it at the end of the day. For most, their job is not an all-consuming locus of identity and focus of their concerns.

Strikingly, during the COVID-19 pandemic that began in 2020, an opposing folk cultural description arose: Americans no longer have a good work ethic. As employers had trouble filling low-wage jobs, one McDonald's restaurant posted a sign that went viral: "We are short-staffed. Please be patient with the staff that did show up. Nobody wants to work anymore."[2] The generalization "Nobody wants to work anymore" is also wrong. Now we know that most dropouts from the labor force since the beginning of the pandemic were seniors age sixty-five and older.[3]

Although neither of these broad generalizations (Americans are workaholics! Americans don't want to work nowadays!) is accurate as a description of the public, they do reveal the values and anxieties of the commentators. In the preceding chapters, I explored the work motivations of ordinary Americans from a wide range of backgrounds. In the first two parts of this concluding chapter, I turn the tables, studying the influential words of politicians, policy makers, scholars, journalists, and others who make pronouncements like the ones just quoted. What are their assumptions about most people's work motivations, and what are their values about the place of work in a good life? I explain the competing work policies they call for and the policies many of my interviewees would support if they could intervene in these debates. For example, should unemployment benefits and other social welfare assistance be restricted or expanded? Which would be a better society: one with full employment or one with expanded government income supports so adults do not need to work as much?

In the last section, I turn to possible future meanings of working and not working. Like other commentators, I take into account automation and AI, remote work, insecure jobs, and nonmarket options for sustaining a living. However, we cannot assume that these new ways of working will be experienced the same way in the future as they are now. Thus, I set out all the factors we need to consider to better understand how changing contexts could shape work meanings.

Unemployment Benefits: Before, during, and after the COVID-19 Pandemic

In the spring of 2020, COVID-19 began its deadly invasion of the United States. Many states responded by issuing stay-at-home orders, shuttering all businesses except those that were deemed essential and those that could continue with their employees working from home. By April 2020, the unemployment rate was a staggering 14.8 percent.[4] Even after businesses were allowed to reopen, health care concerns, lack of childcare, and supply chain disruptions kept many out of work.

Through the summer and fall of 2020, reporters around the country asked some of those laid-off workers how they were coping while they were out of work and, once they were able to return, how they felt about working again. An immigrant from El Salvador who had been a bartender in Las Vegas before the casinos closed told a reporter, "Sometimes one feels afflicted, desperate, because we want to work. We don't want unemployment benefits, free money for no work. We want to feel useful." A young Native man in Arizona who had become a Level 2-certified sommelier missed his job. He spoke of how wine had become his "window to the world, this way for me to travel" to which he otherwise had no access. A Black woman in her fifties cried for joy when she returned to her job at the Grand Rapids, Michigan, visitor center after being furloughed for months. She loved her job: "It seemed like a fairy tale because I just love being a team member where I can help people." She commented, "I hate being stuck at home. I hate not being able to go to work, not so much for the money, but just for a part of my sanity. After so much time, you've done all the projects at your house, so what else is there to do?"[5]

Their comments echo some of the same themes I heard in my research. I spoke with immigrants like the bartender from El Salvador who were reluctant to take government benefits because they wanted to "feel useful." My participants had additional reasons for wanting to work. Like the Arizona sommelier and the Michigan woman who worked in a visitor center, working could be enjoyable for them. Several of my participants said that working regularly could be a form of self-care. A surprising number said one of their past jobs had been "fun," either because they enjoyed the tasks or because they liked socializing with their coworkers. Unfortunately, the perspective of laid-off workers was rarely heard during the contentious debates about unemployment benefits in the first year of the COVID-19 pandemic.

As I discussed in chapter 4, recipients of unemployment benefits occupy an unstable place in a widely shared American cultural model that imagines a binary division between the "deserving" and the "undeserving" poor. In general, unemployment benefit recipients are considered "deserving" because the only way to qualify for those benefits is to have been working and to have lost their job through no fault of their own. However, if the unemployed remain out of work for many weeks, then some politicians and other commentators start criticizing them for "loafing" at the taxpayers' expense. Thus, unemployment benefits are designed to be short-term and of limited financial assistance. In most states, unemployment benefits end after twenty-six weeks. After the Great Recession of 2007–9, some state legislatures, facing pressure from business interests, lowered benefit periods to only twelve weeks and created other application barriers. Nationally, only 27 percent of jobless workers qualified for unemployment benefits in 2019, and in some states just 15 percent qualified. Furthermore, state unemployment benefit programs are designed to replace only about half the worker's former wages, and the maximum benefit is capped, so many of the unemployed receive much less than half of what they had earned.[6] For minimum-wage workers who are barely getting by even when they are working, an unemployment benefit of half what they had been earning is completely inadequate.[7] Freelance workers, independent contractors, and the self-employed, including workers who obtain gigs through online platforms, are normally ineligible for unemployment benefits.[8]

A recession created by the response to a public health emergency is not a normal situation. The COVID-19 pandemic overwhelmed the social body's feeble defense, "That is how it's always been done," forcing at least temporary changes not only in how work is conducted but also in the way the government responds to widespread unemployment.

At the beginning of the COVID-19 pandemic, sympathy for those who lost their incomes, along with worries that the economy would go into a deeper recession as the unemployed curtailed their spending, spurred the largest expansion of unemployment benefits in US history.[9] In March 2020, Congress passed the CARES (Coronavirus Aid, Relief, and Economic Security) Act. It not only extended unemployment benefits for an additional thirteen weeks, as is typical during recessions,[10] but also for the first time made unemployment benefits available to those who would not normally qualify because they were freelancers or gig workers or had insufficient prior earnings. Furthermore, the CARES Act added $600 a week to displaced workers' unemployment benefit through the end of July 2020, regardless of their prior incomes.[11]

That $600 a week flat benefit enhancement was chosen as a fast and easy fix. To quickly stimulate the economy under the unusual circumstances of the pandemic, policy makers wanted to fully replace workers' lost wages. Because they could not rely on the states' outdated IT programs to quickly perform those individual calculations for each worker, federal policy makers fell back on the simple expedient of calculating the difference between the average national wage before the pandemic and the average unemployment insurance benefit. That is how they arrived at the figure of $600, which was added to the weekly check of everyone who qualified for unemployment benefits. It supplemented the state unemployment insurance benefits, which averaged $387 a week, giving the average laid-off worker $987 a week in unemployment benefits for the first few months of the pandemic.[12]

Six hundred dollars a week is the amount someone would receive if they worked a forty-hour week at $15 an hour. The federal minimum wage in the United States in 2020 was less than half that amount at $7.25 an hour. For several years low-wage workers had been engaged in strikes and protests for a minimum wage of $15 an hour. By a cosmic coincidence, the CARES Act temporarily fulfilled the goal of the Fight for $15 movement—but for those who were unemployed, rather than for those who were working. During the pandemic, workers in low-wage service jobs who had been earning less than $15 an hour made up a large share of the unemployed.[13] Some University of Chicago economists reported that while the $600 unemployment supplement was in place (from April through the end of July 2020), 76 percent of those on unemployment compensation were eligible for more money from unemployment than they had earned while working.[14] It was a remarkable moment in the history of the US welfare state. For a brief time, unemployment benefits, which are usually woefully inadequate, came to as much as or more than low-income workers had earned before they lost their jobs.

The backlash was predictable. Low-wage employers who were ready to re-hire workers over the summer of 2020 complained they were having difficulty finding willing workers; conservative politicians and other policy makers argued that the large unemployment benefit was clearly a work disincentive and had to be reduced to force the unemployed to take jobs.[15]

When they designed the first CARES Act in March 2020, policy makers thought that the pandemic would end after a few weeks. That optimistic prediction was wrong. When the CARES Act was about to expire at the end of December 2020, Congress agreed to extend unemployment benefits until mid-March 2021, and they compromised on a smaller $300 weekly benefit supplement. The American Rescue Plan that passed the new Congress in mid-March ensured funding for states to provide these enhanced unemployment benefits through the first week of September 2021.[16]

Vaccines were developed at the end of 2020. In 2021 restaurants, stores, and other businesses that had been shuttered began reopening, but there were still not enough workers to fill all the job vacancies. The shortages were particularly acute in lower-wage, in-person leisure and hospitality jobs.[17] Once again, business owners and conservative commentators blamed the extended and enhanced unemployment benefits for creating the shortages. As one pub owner put it, "The government is making it easy for people to stay home and get paid. You can't really blame them much. But it means we have hours to fill and no one who wants to work."[18] In response, twenty-six governors either discontinued the $300 enhanced benefit or cut off the additional weeks of unemployment benefits.[19] When the governor of Wyoming announced that his state would end those benefits, he stated, "Incentivizing people not to work is just plain un-American."[20]

The word choices of the pub owner ("The government is making it easy for people to stay home and get paid. You can't really blame them much") and the Wyoming governor ("Incentivizing people not to work") are revealing. These comments are based on a *rational choice work decision* cultural model. It is one of two popular US cultural models that explain why people might choose not to work.

According to the second model, the *ingrained bad work ethic* model, there is a "class of people who simply don't want to work," as a businessman put it in an editorial. This discriminatory model casts aspersions on whole groups, such as people in poverty (especially people of color in poverty) or young people.

For example, older adults like that businessman are prone to disparage "a generation of slackers who would rather sit at home watching reality TV than to rejoin the real world where people work to make a living."[21] Among politicians, the ingrained bad work ethic model is more often voiced by conservatives than liberals.

However, one need not be a political conservative to suspect that any rational person would rather stay home if they could receive as much money as they would by making the effort to go to work. The *rational choice work decision* model assumes that choices about taking a job are based on short-term cost/benefit calculations. If we add the assumption that most people consider working an unpleasant necessity undertaken solely for a paycheck, then it follows that people would prefer staying at home if they received enough money from other sources.[22] These are the unspoken beliefs that lie behind the rhetoric that unemployment benefits are "incentivizing people not to work."[23]

As the psychologist Barry Schwartz argues forcefully, the flaw in this rational choice model is that it focuses on economic reasons for working, ignoring the additional nonfinancial benefits that matter for so many people.[24] Those with a diligent 9-to-5 work ethic want to feel productive and have a structure for their days and weeks. Many want to be valued members of a group who are recognized for their contributions. Some men feel they are failing to live up to cultural expectations of manhood if they are out of work. Both men and women say they would feel better about themselves if they were working or that having a job would make them feel a part of mainstream society. And many enjoy at least some aspects of their jobs.

Motivations for working, abstractly, could be enhanced or outweighed by the working conditions of a particular job. Some of my participants' jobs caused them injuries, subjected them to harassment from coworkers or managers, or required them to engage in repugnant business practices. In those cases, going to work had serious costs. However, it was far more common for them to describe jobs they had liked than ones they had disliked.

To be sure, the pay and fringe benefits they received from their job mattered as well. I do not mean that the financial rewards of working are irrelevant in decisions about whether to go to work. My point is that they are only one consideration.

One could reply that my interviewees and the examples quoted earlier of workers laid off during the pandemic may not be representative. It is quite likely that those who had previously been working hard for poverty-level wages appreciated the enhanced unemployment benefits, which gave them enough money to live on for a change. No doubt some may have delayed their return to work for that reason. However, several careful economic analyses have shown that the effects of the enhanced benefits on returns to work were small.[25] Strikingly, half of those who received the $600 a week benefit supplement returned to work before the supplements expired, even though three-quarters of the unemployed were receiving more money from unemployment benefits than they had been paid when they were working.[26] In other words, a large share of those thrown out of work early in the pandemic elected to forgo higher incomes in order to work again.

The real reasons for labor shortages predate the COVID-19 pandemic: lower birthrates, retirements of older workers in the large Baby Boomer generation, and immigration restrictions.[27] In the early 2000s there were between two and three workers per job opening, rising to more than six in 2009, but by the end of 2021, that ratio fell to a half-worker available for every opening.[28] Many other factors affected the labor market during the first two years of the pandemic, including closed schools and daycare centers, which made it difficult for parents of young children (mothers especially) to work, and the continuing fear of infection, a particular concern for older workers.

Labor shortages were difficult for small business owners, but they gave workers more bargaining power. When there are fewer workers than job openings, they can demand higher wages. One ice cream parlor that had no applicants for $7.25 an hour (plus tips) jobs as scoopers was flooded with applicants after the owner raised the starting wage to $15 an hour.[29] It should not be surprising that when labor markets give workers more options, they will be choosier about their jobs. In general, Americans, like my participants, do want to work, but they also want more say about their working conditions. The tight labor market and workers' anger about their treatment during the pandemic fed an upsurge in labor organizing in the United States, as well as in public support for unions.[30]

What are the practical implications for unemployment benefits? No one is advocating for paying the jobless more than they earned when working. Still, unemployment benefits can be more generous, especially for low-income workers, with little overall effect on employment levels.[31] There should be a national minimum unemployment benefit level that should increase as average wages increase, as well as a national minimum number of weeks of benefits.[32] Some research shows that a longer period of unemployment benefits lets workers find a better employer, a more suitable job for their skills, and higher wages.[33] The problem is not that we provide too much to the unemployed but that we pay low-wage workers too little.

A work ethic is not all or nothing that one either has or does not. There are multiple work ethics, and the specific job matters as much as or more so than devotion to labor in the abstract. I build on those observations in the next section, where I consider competing laborist and post-work visions for the future.

Work Policies, Cultural Models, and Unlikely Bedfellows

Debates about whether unemployment benefits affect labor force participation are technical discussions bristling with terms like "reservation wage" and "liquidity effects." These technical arguments simply take for granted an affirmative answer to a basic social question: Is a good society one in which all adults are working for wages, unless they are in school, retired, or occupied with family responsibilities? When scholars argue (as I did in the last section) that more generous unemployment benefits will not stop the jobless from looking for work, we seem to be assuming waged work as the ideal. Whether it should be the ideal is the subject of a lively debate at present, one that cuts across the usual Right–Left divide.

Among those on the political Left, there is contention over which would be better: a society in which all adults capable of going to work were guaranteed a well-paid job, or a society in which adults were not forced to sell their labor to live a decent life. Progressive activists and scholars disagree about which vision of a good society to fight for. The *laborist Left* advocates for the first, the *post-work Left* for the second.

I take the label laborist from post-work theorist Kathi Weeks. Although it is not widely used, it aptly expresses political organizing that "celebrate[s] the worth and dignity of waged work and . . . contend[s] that such work is entitled to respect and adequate recompense."[34] That has been the mainstream view of the labor movement, and it is the foundation of European social democracies.[35] Progressive laborist activists and scholars claim that most people want to work, and the problem is there are not enough good jobs. They advocate for full employment, with the government stepping in to provide such jobs when necessary. Dr. Martin Luther King proclaimed, "We need an economic bill of rights. This would *guarantee a job* to all people who want to work and are able to work." The famous 1963 march on Washington, the occasion for Dr. King's "I Have a Dream" speech, was called the "March on Washington for *Jobs* and Freedom."[36]

The laborist Left shares with political conservatives a preference for a social order in which adults can be self-supporting through waged work. In response to Donald Trump's election in 2016, some laborist policy makers from the Left, Right, and in between, led by the centrist Opportunity America think tank, agreed that more jobs would be the best solution for the grievances of an angry working class whose standard of living fell as a result of deindustrialization in the mid-Atlantic and upper Midwest. Their report states that despite the ideological differences among the policy makers, they agreed that any solutions must begin with getting people to work: "The most important provision of the social contract is work: the opportunity for meaningful, rewarding work and the norm that healthy adults who aren't taking care of children should engage in work." Why is work so important? In addition to producing income, "it's character-forming—a first good choice that usually leads to other good choices and essential values like purpose, diligence, responsibility and self-reliance."[37] For laborists, advances in artificial intelligence and robotics are threats to a society centered on paid work for all.

Where adherents to the laborist Left depart from typical conservative laborists is in their assumptions about whether most adults want to work. Conservative laborists are more likely than those on the Left to assume that many people do not want to work: they believe in the *ingrained bad work ethic* model. They think that shirkers must be forced to work for a living by restricting other means of support. The Opportunity America report adopts the alternative laborist Left assumption that most people do want to work: "For most people, [*working is*] more satisfying than almost any other activity, including consumption."[38] According to this view, the government does not need to force people to work. Instead, the state should provide more jobs and opportunities for job training.

Post-work theorists thoroughly disagree that work is the most satisfying thing people could be doing. These theorists draw a stark distinction between "work time and non-work time, between work and life, between time for what we are obligated to do and time for 'what we will.'"[39] They want less of the first of each pair and more of the second. Yet, the term "post-work" is misleading: they do not propose a future of total leisure. As Kathi Weeks forcefully articulates in *The Problem with Work*, they advocate for much less work time, and they question the assumption that the primary way to support oneself should be through waged labor. Post-work activists and theorists call not for a right to work but for "'the refusal of work.'"[40] By "refusal of work," they mean, "refusal of the ideology of work as [*a person's*] highest calling and moral duty, a refusal of work as the necessary center of social life and means of access to the rights and claims of citizenship."[41] Adopting this perspective, Weeks questions why so many feminists have fought for women to have equal opportunities for waged work instead of demanding more free time.

A key demand of post-work activists is a shorter workweek, say thirty hours, achieved either through a six-hour workday or a four-day workweek, with no

reduction in pay. To give people greater options, including the ability to refuse unfulfilling jobs, post-work theorists also champion a universal basic income (UBI): a monthly or annual cash grant from the government to every
adult.[42] Some on the laborist Left also support a UBI because it would help
workers bargain for better wages and working conditions. By contrast, post-
work activists argue that "even the best job is a problem when it monopolizes
so much of life."[43] Instead, they hope that receiving a UBI will enable people
to work less, giving them time "to consider and experiment with different
kinds of lives."[44] From a post-work perspective, advances in automation are
welcome if the result is more free time for people to do what they want. In
supporting freedom to decide how to use one's time, post-work theorists are
joined by some libertarian conservatives who prefer a (low) guaranteed basic
income instead of government social welfare programs that come with layers
of regulation.[45]

Post-work theorists seek to liberate people from having to work long hours
to earn a living, while most political conservatives who are not libertarian want
to require adults to work for a living instead of receiving money from the government. However, their underlying assumptions about work and human
motivation are the same. Writers on both sides accept the rational choice work
decision premise that any rational person would prefer staying at home if they
received enough money so that they did not have to work. Both assume that
waged work is not intrinsically enjoyable. Post-work theorists Stanley Aronowitz and William DiFazio state that explicitly: "When they are given the opportunity, workers—skilled and unskilled alike—are pleased to be relieved of
participation in the labor process provided they are guaranteed an income adequate to the current 'decent' standard of living."[46] They assume that people
work only to obtain a "decent" standard of living, and if they could reach that
living standard without paid employment, they would not work. According
to Aronowitz and DiFazio, they should not have to.

Kathi Weeks has a subtler argument. As I explained in chapter 6, she recognizes that one answer to her question, "Why do we work so long and so
hard?" is that "we work because we want to: work provides a variety of satisfactions—in addition to income, it can be a source of meaning, purpose, structure, social ties, and recognition." She argues, however, that wanting to work
hard is not inherent to humans; instead, it was inculcated in Europe and the
United States with the Protestant work ethic. Thus, although people may consent to work long hours, this is a manufactured consent.[47] That people do not
naturally want to work is also implicit in formulations such as the distinction
she draws between "work time and non-work time, between work and life,
between time for what we are obligated to do and time for 'what we will.'"

Waged work is equated with "what we are obligated to do," whereas activities outside work are "what we will."

My research leads me to a position between laborist and post-work ideologies. I disagree with post-work theorists Aronowitz and DiFazio that "when they are given the opportunity, workers—skilled and unskilled alike—are pleased to be relieved of participation in the labor process." That is not true, and such claims reinforce the narrative of many conservative commentators that recipients of government social assistance have to be bludgeoned into working because their natural preference is to avoid that effort. When I asked my participants what sorts of policies they would enact if they were in charge, many proposed measures to create more jobs, much like the proposals of the laborist Left. Few opposed work to "life"; most viewed the right sort of job as part of a good life. Other researchers have found the same, including among people who receive income supports from the state in societies as diverse as Norway and South Africa, as well as the United States.[48]

However, the laborists' claim, "For most people, [*work is*] more satisfying than almost any other activity, including consumption," is questionable as well. Waged work can indeed be highly satisfying, but so can relaxation, leisure activities, time with friends and family, community involvement, and religious and spiritual practices.[49] Most of my participants did not live to work, and among those who had previously done so, many later changed their priorities. Post-work theorists are absolutely right to insist on a better balance between work time and time for other activities. Many of my participants disliked jobs that required long hours. From my research, I would predict that post-work proposals to shorten the workweek, without a decrease in pay, would prove very popular with workers. Recent studies of workplaces that are trying a thirty-two-hour workweek have found employees more energized and employers ready to continue the practice.[50]

Overtime protections are too weak in the United States. In 2020 the Department of Labor expanded the category of workers entitled to overtime pay, but salaried workers paid at least $684 a week can still be forced to work long hours without additional compensation.[51] More workers should be entitled to overtime pay. The United States could adopt the overtime regulations in the European Union, which mandates an average workweek of no longer than forty-eight hours in all member states, with exceptions for only a few occupations.[52]

US workers also need mandated paid vacations and holidays. The United States is the only wealthy country in the world without federally mandated vacation pay or holiday pay. Nearly one-quarter of US workers, typically those in low-wage positions, receive neither.[53] A posting on Reddit by someone outside the United States asked Americans on the discussion website, "How do y'all stay sane with so few holidays and vacation time?" The top-voted comments of more than 15,000 responses were variations on "We don't—it's driving us crazy" (r/antiwork, January 17, 2023).

Descriptions of Americans as driven by a Puritan work ethic are dangerous because they suggest that most Americans want to work long hours and do not care whether they have paid vacations and holidays. One economist commented in 2001, "It's unique to Americans that they continue to increase their working hours, while hours are declining in other industrialized nations . . . It has a lot to do with the American psyche, with American culture. American workers are eager to make the best impression, to put in the most hours."[54] That is true of some American workers but not most. The very long hours that managers and professionals have to work may explain my findings that many welcomed a break and a chance to rethink their priorities when they lost their job.[55] Wanting a break is not limited to a new "generation of slackers."[56] When Edward Wight Bakke studied unemployed blue-collar working men in the United States during the Great Depression in the 1930s, he found that, initially, those workers appreciated their layoffs "as a chance for a short holiday."[57]

Post-work theorists are also right to fight for social welfare protections (for example, health care, paid sick leave, and paid family leave) that are not tied to full-time standard employment. That is important because, as I explain in the next section on the future of work, linking such necessary protections to standard employment leaves out the large and growing category of independent contractors, freelancers, and gig workers.

There is another problem with all the work ideologies I have described so far. Although the laborist Left along with most conservatives say Americans work too little, and post-work theorists disagree, saying Americans work too much, all sides speak of work abstractly, rather than about the characteristics of specific jobs. True, labor unions try to improve material aspects of jobs—pay, fringe benefits, and safe working conditions—but usually they do not address all the features that make jobs enjoyable or drudgery. To explore that issue, we need the insights of other theorists.

Contributive justice theorists see work as *potentially* a source of meaning or fulfillment. Their political goal is not less work or better remunerated work but more satisfying work. This leads them to consider what makes a job meaningful and whether there is equal opportunity to obtain meaningful jobs, a social justice issue they take to be of paramount importance after minimal economic needs are met.[58] I agree that we need to stop talking about work abstractly and instead look at what matters to workers in a job, which is a good segue to considering the future of work.

Future Meanings of Working, Not Working, and the Ambiguous In-Between

Does my research give us a basis for predicting how US Americans or people elsewhere might think about working and not working in the future? And are those the only two choices?

Predicting the future of work meanings is doubly hazardous because it requires predicting not only how the world will change but also how people might feel about those changes. Predicting how the world will change is very difficult by itself. For example, we can imagine the potential of AI and robotics to alter or displace human labor, but the availability of a technology does not determine which employers will adopt it, whether state policies will promote or constrain its adoption, or how workers will respond politically.[59] Furthermore, the future of work cannot be reduced to AI and automation.[60] For example, will parents be allowed or encouraged to use genetic engineering to improve their offspring's opportunities for remunerative occupations?[61] What demographic changes are coming, and what impact will those shifts have on the workforce of different nations? How will societies adapt to climate change and the upheavals it causes? How might new technologies and policies about them shape where people work, when they work, and relations between workers and employers?

The importance of humility about the limits of our ability to predict the future became exceedingly clear as I was finishing this book. For years, futurists had been pondering the possibility that human labor would be displaced by advances in AI and automation. Who foresaw that the public health response to a microscopic virus would suddenly throw a half-billion people out of work around the world and disrupt assumptions about how work is conducted?[62] Now, working from home has forced its way into conversations about the future of work.

Even if we could accurately predict such changes, we would not know what meanings they would hold for people in the future. We do not know whether our counterparts in 2030 or 2040 or 2050 will interpret new situations with the same assumptions and values about the place of waged work in a good life that we have now or whether new circumstances will give rise to different assumptions and values. Most likely, it will be a mix of old and new.

It is tempting to use the past as a guide to the future. For example, the journalist Derek Thompson wondered how Americans would deal with high levels of technological unemployment: "a new normal, where the expectation that work will be a central feature of adult life dissipates for a significant portion of society." To answer that question, he considered the example of

Youngstown, Ohio, in the late 1970s and early 1980s, when steel mill owners moved jobs abroad, throwing fifty thousand people out of work. The result was a "psychological and cultural breakdown" reflected in high rates of "depression, spousal abuse, and suicide," which Thompson suggests we could see in a future in which most labor is performed by sophisticated AI programs and tireless robots.[63] However, those who lost well-paid factory jobs several decades ago were unemployed in what has been termed a "work society," based on the norm that adults (at least, adult men) would spend the majority of their waking hours in full-time employment for forty or more years. If waged work ceased to be a central feature of adult life, we could expect new ways of living, thinking, and feeling.

I am agnostic about whether AI and automation will cause high levels of unemployment in the future. Over the last decade, experts' forecasts have shifted—from estimates that nearly half of all jobs in the United States could be automated in the next ten to twenty years, to carefully reasoned explanations that occupational transformation is more probable than massive unemployment, only to swing back to renewed worries about the value added by human labor given the increasing sophistication of machine learning.[64] Any prediction I made now could be outdated in a few years. Nor is widespread technological unemployment the only looming possibility to consider. Among the other trends I just discussed, the proliferation of ways of earning a living other than through standard employment is especially important. That is why I labeled this section "future meanings of working, not working, and in-between." By "in-between," I mean alternatives to both full-time employment and full-time unemployment.[65]

I do not have the expertise to predict the future, nor do I claim that my participants' work meanings are timeless and universal. They are only one group of people at one slice of time. Instead, I describe seven factors that affect people's thoughts and feelings about work: (1) predominant types of livelihoods, (2) workers' expectations of job availability, (3) workers' attitudes about the types of jobs and working conditions available to them, (4) nonmarket options for sustaining a living, (5) consumption norms, (6) other meanings of work in a good life, and (7) the individual's identities. I discuss the first factor in detail and the others more briefly. These factors foreground the diversity of people's situations and meanings, today and in the future.

Predominant Types of Livelihoods

"Work" has not always meant what the anthropologists James Ferguson and Tania Li say came to be thought of as the "proper job" under industrial capitalism. Earning a living by selling one's labor—rather than through subsistence agriculture, tributary modes of production like European feudalism, and other subsistence strategies—is a historic exception. Standard employment—"year-round, full-time wage employment with a single employer . . . and with the expectation of durable attachment"—is even rarer.[66] Even in the Global North in the twentieth century, disadvantaged groups, such as migrants, ethnic minorities, and women, have often labored for pay without the protections of standard employment. Currently, more than half the people in the world work in what the International Labor Organization calls the informal economy of unregulated economic activity, making a living from improvised combinations of contingent labor and sales of specialized services and their own products.[67] Contingent employment and self-employment are also becoming more common in the post-Fordist Global North. This is not as dramatic as sci-fi images of androids lounging in break rooms, but it is consequential. There are struggles underway to shape what work will be like in a gig economy of irregular work.

There is no doubt that such a shift is occurring in the United States and elsewhere in the Global North. Employers are cutting costs by eliminating direct employees and instead hiring temporary agency and contract firm workers, freelancers, anonymous online gig workers, and other independent contractors.[68] Observers trace the beginnings of this shift to the mid-1970s and 1980s as neoliberal ideologies, shareholder pressures, and global competition led large companies to push for more "flexible" labor arrangements. New information and communication technologies have made it easier for employers to break up jobs into microtasks that can be contracted out—perhaps to workers whom they never meet.[69]

In the United States, the number of employees working for temporary services firms increased nearly 40 percent from 2011 to 2022.[70] In 2022 more than one-third of US survey respondents were contract, freelance, temporary, or digital platform gig workers, up from a little more than one-quarter in 2016. Nearly three-quarters of those independent workers had no other job.[71]

More workers are also choosing to work for themselves. In 2017, the percentage of adults reporting self-employment income on their taxes reached the highest level since the IRS started collecting that information in 1957. A Gallup survey conducted at the end of 2019 estimated that 28 percent of US workers have some form of self-employment, with about half relying on self-employment as their primary source of income.[72]

Not everyone who is counted as self-employed in official statistics chose that status. A growing trend is for employers to classify their workers as independent contractors rather than employees. Doing so enables employers to save about 30 percent of their labor costs because they do not have to pay overtime, fringe benefits, or their share of payroll taxes.[73] Such misclassified independent contractors typically include gig workers on digital platforms, many construction workers, short- and long-haul truck drivers, in-home care workers, fitness trainers, and loan officers.[74] This is a blurry category some researchers call "dependent contractors" because such workers are often not free to set their pay rate or working conditions.[75]

If, in the future, most workers are self-employed or have temporary positions, the whole nature of work in the Global North will change. Adults' lives may cease to be structured by shared work hours, workdays, or even work years. Researchers like me will not conduct interviews asking how the unemployed feel about being out of work because formal unemployment will be as rare as formal employment. Instead, there will be a constant scramble for income-producing opportunities without the clear boundaries of either having a job or being unemployed.

Some post-work progressives cheer the prospect of a future in which irregular work is the norm. By contrast, those on the laborist Left call for more labor protections from precarious employment.[76] Among the latter, there are different views about how best to protect misclassified independent contractors who rely on a single employer or platform for their income. Should they be considered employees, with all the legal protections of standard employment, even if that means they cannot set their own hours? Or should a new employment category be created for them, as exists in Canada and some other countries?[77]

In the mid-1990s, the Freelancers Union was established in the United States to offer affordable health insurance and other benefits to self-employed workers and to advocate on their behalf. During the COVID-19 pandemic, it succeeded in extending unemployment benefits to the self-employed.[78] Some European countries have established voluntary unemployment insurance plans for the self-employed or have separate financial protection systems for them (including misclassified independent contractors), so they can receive family leave, sick pay, and pensions when they retire.[79]

It is important to recognize variation in the broad category of precarious work. There are different material and immaterial costs and benefits of being a temporary agency worker, on-call worker, misclassified independent contractor, true independent contractor or freelancer, and owner of a small business.[80] Furthermore, even those in the same kind of position vary in their feelings about it because they have different goals. One study found that full-time Uber and Lyft drivers struggled to make a living, leaving them much less satisfied than part-time drivers for whom it was a second income or the "hobbyists" who drove because they enjoyed the social contacts more than because they needed the money.[81] Jagat Bodhi, a telecommunications technician I interviewed in this project, resented being forced to become a contractor constantly scrambling for work when his company fired full-time employees, as he had been previously. He felt that as a contractor, "You're just a number. You are easily replaced." By contrast, a Black telecommunication engineer I interviewed for an earlier study left standard employment to become a contractor because of the discrimination he had experienced at work. This engineer sought to minimize his workplace attachments, preferring the life of a contractor where "you go in, you do your job, you get paid, you leave." I also found that because labor protections in the United States are minimal even for standard employment, the standard/nonstandard distinction was not always salient to my participants nor what mattered most to them.[82]

In sum, the meanings of "precarious employment" depend on what workers take as normal, which is not the same for everyone and will likely change in the future.

Workers' Expectations of Job Availability and Duration without Work

A factor that affects the experience of not working is whether workers anticipate being without work and how they imagine their future opportunities.[83]

As I noted earlier in this chapter, Bakke's longitudinal study of factory workers who were unemployed during the Great Depression in the 1930s found that, at first, workers were not worried: they were accustomed to short periods without work. It was typical in that period for factories to lay off workers when sales dropped and to rehire them as business improved.[84] At present, job instability is the norm among financial analysts on Wall Street and high-tech workers. Ethnographers observe that laid-off workers in those fields are not very worried because they expect to find a similar job with relative ease.[85] Workers can prepare, financially and psychologically, for that kind of normalized frictional unemployment, and they are buoyed by good prospects for the future.

By contrast, when job loss is the result of the demise of an industry in the absence of other good job opportunities, workers may be unprepared financially and unable to imagine a path forward. The wrenching effects of permanent shifts in the local economy have been documented for factory closings in the United States and Europe and after privatization of formerly state-supported industries in postsocialist China and Romania.[86] This sort of structural unemployment seems the most difficult to bear.

To judge from my research, the psychological effects of cyclical unemployment are initially like frictional unemployment because it is hard to know how long a downturn will last. The factory workers whom Bakke studied early in the Great Depression had no way of knowing it would last ten years. The job seekers I interviewed in the aftermath of the Great Recession, the most severe downturn in the US economy since the Great Depression, could not know that it would be nearly six and a half years before employment levels returned to pre-recession levels.[87] My participants initially thought that their current period of unemployment would be like previous times they had been out of work, when labor markets were better, so they expected to find another job in the same field before long. As time passed, their feelings changed. Their savings may have been sufficient for several months of joblessness but not for a year or more, and they faced difficult decisions with no idea of what the future would bring. Did they need to tap into their retirement savings? Should they train for a different occupation? Should they sell their home and move to less expensive housing? They were mired in uncertainty, unsure how to feel or plan.

Although being out of work during a severe economic downturn is difficult in many respects, it may come with somewhat less social stigma and greater support from the state, community groups, and family members. Lasting structural unemployment could eventually have the same effect. I am reminded of Daniel Mains's ethnography of young men without jobs in urban Ethiopia at a time of chronic, high unemployment rates. When Mains asked if they felt shame about being out of work, they replied that "a condition shared by so many people could not be considered shameful."[88] That outlook may be common if there is widespread technological unemployment in the future.

Workers' Attitudes about the Types of Jobs and Working Conditions Available to Them

The kinds of jobs and working conditions available in the future will also affect how people feel about working. As the technology journalist Kevin Roose puts it, we need to write "more about AI's effects on the *quality* of jobs, rather than just the quantity of them."[89]

The ease of digital platforms for consumers hides the backstage human labor on which these transactions depend. For example, e-commerce currently requires an army of low-wage warehouse workers. Warehouse work is plentiful in southern California, a logistics hub for trans-Pacific trade, but for two of my interviewees, those were the worst jobs they had ever held. Summer Carrington developed foot pain from running around the concrete floors of a huge Amazon fulfillment center to pull orders under strict time limits. She said the workers were given few breaks to sit, and they were closely monitored for theft. She was just as glad when she was not rehired after the holiday-season rush. Those jobs are likely to be automated in the future.

However, automation still requires human oversight. Digital platforms rely on people to train AI programs, remove unacceptable content on social media, fix technical glitches, and rate search engine and chatbot responses for appropriateness. The anthropologist Mary Gray and computer scientist Siddharth Suri call this invisible human labor "ghost work." They describe one woman who checks 1,100 news snippets an hour through Amazon's Mechanical Turk, quickly categorizing each one as "sports," "politics," or some other category, for two cents per task. Her other assignments included checking pictures that were flagged as offensive on social media. It sounds boring to me, but that woman said she liked the variety of tasks, and she could watch TV shows or listen to music to help pass the time.[90] By contrast, some content raters hired by subcontract firms working for Google, YouTube, and other platforms reported being traumatized by the grisly content they deleted and are seeking to organize to increase their low pay.[91]

Unlike warehouse workers, ghost workers can work from home or anywhere else they can go online. The rise of computer-mediated jobs and the COVID-19 pandemic have undermined one of the basic conditions of paid employment from the mid-nineteenth century on—that it requires congregating in a central location separate from the workers' homes. By July 2022, approximately 30 percent of paid workdays in the United States were being performed remotely, up from only 5 percent before COVID-19.[92] It is a huge shift for workers whose tasks depend primarily on computers and telephones.

From the reports so far, whether workers like remote work depends on their personal situations. Those who had long commutes are grateful for this option, as are parents of young children and workers with mobility impairments.[93] In the United States, some workers of color reported feeling relieved by being able to avoid the microaggressions or outright discrimination they experienced in their workplaces.[94] On the other side, there are also reports of new hires feeling adrift and workers missing social interaction. One international survey found that more than eight in ten workers would be motivated to return to the office to socialize with coworkers. The youngest (Gen Z) workers were especially eager to reconnect with work friends and older mentors,[95] reminding me of a college student interviewee who said that, after she graduated, she wanted to work for a company where she would be expected to hang out with colleagues after work hours because that was how she would make friends in a new city. As I explained in the last chapter, many of my unemployed participants of all ages and family situations missed the casual friendly interactions that had made going to work fun for them. If remote work remains common, will working hours become a time for strictly business, as is the norm in some countries now?[96] And if that happens, will workers compensate by finding other opportunities for social interactions beyond their household?

One question for the future is how remote work will affect the balance between workers' independence and managers' oversight. At present, some employers are trying to monitor their remote workers through "bossware" surveillance programs that can be highly invasive and installed without the worker's consent or even knowledge.[97] We can imagine future scenarios of virtual reality meetings attended by avatars, with employees using chatbots to make their avatars speak in their absence and bosses trying to detect whether their employee is really present.

Remote work can also break down the separation of spheres between home and work. One possible effect is a shift in the gendering of home as women's domain and work outside the home as men's domain. Expectations about who is responsible for childcare and housework may change as well, although not necessarily.

One scholar writing about remote work worries, "The conversion of the home environment into a work environment has tended to corrupt the sanctity of the home" as a place "that allows the stresses of work to melt away and permits workers to enjoy time with family separated from work pressures or activities."[98] That separation is important in some societies,[99] but it overly idealizes home life. The sociologist Arlie Hochschild found that some American women did not want to take parenting leave because going to work was less stressful than staying home.[100] Will normalizing remote work keep women, especially mothers of young children, at home when they would prefer to get away for several hours every day?

For most of human history and in much of the world today, it would be odd to view home as a sanctuary away from work. For example, Seo Young Park studied South Korean garment manufacturers who create fast-fashion clothes in home factories. The garment workers chat with friends and watch their small children on the workshop floor while they are sewing. The owners slip away briefly to cook for their family and workers and then return to their sewing machines to meet their late-night deadlines. For the owners of the home factories, spatial and temporal boundaries between home and work are fluid.[101] My interviewees with a diligent 9-to-5 work ethic wanted those boundaries to be well defined, but future workers may feel differently.

Beyond the issue of where people will work in the future, there remains the key concern of whether their tasks will be engaging. Ideally, routine, boring functions will be automated, leaving humans only creative and stimulating tasks. However, Gray and Suri's description of ghost work suggests it is likely that the jobs left for humans in the future will not all be creative and interesting. As contributive justice theorists have stressed, that should be a focus for labor organizing in the future.

Nonmarket Options for Sustaining a Living

How people feel about waged work also depends on what other ways they can sustain a living and how they feel about those alternatives.

The two feminist theorists who publish under the name J. K. Gibson-Graham argue that we do not need a socialist revolution to create alternatives to waged work. Those alternatives already exist and include self-provisioning (for example, through scavenging, sewing, crafting, gardening, or hunting) and resource exchanges (for example, reciprocal work exchanges and cooperatives, co-living collectives, in-kind payments, and gifts).[102] They urge political change that enlarges the place of these nonmarket alternatives, challenging the hegemony of profit-making firms with their dependence on exploited labor and invented consumption "needs."

Interestingly, all the alternatives named by Gibson-Graham are ways of maintaining self-sufficiency or reciprocity, rather than one-way dependence. Americans have been characterized as rugged individualists who are unwilling to receive financial assistance, and many of my participants said that was true of them. However, they were able to accept financial assistance if it was part of an ongoing reciprocal relationship. Money from their parents could be repaid with physical assistance; donations from their faith community could be repaid with volunteer hours; extended unemployment benefits from the state were a fair exchange for their past tax payments and labor.

If in the future it becomes more difficult to sustain a living from waged work, I predict not only greater pressure for state income support but also greater expectations for financial support from family members and community groups, along with ways of interpreting such support as consistent with a morally worthy life.

Consumption Norms

People work not only to live but also to live well. How people feel about waged work in the future will also depend on consumption norms. An adequate income is not just one that keeps a person alive; it is one that enables a person to live in the manner that is socially expected.

How my unemployed participants felt about their current levels of consumption depended on their levels of debt, previous consumption highs and lows, the kinds of consumption needed to maintain their social relationships, and what served as a basis of their class identities, including symbolically significant forms of consumption. Some had taken on high levels of debt, which made them anxious. When they lost their jobs, many stopped accumulating debt for discretionary expenses, which helped them feel more relaxed.[103] Many of those who had previously been well-off, however, had trouble adapting to a drastically reduced income. They could not keep up with friends whose ways of socializing required a level of spending my unemployed participants could no longer afford. Some were embarrassed by their visibly reduced consumption, which had been central to their self-identification as "middle class" or as a "have" (rather than a "have-not") in society. Home ownership is an especially freighted key symbol at present in the United States.[104] Among some of my married interviewees, when unemployment made it impossible to pay the mortgage on their home, divorce followed soon after. By contrast, for those who had been unhoused, simply obtaining a decent place to reside made them more secure even if their income remained very low. As other researchers have found, downward mobility is more difficult to adjust to than precarity as a normal state.[105]

The social analyst Peter Frase argues that how well people will live a future of climate change and automation depends on whether there is overall abundance or scarcity and whether wealth and power are distributed equally or hierarchically. If everyone lived very simply, that would be the norm to which all would eventually adjust. Perhaps home ownership would cease to be a common symbol of a successful life. However, if there were great income inequality, it would be difficult for the majority to live without any of the comforts or pleasures they observed among the well-off.[106]

Other Meanings of Work in a Good Life

Social meanings of consumption take us to the larger place of work in a good life. A life can be "good" because it is pleasurable or because it is morally worthy.[107] How does work fit into a good life in either of those senses now, and how might those meanings change in the future?

As I explained, in the United States today there are three dominant ways of thinking about work as a moral duty. The first is that adults have the obligation to support themselves and their families (working to live). The second is that adults should spend a conventionally fixed part of their days and weeks applying themself conscientiously to paid work or other productive activities (a diligent 9-to-5 work ethic). The third is that adults should make their paid work the center of their identity and interests, devoting as much time as necessary to be successful (a living-to-work ethic). The second and third are the historic developments Weber termed the Protestant work ethic. The third (what I call a living-to-work ethic) takes the imperative to be productive to its Puritan extreme, which Weber believed was peculiar because it subordinates the rest of life to work, instead of the reverse. He believed that ethic had disappeared by the early twentieth century, although others contend that there is a new Puritan work ethic enjoining managers and professionals in particular to devote long hours to their jobs.[108]

Each notion of work as a moral duty could shift in the future, depending on the first five factors I discussed. For example, a duty to be self-supporting could shift to a duty to *try* to be self-supporting, or a duty to contribute to one's collective living group, or a duty to be self-supporting only for certain expenses (for example, responsible for earning disposable income but not for necessities like housing, food, and health care).

If self-employment and gig work become more common, a diligent 9-to-5 work ethic will change. Conventional hours for being productive may become much shorter or fade away. More importantly, what counts as honorable productive activity could expand to encompass the nonmarket forms of provisioning Gibson-Graham discussed as well as community volunteer work, as a substitute for and not just an adjunct to paid work. The future of volunteerism should be reimagined along with the future of work.[109]

A blurring of daily and weekly temporal rhythms could extend to the life course. The sociologist Phyllis Moen calls for changing the common assumption that lives should march along from formal education to paid work to retired leisure, the "outdated learn-earn-leisure lockstep."[110] One of my participants, Alice Joyner, was looking to begin a new career as a family counselor at the age of seventy-eight. She was inspired by her grandmother, who was still farming when she was eighty. Her grandmother used to say she was "in her use." Alice misheard at first: "I thought she was trying to say *youth*. But she knew what she was saying." For Alice, "it's good to feel useful all your life."[111] Social policies can break up the learn-earn-leisure lockstep in more ways than by encouraging additional years of paid employment. There should also be more opportunities for lifelong education, as well as more vacations and sabbaticals in the middle decades of life.[112]

How might a living-to-work ethic change if work outside of standard employment became common? Someone who is self-employed may have to work long hours to make a sufficient income. However, that is not a living-to-work ethic, in which one has a moral duty to work constantly. The living-to-work model of a morally good life may be changing or perhaps was never common. Nearly all my participants stated emphatically that it is morally wrong to put one's work ahead of everything else in life. Many of those who previously had a living-to-work ethic said a lesson they learned from being out of work was that their priorities had been misguided. They were joined in that view by those with a diligent 9-to-5 work ethic, who emphasized that one should be conscientious while on the job but not let one's work take over one's life.

Current wellness discourses create a new imperative, one that has elements of both morality and pleasure: we *ought* to protect our health, and we will feel better if we do. For the unemployed who had formerly worked long hours, working less was healthier. By contrast, many of those who had previously worked fixed hours said that not working was harmful to their health. One participant gave the analogy of a vehicle that becomes rusty through disuse. From both ends I saw a convergence on the value of work as one part of a fulfilling life, but only if it is kept in balance.

The right kind of work could also be enjoyable. Most of my participants did not see work as all grim duty and life outside work as all pleasure. When they spoke of finding fun in or at their jobs, they envisioned work as part of a good life in all senses. Whether jobs will continue to be fun in the future, however, remains to be seen.

It also remains to be seen whether a moral imperative to be productive persists in the United States and perhaps many other societies, with "productivity" expanded to include self-care and other nonremunerative activities. Another possibility I saw among my participants is that a productivity ethos is replaced by its frenetic doppelganger, a staying-busy ethos.[113] It was common for my interviewees to say they were "staying busy" if they had a day full of scheduled activities. Only one said they preferred to relax.

The Individual's Identities

Lastly, how people feel about working, not working, or working sometimes depends on their socially defined identities and on their personally meaningful self-representations, the core of who they think they are. To recap earlier chapters, when it comes to attitudes about waged work some of the most relevant social identities in the United States currently are defined by gender, household role, age, nativity (immigrant or native-born), and class. For example, at present, dominant gender roles put more pressure on married men to remain in the workforce than on married women. Some men I interviewed (both straight and gay) felt that being unemployed made them "less of a man," but no woman I interviewed felt that being unemployed made them less of a woman, although they felt diminished as persons. Parents—both male and female—faced pressures if they were the head of the household that were not felt by nonparents, both to provide for their children and to set a good example for them. Among middle-class Americans there is less pressure for emerging adults in their twenties to be self-supporting than in the past. Immigrants of all ages, however, especially those trying to attain citizenship, face strong internal and external pressures to find paid work and eschew state supports. People differ as well in what they see as the core of their class identities—whether that is based on the kind of work they do, their income and consumption, their diligent efforts to support themself and their family, or a mix of those.

Any of those meanings could change in the future.

There are many other possible personal meanings of working. For some of my interviewees, staying busy with work was a way to take their mind off personal trauma. For others, especially for some immigrants from Asia and Latin America, the money they earned enabled them to fulfill obligations to their natal family. Many took pleasure from what they could create or contribute through their jobs. For those with an occupational passion, their ideal job would be a realization of what they were meant to do in life. Although new cultural models of the place of work in a good life may arise in the future, I would expect continuing diversity in what pulls at our hearts.

No ethnography can be a study of the future. We can only describe the way people think, feel, and act now, and those ways of being in the world could change. The best way to be prepared is to shed our preconceptions about what is possible. If we pay attention to the diversity in values and practices that are already present, we can imagine fresh alternatives.

Appendix

Participants

PSEUDONYM	GENDER	FIRST-GENERATION IMMIGRANT?	RACIAL/ETHNIC IDENTITY	JOB BEFORE FIRST INTERVIEW
Abel Jimenez	M	yes (Mexico)	Latino	ran small food market / vegetable delivery
Alfredo Reyes	M	yes (El Salvador)	Latino	baker
Alice Joyner	F	no	Black	Christian Science nurse / student
Amber Washington	F	no	Black	social service agency administrator
Anastasia Tang	F	yes (Southeast Asia)	Southeast Asian American	HR manager
Ann Lopez	F	no	Latino	IT worker
Auguste Salander	M	no	white	pizza delivery
Carl Mathews	M	no	Black	City of LA., security officer
Caroline James	F	no	white	senior VP, HR, entertainment company
Celeste Rue	F	no	mixed (European/American Indian /Latino)	admin assistant (temp)
Charles Toppes	M	no	white	director manufacturing operations, furniture company
Charlie Mike Romero	M	yes (El Salvador)	mixed (Latino/Asian)	database administrator for bank
Chipper Goodman	M	no	white	bouncer at a club (part-time)
Daniel Horn	M	no	white	contractor
Della Jones	F	no	white	public school teacher
Elizabeth Montgomery	F	no	white	sales, high end office furniture
Emily Quinn	F	no	white	exec asst, construction company
Feliciano Salas	M	yes (Mexico)	Latino	roofer / day laborer

PSEUDONYM	GENDER	FIRST-GENERATION IMMIGRANT?	RACIAL/ETHNIC IDENTITY	JOB BEFORE FIRST INTERVIEW
Fred Hernandez	M	1.5* (Mexico)	Latino	DUI counselor
Gabriella Gomez	F	1.5 (Mexico)	Latino	yoga teacher, massage therapist, retail clerk (part-time)
Ginger Thi	F	no	East Asian American	secretary/temp
Hillary Edwards	F	no	Black	banker
Ichabod Jones	M	no	Latino	social services program director
Isabel Navarro	F	yes (Mexico)	Latino	esthetician, self-employed/disabled
Jackie Gallardo	F	1.5 (Mexico)	Latino	warehouse work (temp)
Jagat Bodhi	M	yes (Uganda, England)	South Asian American	telecommunications technician
Jake Taylor	M	no	white	warehouse operations manager
Jim Wade	M	no	white	service advisor auto parts store, census worker (short-term)
John Davis	M	no	mixed (Black/American Indian/European)	senior VP, organization development, financial services company
Jorge Paiz	M	yes (Guatemala)	Latino	construction worker
José Navarro	M	yes (Mexico)	Latino	food vendor, athletic stadiums
Katarina Spelling	F	no	white	branch manager, social services organization, then communications coordinator, nonprofit organization (part-time)
Kham Sy Phouphan	M	yes (Laos)	Southeast Asian American	machine operator, lighting company
Krystal Murphy	F	no	white	admin assistant, financial services company
La dama de abril	F	Yes (Colombia, Venezuela)	Latino	housecleaning business
Linda McDaniel	F	no	white	executive assistant, construction company
Lisa Rose	F	no	white	associate VP, nonprofit organization
Lucy Guerrero	F	yes (Colombia, Venezuela)	Latino	HR office work, courier company
Luis Segura	M	yes (Mexico)	Latino	gardener/day laborer
Magenta Love	F	no	Black	health information consultant/cosmetology teacher (part-time)
Marcus Walker	M	no	Black	assembly worker

PSEUDONYM	GENDER	FIRST-GENERATION IMMIGRANT?	RACIAL/ETHNIC IDENTITY	JOB BEFORE FIRST INTERVIEW
Maria Carrera	F	yes (Ecuador)	Latino	manufacturing operations supervisor
Mary Brown	F	no	Black	student advisor in outreach program
Mickey Muller	M	no	white	electrical engineer
Miguel Vargas	M	yes (Mexico)	Latino	account manager, cosmetics company
Miriam Ramos	F	no	mixed (Latino/American Indian)	hairdresser
Mona Childs	F	no	Declined to state	marketing for senior housing
Monserrat León	F	yes (Mexico)	Latino	waitress
Natalie Harper	F	no	white	grant specialist
Paula Jackson	F	1.5 (Cuba)	Latino	phlebotomist
Pepper Hill	F	no	white	director of consulting for a large nonprofit
Phoenix Rises	F	no	Black	special ed teacher
Ralph Edwards	M	no	Black	sales for credit card processor
Rebecca Robinson	F	no	white	admin assistant (temp)
ReNé McKnight	F	no	Black	customer support, call center
Robert Milner	M	no	Latino	supply chain strategist
Sam Lennon	F	no	mixed (white/American Indian)	cashier, counter assistant, deli
Stacie McCarthy	F	no	white	loan processor/funder
Stephen Smith	M	no	white	senior director, development and finance, large company in leisure industry
Summer Carrington	F	no	white	asset manager at bank
Terrance West	M	no	Black	shipping/receiving clerk
Theresa Allen	F	no	white	waitress/homemaker
Tom Dunn	M	no	white	IT recruiter
Tony DeLuca	M	no	white	VP, HR, entertainment company

Note: Two of my pilot interviewees are mentioned in the text: Bob Roberts, male, nonimmigrant, white, lobbyist for a nonprofit; Earl Apache Longwolf, male, nonimmigrant, mixed (American Indian/Black), welder.

* Leslie Berestein Rojas, "Gen 1.5: Where an Immigrant Generation Fits In," KPCC, March 21, 2012, http://www.scpr.org/blogs/multiamerican.

Notes

Preface and Note on Terminology

1. Rani Molla, "Quiet Hiring and the Endless Quest to Coin Terms about Work," *Vox*, updated January 12, 2023, https://www.vox.com/recode/23548422/quiet-quitting-hiring-great-resignation-words-about-work.

2. Claudia Strauss, "Not-So Rugged Individualists: U.S. Americans' Conflicting Ideas about Poverty," in *Work, Welfare, and Politics: Confronting Poverty in the Wake of Welfare Reform*, ed. Frances Fox Piven, Joan Acker, Margaret Hallock, and Sandra Morgen (Eugene: University of Oregon Press, 2002), 55–69; Claudia Strauss, *Making Sense of Public Opinion: American Discourses about Immigration and Social Programs* (New York: Cambridge University Press, 2012).

3. Rakin Rahman, "The Top 5 Ports in the United States 2022," *Port Technology International*, December 13, 2022, https://www.porttechnology.org/news/the-top-5-ports-in-the-united-states/.

4. Susan A. Phillips, "Op-Ed: We Mapped the Warehouse Takeover of the Inland Empire: The Results Are Overwhelming," *Los Angeles Times*, May 1, 2022, https://www.latimes.com/opinion/story/2022-05-01/inland-empire-warehouse-growth-map-environment.

5. Los Angeles County Economic Development Corporation, *Manufacturing: Still a Force in Southern California* (Los Angeles: Los Angeles County Economic Development Corporation, 2011), 2, https://laedc.org/reports/Manufacturing_2011.pdf.

6. Ruth Mantell and MarketWatch, "Home Prices off Record 18% in Past Year, Case-Shiller Says," *Market Watch*, December 30, 2008, https://www.marketwatch.com/story/home-prices-off-record-18-in-past-year-case-shiller-says.

7. Unemployment rates were higher than 12% in Los Angeles, San Bernardino, and Riverside Counties. "County Unemployment Rates, 2011 Annual Average," California Employment Development Department, October 2015, https://www.labormarketinfo.edd.ca.gov/file/Maps/County_UR_2011BM2014.pdf.

8. See, for example, Council of Economic Advisors, *Expanding Work Requirements in Non-Cash Welfare Programs* (Washington, DC: Council of Economic Advisors, July 2018), expanding-Work-Requirements-in-Non-Cash-Welfare-Programs.pdf (archives.gov).

9. Leo H. Carney, "Proposed Ciba Plant Stirs Controversy," *New York Times*, October 21, 1984, https://www.nytimes.com/1984/10/21/nyregion/proposed-ciba-plant-stirs-controversy.html.

10. Claudia Strauss, "What Makes Tony Run? Schemas as Motives Reconsidered," in *Human Motives and Cultural Models*, ed. Roy D'Andrade and Claudia Strauss (Cambridge: Cambridge University Press, 1992), 197–224.

11. Edna Bonacich and Juan David De Lara, "Economic Crisis and the Logistics Industry: Financial Insecurity for Warehouse Workers in the Inland Empire," IRLE Working Papers (Institute for Research on Labor and Employment, UCLA, 2009), https://escholarship.org/uc/item/8rn2h9ch; Alemayehu Bishaw and Kayla Fontenot, "Poverty: 2012 and 2013" (US Census Bureau, Washington, DC, September 2014), https://www2.census.gov/library/publications/2014/acs/acsbr13-01.pdf.

12. In 2019, 34% of the population in Los Angeles County was foreign born as was 21% in San Bernardino County. US Census Bureau, "Los Angeles County, California," accessed May 23, 2021, https://data.census.gov/cedsci/profile?q=Los%20Angeles%20County,%20California&g=0500000US06037; and US Census Bureau, "San Bernardino County, California," accessed May 23, 2021, https://data.census.gov/cedsci/profile?q=San%20Bernardino%20County,%20California&g=0500000US06071. A few lived in the cities of Los Angeles, San Bernardino, or Riverside; the rest resided in the suburbs of those cities. The majority lived in Los Angeles County or San Bernardino County, but there were also a few from Orange, Ventura, and Riverside Counties.

13. Among the study participants twenty-four identify as white, nineteen as Latino/a, eleven as Black, four as Asian American, and five as mixed, including four with traceable American Indian ancestry. One preferred not to say. Of the immigrants, ten were from Mexico, four from Central America or the Caribbean, three from South America, two from Southeast Asia, and one from East Africa and the United Kingdom. Three were 1.5-generation immigrants, meaning they immigrated as children. See the appendix.

14. "U.S. Immigrant Population and Share over Time, 1850–Present," Migration Policy Institute, accessed July 29, 2021, https://www.migrationpolicy.org/programs/data-hub/charts/immigrant-population-over-time.

15. This image privileges immigration to the East Coast of the United States, omitting the extensive East Asian immigration to the United States in the nineteenth century and the change in the borders of United States after the Treaty of Guadalupe Hidalgo in 1848, resulting in thousands of Mexican citizens becoming US residents.

16. We did not attempt follow-up interviews with Claudia C.'s interviewees, so the average interview hours were shorter for them.

17. Kathi Weeks, *The Problem with Work: Feminism, Marxism, Antiwork Politics, and Postwork Imaginaries* (Durham, NC: Duke University Press, 2011), 47. Weeks took the quote from Max Weber, "Science as a Vocation."

18. The pilot interviews were conducted in Rhode Island and southeastern Massachusetts.

19. My son's path is common among younger workers. One global survey found that 53% of respondents born between 1997 and 2007 want to have their own business. Jared Lindzon, "Why Gen Z Is so Keen on Entrepreneurship, and What That Means for Employers," *Fast Company*, May 11, 2021, https://www.fastcompany.com/90631769/why-gen-z-is-so-keen-on-entrepreneurship-and-what-that-means-for-employers.

20. Jean Guerrero, "The Term Latinx Wasn't Made by 'Woke' Whites: Stop Erasing Its Creators," *Los Angeles Times*, January 27, 2022, https://www.latimes.com/opinion/story/2022-01-27/op-ed-latinx-white-elites-marginalized-creators; Vanesha

McGee, "Latino, Latinx, Hispanic, or Latine? Which Term Should You Use?" *Bestcol-leges.com*, updated September 23, 2022, https://www.bestcolleges.com/blog/hispanic-latino-latinx-latine/#:~:text=Latine%20came%20to%20mainstream%20use,use%20of%20%22e%22%20instead.

21. John Daniszewski, "Why We Will Lowercase White," Associated Press, July 20, 2020, https://blog.ap.org/announcements/why-we-will-lowercase-white.

1. Multiple Meanings of Work in the United States

1. Charles Ward, "Protestant Work Ethic That Took Root in Faith Is Now Ingrained in Our Culture," *Houston Chronicle*, September 1, 2007, https://www.chron.com/life/houston-belief/article/Protestant-work-ethic-that-took-root-in-faith-is-1834963.php.

2. All names of participants are pseudonyms, usually chosen by them.

3. Susan Adams, "America's Worst Cities for Finding a Job," *Forbes*, November 23, 2011, http://www.forbes.com/sites/susanadams/2011/11/23/americas-worst-cities-for-finding-a-job/.

4. [. . .] means a deletion from an interview excerpt. See the Transcription Key in the front matter.

5. On the utopian/dystopian divide in writing about the future, see Samuel Gerald Collins, "Working for the Robocracy: Critical Ethnography of Robot Futures," *Anthropology of Work Review* 39, no. 1 (2018), https://doi.org/10.1111/awr.12131.

6. Stanley Aronowitz and William DiFazio, *The Jobless Future: Sci-Tech and the Dogma of Work* (Minneapolis: University of Minnesota Press, 1994), 335. See also Weeks, *The Problem with Work*.

7. Peter Frase, "Against Jobs, for Full Employment," *Jacobin*, July 27, 2011, https://jacobinmag.com/2011/07/against-jobs-for-full-employment/.

8. Erik Brynjolfsson and Andrew McAfee, *The Second Machine Age: Work, Progress, and Prosperity in a Time of Brilliant Technologies*, 2nd ed. (New York: Norton, 2016), 234, 235.

9. Marie Jahoda, "Work, Employment, and Unemployment: Values, Theories, and Approaches in Social Research," *American Psychologist* 36, no. 2 (1981): 189, https://doi.org/10.1037//0003-066X.36.2.184.

10. John A. Garraty, *Unemployment in History: Economic Thought and Public Policy* (New York: Harper & Row, 1978), 5.

11. In a famous essay, anthropologist Marshall Sahlins draws on some time studies of hunters and gatherers to emphasize their considerable leisure time, contrary to popular perceptions. There have been criticisms of what kinds of labor were omitted from his calculations, but the general point stands. Marshall Sahlins, "The Original Affluent Society," in his *Stone Age Economics* (Chicago: Aldine, 1972), 1–39. See also James Suzman, *Work: A Deep History, from the Stone Age to the Age of Robots* (New York: Penguin, 2021).

12. Garraty, *Unemployment in History*, 5.

13. Garraty cites Pierre Bourdieu's finding that in the 1960s seasonal agricultural laborers in northern Algeria considered themselves to be unemployed during the months they were not working, but those in southern Algeria did not. The northern area (Kabylia) had a long history of emigration to France, which is dominated by a wage economy. Bourdieu writes that the absence of a predominant wage economy in

the south meant they "'had not discovered the idea [of] unemployment.'" Pierre Bourdieu, *Travail et travailleurs en Algérie: Étude sociologique* (Paris: Editions de la Maison des sciences de l'Homme, 1963), 52, 303–4, quoted in Garraty, *Unemployment in History*, 6.

14. William Monteith, Dora-Olivia Vicol, and Philippa Williams, "Work beyond the Wage," in their edited book, *Beyond the Wage: Ordinary Work in Diverse Economies* (Bristol: Bristol University Press, 2021), 3–4.

15. Tocqueville excluded slave owners in the South from these generalizations. Alexis de Tocqueville, "Why Americans Consider All Occupations Honorable," in *Democracy in America*, vol. 2, trans. George Lawrence, ed. J. P. Mayer (Garden City, NY: Doubleday, 1969), 550.

16. Tocqueville, *Democracy in America*, 550.

17. Caitrin Lynch and Daniel Mains, "Epilogue: Rethinking the Value of Work and Unemployment," in *Anthropologies of Unemployment: New Perspectives on Work and Its Absence*, ed. Jong Bum Kwon and Carrie M. Lane (Ithaca: Cornell University Press, 2016), 223–27; "International Labor Laws and Minimum Age Requirements," Blue Marble Payroll, June 25, 2018, https://bluemarblepayroll.com/international-labor-laws -minimum-age-requirements/; Eversheds Sutherland, "Compulsory Retirement: An International Comparison," *Lexology*, April 11, 2014, https://www.lexology.com /library/detail.aspx?g=6a6150 b.c.-0825-4166-9e52-d6589c6ee237. See also Ida Susser, "The Construction of Poverty and Homelessness in US Cities," *Annual Review of Anthropology* 25, no. 1 (1996): 413–14, https://doi.org/10.1146/annurev.anthro.25.1.411.

18. Derek Thompson, "A World without Work," *The Atlantic*, July/August 2015, https://www.theatlantic.com/magazine/archive/2015/07/world-without-work /395294/.

19. See also Francis Grund, *The Americans in Their Moral, Social, and Political Relations: Two Volumes in One* (Boston: Marsh, Capen and Lyon, 1837; New York: Augustus M. Kelly, 1971).

20. Judith N. Shklar, *American Citizenship: The Quest for Inclusion* (Cambridge, MA: Harvard University Press, 1991), 1.

21. L. Robert Kohls, *The Values Americans Live By* (Washington, DC: Meridian Intercultural Orientation Program, 1984), 6.

22. Thompson, "A World without Work"; Derek Thompson, "Workism Is Making Americans Miserable," *The Atlantic*, February 24, 2019, https://www.theatlantic.com /ideas/archive/2019/02/religion-workism-making-americans-miserable/583441/.

23. Capitol Hill Dweller, comment about "Is It Great to Be a Worker in the U.S.? Not Compared with the Rest of the Developed World," *Washington Post*, July 4, 2018, https://www.washingtonpost.com/news/wonk/wp/2018/07/04/is-it-great-to-be-a -worker-in-the-u-s-not-compared-to-the-rest-of-the-developed-world/?utm_term= .bec1d6359510. (Comment no longer available.)

24. Akihito Shimazu et al., "Workaholism vs. Work Engagement: The Two Different Predictors of Future Well-Being and Performance," *International Journal of Behavioral Medicine* 22, no. 1 (2015), https://doi.org/10.1007/s12529-014-9410-x.

25. For a related but different categorization of work ethics, see Paul Heelas, "Work Ethics, Soft Capitalism and the 'Turn to Life,'" in *Cultural Economy: Cultural Analysis and Commercial Life*, ed. Paul Du Gay and Michael Pryke (London: Sage, 2002), 78–96.

26. Max Weber, *The Protestant Ethic and the Spirit of Capitalism*, trans. Talcott Parsons (1904–5; New York: Charles Scribner's Sons, 1958).

27. On the discursive construction of class, see Sherry Ortner, "Identities: The Hidden Life of Class," *Journal of Anthropological Research* 54, no. 1 (1998), https:// doi.org / 10.1086 / jar.54.1.3631674. On multiple meanings of being "middle class" globally, see Rachel Heiman, Carla Freeman, and Mark Liechty, eds., *The Global Middle Classes: Theorizing through Ethnography* (Santa Fe: School for Advanced Research Press, 2012).

28. Lila Abu-Lughod, "Writing against Culture," in *Recapturing Anthropology: Working in the Present*, ed. Richard G. Fox (Santa Fe: School of American Research Press, 1991), 137–62.

29. Council of Economic Advisors, *Expanding Work Requirements in Non-Cash Welfare Programs* (Washington, DC: Council of Economic Advisors, July 2018), https:// trumpwhitehouse.archives.gov / briefings-statements / cea-report-expanding-work -requirements-non-cash-welfare-programs /.

30. The 2018 Council of Economic Advisors report also fails to mention the weak overtime protections that force many Americans to work long hours whether they want to or not. Jerry A. Jacobs and Kathleen Gerson, *The Time Divide: Work, Family, and Gender Inequality* (Cambridge, MA: Harvard University Press, 2004).

31. That is why it is problematic to conduct cross-cultural research by comparing people in different countries with no further specification of their social locations.

32. Claudia Strauss and Naomi Quinn, *A Cognitive Theory of Cultural Meaning* (Cambridge: Cambridge University Press, 1997).

33. Robert A. LeVine, *Culture, Behavior, and Personality: An Introduction to the Comparative Study of Psychosocial Adaptation*, 2nd ed. (New Brunswick, NJ: AldineTransaction, 1982), 293.

34. Strauss and Quinn, *A Cognitive Theory of Cultural Meaning*, chapter 2; Claudia Strauss, "The Complexity of Culture in Persons," in *Advances in Culture Theory from Psychological Anthropology*, ed. Naomi Quinn (New York: Palgrave, 2018), 109–38.

35. Claudia Strauss, "Cultural Standing in Expression of Opinion," *Language in Society* 33, no. 2 (2004), https:// doi.org / 10.1017 / S004740450433201X.

36. Naomi Quinn and Dorothy Holland, "Culture and Cognition," in *Cultural Models in Language and Thought*, ed. Dorothy Holland and Naomi Quinn (Cambridge: Cambridge University Press, 1987), 3–40.

37. For methods of analyzing cultural models see Naomi Quinn, ed., *Finding Culture in Talk: A Collection of Methods* (New York: Palgrave, 2005).

38. Christine Jeske, *The Laziness Myth: Narratives of Work and the Good Life in South Africa* (Ithaca: Cornell University Press, 2020), 8–11.

39. Andrew E. Clark, "Unemployment as a Social Norm: Psychological Evidence from Panel Data," *Journal of Labor Economics* 21, no. 2 (2003), https:// doi.org / 10.1086 / 345560; Jennie E. Brand, "The Far-Reaching Impact of Job Loss and Unemployment," *Annual Review of Sociology* 41 (2015): 366, https:// doi.org / 10.1146 / annurev -soc-071913-043237.

40. See, for example, Katherine M. Dudley, *The End of the Line: Lost Jobs, New Lives in Postindustrial America* (Chicago: University of Chicago Press, 1994); Katherine Newman, *Falling from Grace: Downward Mobility in the Age of Affluence* (Berkeley: University

of California Press, 1988); Gregory Pappas, *The Magic City: Unemployment in a Working-Class Community* (Ithaca: Cornell University Press, 1989). For studies of recent factory closings, see Victor Tan Chen, *Cut Loose: Jobless and Hopeless in an Unfair Economy* (Oakland: University of California Press, 2015); Farah Stockman, *American Made: What Happens to People When Work Disappears* (New York: Random House, 2021).

41. "Unemployment—The Economic Lowdown Podcast Series, Episode 5," Federal Reserve Bank of St. Louis, accessed May 25, 2021, https://www.stlouisfed.org/education/economic-lowdown-podcast-series/episode-5-unemployment.

42. Tejvan Pettinger, "Structural Unemployment," *Economics Help*, August 7, 2019, https://www.economicshelp.org/blog/27657/unemployment/structural-unemployment/.

43. Christine J. Walley, *Exit Zero: Family and Class in Postindustrial Chicago* (Chicago: University of Chicago Press, 2013), 72–73.

44. Walley, *Exit Zero*, 68.

45. Aronowitz and DiFazio, *The Jobless Future*, 27. Those guarantees were not available to many women and workers of color in the informal economy. Sharryn Kasmir, "The Anthropology of Labor," in *Oxford Research Encyclopedia of Anthropology* (Oxford: Oxford University Press, 2020), https://doi.org/10.1093/acrefore/9780190854584.013.97.

46. Sherry Lee Linkon argues that "post-Fordist" is a more accurate term than "postindustrial" to describe the current economy. Manufacturing continues but with fewer workers. Sherry Lee Linkon, *The Half-Life of Deindustrialization: Working-Class Writing about Economic Restructuring* (Ann Arbor: University of Michigan Press, 2018), 5.

47. Dennis Arnold and Joseph R. Bongiovi, "Precarious, Informalizing, and Flexible Work: Transforming Concepts and Understandings," *American Behavioral Scientist* 57, no. 3 (2013): 294–95, https://doi.org/10.1177/0002764212466239. See also the discussion of flexible capitalism in David Harvey, *The Condition of Postmodernity: An Inquiry into the Conditions of Cultural Change* (Oxford: Blackwell, 1989).

48. Karen Ho, *Liquidated: An Ethnography of Wall Street* (Durham, NC: Duke University Press, 2009), esp. chap. 3.

49. Ho, *Liquidated*, 75, 85, 217, 222.

50. Carrie M. Lane, "Man Enough to Let My Wife Support Me: How Changing Models of Career and Gender Are Reshaping the Experience of Unemployment," *American Ethnologist* 36, no. 4 (2009): 685–86, https://doi.org/10.1111/j.1548-1425.2009.01203.x. See also Carrie M. Lane, *A Company of One: Insecurity, Independence, and the New World of White-Collar Unemployment* (Ithaca: Cornell University Press, 2011). Gershon found that knowledge economy workers and those who managed them in the San Francisco Bay Area expected jobs to be short-lived. Ilana Gershon, *Down and Out in the New Economy: How People Find (or Don't Find) Work Today* (Chicago: University of Chicago Press, 2017).

51. None of my participants used this term, but a member of the audience brought it up during a talk I gave. Appreciating a short time out of work is not new. When Bakke studied unemployed blue-collar working men in the United States during the Great Depression in the 1930s, he learned that they were used to periodic layoffs. Bakke commented, "Since he [*the unemployed worker*] has had the same experience before, he is likely to expect the layoff to be merely temporary and to regard it as a chance for a short holiday." E. Wight Bakke, *Citizens without Work: A Study of the Effects of Unemployment upon the Workers' Social Relations and Practices* (New Haven, CT: Yale University Press, 1940), 155.

52. Lane, *Company of One*, 46.

53. "Unemployment—The Economic Lowdown Podcast."

54. For more detail on how class, race, and gender privilege can create better unemployment experiences and better outcomes when working again, see Sarah Damaske, *The Tolls of Uncertainty: How Privilege and the Guilt Gap Shape Unemployment in America* (Princeton: Princeton University Press, 2021).

55. See also Chen, *Cut Loose*.

56. "Unemployment—The Economic Lowdown Podcast."

57. Damaske, *The Tolls of Uncertainty*, 32–33; Steven. H. Lopez and Lora A. Phillips, "Unemployed: White-Collar Job Searching after the Great Recession," *Work and Occupations* 46, no. 4 (2019): 504, https://doi.org/10.1177/0730888419852379.

58. "Civilian Unemployment Rate, Seasonally Adjusted," US Bureau of Labor Statistics, accessed May 25, 2021, https://www.bls.gov/charts/employment-situation/civilian-unemployment-rate.htm; "County Unemployment Rates, 2011 Annual Average," California Employment Development Department, https://www.labormarketinfo.edd.ca.gov/file/Maps/County_UR_2011BM2014.pdf.

59. Rand Ghayad, "The Jobless Trap," Northeastern University, Boston, 2013, http://citeseerx.ist.psu.edu/viewdoc/download?doi=10.1.1.692.6736&rep=rep1&type=pdf. But see Lee Dye, "Unemployment: UCLA Study Shows Stigma of Joblessness Is Immediate," *ABC News*, April 5, 2011, https://abcnews.go.com/Technology/unemployment-stigma-begins-quickly-makes-job-search-harder/story?id=13302693.

60. Evan Cunningham, "Great Recession, Great Recovery? Trends from the Current Population Survey," *Monthly Labor Review* 141, no. 4 (April 2018), https://doi.org/10.21916/mlr.2018.10.

61. "Average (Mean) Duration of Unemployment [UEMPMEAN]," US Bureau of Labor Statistics, Federal Reserve Bank of St. Louis, January 31, 2023, https://fred.stlouisfed.org/series/UEMPMEAN.

62. Mason Ameri et al., "The Disability Employment Puzzle: A Field Experiment on Employer Hiring Behavior," *ILR Review* 71, no. 2 (2018), https://doi.org/10.1177/0019793917717474.

David Neumark, Ian Burn, and Patrick Button, "Is It Harder for Older Workers to Find Jobs? New and Improved Evidence from a Field Experiment," *Journal of Political Economy* 127, no. 2 (April 2019), https://doi.org/10.1086/701029. Marianne Bertrand and Sendhil Mullainathan, "Are Emily and Greg More Employable than Lakisha and Jamal? A Field Experiment on Labor Market Discrimination," *American Economic Review* 94, no. 4 (2004), https://doi.org/10.1257/0002828042002561; Sonia K. Kang, Katherine A. DeCelles, András Tilcsik, and Sora Jun, "Whitened Résumés: Race and Self-Presentation in the Labor Market," *Administrative Science Quarterly* 61, no. 3 (September 2016), https://doi.org/10.1177/0001839216639577. For a finding of no discrimination based on apparent Latino and African American surnames, see Rajeev Darolia et al., "Race and Gender Effects on Employer Interest in Job Applicants: New Evidence from a Resume Field Experiment," *Applied Economics Letters* 23, no. 12 (2016), https://doi.org/10.1080/13504851.2015.1114571. András Tilcsik, "Pride and Prejudice: Employment Discrimination against Openly Gay Men in the United States," *American Journal of Sociology* 117 (2011), https://doi.org/10.1086/661653; Emma Mishel, "Discrimination against Queer Women in the U.S. Workforce: A Résumé Audit Study," *Socius: Sociological*

Research for a Dynamic World 2 (2016), https://doi.org/10.1177/2378023115621316. Bradley R. E. Wright, Michael Wallace, John Bailey, and Allen Hyde, "Religious Affiliation and Hiring Discrimination in New England: A Field Experiment," *Research in Social Stratification and Mobility* 34 (2013), https://doi.org/10.1016/j.rssm.2013.10.002. Those who indicated participating in college atheist and Evangelical Christian groups also received somewhat fewer calls. There is an extensive international overview of these studies in Stijn Baert, "Hiring Discrimination: An Overview of (Almost) All Correspondence Experiments since 2005" (IZA Discussion Papers, No. 10738, Institute of Labor Economics (IZA), Bonn, 2017), https://docs.iza.org/dp10738.pdf. There is an updated registry on his website as well: https://users.ugent.be/~sbaert/research_register.htm.

63. Amanda Agan and Sonja Starr, "Ban the Box, Criminal Records, and Racial Discrimination: A Field Experiment," *Quarterly Journal of Economics* 133, no. 1 (2017), https://doi.org/10.1093/qje/qjx028.

64. Amy Traub, *Discredited: How Employment Credit Checks Keep Qualified Workers out of a Job* (New York: Dēmos, 2014), https://www.demos.org/research/discredited-how-employment-credit-checks-keep-qualified-workers-out-job.

65. Jack R. Friedman, "Shame and the Experience of Ambivalence on the Margins of the Global: Pathologizing the Past and Present in Romania's Industrial Wastelands," *Ethos* 35, no. 2 (2007): 248, https://doi.org/10.1525/eth.2007.35.2.235. The "violence of everyday life" is an allusion to Nancy Scheper-Hughes, *Death without Weeping: The Violence of Everyday Life in Brazil* (Berkeley: University of California Press, 1992). See also Brand, "Far-Reaching Impact of Job Loss and Unemployment."

66. Friedman, "Shame and the Experience of Ambivalence"; Jie Yang, *Unknotting the Heart: Unemployment and Therapeutic Governance in China* (Ithaca: Cornell University Press, 2015).

67. Kelly McKowen, "Substantive Commitments: Reconciling Work Ethics and the Welfare State in Norway," *Economic Anthropology* 7, no. 1 (2020), https://doi.org/10.1002/sea2.12169. In 2014 I interviewed two unemployed Danish women who said that their country's generous welfare state created social pressure to be a contributing taxpayer. One stated, "Now, in people I talk to, they feel that you—somehow you're profiting on the system, that you get paid without doing anything." This is better by far than starving, but they said it felt "shameful."

68. Pieter Serneels, "The Nature of Unemployment among Young Men in Urban Ethiopia," *Review of Development Economics*, 11, no. 1 (2007): 174, https://doi.org/10.1111/j.1467-9361.2007.00389.x.

69. Daniel Mains, *Hope Is Cut: Youth, Unemployment, and the Future in Urban Ethiopia* (Philadelphia: Temple University Press, 2012), 4. See also Clark, "Unemployment as a Social Norm."

70. Jeske, *The Laziness Myth*. See also Craig Jeffrey, *Timepass: Youth, Class, and the Politics of Waiting in India* (Stanford: Stanford University Press, 2010). For a different perspective on South Africa, see E. Fouksman, "The Moral Economy of Work: Demanding Jobs and Deserving Money in South Africa." *Economy and Society* 49, no. 2 (2020), https://doi.org/10.1080/03085147.2019.1690276.

71. Kay Lehman Schlozman and Sidney Verba, *Injury to Insult: Unemployment, Class, and Political Response* (Cambridge, MA: Harvard University Press, 1979), 104. See also David B. Grusky, Bruce Western, and Christopher Wimer, "The Consequences

of the Great Recession," in their edited book *The Great Recession* (New York: Russell Sage Foundation, 2011), 10.

72. Newman, *Falling from Grace*, 77. Newman's careful analysis shows that although unemployed managers had alternative explanations for their unemployment (for example, age discrimination), the dominant meritocratic individualist discourses in the business community still undermined their self-worth. On self-blame among the unemployed, see also Chen, *Cut Loose*; Ofer Sharone, *Flawed System/Flawed Self: Job Searching and Unemployment Experiences* (Chicago: University of Chicago Press, 2014).

73. See also Lane, *Company of One*, 9. Interestingly, Damaske found that unemployed women in her study exhibited more self-blame than the unemployed men. Damaske, *The Tolls of Uncertainty*. Lopez and Phillips found both self-blame and system blame among white-collar job seekers in the aftermath of the Great Recession. Lopez and Phillips, "Unemployed."

74. In chapter 2 I discuss wellness discourses and practices that counter a living-to-work ethic.

75. I give more details in chapters 2 and 4. See also Lopez and Phillips, "Unemployed," 489ff.

76. Claudia Strauss, "Engaged by the Spectacle of Protest: How Bystanders Became Invested in Occupy Wall Street," in *Political Sentiments and Social Movements: The Person in Politics and Culture*, ed. Claudia Strauss and Jack Friedman (New York: Palgrave, 2018), 33–60.

77. Bakke, *Citizens without Work*, 21–22.

78. Tanya Luhrmann, *When God Talks Back: Understanding the American Evangelical Relationship with God* (New York: Vintage, 2012).

79. Raymond Garrett-Peters, "'If I Don't Have to Work Anymore, Who Am I?' Job Loss and Collaborative Self-Concept Repair," *Journal of Contemporary Ethnography* 38, no. 5 (2009), https://doi.org/10.1177/0891241609342104. The importance of religious beliefs for job seekers is also touched on by Lane, *Company of One*, 90; Richard Sennett, *The Corrosion of Character* (New York: Norton, 1998), 130; Wendy Patton and Ross Donohue, "Coping with Long-Term Unemployment," *Journal of Community & Applied Social Psychology* 8, no. 5 (1998): 338, https://doi.org/10.1002/(SICI)1099-1298 (1998090)8:53.0.CO;2–6.

80. Barbara Ehrenreich, *Bright-Sided: How the Relentless Promotion of Positive Thinking Has Undermined America* (New York: Metropolitan Books, 2009).

81. Claudia Strauss, "Positive Thinking about Being out of Work in Southern California after the Great Recession," in *Anthropologies of Unemployment: New Perspectives on Work and Its Absence*, ed. Jong Bum Kwon and Carrie M. Lane (Ithaca: Cornell University Press, 2016), 171–90. Positive thinking discourse was also noted among job seekers by Sharone, *Flawed System/Flawed Self*, 38–39; Lane, *Company of One*, 161–62; and Gershon, *Down and Out*, 24. Positive thinking discourse is not limited to the United States. Patton and Donahue heard some positive thinking among those coping well with long-term unemployment in Australia. Patton and Donohue, "Coping with Long-Term Unemployment," 338.

82. "Definition of Work," *Merriam-Webster*, https://www.merriam-webster.com/dictionary/work, accessed May 3, 2022.

83. John W. Budd, *The Thought of Work* (Ithaca: Cornell University Press, 2011), 2; André Gorz, *Reclaiming Work: Beyond the Wage-Based Society*, trans. Chris Turner (Cambridge: Polity Press, 1999), 3; Jeske, *The Laziness Myth*, 10–11.

84. Mechthild von Vacano, personal communication, June 1, 2018.

85. Budd, *The Thought of Work*, 2.

86. All labor force statistics also exclude active-duty military from those who are employed, as well as those in prison or otherwise institutionalized. "How the Government Measures Unemployment," US Bureau of Labor Statistics, October 8, 2015, https://www.bls.gov/cps/cps_htgm.htm#employed.

87. Carrie M. Lane, "The Limits of Liminality: Anthropological Approaches to Unemployment in the United States," in *Anthropologies of Unemployment: New Perspectives on Work and Its Absence*, ed. Jong Bum Kwon and Carrie M. Lane (Ithaca: Cornell University Press, 2016), 29–31; Lynch and Mains, "Epilogue," 214–15.

88. "Unemployment—The Economic Lowdown Podcast."

89. Zygmunt Bauman, *Work, Consumerism and the New Poor,* 2nd ed. (Berkshire, UK: Open University Press, 2005), 1.

90. Jeske, *The Laziness Myth*, 24.

2. Two Protestant Work Ethics (Living to Work or Working Diligently)

1. Weeks, *Problem with Work*, 1, 11, 2, 11, 38ff.

2. Sometimes this is called "misery poker," one definition of which is "a game played between people that have ridiculous amounts of work. It is played by calling, raising and betting assignments. It is often played by college students." Example: "It's unbelievable, but I just lost misery poker to Christina. I had a term paper, a test in art history, and a lab but she raised me a history paper" ("Misery Poker," definition by Leah Beah, Urban Dictionary, March 29, 2009, https://www.urbandictionary.com/define.php?term=misery+poker). See also Elizabeth Bernstein, "Misery Poker: It's One Game Worth Losing," *Wall Street Journal*, June 16, 2009, http://www.wsj.com/articles/SB124511445043317379. A professor at a state university thought that attitude was not as common there. Alma Gottlieb, comment to author, November 20, 2020.

3. Fâtima @r0sewater, posted on Twitter and reposted on other platforms.

4. Musk and Mayer were quoted in Erin Griffith, "Why Are Young People Pretending to Love Work?" *New York Times*, January 26, 2019, https://www.nytimes.com/2019/01/26/business/against-hustle-culture-rise-and-grind-tgim.html.

5. Dan Lyons, "In Silicon Valley, Working 9 to 5 Is for Losers," *New York Times*, August 31, 2017, https://www.nytimes.com/2017/08/31/opinion/sunday/silicon-valley-work-life-balance-.html?_r=0.

6. Quoted in Lyons, "In Silicon Valley, Working 9 to 5 Is for Losers."

7. Jim Edwards, "Reddit's Alexis Ohanian Says 'Hustle Porn' is 'One of the Most Toxic, Dangerous Things in Tech Right Now,'" *Business Insider*, November 6, 2018, https://www.businessinsider.com/reddit-alexis-ohanian-hustle-porn-toxic-dangerous-thing-in-tech-2018-11; Jennifer Earl, "Reddit Co-Founder Alexis Ohanian Blasts 'Hustle Porn' on Social Media: It's 'Really Toxic,'" *Fox Business*, May 27, 2019, https://www.foxbusiness.com/business-leaders/reddit-co-founder-alexis-ohanian-hustle-porn-toxic.

8. Thorstein Veblen, *The Theory of the Leisure Class* (1899; repr. Mineola, NY: Dover, 1994), 25.

9. Silvia Bellezza, Neeru Paharia, and Anat Keinan, "Conspicuous Consumption of Time: When Busyness and Lack of Leisure Time Become a Status Symbol," *Journal of Consumer Research* 44 (2017), https://doi.org/10.1093/jcr/ucw076.

10. Charlie Giattino, Esteban Ortiz-Ospina, and Max Roser, "Working Hours," *OurWorldInData.org*, December 2020, https://ourworldindata.org/working-hours.

11. Lydia Saad, "The '40-Hour' Workweek Is Actually Longer—by Seven Hours," Gallup, August 29, 2014, https://news.gallup.com/poll/175286/hour-workweek-actually-longer-seven-hours.aspx; Claire Cain Miller, "Women Did Everything Right: Then Work Got 'Greedy,'" *New York Times*, April 26, 2019, https://www.nytimes.com/2019/04/26/upshot/women-long-hours-greedy-professions.html?searchResultPosition=4.

12. Saad, "The '40-Hour' Workweek Is Actually Longer." Those figures are just for full-time workers, not including those who work two or more part-time jobs.

13. In that respect, I agree with Weeks, *Problem with Work*, 54.

14. "Following Weber, productivism can be seen as an ethos in which 'work,' as paid employment, has been separated out in a clear-cut way from other domains of life. Work becomes a standard-bearer of moral meaning—it defines whether or not individuals feel worthwhile or socially valued." Anthony Giddens, *Beyond Left and Right: The Future of Radical Politics* (Stanford: Stanford University Press, 1994), 175.

15. I pondered whether to use "ethos" (a "characteristic spirit") instead of "ethic" ("a set of moral principles"), https://en.oxforddictionaries.com. I decided to keep "ethic" because it expresses the moral element of this outlook, but I could also see an argument for "ethos" as a way of thinking that goes beyond morality.

16. Alison Doyle, "Difference between an Exempt and a Non-Exempt Employee," The Balance Careers, November 22, 2020, https://www.thebalancecareers.com/exempt-and-a-non-exempt-employee-2061988; Lisa Nagele-Piazza, "Are Your Pay Rates Compliant for 2020?" SHRM, February 3, 2020, https://www.shrm.org/resourcesandtools/legal-and-compliance/state-and-local-updates/pages/are-your-pay-rates-compliant-for-2020.aspx.

17. Weber, *Protestant Ethic*, 24.

18. Weber, *Protestant Ethic*, 66–67.

19. Weber, *Protestant Ethic*, 68.

20. Weber, *Protestant Ethic*, 69.

21. Weber, *Protestant Ethic*, 60.

22. Weber, *Protestant Ethic*, 157.

23. Weber, *Protestant Ethic*, 157.

24. Weber, *Protestant Ethic*, 157–58.

25. George Lakoff and Mark Johnson, *Metaphors We Live By* (Chicago: University of Chicago Press, 1980), 7–9.

26. Weber, *Protestant Ethic*, 48, 49.

27. Weber, *Protestant Ethic*, 182.

28. Weber, *Protestant Ethic*, 170.

29. Weber, *Protestant Ethic*, 181.

30. Weber, *Protestant Ethic*, 70; also, 283n115.

31. Weber, *Protestant Ethic*, 71.

32. Weber, *Protestant Ethic*, 53. To be precise, Weber saw the Protestant work ethic as highly rational in its methods but irrational in its ultimate aims.

33. Weber indicates that, for German observers, American businessmen had long served as exemplars of those devoted to making money above all else. Weber, *Protestant Ethic*, 51.

34. See the literature review in Adrian Furnham, "The Protestant Work Ethic: A Review of the Psychological Literature," *European Journal of Social Psychology* 14, no. 1 (January/March 1984), https://doi.org/10.1002/ejsp.2420140108.

35. Robert Bellah, "Reflections on the Protestant Ethic Analogy in Asia," in his *Beyond Belief: Essays on Religion in a Post-Traditionalist World* (Berkeley: University of California Press, 1970), 53–63.

36. Weeks, *Problem with Work*, 39.

37. Weber, *Protestant Ethic*, 81. Those are Weber's words, not Luther's.

38. Weber, *Protestant Ethic*, 62. See also Weeks, *Problem with Work*, 39, 44.

39. Weber, *Protestant Ethic*, 62.

40. Weber, *Protestant Ethic*, 177, 281n101; see also 179. See also Weeks, *Problem with Work*, 8.

41. Weber, *Protestant Ethic*, 80.

42. Weber, *Protestant Ethic*, 127.

43. Weber, *Protestant Ethic*, 127. In a fascinating footnote, Weber departed from the distinction between Protestants and Catholics that he drew in the rest of the book and instead contrasted mystically inclined Germans of all faiths with activity-oriented Americans. In this footnote, he discussed a nineteenth-century caustic portrait of Americans published in Germany (*Der Amerikamude*, 1855), calling it valuable "as a document of the (now long since blurred-over) differences between the German and the American outlook, one may even say of the type of spiritual life which, in spite of everything, has remained common to all Germans, Catholic and Protestant alike, since the German mysticism of the Middle Ages, as against the Puritan capitalistic valuation of action." Weber, *Protestant Ethic*, 192n3.

44. Weber, *Protestant Ethic*, 53.

45. I realize that "long hours" is a vague term; what seems long to one worker or researcher may not seem long to another. I relied on my participants' self-descriptions of having devoted more time on their jobs than, in retrospect, they felt was necessary or desirable, given all the ways they could have spent their time. Later in this section, I explain why standardized measures of work centrality would have been of questionable value for those out of work.

46. Robert R. Hirschfeld and Hubert S. Field, "Work Centrality and Work Alienation: Distinct Aspects of a General Commitment to Work," *Journal of Organizational Behavior* 21, no. 7 (2000), https://doi.org/10.1002/1099-1379(200011)21:73.0.CO;2-W.

47. We did not obtain each participant's previous work hours, so I cannot say with certainty which ones had typically worked longer than fifty hours a week when they were employed.

48. Strauss, "Positive Thinking about Being out of Work in Southern California after the Great Recession."

49. These are Ehrenreich's glosses. Barbara Ehrenreich, *The Hearts of Men: American Dreams and the Flight from Commitment* (Garden City, NY: Anchor Press / Doubleday, 1983), 89, 94, 96.

50. Emory L. Cowen, "In Pursuit of Wellness," *American Psychologist* 46, no. 4 (1991): 404, https:// doi.org / 10.1037 / 0003-066X.46.4.404.

51. Elizabeth Montgomery's attempt to live in the present may be a current secular version of Buddhist ideas. Alma Gottlieb, comment to author, August 2019.

52. David McGillivray, "Fitter, Happier, More Productive: Governing Working Bodies through Wellness," *Culture and Organization* 11, no. 2 (2005), https:// doi.org / 10 .1080 / 14759550500091036. See also J. A. English-Lueck and Miriam Lueck Avery, "Intensifying Work and Chasing Innovation: Incorporating Care in Silicon Valley," *Anthropology of Work Review* 38, no. 1 (2017), https:// doi.org / 10.1111 / awr.12111; J. A. English-Lueck, *Being and Well-Being: Health and the Working Bodies of Silicon Valley* (Stanford, CA: Stanford University Press, 2010).

53. Bryan Robinson, quoted in Kathleen Doheny, "Working Yourself to Death: Long Hours Bring Risks," WebMD, July 16, 2018, https:// www.webmd.com / balance / stress-management / news / 20180716 / working-yourself-to-death-long-hours-bring -risks.

54. W. Oates, *Confessions of a Workaholic: The Facts about Work Addiction* (New York: World, 1971), 11, quoted in Wilmar B. Schaufeli, Toon W. Taris, and Arnold B. Bakker, "Dr. Jekyll or Mr. Hyde? On the Differences between Work Engagement and Workaholism," in *Research Companion to Working Time and Work Addiction*, ed. Ronald J. Burke (Cheltenham, UK: Elgar, 2006), 193. Other researchers emphasize not long hours but rather that "workaholics struggle to psychologically detach from work." Nancy P. Rothbard and Lieke ten Brummelhuis, "How Being a Workaholic Differs from Working Long Hours," Pocket, accessed July 19, 2021, https:// getpocket.com / explore / item / how-being-a-workaholic-differs-from-working-long-hours?utm_source=pocket _mylist. Originally published in *Harvard Business Review*, March 4, 2018.

55. "Welcome to Workaholics Anonymous," Workaholics Anonymous, 2021, http:// www.workaholics-anonymous.org /.

56. Suzan Lewis, Richenda Gambles, and Rhona Rapoport, "The Constraints of a 'Work–Life Balance' Approach: An International Perspective, *International Journal of Human Resource Management* 18, no. 3 (2007): 360, https:// doi.org / 10.1080 / 095851906011 65577. I use this term for convenience, despite agreeing with the excellent analysis in David E. Guest, "Perspectives on the Study of Work-Life Balance," *Social Science Information* 41, no. 2 (2002): 261–63, https:// doi.org / 10.1177 / 053901840204100200. Guest points out it is not clear what we mean by "work," "life," or "balance"—or why work is opposed to life, instead of being part of it.

57. Lewis et al., "Constraints of a 'Work–Life Balance' Approach," 361.

58. Sharon Hays, *The Cultural Contradictions of Motherhood* (New Haven, CT: Yale University Press, 1996); Annette Lareau, *Unequal Childhoods: Class, Race, and Family Life* (Berkeley: University of California Press, 2011); Anne-Marie Slaughter, *Unfinished Business: Women Men Work Family* (New York: Random House, 2015).

59. Jacques Freyssinet and François Michon, "Overtime in Europe" (Eurofound, Luxembourg, June 30, 2003), https:// www.eurofound.europa.eu / publications / report / 2003 / overtime-in-europe.

See also Edward Fischer, *The Good Life: Aspiration, Dignity, and the Anthropology of Wellbeing* (Stanford, CA: Stanford University Press, 2014), 107–8, on successful labor organizing in Germany to shorten workweek hours while holding wages steady, along with the cultural value of *Feierabend* (quitting time).

60. Erin Reid, "Why Some Men Pretend to Work 80-Hour Weeks," *Harvard Business Review*, April 28, 2015, https://hbr.org/2015/04/why-some-men-pretend-to-work-80-hour-weeks. See also Miller, "Women Did Everything Right: Then Work Got 'Greedy.'"

61. McKinsey & Company, *Women in the Workplace: 2020* (New York: McKinsey & Company, 2020), 24, https://www.mckinsey.com/featured-insights/diversity-and-inclusion/women-in-the-workplace.

62. Wilmar B. Schaufeli, Toon W. Taris, and Arnold B. Bakker, "It Takes Two to Tango: Workaholism Is Working Excessively and Working Compulsively," in *The Long Work Hours Culture: Causes, Consequences and Choices*, ed. Ronald J. Burke and Cary L. Cooper (Bingley, UK: Emerald, 2008), 204.

63. Schaufeli et al., "Dr. Jekyll or Mr. Hyde?" 193–94.

64. Shimazu et al., "Workaholism vs. Work Engagement." These mental and physical health correlations were weak but statistically significant. See also the twenty questions at "Welcome Newcomers!," Workaholics Anonymous, 2021, http://www.workaholics-anonymous.org/newcomers.

65. See Guest, "Perspectives on the Study of Work-Life Balance," 260, for critiques of disease models of workaholism.

66. Weber hinted at possible enjoyment from work when he wrote, "In the United States, the pursuit of wealth, stripped of its religious and ethical meaning, tends to become associated with purely mundane passions which often actually give it the character of sport." Weber, *Protestant Ethic*, 182.

67. See the discussion of a "career" approach to choosing a job or occupation in chapter 6.

68. "All Employees, Total Nonfarm [PAYEMS]," U.S. Bureau of Labor Statistics, retrieved from FRED, Federal Reserve Bank of St. Louis, April 8, 2023, https://fred.stlouisfed.org/series/PAYEMS.

69. Elizabeth Dwoskin, "The Fight over Retraining the Unemployed," *Bloomberg Businessweek*, April 12, 2012, http://www.bloomberg.com/bw/articles/2012-04-09/the-fight-over-retraining-the-unemployed.

70. For descriptions of contemporary US job search rituals, see Barbara Ehrenreich, *Bait and Switch: The (Futile) Pursuit of the American Dream* (New York: Henry Holt, 2005); Lane, *Company of One*, 74–77.

71. Gina Belli, "How Many Jobs Are Found through Networking, Really?" Payscale, April 6, 2017, https://www.payscale.com/career-news/2017/04/many-jobs-found-networking.

72. Sharone found class differences: US blue-collar workers more often ignored career counselors' advice and relied on methods that had worked for them in the past, such as personal contacts. Sharone, *Flawed System/Flawed Self*, chap. 6.

73. Sharone, *Flawed System/Flawed Self*, 109.

74. On conspicuous busyness as a US salaried worker's status symbol, see Bellezza et al., "Conspicuous Consumption of Time."

75. On the variety of ways contemporary Americans stay busy, see Charles N. Darrah, James M. Freeman, and J. A. English-Lueck, *Busier than Ever! Why American Families Can't Slow Down* (Stanford, CA: Stanford University Press, 2007).

76. See chapter 1 for an explanation of cultural standing; also Strauss, "Cultural Standing in Expression of Opinion."

77. Strauss, "Cultural Standing in Expression of Opinion," 181.

78. Hochschild reports hearing a corporate employee use that very phrase: "I work to live; I don't live to work." Arlie Russell Hochschild, *The Time Bind: When Work Becomes Home and Home Becomes Work* (New York: Metropolitan Books, 2000), 35. Rejection of workaholism may be what I have termed a "conventional discourse." Strauss, *Making Sense of Public Opinion*.

79. These are not the same as what other researchers call "9-to-5" employees, who are not engaged with their jobs. Marisa Salanova, Mario Del Líbano, Susana Llorens, and Wilmar B Schaufeli, "Engaged, Workaholic, Burned-Out or Just 9-to-5? Toward a Typology of Employee Well-Being," *Stress and Health* 30, no. 1 (2014): 77, https://doi.org/10.1002/smi.2499.

80. See also Sharone, *Flawed System/Flawed Self*, 157.

81. Jahoda, "Work, Employment, and Unemployment," 188.

82. Strauss, *Making Sense of Public Opinion*, 205–7, 247–53.

83. Lauren Berlant, *Cruel Optimism* (Durham, NC: Duke University Press, 2011), 170–71.

84. Jahoda, "Work, Employment, and Unemployment,"189.

85. Lucien Febvre, cited in E. P. Thompson, "Time, Work-Discipline, and Industrial Capitalism," *Past & Present* 38 (1967): 60n13.

86. Thompson, "Time, Work-Discipline," 60.

87. Thompson, "Time, Work-Discipline," 95.

88. Thompson, "Time, Work-Discipline," 96.

89. Heejung Chung and Tanja Van der Lippe, "Flexible Working, Work–Life Balance, and Gender Equality: Introduction," *Social Indicators Research* 151, no. 2 (2020): 369–70, https://doi.org/10.1007/s11205-018-2025-x.

90. David L. Blustein, "The Role of Work in Psychological Health and Well-Being: A Conceptual, Historical, and Public Policy Perspective," *American Psychologist* 63, no. 4 (2008), https://doi.org/10.1037/0003-066X.63.4.228.

91. See also Jahoda on "status and identity" as intangible work benefits. Jahoda, "Work, Employment, and Unemployment," 189.

92. An anthropologist who interviewed unemployed Norwegians has similar findings: "To live in accordance with the employment ethic is not to work hard per se but rather to achieve that sense of ordinariness, fulfillment, and moral satisfaction that comes with having a job." McKowen, "Substantive Commitments," 124. Interestingly, however, it seems that "the moral satisfaction" that McKowen describes comes from contributing taxes to the welfare state, not from productivist values.

93. Nicholas Bloom, "How Working from Home Works Out" (Stanford Institute for Economic Policy Research, June 2020), 2, https://siepr.stanford.edu/research/publications/how-working-home-works-out.

94. Kim Parker, Juliana Horowitz and Rachel Minkin, "How the Coronavirus Outbreak Has—and Hasn't—Changed the Way Americans Work" (Pew Research Center,

December 2020), https://www.pewresearch.org/social-trends/2020/12/09/how-the
-coronavirus-outbreak-has-and-hasnt-changed-the-way-americans-work; Hilary Osborne, "Home Workers Putting in More Hours since Covid, Research Shows," *The
Guardian*, February 4, 2021, https://www.theguardian.com/business/2021/feb/04
/home-workers-putting-in-more-hours-since-covid-research; Jenesse Miller, "COVID-19
Has Hit Women Hard, Especially Working Mothers," *USCNews*, June 18, 2020, https://
news.usc.edu/171617/covid-19-women-job-losses-childcare-mental-health-usc-study.

95. Bloom, "How Working from Home Works Out," 7. For alternative ways of
combining working from home with socializing with other people, see Seo Young Park,
"Stitching the Fabric of Family: Time, Work, and Intimacy in Seoul's Tongdaemun
Market," *Journal of Korean Studies* 17, no. 2 (2012), https://doi.org/10.1353/jks.2012
.0023. I return to this topic in chapters 6 and 7.

96. Lane heard the same in her research with unemployed high-tech workers. Lane,
"Limits of Liminality," 27. See also this discussion on Reddit: https://www.reddit.com/r
/AskReddit/comments/42g9i2/unemployed_people_of_reddit_what_do_you_do_all
_day/.

97. Michael G. Flaherty, "Time Work: Customizing Temporal Experience," *Social
Psychology Quarterly* 66, no. 1 (2003): 20, https://doi.org/10.2307/3090138; Garrett-
Peters, "If I Don't Have to Work Anymore, Who Am I?," 562.

98. See Sharone, *Flawed System/Flawed Self*; and Lane, "Limits of Liminality" for
similar observations.

99. For a different finding, see Sharone, *Flawed System/Flawed Self*, 116.

100. Kohls, "The Values Americans Live By," 6.

101. Strauss, "What Makes Tony Run?"; Reid, "Why Some Men Pretend to Work
80-Hour Weeks"; Saad, "The "40-Hour" Workweek Is Actually Longer."

102. Brigid Schulte, *Overwhelmed: Work, Love, and Play When No One Has the Time*
(New York: Sarah Crichton Books, 2014), 44ff.

103. Shayla Love, "The Cult of Busyness," *Vice*, June 7, 2021, https://www.vice
.com/en/article/k78wpz/covid-changed-our-relationship-to-busyness-can-we-keep
-it-that-way-v28n2?utm_source=pocket-newtab.

3. Working to Live Well

1. Anna Jefferson, "'Not What It Used to Be': Schemas of Class and Contradiction
in the Great Recession," *Economic Anthropology* 2, no. 2 (2015): 312, https://doi.org
/10.1002/sea2.12033.

2. Weber, *Protestant Ethic*, 71.

3. Weber, *Protestant Ethic*, 181. The "iron cage" metaphor was chosen by Talcott
Parsons, who translated *The Protestant Ethic and the Spirit of Capitalism* into English. A
better translation, according to Peter Baehr, would have been "shell as hard as steel,"
which has subtly different connotations. Peter Baehr, "The 'Iron Cage' and the 'Shell
as Hard as Steel': Parsons, Weber, and the *Stahlhartes Gehäuse* Metaphor in *The Protestant Ethic and the Spirit of Capitalism*," *History and Theory* 40 (May 2001), https://doi
.org/10.1111/0018-2656.00160.

4. Grant McCracken, *Culture and Consumption: New Approaches to the Symbolic Character of Consumer Goods and Activities* (Bloomington: Indiana University Press, 1988), 4–9.

5. Daniel Miller, "Consumption Studies as the Transformation of Anthropology," in *Acknowledging Consumption: A Review of New Studies,* ed. Daniel Miller (London: Routledge, 1995), 263–92, especially 278.

6. "City of Los Angeles Security Officer Yearly Salaries in California," Indeed, accessed June 14, 2021, https://www.indeed.com/cmp/City-of-Los-Angeles/salaries/Security-Officer/California.

7. Carl Mathews's desire for the pleasures of lavish consumption is different from seeing consumption as a signal of a middle-class class identity, although that mattered to him as well. For more on the way some middle-class Blacks like him signal their class identity in different contexts, see Karyn R. Lacy, *Blue-Chip Black: Race, Class, and Status in the New Black Middle Class* (Berkeley: University of California Press, 2007).

8. That was common. Michael Calhoun, "Lessons from the Financial Crisis: The Central Importance of a Sustainable, Affordable and Inclusive Housing Market" (Brookings Center on Regulation and Markets, September 5, 2018), https://www.brookings.edu/research/lessons-from-the-financial-crisis-the-central-importance-of-a-sustainable-affordable-and-inclusive-housing-market/.

9. Carl still had friends. Our interviews were frequently interrupted by their calls.

10. "The American dream," Merriam-Webster, accessed June 14, 2021, https://www.merriam-webster.com/dictionary/the%20American%20dream.

11. Tocqueville, "The Taste for Physical Comfort in America," vol. 2 in *Democracy in America*, 531.

12. In 2011, when I conducted my research, a bare majority (51%) of adults lived in middle-income households, down from 61 percent of adults in 1971. The Pew Research Center defines middle-income households as "two-thirds to double the national median, after incomes have been adjusted for household size." Rakesh Kochhar, "The American Middle Class Is Stable in Size, but Losing Ground Financially to Upper-Income Families" (Pew Research Center, September 6, 2018), https://pewrsr.ch/2FxKvLs.

13. Tocqueville, "The Taste for Physical Comfort in America," vol. 2 in *Democracy in America*, 531.

14. My research assistant Rylie Fong pointed out that Veblen's theory is compatible with Tocqueville's. Tocqueville focuses on the importance of material acquisitions for a mobile middle-class, whereas Veblen explains what kinds of material acquisitions are desired. Rylie Fong, comment to author, June 16, 2021.

15. Veblen, *Theory of the Leisure Class*, 52.

16. Veblen, *Theory of the Leisure Class*, 54–55.

17. Chad Stone et al., "A Guide to Statistics on Historical Trends in Income Inequality" (Center on Budget and Policy Priorities, Washington, DC, updated January 13, 2020), 9–10, https://www.cbpp.org/research/poverty-and-inequality/a-guide-to-statistics-on-historical-trends-in-income-inequality. The second set of figures considers income after taxes and government transfer payments.

18. Juliet B. Schor, *The Overspent American: Why We Want What We Don't Need* (New York: Harper, 1998), 12.

19. Schor, *Overspent American*, 9–10, 11–12. The large range of estimates in spending increases is due to different ways of controlling for inflation.

20. Bauman, *Work, Consumerism*, 23–24, 25–26.

21. Bauman, *Work, Consumerism*, 1.

22. Chen, *Cut Loose*, 216–18.

23. Daniel Horowitz, *The Anxieties of Affluence: Critiques of American Consumer Culture, 1939–1979* (Amherst: University of Massachusetts Press, 2004), 2–3. See also Daniel Miller's suggestion that anthropologists have been influenced by "a generalised puritanism which assumes that the desire for goods is based on an irrational materialism." Miller, "Consumption Studies as the Transformation of Anthropology," 269.

24. Eric Etheridge, "Rich Santelli: Tea Party Time," *New York Times*, February 20, 2009, https://opinionator.blogs.nytimes.com/2009/02/20/rick-santelli-tea-party-time/.

25. Anne Meneley, "Consumerism," *Annual Review of Anthropology* 47 (2018): 118, https://doi.org/10.1146/annurev-anthro-102116-041518.

26. Owen Kelly, "Understanding Compulsive Shopping Disorder," Verywell Mind, September 17, 2020, https://www.verywellmind.com/what-is-compulsive-shopping-disorder-2510592.

27. Meneley, "Consumerism," 119–21.

28. BER Staff, "Rise of Thrifting: Solution to Fast Fashion or Stealing from the Poor?" post at website of *Berkeley Economic Review*, November 19, 2019, https://econreview.berkeley.edu/rise-of-thrifting-solution-to-fast-fashion-or-stealing-from-the-poor/.

29. According to a reference librarian at the Claremont Colleges, "The quote is attributed to the reference *Ben Franklin, Advice to a Young Tradesman* (1748). However, I found the text of *Advice to a Young Tradesman*, 1748 in several places and this particular quote is not contained in that text." Mary Martin, email message to author, September 11, 2020.

30. "Our Mission" and homepage of the New Dream website, accessed June 14, 2021, https://newdream.org/ and https://newdream.org/about-us.

31. Kate Bowler, *Blessed: A History of the American Prosperity Gospel* (Oxford: Oxford University Press, 2013), 39–40, 78. Bowler explains why she uses this term, although contemporary prosperity preachers do not. Bowler, *Blessed*, 249–51.

32. Marla F. Frederick, *Between Sundays: Black Women and Everyday Struggles of Faith* (Berkeley: University of California Press, 2003), 142, 146–53.

33. Quoted (no source given) in Bowler, *Blessed*, 200.

34. Rhonda Byrne, *The Secret* (New York: Atria, 2006), 99.

35. Byrne, *The Secret*, 103, 107ff.

36. For fascinating and contrasting international studies of good life aspirations, see Fischer, *The Good Life*; Jeske, *The Laziness Myth*; McKowen, "Substantive Commitments," 129.

37. According to one cultural historian the ideal before World War II was an urban penthouse, but the suburban single-family home became established as a cultural ideal after the war. David Marc, cited in Stephanie Coontz, *The Way We Never Were: American Families and the Nostalgia Trap* (New York: Basic Books, 1992), 25. On the importance of homeownership in the United States, see Jefferson, "'Not What It Used to Be,'" 312; Constance Perin, *Everything in Its Place: Social Order and Land Use in America* (Princeton, NJ: Princeton University Press, 1977), especially 44–49; Nicholas W. Townsend, *The Package Deal: Marriage, Work and Fatherhood in Men's Lives* (Philadelphia: Temple University Press, 2002), 138. As Alma Gottlieb and Beverly Haviland pointed out to me, a single-family home and a car are valued, in part, for the privacy and independence they provide. Comments to author, October 17, 2019.

38. That consumption is opposed to caring about sociality is one of the "myths" of consumption discussed by Daniel Miller, "Consumption as the Vanguard of History," in *Acknowledging Consumption: A Review of New Studies*, ed. Daniel Miller (London: Routledge, 1995), 20–21.

39. Andrew Hernandez, "American Dream," Urban Dictionary, November 28, 2004, https://www.urbandictionary.com/define.php?term=American%20Dream.

40. Hernandez, "American Dream." His definition ended "or don't agree with capitolism." I suspect that was an unintentional misspelling, rather than the slang term "capitolism" meaning "an ironic reference to an economy in which market forces are subsumed to political interests in Washington." Marcellus_vrw, Urban Dictionary, March 11, 2009, https://www.urbandictionary.com/define.php?term=Capitolism.

41. William A. Gamson and Andre Modigliani, "Media Discourse and Public Opinion on Nuclear Power: A Constructionist Approach," *American Journal of Sociology* 95, no. 1 (1989): 3, https://doi.org/10.1086/229213. It could also be a "key symbol." The anthropologist Sherry Ortner gives as example of a key symbol "'work' in the Protestant ethic." Sherry B. Ortner, "On Key Symbols," *American Anthropologist* 75, no. 5 (1973): 1339, https://doi.org/10.1525/aa.1973.75.5.02a00100.

42. Avi Friedman and David Krawitz, *Peeking through the Keyhole: The Evolution of North American Homes* (Montreal: McGill-Queen's University Press, 2002), 76; "Highlights of Annual 2020 Characteristics of New Housing," U.S. Census Bureau, accessed July 30, 2021, https://www.census.gov/construction/chars/highlights.html.

43. "White picket fences" can be a metaphor for a happy life. One my participants, Emily Quinn, commented that she could not tell her sister how difficult it was to be out of work: "My sister is, 'If it's not white picket fences and roses I really don't wanna talk about it.'"

44. Les Christie, "America's Homes Are Bigger than Ever," CNN Money, June 5, 2014, https://money.cnn.com/2014/06/04/real_estate/american-home-size/.

45. Schor, *The Overspent American*, 113.

46. Meneley, "Consumerism," 118.

47. Pierre Bourdieu, *Distinction: A Social Critique of the Judgement of Taste*, trans. Richard Nice (Cambridge, MA: Harvard University Press, 1984).

48. Atif Mian and Amir Sufi, *House of Debt: How They (and You) Caused the Great Recession, and How We Can Prevent It from Happening Again* (Chicago: University of Chicago Press, 2014).

49. Austin Nichols, Josh Mitchell, and Stephan Lindner, "Consequences of Long-Term Unemployment" (Urban Institute, Washington, DC, 2013), 3, https://www.urban.org/sites/default/files/publication/23921/412887-Consequences-of-Long-Term-Unemployment.PDF.

50. "Estimate of Median Household Income for Los Angeles County, CA," Federal Reserve Bank of St. Louis, updated December 10, 2020, https://fred.stlouisfed.org/series/MHICA06037A052NCEN; "Estimate of Median Household Income for San Bernardino County, CA," Federal Reserve Bank of St. Louis, updated December 10, 2020, https://fred.stlouisfed.org/series/MHICA06071A052NCEN.

51. Their past and current incomes were obtained on a form with the income ranges shown in figures 3.4 and 3.5. To estimate the decline, I took the midpoint of each range, using $8,500 for those who checked the bottom category of less than $12,000/year

and $600,000 for those who checked the top category of more than $500,000/year. If they volunteered the exact amount of their income, I used that figure instead.

52. Jessica Godofsky, Carl Van Horn, and Cliff Zukin, *American Workers Assess an Economic Disaster* (New Brunswick, NJ: John J. Heldrich Center for Workforce Development, Rutgers University, 2010), 7. The problem was particularly acute in southern California. During the Great Recession, the US Bankruptcy Court district for Southern California had the highest increase in bankruptcy filings of any court in the country. Jonathan Lansner, "The Recession That Cut California Deeply Isn't Fully Forgotten," *Orange County Register*, September 17, 2018, https://www.ocregister.com /2018/09/17/the-recession-that-cut-california-deeply-isnt-fully-forgotten/.

53. That is why it is important to get to know participants over multiple interviews and use a variety of prompts. Although Auguste Salander's good life image spoke of material desires that he seemed uninterested in during the interviews, in other cases, it was the reverse. For example, Carl Mathews's response to the good life question was "having God in your life" and "live within your means," along with other prudent financial advice—but nothing about making his home a palace.

54. The most recent research backs up Jim Wade's assessment, "Money does buy happiness." People with higher incomes are more likely to say they are happier or, at least, that they are more satisfied with their life, whether comparing across countries or within them. Betsey Stevenson and Justin Wolfers, "Economic Growth and Subjective Well-Being: Reassessing the Easterlin Paradox" (Brookings Papers on Economic Activity, no. 14282, 2008), https://users.nber.org/~jwolfers/papers/EasterlinParadox .pdf; Erik Linqvist, Robert Östling, and David Cesarini, "Long-Run Effects of Lottery Wealth on Psychological Well-Being" (NBER Working Paper No. 24667, May 2018), https://doi.org/10.3386/w24667. See also Justin Wolfers, "Money Really Does Lead to a More Satisfying Life," *New York Times*, August 24, 2018, https://www.nytimes .com/2018/08/24/business/money-satisfaction-lottery-study.html. Linqvist et al. found a robust correlation between higher incomes from lottery winnings and life satisfaction (responses to "Taking all things together in your life, how satisfied would you say that you are with your life these days?") but not as strong a correlation to current happiness (responses to "All things considered, how happy would you say that you are?"). Stevenson and Wolfers, in contrast, found that both increased happiness and life satisfaction correlated with higher income in cross-national samples.

55. "Daily Practice," Soka Gakkai International—USA, accessed June 14, 2021, http://www.sgi-usa.org/member-resources/member-activities/daily-practice/.

56. "Golden Words by Daisaku Ikeda, Golden Words No. 711," https://m.facebook .com/goldenzones/photos/a.157302158013887/1039735003103927/?type=3&source =48.

57. Casey Leins, "Cities with the Most Homelessness," *U.S. News & World Report*, December 18, 2019, https://www.usnews.com/news/cities/slideshows/cities-with -the-most-homelessness-in-the-us?slide=4.

58. That 40 percent figure includes Stephen Smith's wife. If she were excluded because I learned about her fears secondhand, it would still be a striking 30 percent of those with former annual household incomes of $200,000 or more expressed such worries in the interviews. I cannot see why those with household incomes below $200,000 would be more likely to keep any such fears to themselves.

59. Similarly, Marianne Cooper was surprised to find considerable financial anxiety among affluent northern Californians in the research she conducted shortly before the Great Recession. Cooper, *Cut Adrift: Families in Insecure Times* (Berkeley: University of California Press, 2014), chap. 4.

60. Tocqueville, "The Taste for Physical Comfort in America," vol. 2 in *Democracy in America*, 531.

61. Cooper found that her affluent participants were particularly knowledgeable about economic trends such as the growing gap between rich and poor in the United States. She speculates that may account for their surprising financial anxieties. Cooper, *Cut Adrift*, 96, 107. In my research, conducted six years after hers, I heard the idea that the middle class is disappearing voiced by participants of all classes.

62. Alejandro Portes and Rubén G. Rumbaut, *Immigrant America: A Portrait* (Berkeley: University of California Press, 2014), 2.

63. Ana Gonzalez-Barrera, "More Mexicans Leaving than Coming to the U.S." (Pew Research Center, Washington, DC, November 19, 2015), https://www.pewresearch.org/hispanic/wp-content/uploads/sites/5/2015/11/2015-11-19_mexican-immigration__FINAL.pdf. For an ethnographic description, see Frances Abrahamer Rothstein, "Labor on the Move: Kinship, Social Networks, and Precarious Work among Mexican Migrants," in *Anthropologies of Unemployment: New Perspectives on Work and Its Absence*, ed. Jong Bum Kwon and Carrie M. Lane (Ithaca: Cornell University Press, 2016), 155–70.

64. Martijn Hendriks, "The Happiness of International Migrants: A Review of Research Findings," *Migration Studies* 3, no. 3 (2015): 361, https://doi.org/10.1093/migration/mnu053.

65. Kristyn Frank and Feng Hou, "Over-Education and Well-Being: How Does Education-Occupation Mismatch Affect the Life Satisfaction of University-Educated Immigrant and Non-Immigrant Workers?" *Ethnicity & Health* 23, no. 8 (2018), https://doi.org/10.1080/13557858.2017.1316832. The anthropologist Susanna Rosenbaum found another frame of reference for immigrants who had lived in the United States for many years, some of whom compared their present situation not only with their life in their home country but also with their lives when they first arrived in the United States. Rosenbaum, *Domestic Economies: Women, Work, and the American Dream in Los Angeles* (Durham, NC: Duke University Press, 2017).

66. Hendriks, "Happiness of International Migrants," 347.

67. Hendriks, "Happiness of International Migrants," 361–62.

68. Regarding the importance of a subjective sense of belonging, see Rosenbaum, *Domestic Economies*, 12.

69. From 2010 to 2014, Latinos (immigration generation unspecified) in large urban counties in California had a median household income of $48,373. California Senate Office of Research, "A Statistical Picture of Latinos in California: 2017 Update" (California Senate Office of Research, Sacramento, CA, July 2017), 7–8, https://latinocaucus.legislature.ca.gov/sites/latinocaucus.legislature.ca.gov/files/forms/Statistical%20Picture%20of%20Latinos%20in%20California%20-%202017%20Update.pdf.

70. Typical home prices from https://www.zillow.com/irvine-ca/home-values/ and https://www.zillow.com/pomona-ca/home-values/, accessed March 12, 2023.

71. Anastasia requested that I not identify the country she came from to protect her confidentiality.

72. Anastasia's narrative suggests that the "dual frame of reference" theory should be expanded to add return migrants, because she compared herself not only to those who stayed in the home country and to the native-born in her new host country but also to return migrants. A fourth possible reference group consists of other immigrants (first-generation or later generation) in the host country; a fifth could be themselves at an earlier time. Rosenbaum, *Domestic Economies*. For research on the mental health effects of unemployment and underemployment on highly educated immigrants, see Jennifer Asanin Dean and Kathi Wilson, "'Education? It Is Irrelevant to My Job Now. It Makes Me Very Depressed . . .': Exploring the Health Impacts of Under / Unemployment among Highly Skilled Recent Immigrants in Canada," *Ethnicity & Health* 14, no. 2 (2009), https:// doi.org/ 10.1080/ 13557850802227049.

73. The interview was conducted in 2012, before the violence that later forced many Salvadorans to flee. For median incomes in El Salvador at the time, see "Household Income up 10% in El Salvador," CentralAmericaData, September 1, 2014, https:// www.centralamericadata.com/ en/ article/ home/ Household_Income_Up_10_in_El _Salvador.

74. Portes and Rumbaut, *Immigrant America*, 54, 57.

75. Both are Catholic, although neither attended Mass.

76. Octavio Blanco, "Immigrant Workers Are Most Likely to Have These Jobs," CNN, March 16, 2017, https:// money.cnn.com/ 2017/ 03/ 16/ news/ economy/ immigrant-workers-jobs/ index.html; Rosenbaum, *Domestic Economies*, 8.

77. The average cost of homes in Irvine would have been a little lower at the time we spoke.

4. Working to Just Live

1. For an exploration of current ways of making a living beyond standard waged employment, see William Monteith, Dora-Olivia Vicol, and Philippa Williams, eds., *Beyond the Wage: Ordinary Work in Diverse Economies* (Bristol, UK: Bristol University Press, 2021).

2. Susser, "Construction of Poverty and Homelessness," 413–14.

3. David Davenport and Gordon Lloyd, "Rugged Individualism: Dead or Alive?" (Defining Ideas, Hoover Institution, Stanford University, Stanford, January 10, 2017), https:// www.hoover.org/ research/ rugged-individualism-dead-or-alive-0. The term "rugged individualism" was popularized by Herbert Hoover. Hoover, "'Rugged Individualism' Campaign Speech," Digital History (1928; 2021), https:// www.digitalhistory .uh.edu/ disp_textbook.cfm?smtID=3&psid=1334.

4. Nancy Fraser and Linda Gordon, "A Genealogy of Dependency: Tracing a Keyword of the US Welfare State," *Signs: Journal of Women in Culture and Society* 19, no. 2 (1994): 320, https:// doi.org/ 10.1086/ 494886. On American kin systems, see Francis L. K. Hsu, "Rugged Individualism Reconsidered," in his *Rugged Individualism Reconsidered: Essays in Psychological Anthropology* (Knoxville: University of Tennessee Press, 1983), 3–17.

5. "A Shocking 52% of Unemployed Americans Have Exhausted Their Benefits," *Business Insider*, November 6, 2011, https:// www.businessinsider.com/ a-shocking-52 -of-unemployed-americans-have-exhausted-their-unemployment-benefits-2011-11.

6. In 2013, only half of Americans had $400 in cash to cover an emergency expense. By 2018 nearly 40 percent still lacked that much cash for emergencies. Board of Governors of the Federal Reserve System, *Report on the Economic Well-Being of U.S. Households in 2018* (Washington, DC: Board of Governors of the Federal Reserve System, May 2019), https://www.federalreserve.gov/publications/2019-economic-well-being-of-us-households-in-2018-dealing-with-unexpected-expenses.htm. For recommendations about savings, see, for example, Matthew Goldberg, "How to Start (and Build) an Emergency Fund," Bankrate, January 25, 2021, https://www.bankrate.com/banking/savings/starting-an-emergency-fund/.

7. Perhaps surprisingly for those who consider Japan a more sociocentric, group-oriented society than the United States, it has been more difficult for the unemployed and precariously employed there to obtain assistance from the state or their families; without work, some have starved to death. See Anne Allison, *Precarious Japan* (Durham, NC: Duke University Press, 2013).

8. Kaiser Family Foundation/NPR, "Long-Term Unemployed Survey" (Henry J. Kaiser Family Foundation, Menlo Park, CA, 2011), 19, https://www.kff.org/other/poll-finding/long-term-unemployed-survey/.

9. From 2000 to 2010, rents in the city of Los Angeles rose by 31 percent after correcting for inflation while incomes rose only a little more than 1 percent. The median home cost $400,000 by the end of 2012, but a Los Angeles household with a median income could afford a home that cost no more than $190,000 (using standard measures of home affordability). Los Angeles Department of City Planning, *Housing Element 2013–2021* (Los Angeles: Department of City Planning, 2013), xiv, https://planning.lacity.org/odocument/05b5d571-9bde-43c7-99e4-1aa6b656a7e9/HousingElement_20140321.pdf.

10. Christine Flanagan and Mary Schwartz, "Rental Housing Market Condition Measures: A Comparison of U.S. Metropolitan Areas from 2009 to 2011" (US Census Bureau, Washington, DC, April 2013), https://www2.census.gov/library/publications/2013/acs/acsbr11-07.pdf. For current housing costs in Los Angeles County, see "Los Angeles County, CA," City-Data.com, http://www.city-data.com/county/Los_Angeles_County-CA.html#ixzz3uWqQCohl.

11. Richard Florida, "The U.S. Spends Far More on Homeowner Subsidies than It Does on Affordable Housing," Bloomberg Citylab, April 17, 2015, https://www.citylab.com/equity/2015/04/the-us-spends-far-more-on-homeowner-subsidies-than-it-does-on-affordable-housing/390666/.

12. Florida, "The U.S. Spends Far More on Homeowner Subsidies"; "Housing Choice Vouchers Fact Sheet," US Department of Housing and Urban Development, accessed April 15, 2023, https://www.hud.gov/program_offices/public_indian_housing/programs/hcv/about/fact_sheet#3.

13. Julia Wick, "The Waiting List for Section 8 Vouchers in L.A. Is 11 Years Long," *LAist*, April 4, 2017, https://laist.com/2017/04/04/section_8_waiting_list.php.

14. Mian and Sufi, *House of Debt.*

15. Calhoun, "Lessons from the Financial Crisis."

16. Kaiser Family Foundation/NPR, "Long-Term Unemployed Survey," 18.

17. "5 Charts about Public Opinion on Medicaid," Kaiser Family Foundation, March 30, 2023, https://www.kff.org/medicaid/poll-finding/data-note-5-charts-about-public-opinion-on-medicaid/.

18. "Average Cost of Employer-Sponsored Health Insurance," eHealth, updated January 11, 2021, https://www.ehealthinsurance.com/resources/small-business/average-cost-of-employer-sponsored-health-insurance.

19. "How Does the Tax Exclusion for Employer-Sponsored Health Insurance Work?" Tax Policy Center, Urban Institute and Brookings Institution, 2022, https://www.taxpolicycenter.org/briefing-book/how-does-tax-exclusion-employer-spons ored-health-insurance-work.

20. Diane Rowland and Rachel Garfield, "Health Insurance for Unemployed Workers," Medscape, accessed March 3, 2021, https://www.medscape.com/viewarticle/423660_5. During the Great Recession, there were federal subsidies to help the unemployed with their COBRA costs, but those subsidies had expired by the time I began my research. US Treasury Department, "COBRA Insurance Coverage since the Recovery Act: Results from New Survey Data" (US Treasury Department, Washington, DC, May 2010), 2, https://home.treasury.gov/system/files/226/COBRA_Insurance_Coverage _since_the_Recovery_Act_Results_from_New_Survey_Data_MAY2010.pdf.

21. "Overview of the Affordable Care Act and Medicaid," MACPAC (Medicaid and CHIP Payment and Access Commission), 2023, https://www.macpac.gov/subtopic/overview-of-the-affordable-care-act-and-medicaid/.

22. Garrett Therolf, "County Faulted in Death at King," Los Angeles Times, December 4, 2008, https://www.latimes.com/archives/la-xpm-2008-dec-04-me-king4-story.html.

23. See also Mike Dang, "Their Children Are Their Retirement Plans," New York Times, updated Jan. 23, 2023, https://www.nytimes.com/2023/01/21/business/retirement-immigrant-families.html?searchResultPosition=1.

24. Their actions fit the oft-described value of familismo: "loyalty, solidarity, and reciprocity among family members." Esther J. Calzada, Catherine S. Tamis-LeMonda, and Hirokazu Yoshikawa, "Familismo in Mexican and Dominican Families from Low-Income, Urban Communities," Journal of Family Issues 34, no. 12 (2013): 1697, https://doi.org/10.1177/0192513X12460218. Careful studies have shown problems with blanket assumptions of familismo among immigrants and later generations of Latinos in the United States. Carolyn Smith-Morris et al., "An Anthropology of Familismo: On Narratives and Description of Mexican/Immigrants," Hispanic Journal of Behavioral Sciences 35, no. 1 (2013), https://doi.org/10.1177/0739986312459508, and Agius Vallejo's research, described next.

25. Jody Agius Vallejo, Barrios to Burbs: The Making of the Mexican American Middle Class (Stanford, CA: Stanford University Press 2012), 71.

26. Agius Vallejo, Barrios to Burbs, 76, 89.

27. Catherine Rampell, "It Takes a B.A. to Find a Job as a File Clerk," New York Times, February 19, 2013, https://www.nytimes.com/2013/02/20/business/college-degree-required-by-increasing-number-of-companies.html?pagewanted=all&_r=0; Catherine Rampell, "Degree Inflation? Jobs That Newly Require B.A.'s," New York Times, December 4, 2012, https://economix.blogs.nytimes.com/2012/12/04/degree-inflation-jobs-that-newly-require-b-a-s/. Those were the conditions when I conducted my research. A tighter labor market after 2020 may have led to a relaxation in the credentials employers required. Neil Irwin, "Workers Are Gaining Leverage over Em-

ployers Right before Our Eyes," *New York Times*, updated June 6, 2021, https://www
.nytimes.com/2021/06/05/upshot/jobs-rising-wages.html.

28. Esteban Ortiz-Ospina and Max Roser, "Marriages and Divorces," Our World in
Data, 2020, https://ourworldindata.org/marriages-and-divorces.

29. "Historical Marital Status Tables," US Census Bureau, accessed April 15, 2023,
https://www.census.gov/data/tables/time-series/demo/families/marital.html.

30. Katherine S. Newman, *The Accordion Family: Boomerang Kids, Anxious Parents,
and the Private Toll of Global Competition* (Boston: Beacon Press, 2012). Newman also
investigated Scandinavian countries where the situation is different because there is
government support for independent living. See also Norma Mendoza-Denton and
Aomar Boum, "Breached Initiations: Sociopolitical Re-Sources and Conflicts in
Emergent Adulthood," *Annual Review of Anthropology* 44, no. 1 (2015), https://doi.org
/10.1146/annurev-anthro-102214-014012.

31. Jonathan Vespa, "A Third of Young Adults Live with Their Parents," Census.gov,
revised October 8, 2021, https://www.census.gov/library/stories/2017/08/young
-adults.html.

32. Adam Davidson, "It's Official: The Boomerang Kids Won't Leave," *New York
Times Magazine*, June 20, 2014, http://www.nytimes.com/2014/06/22/magazine/its
-official-the-boomerang-kids-wont-leave.html. However, Townsend's research with
middle-class baby-boomer-generation men in California found that, although they portrayed themselves as independent from their parents right out of school, 70 percent
received help from relatives when buying their first home. Townsend, *The Package
Deal*, 149, 220n2.

33. Newman, *The Accordion Family*, xvii.

34. Asian and Latino immigration is also driving that trend, but multigenerational
households have increased among whites since 1971. Interestingly, Pew defines "adult
children" as twenty-five years old or older, perhaps in recognition of changing norms
about when young people become "adults." D'Vera Cohn et al., "Financial Issues Top
the List of Reasons U.S. Adults Live in Multigenerational Homes" (Pew Research Center, Washington, DC, March 2022), https://www.pewresearch.org/social-trends/2022
/03/24/the-demographics-of-multigenerational-households/.

35. Newman, *The Accordion Family*, 5–21. The anthropologist Eileen Anderson-Fye
told me that every year she asks the students in her course on adolescence if they are
adults. All are traditional college-age students. In the past, only one or two students per
class thought they were adults (e.g., if they had a child). When she would ask what it
took to be an adult, they would say "earning a living." In 2015, for the first time, a majority said they were adults. Their criterion has shifted to making their own decisions
for their future, not earning their own living. That fits the trend Newman observed of
moving away from fixed markers of adulthood to a subjective sense of responsibility for
one's own life. Conversation with the author, March 31, 2016.

36. Jeffrey Jensen Arnett, "Emerging Adulthood: A Theory of Development from
the Late Teens through the Twenties," *American Psychologist* 55, no. 5 (2000), https://doi
.org/10.1037/0003-066X.55.5.469.

37. Jennifer Finney Boylan, "What to Expect the 264th Month," *New York Times*,
May 30, 2018, https://www.nytimes.com/2018/05/30/opinion/what-to-expect-the

-264th-month.html?partner=IFTTT. A 2005 Pew Research Center poll found that across the generations, one-third of respondents thought it was a parent's responsibility to let an adult child live in the parent's home. Pew Research Center, "From the Age of Aquarius to the Age of Responsibility: Baby Boomers Approach Age 60" (Pew Research Center, Washington, DC, December 8, 2005), 3.

38. Newman, *The Accordion Family*, xvi, xxii.

39. Walter Hamilton, "Great Recession Has New Wrinkles for Older Workers," *Los Angeles Times*, November 10, 2013, https://www.latimes.com/business/la-fi-older -jobs-20131110-story.html.

40. Emily Brandon, "Why Older Workers Can't Get Hired," *U.S. News and World Report*, May 18, 2012, http://money.usnews.com/money/blogs/planning-to-retire /2012/05/18/why-older-workers-cant-get-hired; US Government Accountability Office, "Unemployed Older Workers: Many Experience Challenges Regaining Employment and Face Reduced Retirement Security" (Report to the Chairman, Special Committee on Aging, US Senate, Washington, DC, May 15, 2012), https://www.gao .gov/products/gao-12-445. See also Richard Sennett, *The Culture of the New Capitalism* (New Haven: Yale University Press, 2006), 94ff.

41. Leslie Patton, "Senior Citizens Are Replacing Teenagers as Fast-Food Workers," Bloomberg, November 5, 2018, https://www.bloomberg.com/news/articles/2018-11 -05/senior-citizens-are-replacing-teenagers-at-fast-food-joints.

42. "Older Workers," US Bureau of Labor Statistics, July 2008, https://www.bls.gov /spotlight/2008/older_workers/.

43. Pew Research Center, "From the Age of Aquarius," 3.

44. Mains, *Hope Is Cut*, 142–43.

45. Marcel Mauss, *The Gift: Forms and Functions of Exchange in Archaic Societies*, trans. Ian Cunnison (1925; repr. New York: W. W. Norton, 1967), 63.

46. Tocqueville, "On the Use Which the Americans Make of Associations in Civil Life," vol. 2 in *Democracy in America*, 513–17.

47. Thomas Rotolo, "Trends in Voluntary Association Participation," *Nonprofit and Voluntary Sector Quarterly* 28, no. 2 (June 1999), https://doi.org/10.1177/089976409 9282005. Many mutual aid groups arose to provide food and other assistance during the COVID-19 recession of 2020, but I have not found reports of those during the Great Recession. Kimiko de Freytas-Tamura, "How Neighborhood Groups Are Stepping in Where the Government Didn't," *New York Times*, updated March 6, 2021, https://www .nytimes.com/2021/03/03/nyregion/covid-19-mutual-aid-nyc.html.

48. The only social problem that could occur is running into a volunteer one knows, as happened to Della Jones one time. That encounter was upsetting for her because it reminded her that she used to be a volunteer along with that former friend. She said she went back to her car and started crying because "I just miss them and I miss that and everything that could have been."

49. Thomas Humphrey Marshall, "Citizenship and Social Class," excerpted in *Citizenship and Social Class*, Vol. 2, ed. Thomas Burton Bottomore and Thomas Humphrey Marshall (1950; repr. London: Pluto Press, 1992), 30.

50. Summarized by John E. Hansan, "Poor Relief in Early America" (VCU Libraries Social Welfare History Project, Virginia Commonwealth University, 2011), https:// socialwelfare.library.vcu.edu/programs/poor-relief-early-amer/.

51. An influential example is Charles A. Murray, *Losing Ground: American Social Policy, 1950–1980* (New York: Basic Books, 1984). Murray particularly criticized programs targeted to the poor. Interestingly, in recent years Murray has been a proponent of a universal basic income in place of such targeted welfare programs. Charles Murray, *In Our Hands: A Plan to Replace the Welfare State* (Washington, DC: American Enterprise Institute for Public Policy Research, 2016).

52. Agricultural workers and domestic workers—the primary occupations of Black men and women in the South—were excluded from the provisions of the 1935 Social Security Act. On racial and gender restrictions in US social welfare in the early to mid-twentieth century, see Fraser and Gordon, "A Genealogy of Dependency," 321–22. For an argument that the exclusion was not racially motivated, see Larry DeWitt, "The Decision to Exclude Agricultural and Domestic Workers from the 1935 Social Security Act," *Social Security Bulletin* 70, no. 4 (2010), https://www.ssa.gov/policy/docs/ssb/v70n4/v70n4p49.html.

53. Michael B. Katz, *The Undeserving Poor: America's Enduring Confrontation with Poverty*, 2nd ed. (Oxford: Oxford University Press, 2013), 8.

54. Damaske argues that the unemployed have long been viewed with suspicion in the United States. Damaske, *Tolls of Uncertainty*, 103, 226. I agree they can fall under suspicion, but they are treated better in the US social welfare system than some other groups facing economic insecurity.

55. Stephan Leibfried, "Towards a European Welfare State? On Integrating Poverty Regimes into the European Community," in *Social Policy in a Changing Europe*, ed. Zsuzsa Ferge and Jon Eivind Kolberg (Frankfurt am Main: Campus Verlag, 1992), 252.

56. Center on Budget and Policy Priorities, "Policy Basics: Temporary Assistance for Needy Families" (Center on Budget and Policy Priorities, Washington, DC, updated March 1, 2022), 3–4, https://www.cbpp.org/research/family-income-support/temporary-assistance-for-needy-families.

57. The key legislation was The Personal Responsibility and Work Opportunity Reconciliation Act (PRWORA) of 1996. "A Short History of SNAP," US Department of Agriculture, Food and Nutrition Service, September 11, 2018, https://www.fns.usda.gov/snap/short-history-snap.

58. Compare Table 13 and Table 19, Christopher Howard et al., "The Polls-Trends: Poverty," *Public Opinion Quarterly* 81, no. 3 (2017): 781, 785, https://doi.org/10.1093/poq/nfx022. See also Strauss, *Making Sense of Public Opinion*, 209, summarizing General Social Survey polls from 1984 to 2010. There I propose that these confusing survey findings are the result of multiple vernacular discourses acquired by the American public and of cultural schemas that do not conform to elite ideologies. US social welfare spending also includes a variety of targeted tax breaks, including ones to help low-income wage earners (the earned income tax credit), parents (the child tax credit), and homeowners (the home mortgage interest deduction), as well as tax subsidies for employer-provided health insurance. Those tax deductions, credits, and exemptions operate invisibly. They rarely enter public discourse; when they do, they are framed as part of tax policy, not as social welfare programs. As a result, those benefiting from these breaks do not question their entitlement to them, nor are they questioned by others.

59. The near-poor in this study include those with incomes below 150% of the federal poverty level. Mark Robert Rank, Thomas A. Hirschl, and Kirk A. Foster, *Chasing*

the American Dream: Understanding What Shapes Our Fortunes (Oxford: Oxford University Press, 2014), Table B2, 190, drawing on the longitudinal Panel Study of Income Dynamics in the United States from 1968 to 2009.

60. US Department of Health and Human Services, Office of the Assistant Secretary for Planning and Evaluation, *Poverty in the United States: 50-Year Trends and Safety Net Impacts*, by Ajay Chaudry et al. (Washington, DC: March 2016), https://aspe.hhs.gov/system/files/pdf/154286/50YearTrends.pdf, 27; Martin Gilens, *Why Americans Hate Welfare: Race, Media, and the Politics of Antipoverty Policy* (Chicago: University of Chicago Press,1999), 68. The survey research Katz cites emphasizes cultural models of the poor as Black. Others have noted that immigrants, especially from Latin America, have also been imagined as among the undeserving poor. Katz, *Undeserving Poor*, 9.

61. Gilens, *Why Americans Hate Welfare*, 103.

62. Gilens found the same pattern for three years of television news coverage of poverty. Gilens, *Why Americans Hate Welfare*, 114, 131.

63. Although Oscar Lewis formulated the construct of a "culture of poverty," his version of it was not about inherent racial traits—unlike, for example, the later arguments of Lawrence Mead. Oscar Lewis, "The Culture of Poverty," *Scientific American* 215, no. 4 (1966); Lawrence M. Mead, *The New Politics of Poverty: The Nonworking Poor in America* (New York: Basic Books, 1992).

64. Center on Budget and Policy Priorities, "Policy Basics: Unemployment Insurance" (Center on Budget and Policy Priorities, Washington, DC, updated October 4, 2021), https://www.cbpp.org/research/economy/unemployment-insurance; "FY 2019 Characteristics and Financial Circumstances of TANF Recipients Data," US Department of Health & Human Services, Office of Family Assistance, November 16, 2020, https://www.acf.hhs.gov/ofa/data/ofa-releases-fy-2019-characteristics-and-financial-circumstances-tanf-recipients-data.

65. Liz Schott, "State General Assistance Programs Very Limited in Half the States and Nonexistent in Others, Despite Need" (Center on Budget and Policy Priorities, Washington, DC, updated July 2, 2020), https://www.cbpp.org/research/family-income-support/state-general-assistance-programs-very-limited-in-half-the-states.

66. Center on Budget and Policy Priorities, "Policy Basics: Unemployment Insurance." After the Great Recession, some state legislatures reduced benefit periods to only twelve weeks. Michele Evermore, "Unemployment Insurance during COVID-19: The CARES Act and Role of UI during the Pandemic," Testimony June 9, 2020. National Employment Law Project, https://www.nelp.org/publication/unemployment-insurance-covid-19-cares-act-role-ui-pandemic/.

67. Hannah Shaw and Chad Stone, "Key Things to Know about Unemployment Insurance" (Center on Budget and Policy Priorities, Washington, DC, updated December 20, 2011), https://www.cbpp.org/research/key-things-to-know-about-unemployment-insurance.

68. Chad Stone, "Congress Should Renew Emergency Unemployment Compensation before the End of the Year" (Center on Budget and Policy Priorities, Washington, DC, updated November 21, 2013), https://www.cbpp.org/research/congress-should-renew-emergency-unemployment-compensation-before-the-end-of-the-year.

69. Glassdoor, *Which Countries in Europe Offer the Fairest Paid Leave and Unemployment Benefits?* (Mill Valley, CA: Glassdoor, 2016), 11, 14, https://www.glassdoor.com/research/app/uploads/sites/2/2016/02/GD_FairestPaidLeave_Final-2.pdf.

70. Ed Bolen and Stacy Dean, "Waivers Add Key State Flexibility to SNAP's Three-Month Time Limit" (Center on Budget and Policy Priorities, Washington, DC, updated February 6, 2018), https://www.cbpp.org/research/food-assistance/waivers-add-key-state-flexibility-to-snaps-three-month-time-limit.

71. Maureen Pirog, Edwin Gerrish, and Lindsey Bullinger, "TANF and SNAP Asset Limits and the Financial Behavior of Low-Income Households" (Report to the Pew Charitable Trusts, May 2017), http://www.pewtrusts.org/~/media/Assets/2017/09/TANF_and_SNAP_Asset_Limits_and_the_Financial_Behavior_of_Low_Income_Households.pdf.

72. Thomas S. Weisner et al., "'I Want What Everybody Wants': Goals, Values, and Work in the Lives of New Hope Families," in *Making It Work: Low-Wage Employment, Family Life, and Child Development*, ed. Hirokazu Yoshikawa, Thomas S. Weisner, and Edward D. Lowe (New York: Russell Sage Foundation, 2005), 151.

73. Damaske found that her male interviewees waited longer than her female interviewees before throwing themselves into their job search. Damaske, *Tolls of Uncertainty*, 162–65.

74. "SNAP: Frequently Asked Questions," SNAP to Health! 2023, https://www.snaptohealth.org/snap/snap-frequently-asked-questions/#myths.

75. Aimee Picchi, "7 Things You May Not Know about Food Stamps," CBS News, February 16, 2018, https://www.cbsnews.com/news/7-things-you-may-not-know-about-food-stamps/. Beverly Haviland stressed to me the importance of public visibility or invisibility of social welfare benefits. Comments to author, February 7, 2020.

76. Alma Gottlieb found that when she suggested to some graduate students that they go on food stamps, they always resisted the idea, even though they were eligible because of their low incomes. She helped me recognize the importance of class identities in her comments on an earlier draft of this chapter. Comments to author, February 13, 2020.

77. Mona Childs also had productivist and consumerist class identities, as I explained in chapters 2 and 3. See also Jefferson, "'Not What It Used to Be,'" 316.

78. It is interesting that three of the nine women in my study who eventually received food stamps initially expressed resistance to doing so, but none of the five men who received food stamps expressed the same concerns.

79. Mark R. Rank, "A View from the Inside Out: Recipients' Perceptions of Welfare," *Journal of Sociology & Social Welfare* 21, no. 2 (May 1994).

80. The unemployed Americans whom Carrie Lane interviewed also normalized unemployment benefits, with the one exception of a twenty-five-year-old engineer "who had moved back in with his parents following his layoff" and refused to take unemployment benefits, "which he saw as 'too socialist.'" Lane, *Company of One*, 57.

81. Katz, *Undeserving Poor*, 8.

82. Grusky, Western, and Wimer, "The Consequences of the Great Recession," 10. See also Schlozman and Verba, *Injury to Insult*, 145, 363.

83. Stanley Feldman and Marco R. Steenbergen, "The Humanitarian Foundation of Public Support for Social Welfare," *American Journal of Political Science* 45, no. 3 (2001), https://doi.org/10.2307/2669244.

84. See also Lopez and Phillips, "Unemployed."

85. I describe my participants' diverse responses to the Occupy Movement in Strauss, "Engaged by the Spectacle of Protest."

86. Elsewhere I call this the "Contributors Deserve Benefits" conventional discourse. Strauss, *Making Sense of Public Opinion*, 273–76.

87. The maximum in California at that time was actually $1,800 a month. California Employment Development Department, "A Guide to Benefits and Employment Services" (DE 1275A Rev. 49 (2–12), California Employment Development Department, Sacramento, CA), 9, https://www.edd.ca.gov/pdf_pub_ctr/de1275a.pdf.

88. Glassdoor, "Which Countries in Europe Offer the Fairest Paid Leave and Unemployment Benefits?" 14.

89. Strauss, "Not-So Rugged Individualists."

90. They could still be embarrassed about it, however. Theresa Allen described the process of applying: "It's depressing, it's one step above jail, the people that you're sitting with." Some of my participants, especially immigrants whom I discuss next, never considered applying.

91. Interpretation offered by Beverly Haviland, comments to author, February 7, 2020.

92. I am not counting four other participants who were brought to the United States when they were young. Ong uses the term "'cultural citizenship' to refer to the cultural practices and beliefs produced from negotiating the often ambivalent and contested relations with the state and its hegemonic forms that establish the criteria of belonging." Aihwa Ong, "Cultural Citizenship as Subject-Making: Immigrants Negotiate Racial and Cultural Boundaries in the United States," *Current Anthropology* 37, no. 5 (1996): 738, https://doi.org/10.1086/204560.

93. Tanya Broder and Gabrielle Lessard, "Overview of Immigrant Eligibility for Federal Programs" (National Immigration Law Center, Los Angeles, updated March 2023), https://www.nilc.org/issues/economic-support/overview-immeligfedprograms/. For current exceptions regarding Medicaid eligibility in California, see "Information for Immigrants," Covered California, 2023, https://www.coveredca.com/learning-center/information-for-immigrants/.

94. Van Hook and Bean found that in the early 1990s Mexican immigrants had significantly shorter durations on welfare (cash assistance for low-income families) than US-born whites or African Americans. Mexican immigrants also had shorter welfare durations than other Latinos in their data. They attribute it to Mexican immigrants' work-based reasons for emigrating. I suspect the explanation may include other factors, such as control of informal hiring networks in many low-wage industries. Jennifer Van Hook and Frank D. Bean, "Explaining Mexican-Immigrant Welfare Behaviors: The Importance of Employment-Related Cultural Repertoires," *American Sociological Review* 74, no. 3 (2009), https://doi.org/10.1177/000312240907400305.

95. US Immigration and Naturalization Service, "Field Guidance on Deportability and Inadmissibility on Public Charge Grounds," *Federal Register* 64, no. 101 (March 26, 1999), https://www.govinfo.gov/content/pkg/FR-1999-05-26/pdf/99-13202.pdf.

96. National Immigration Law Center, *Overview of Immigrant Eligibility for Federal Programs*, 11–12. Their concerns were understandable because the rules are not stable. Public charge rules proposed by the Trump administration included SNAP benefits in public

charge deliberations. Pam Fessler and Joel Rose, "Trump Administration Rule Would Penalize Immigrants for Needing Benefits," NPR, August 12, 2019, https://www.npr.org /2019/08/12/748328652/trump-administration-rule-would-penalize-immigrants-for -using-benefits.

97. Pat Gowens, "Welfare, Learnfare-Unfair! A Letter to My Governor," *Ms.* (September–October 1991), 90–91. Quoted in Fraser and Gordon, "A Genealogy of Dependency," 333.

98. Beckman and Mazmanian emphasize the practical and emotional benefits of contemporary Americans' mutual aid arrangements. Christine M. Beckman and Melissa Mazmanian, *Dreams of the Overworked: Living, Working, and Parenting in the Digital Age* (Stanford, CA: Stanford University Press, 2020).

99. Mauss, *The Gift*, 65.

100. McKowen, "Substantive Commitments."

101. Nancy Fraser and Linda Gordon, "Contract versus Charity: Why Is There No Social Citizenship in the United States?" *Socialist Review* 22, no. 3 (1993): 63–64.

5. Gendered Meanings of Unemployment

1. Brynjolfsson and McAfee, *Second Machine Age*, 234.

2. "Labor Force Participation Rate, Female (% of Female Population Ages 15+) (modeled ILO estimate)," World Bank, updated February 21, 2023, https://data .worldbank.org/indicator/SL.TLF.CACT.FE.ZS?view=map.

3. Women comprised 47% of the civilian labor force in 2021. "Women in the Workforce: United States (Quick Take)," Catalyst, August 29, 2022, https://www.catalyst .org/research/women-in-the-workforce-united-states/; Mitra Toossi, "A Century of Change: The U.S. Labor Force, 1950–2050," *Monthly Labor Review* (May 2002): 15, https://www.bls.gov/opub/mlr/2002/05/art2full.pdf; "Working Wives in Married-Couple Families, 1967–2011," US Bureau of Labor Statistics, June 2, 2014, https://www .bls.gov/opub/ted/2014/ted_20140602.htm. These statistics refer to heterosexual couples only; comparable data for same-sex couples will begin with data gathered in the January 2020 Current Population Survey (Karen Kosanovich, Economist, Office of Employment and Unemployment Statistics, Bureau of Labor Statistics, email to author, March 27, 2020).

4. "Women in the Labor Force: A Databook," US Bureau of Labor Statistics, December 2019, https://www.bls.gov/opub/reports/womens-databook/2019/home .htm.

5. Diane Coyle, "Working Women of Color Were Making Progress. Then the Coronavirus Hit," *New York Times*, January 14, 2021, https://www.nytimes.com/2021/01 /14/opinion/minority-women-unemployment-covid.html.

6. Nicole Bateman and Martha Ross, "Why Has COVID-19 Been Especially Harmful for Working Women?" (Brookings Institution, October 2020), https://www .brookings.edu/essay/why-has-covid-19-been-especially-harmful-for-working -women/; Tim Henderson, "Mothers Are 3 Times More Likely than Fathers to Have Lost Jobs in Pandemic," *Stateline*, September 28, 2020, https://www.pewtrusts.org/en /research-and-analysis/blogs/stateline/2020/09/28/mothers-are-3-times-more -likely-than-fathers-to-have-lost-jobs-in-pandemic.

7. Jenesse Miller, "COVID-19 Has Hit Women Hard, Especially Working Mothers," *USCNews*, June 18, 2020, https://news.usc.edu/171617/covid-19-women-job-losses-childcare-mental-health-usc-study.

8. Brooke Jarvis, "Did Covid Change How We Dream?" *New York Times*, updated November 4, 2021, https://www.nytimes.com/2021/11/03/magazine/pandemic-dreams.html. One of my students interviewed a professional mother trying to work from home during the pandemic while supervising the remote schooling of her two elementary-school children. That mother commented, "I was like, 'Oh, I'm not doing my job well, but I'm also not parenting, and I'm not teaching anyone, and everything is a disaster.'" Alice Richards, interview with "April," shared with permission.

9. McKinsey & Company, *Women in the Workplace: 2020*, 6.

10. Shelley J. Correll, Stephen Bernard, and In Paik, "Getting a Job: Is There a Motherhood Penalty?" *American Journal of Sociology* 112, no. 5 (2007), https://doi.org/10.1086/511799. See also McKinsey, *Women in the Workplace*, 20.

11. Helaine Olen, "Opinion: A Lousy Myth about Moms, Kids and Work Makes a Comeback: Republicans Are Running with It," *Washington Post*, May 9, 2021, https://www.washingtonpost.com/opinions/2021/05/09/just-time-mothers-day-lousy-myth-about-moms-kids-work-makes-comeback-republicans-are-running-with-it/.

12. For an analysis of the constraints that lead educated married women to leave the workforce, see Pamela Stone, *Opting Out? Why Women Really Quit Careers and Head Home* (Berkeley: University of California Press, 2007).

13. See also Benjamin M. Seitz et al., "The Pandemic Exposes Human Nature: 10 Evolutionary Insights," *PNAS* 117, no. 45 (November 10, 2020): 27770 (Insight 5), https://doi.org/10.1073/pnas.2009787117.

14. Most twentieth-century studies of the unemployed focus on men's experiences. Some include women, but gender is not the focus of their analysis. For two exceptions, see Paula Rayman, "Women and Unemployment," *Social Research* 54, no. 2 (1987); and Ellen Israel Rosen, *Bitter Choices: Blue-Collar Women in and out of Work* (Chicago: University of Chicago Press, 1987).

15. Lane, "Man Enough to Let My Wife Support Me"; Lane, *Company of One*; Damaske, *Tolls of Uncertainty*. Interestingly, I found almost no expressions of guilty feelings by my female or male interviewees, perhaps because their job losses occurred a few years earlier, during the high unemployment years shortly after the Great Recession. Possibly as a result, there was no difference between my male and female interviewees in forgoing medical insurance or medical care for themselves to save money for their family.

16. Aliya Hamid Rao, *Crunch Time: How Married Couples Confront Unemployment* (Oakland: University of California Press, 2020). See also Karsten I. Paul and Klaus Moser, "Unemployment Impairs Mental Health: Meta-Analyses," *Journal of Vocational Behavior* 74, no. 3 (2009): 266, 272, https://doi.org/10.1016/j.jvb.2009.01.001. On the effects of education, see Gokce Basbug and Ofer Sharone, "The Emotional Toll of Long-Term Unemployment: Examining the Interaction Effects of Gender and Marital Status," *RSF: The Russell Sage Foundation Journal of the Social Sciences* 3, no. 3 (2017): 237–38, https://doi.org/10.7758/rsf.2017.3.3.10. Their analysis of a survey of unemployed adults found that negative moods were less common among college-educated unemployed men than among those without a college education. As they note, negative moods may be unrelated to unemployment or marital tension.

17. Rao, *Crunch Time*, 14.

18. It is possible that the difference from Rao's findings is due to greater economic pressures on my mixed-class suburban California participants than her Philadelphia-area professional middle-class interviewees.

19. Jean L. Potuchek, *Who Supports the Family? Gender and Breadwinning in Dual-Earner Marriages* (Stanford, CA: Stanford University Press, 1997). I take the term "neo-traditional" from Kathleen Gerson, *The Unfinished Revolution: Coming of Age in a New Era of Gender, Work, and Family* (New York: Oxford University Press, 2010), 11.

20. See also Chen, *Cut Loose*.

21. Jessie Bernard, "The Good-Provider Role: Its Rise and Fall," *American Psychologist* 36, no.1 (1981): 2, https://doi.org/10.1037/0003-066X.36.1.1

22. Potuchek, *Who Supports the Family?*, 3. For workforce participation rates of women of color versus white women from 1910–2010, see Martha J. Bailey and Thomas A. DiPrete, "Five Decades of Remarkable but Slowing Change in U.S. Women's Economic and Social Status and Political Participation," 5, https://doi.org/10.7758/rsf.2016.2.4.01.

23. Potuchek, *Who Supports the Family?*, 3; Rayman, "Women and Unemployment," 355–56.

24. Rayman, "Women and Unemployment," 362.

25. Robert A. Margo, "Employment and Unemployment in the 1930s," *Journal of Economic Perspectives* 7, no. 2 (1993): 43, https://doi.org/10.1257/jep.7.2.41.

26. Mirra Komarovsky, *The Unemployed Man and His Family: The Effect of Unemployment upon the Status of the Man in Fifty-Nine Families* (New York: Dryden Press, 1940), 76.

27. Komarovsky, *Unemployed Man and His Family*, 1–2, 46, 14, 16–17, 39, 74.

28. Komarovsky, *Unemployed Man and His Family*, 23. In some of the families, he became closer to his family while he was home, just as I found. Komarovsky, however, interprets an emotionally closer family as the result of the man's desperate efforts to keep his wife and children's love in the absence of the power of a paycheck—an interpretation that may be twisting the evidence to fit her thesis. Komarovsky, *Unemployed Man and His Family*, 13.

29. Strauss, "Cultural Standing in Expression of Opinion," 183.

30. As Pierre Bourdieu would put it, their insistence on being the sole provider was explicit *dogma* and was not the taken-for-granted commonsense that he called *doxa*. As Bourdieu also noticed, the shift from unquestioned doxa to explicitly defended dogma opens the possibility for further social change. Pierre Bourdieu, *Outline of a Theory of Practice*, trans. Richard Nice (Cambridge: Cambridge University Press, 1977).

31. Rayman, "Women and Unemployment," 358, 365.

32. The change may have occurred before the mid-1960s. "Working Wives in Married-Couple Families," US Bureau of Labor Statistics.

33. "Working Wives in Married-Couple Families." Other sources state that on average wives' earnings came to 47 percent of total family income in the United States in 2011. Wenqian Dai, "Dual-Earner Couples in the United States," in *Encyclopedia of Family Studies*, 2016, https://doi.org/10.1002/9781119085621.wbefs406.

34. Potuchek, *Who Supports the Family?*, 4.

35. Townsend, *Package Deal*, 93. See also Michèle Lamont, *The Dignity of Working Men: Morality and the Boundaries of Race, Class, and Immigration* (New York: Russell Sage Foundation, 2000), 34.

36. Rosen, *Bitter Choices*, 97, 103.

37. Potuchek, *Who Supports the Family?*, 2.

38. Townsend, *Package Deal*, 2.

39. Townsend, *Package Deal*, 117.

40. Townsend, *Package Deal*, 93.

41. "Real Median Household Income in the United States [MEHOINUSA672N]," US Census Bureau, retrieved from FRED, Federal Reserve Bank of St. Louis, April 19, 2023, https://fred.stlouisfed.org/series/MEHOINUSA672N. Since 2014, the median household income has been rising.

42. Gerson, *Unfinished Revolution*, 5.

43. David Autor and Melanie Wasserman, "Wayward Sons: The Emerging Gender Gap in Labor Markets and Education" (discussion paper, Blueprint Labs, Massachusetts Institute of Technology, Cambridge, MA, March 2013), https://seii.mit.edu/research/study/wayward-sons-the-emerging-gender-gap-in-labor-markets-and-education/; Bailey and DiPrete, "Five Decades of Remarkable but Slowing Change," 9–10.

44. Anthony P. Carnevale, Nicole Smith, and Artem Gulish, "Women Can't Win: Despite Making Educational Gains and Pursuing High-Wage Majors, Women Still Earn Less than Men" (Center on Education and the Workforce, Georgetown University, Washington, DC, 2018), http://hdl.handle.net/10822/1049530.

45. Autor and Wasserman, "Wayward Sons."

46. Couples could be married, living together unmarried, or engaged.

47. See also Gerson, *Unfinished Revolution*, 138–39.

48. By contrast, Damaske found that middle-class men were more likely than middle-class women or working-class men or women to postpone returning to work. Damaske, *Tolls of Uncertainty*, 157, 162.

49. See also Lynn White and Stacy J. Rogers, "Economic Circumstances and Family Outcomes: A Review of the 1990s," *Journal of Marriage and Family* 62, no. 4 (2000): 1043, https://doi.org/10.1111/j.1741-3737.2000.01035.x.

50. This finding fits the "women's independence" theory that women who have an income sufficient to be self-supporting are less likely to marry. However, according to one literature review, evidence for that theory is weak. White and Rogers, "Economic Circumstances and Family Outcomes," 1041.

51. Cooper found considerable anxiety among the affluent northern California parents she studied about providing for their children's college education and their own retirement. Cooper, *Cut Adrift*, 96–97.

52. See also Komarovsky, *Unemployed Man and His Family*.

53. That does not mean he did half or more of the housework; I did not systematically investigate the time they spent on childcare and housework. Those who have investigated this have found that even if unemployed men increase their efforts at home, they rarely take on the majority of those duties. Instead, they are more likely to frame their increased contributions as "helping" their partner. Rao, *Crunch Time*, chap. 5. For an analysis of "gender display" and "gender-deviance neutralization" in heterosexual couples in which the woman is the higher-income earner, see Oriel Sullivan, "An End to Gender Display through the Performance of Housework? A Review and Reassessment of the Quantitative Literature Using Insights from the Qualitative Literature," *Journal of Family Theory and Review*, 3 (2011): 3, https://doi.org/10.1111/j.1756-2589.2010.00074.x.

54. His situation was different because he and his partner were running a small business together.

55. Interestingly, however, one of the women who was a single mother for many years when her children were young (Lucy Guerrero), realized while she was out of work that she had previously focused on providing an income for her children at the expense of time and emotional attention to them. While she was out of work, she became closer to her younger daughter.

56. Sara Willott and Christine Griffin, "'Wham Bam, Am I a Man?': Unemployed Men Talk about Masculinities," *Feminism & Psychology* 7, no. 1 (1997): 115, 116–17, 121–22, https://doi.org/10.1177/0959353597071012.

57. Although some of the unemployed men in dual-earning couples made statements like that, as Chen found as well. Chen, *Cut Loose*, 135.

58. Komarovsky, *Unemployed Man and His Family*, 24–25.

59. "Working Wives in Married-Couple Families."

60. That man was Marcus Walker. However, he was the one who was out of work, so I do not discuss his situation until later in the chapter.

61. Peter F. Drucker, "They're Not Employees, They're People," *Harvard Business Review* 80, no. 2 (February 2002): 71–72, https://hbr.org/2002/02/theyre-not-employees-theyre-people.

62. This is a good illustration of Rayman's observation: "A paid-work environment that is congenial and supportive in personal terms may be especially important to women who feel their labors at home are not recognized, respected, or appreciated." Rayman, "Women and Unemployment," 375.

63. Komarovsky, *Unemployed Man and His Family*, 39.

64. Deniz Kandiyoti, "Bargaining with Patriarchy," *Gender & Society* 2, no. 3 (1988): 278, https://doi.org/10.1177/089124388002003004.

65. Rosen, *Bitter Choices*, 114–17.

66. Chen, *Cut Loose*, 137–38.

67. The neoclassical model is summarized in Katherine Weisshaar, "Earnings Equality and Relationship Stability for Same-Sex and Heterosexual Couples," *Social Forces* 93, no. 1 (2014): 95, https://doi.org/10.1093/sf/sou065.

68. See studies cited in Dai, "Dual-Earner Couples in the United States"; Weisshaar, "Earnings Equality and Relationship Stability," 96.

69. Weisshaar, "Earnings Equality and Relationship Stability," 106, 118.

70. Newman, *Falling from Grace*, 63. Newman does not state how many gay men participated in her study.

71. Karen Leppel, "Labour Force Status and Sexual Orientation," *Economica* 76, no. 301 (2009): 199, https://doi.org/10.1111/j.1468-0335.2007.00676.x.

72. Dai, "Dual-Earner Couples in the United States."

73. See also Basbug and Sharone, "Emotional Toll of Long-Term Unemployment," 228.

74. Susan L. Brown, quoted in Janet Adamy and Paul Overberg, "Affluent Americans Still Say 'I Do': More in the Middle Class Don't," *Wall Street Journal*, March 8, 2020, https://www.wsj.com/articles/affluent-americans-still-say-i-do-its-the-middle-class-that-does-not-11583691336?mod=djm_memprev_womenIn. See also Mark Mather and Diana Lavery, "In U.S., Proportion Married at Lowest Recorded Levels,"

Population Reference Bureau, September 28, 2010, https://www.prb.org/usmarri agedecline/.

75. Adamy and Overberg, "Affluent Americans Still Say 'I Do.'"

76. Christine R. Schwartz and Robert D. Mare, "Trends in Educational Assortative Marriage from 1940 to 2003," *Demography* 42, no. 4 (2005): 623, https://doi.org/10.1353/dem.2005.0036.

77. See also Lane, "Man Enough to Let My Wife Support Me," 688.

78. Anonymous, "I'm a 'Sugar Baby' Who Gets Paid $500 a Date—Here's What It's Really Like to Date Sugar Daddies and Get Cash, Gifts, and 5-Star Hotel Stays," *Business Insider*, April 3, 2021, https://www.businessinsider.com/sugar-baby-relation ship-sugar-daddy-what-its-like-2019-8.

79. On class differences in unemployment experiences, see also Damaske, *Tolls of Uncertainty*.

80. Sophie Watson, "New Study: Who Should Pay on a First Date?" Elite Singles, August 2019, https://www.elitesingles.com/mag/relationship-advice/who-should-pay -for-date.

81. He had been boasting about his health saying how, in his fifties, he can outrun kids half his age. Maybe he was thinking, "If I'm in such good shape, why aren't women interested in me?" See also Chen, *Cut Loose*, 135.

82. In that survey, for the never-married female respondents, having a steady job was the most important consideration of the survey's fixed-choice responses in choosing a partner, followed closely by "similar ideas about having and raising children." For the men, similar ideas about children were far more important than their potential partner's having a steady job. Wendy Wang and Kim Parker, "Record Share of Americans Have Never Married" (Pew Research Center, Washington, DC, September 24, 2014), http://www.pewsocialtrends.org/2014/09/24/record-share-of-americans-have-never -married/#fn-19804-2.

83. Chen found that single parents in Canada were much less stressed due to more generous state assistance there. Chen, *Cut Loose*, 141–42.

84. Researchers in other societies describe unemployment as attacking men's gender identities. Friedman, "Shame and the Experience of Ambivalence on the Margins of the Global," 251; Yang, *Unknotting the Heart*, 187.

85. Nancy Fraser, "After the Family Wage: A Postindustrial Thought Experiment," in her *Justice Interruptus: Critical Reflections on the "Postsocialist" Condition* (New York: Routledge, 1997), 41–66.

86. Chung and Van der Lippe, "Flexible Working, Work–Life Balance, and Gender Equality," 370–71.

6. Good-Enough Occupations and "Fun" Jobs

1. Alford Young, "New Life for an Old Concept: Frame Analysis and the Reinvigoration of Studies in Culture and Poverty," *Annals of the American Academy of Political and Social Science* 629 (May 2010): 58, https://doi.org/10.1177/0002716209357145. See also Studs Terkel, *Working* (New York: New Press, 2004).

2. Tocqueville, "Why Americans Consider All Honest Callings Honorable," vol. 2 in *Democracy in America*, 551.

3. Karl Marx, *Grundrisse: Foundations of the Critique of Political Economy (Rough Draft)*, trans. Martin Nicolaus (London: Penguin Books, 1973), 104.

4. Sarah J. Ward and Laura A. King, "Work and the Good Life: How Work Contributes to Meaning in Life," *Research in Organizational Behavior* 37 (2017): 64, https://doi.org/10.1016/j.riob.2017.10.001. They are summarizing Michael F. Steger, Bryan J. Dik, and Ryan D. Duffy, "Measuring Meaningful Work: The Work and Meaning Inventory (WAMI)," *Journal of Career Assessment* 20, no. 3 (2012), https://doi.org/10.1177/1069072711436160.

5. The psychologist Barry Schwartz is one of the few scholars of work I have read who recognizes that those with the right kind of job "think the work they do is fun, often in the way that doing crossword puzzles or Sudoku is fun." Barry Schwartz, *Why We Work* (New York: Simon & Schuster, 2015), 1.

6. Jason Topp, "47 Cheap, Fun Things to Do This Weekend," WiseBread, August 3, 2011, https://www.wisebread.com/47-cheap-fun-things-to-do-this-weekend; "Fun Group Activities for Adults," Groupon, February 21, 2019, https://www.groupon.com/articles/fun-group-activities-for-adults.

7. Johan Huizinga, *Homo Ludens: A Study of the Play-Element in Culture* (Boston: Beacon, 1955), 3.

8. Ethel Jorge, email to author, April 24, 2021. Some anthropologists have described fun (*sanuk*) as a key aspect of a good life in Thailand. Hjorleifur Jonsson, "Serious Fun: Minority Cultural Dynamics and National Integration in Thailand," *American Ethnologist* 28, no. 1 (February 2001), https://doi.org/10.1525/ae.2001.28.1.151. However, *sanuk* may suggest comfort and relaxation more than diverting activities. Julia Cassaniti, email to author, March 31, 2023.

9. Robert Myers, "Nuf and E-Nuf among the Nacirema," in *Reflecting on America: Anthropological Views of U.S. Culture*, ed. Clare Boulanger (New York: Pearson Education, 2008), 177 and passim.

10. Michael Moffatt, *Coming of Age in New Jersey: College and American Culture* (New Brunswick, NJ: Rutgers University Press, 1989), 33–34. See also Nancy Lesko, "Individualism and Community: Ritual Discourse in a Parochial High School," *Anthropology & Education Quarterly* 17 (1986), https://doi.org/10.1525/aeq.1986.17.1.05x0977.

11. Clyde Kluckhohn, *Mirror for Man* (New York: McGraw-Hill, 1949), 238, quoted in Myers, "Nuf and E-Nuf," 178.

12. Myers, "Nuf and E-Nuf," 178.

13. The engagement and satisfaction poll results change a little from year to year, but not enough to explain the enormous difference between the satisfaction and engagement findings in these surveys conducted two years apart. Anna Robaton, "Why So Many Americans Hate Their Jobs," CBS News, March 31, 2017, https://www.cbsnews.com/news/why-so-many-americans-hate-their-jobs/; David Spiegel, "85% of American Workers Are Happy with Their Jobs, National Survey Shows," CNBC, April 2, 2019, https://www.cnbc.com/2019/04/01/85percent-of-us-workers-are-happy-with-their-jobs-national-survey-shows.html.

14. "Gallup's Employee Engagement Survey: Ask the Right Questions with the Q12® Survey," Gallup, 2023, https://www.gallup.com/workplace/356063/gallup-q12-employee-engagement-survey.aspx; Jim Harter, "U.S. Employee Engagement Needs a Rebound in 2023," Gallup, January 25, 2023, https://www.gallup.com/workplace

/ 468233 / employee-engagement-needs-rebound-2023.aspx?utm_source=google&utm
_medium=rss&utm_campaign=syndication. See also Beverly Little and Philip Little,
"Employee Engagement: Conceptual Issues," *Journal of Organizational Culture, Communications and Conflict* 10, no. 1 (2006).

15. "Work and Workplace," Gallup, 2023, https: // news.gallup.com / poll / 1720 / work
-work-place.aspx; Sarah Dutton et al., "Women Weigh in on the Presidency and on Their
Own Lives—CBS / NYT poll," updated September 16, 2016, https: // www.cbsnews
.com / news / women-weigh-in-on-the-presidency-and-on-their-lives-cbsnyt-poll /. Both
surveys were of men and women. Another pair of definitions contrasts job "satisfaction"
as measuring satisfaction with work conditions, such as fringe benefits and hours, with
"engagement," which is defined as "a heightened emotional and intellectual connection
that employees have for their job, organization, manager, or coworkers that, in turn, influences them to apply additional discretionary effort to their work." Gad Levanon et al.,
"Job Satisfaction 2021" (Conference Board, New York, 2021), 3, https: // www.conference
-board.org / research / job-satisfaction. However, respondents to job satisfaction surveys
may be considering more than fringe benefits and hours.

16. We also interviewed four 1.5-generation immigrants—those who came to the
United States as young children. I do not include them among the immigrants, although, interestingly, they too did not use "fun" to talk about their work.

17. There is one ambiguous example, discussed below, of a Spanish-speaking participant who used *diversión* (fun) to describe how either he or others looked at work.

18. Google trends show searches for a term by state as a proportion of total online
queries in that state. New York state had one of the lowest proportions of users'
searches for "fun" for the period May 2016–April 2021, accessed April 27, 2021, https: //
trends.google.com / trends / explore?date=today%205-y&geo=US&q=fun.

19. Robert N. Bellah et al., *Habits of the Heart: Individualism and Commitment in
American Life* (Berkeley: University of California Press, 1985); Amy Wrzesniewski
et al., "Jobs, Careers, and Callings: People's Relations to Their Work," *Journal of Research in Personality* 31, no. 1 (March 1997), https: // doi.org / 10.1006 / jrpe.1997.2162.

20. Wrzesniewski et al., "Jobs, Careers, and Callings," 22.

21. For a related outlook, see the description of South Africans who said, "I'm just
a laborer" and who "refused to be wholly identified with [their] job" in Jeske, *Laziness
Myth*, 143.

22. Octavio Blanco, "Immigrant Workers Are Most Likely to Have These Jobs,"
CNN, March 16, 2017, https: // money.cnn.com / 2017 / 03 / 16 / news / economy / immi
grant-workers-jobs / index.html.

23. My research assistant Matthew Barber pointed this out. Comments to author,
July 5, 2020.

24. Clark Molstad, "Choosing and Coping with Boring Work," *Urban Life* 15, no. 2
(1986), https: // doi.org / 10.1177 / 089124168601500204. See also Barbara Garson, *All the
Livelong Day: The Meaning and Demeaning of Routine Work* (Garden City, NY: Doubleday,
1975).

25. Robert C. Ford, Frank S. McLaughlin, and John W. Newstrom, "Questions and
Answers about Fun at Work," *Human Resource Planning* 26, no. 4 (2003), http: //
homepages.se.edu / cvonbergen / files / 2012 / 12 / Questions-and-Answers-about-Fun
-at-Work1.pdf.

26. Ford et al., "Questions and Answers," 20–21.

27. Sharon C. Bolton and Maeve Houlihan, "Are We Having Fun Yet? A Consideration of Workplace Fun and Engagement," *Employee Relations* 31, no. 6, (2009), https://doi.org/10.1108/01425450910991721. On distracting attention from boring work, see Peter Fleming and Andrew Sturdy, "'Being Yourself' in the Electronic Sweatshop: New Forms of Normative Control," *Human Relations* 64, no. 2 (2011): 178, https://doi.org/10.1177/001872671037548. On recruiting high-end workers, see English-Lueck and Avery, "Intensifying Work and Chasing Innovation," 43.

28. "How Silicon Valley Made Work More Stressful," transcript of interview with Dan Lyons, Knowledge@Wharton, February 13, 2019, https://knowledge.wharton.upenn.edu/article/silicon-valley-work-culture/. For post-pandemic changes, see Kate Morgan, "The Death of 'Mandatory Fun' in the Office," BBC, May 19, 2022, https://www.bbc.com/worklife/article/20220517-the-death-of-mandatory-fun-in-the-office.

29. Mary Leighton, "Myths of Meritocracy, Friendship, and Fun Work: Class and Gender in North American Academic Communities," *American Anthropologist* 122, no. 3 (2020): 453, https://doi.org/10.1111/aman.13455.

30. Bolton and Houlihan, "Are We Having Fun Yet?" 565.

31. That implication could be drawn from Wrzesniewski et al.'s comment: "There is strong evidence for the belief that dispositional factors are related to job attitudes. . . . This suggests that the way individuals view work may be a function of stable traits, not just reflections of the work itself." Wrzesniewski et al, "Jobs, Careers, and Callings," 22.

32. See also Young, "New Life for an Old Concept," 63.

33. For further discussion, see Claudia Strauss, "'That Was Just Fun': Small Work Pleasures, Precarious Jobs, and Well-Being." (Under review, *Economic Anthropology*, special issue on Well-Being). For a good overview of nonfinancial work satisfactions, see Schwartz, *Why We Work*.

34. Michael Hardt, "Affective Labor," *boundary 2* 26, no. 2 (1999): 94.

35. The importance of intellectual challenges on the job has been highlighted by contributive justice theorists, such as Andrew Sayer, "Contributive Justice and Meaningful Work," *Res Publica* (2009): 15, https://doi.org/10.1007/s11158-008-9077-8. See also chapter 7.

36. David Graeber, *Bullshit Jobs* (New York: Simon & Schuster, 2018), 9–10, 149–50. He used the term "information worker" for all engaged in immaterial labor, but others distinguish between higher-level "knowledge workers" and lower-level "information workers." "Knowledge Worker versus Information Worker," Blog post, *Business Process Incubator*, September 8, 2014, https://www.businessprocessincubator.com/content/knowledge-worker-versus-information-worker/.

37. MOW International Research Team, *The Meaning of Working* (London: Academic Press, 1987).

38. Aronowitz and DiFazio, *The Jobless Future*, 335.

39. Andrea Muehlebach and Nitzan Shoshan, "Post-Fordist Affect: Introduction," *Anthropological Quarterly* 85, no. 2 (2012): 319, 332.

40. Adam Grant, "Friends at Work? Not So Much," *New York Times*, September 4, 2015, http://www.nytimes.com/2015/09/06/opinion/sunday/adam-grant-friends-at-work-not-so-much.html.

41. Similarly, in China, the work-unit system "was once a source of emotional and communal support for workers." Yang, *Unknotting the Heart*, 14.

42. Clive Thompson, "What if Working from Home Goes on . . . Forever?" *New York Times*, June 9, 2020, https://www.nytimes.com/interactive/2020/06/09/magazine/remote-work-covid.html. See also Bloom, "How Working from Home Works Out."

43. Anne Helen Petersen, "Are You Sure You Want to Go Back to the Office?" *New York Times*, December 23, 2020, https://www.nytimes.com/2020/12/23/opinion/covid-offices-remote-work.html.

44. See, for example, Jeske, *Laziness Myth*, 22.

45. Juan D. De Lara, *Inland Shift: Race, Space, and Capital in Southern California* (Oakland: University of California Press, 2018); Margot Roosevelt, "'The Algorithm Fired Me': California Bill Takes on Amazon's Notorious Work Culture," *Los Angeles Times*, August 31, 2021, https://www.latimes.com/business/story/2021-08-31/la-fi-amazon-warehouse-injuries-ab701-bill-calosha.

46. See also Erika Hayasaki, "Amazon's Great Labor Awakening," *New York Times*, updated March 4, 2021, https://www.nytimes.com/2021/02/18/magazine/amazon-workers-employees-covid-19.html; Roosevelt, "'The Algorithm Fired Me.'"

47. Emma Goldberg, "A Two-Year, 50-Million-Person Experiment in Changing How We Work," *New York Times*, updated April 13, 2022, https://www.nytimes.com/2022/03/10/business/remote-work-office-life.html; Sheela Subramanian, "A New Era of Workplace Inclusion: Moving from Retrofit to Redesign," Futureforum.com, March 11, 2021, https://futureforum.com/2021/03/11/dismantling-the-office-moving-from-retrofit-to-redesign/.

48. Leighton, "Myths of Meritocracy, Friendship, and Fun Work."

49. Wrzesniewski et al., "Jobs, Careers, and Callings," 22.

50. Weber, *Protestant Ethic*, 182.

51. Maddie Lloyd, "How to Answer 'What Are Your Salary Requirements?' (with Examples)," Zippia, February 15, 2021, https://www.zippia.com/advice/what-are-your-salary-requirements/.

52. Those are current annual gross receipts, according to Guidestar.org.

53. See definitions of a "calling" orientation to work in the next section, which include wanting to contribute to the social good. If work orientations are mutually exclusive, then they do not see those with a career orientation as wanting to contribute to the social good. Bellah et al., *Habits of the Heart*, 66; Wrzesniewski et al., "Jobs, Careers, and Callings," 22.

54. Definition of "careerism," Merriam-Webster dictionary, accessed April 29, 2021, https://www.merriam-webster.com/dictionary/careerism.

55. My definition is like Bunderson and Thompson's definition of a calling as "that place in the occupational division of labor in society that one feels destined to fill by virtue of particular gifts, talents, and/or idiosyncratic life opportunities." I altered this definition a little to include negative experiences, which also can shape an occupational passion. J. Stuart Bunderson and Jeffery A. Thompson, "The Call of the Wild: Zookeepers, Callings, and the Double-Edged Sword of Deeply Meaningful Work," *Administrative Science Quarterly* 54, no. 1 (2009): 38, https://doi.org/10.2189/asqu.2009.54.1.32.

56. Weeks, *Problem with Work*, 46, 39; Weber, *Protestant Ethic*, 79, 207n3, 62.

57. Gershon, *Down and Out in the New Economy*, 214.

58. Gershon, *Down and Out in the New Economy*, 215. See also Sharone, *Flawed System/Flawed Self.*

59. Weber wrote about the way Protestant theology was used to provide business owners with industrious workers. Weber, *Protestant Ethic*, 177, 281n101, see also 179.

60. Another possible example is Earl Apache Longwolf. He never used "fun" to talk about welding, but he spoke of the "thrill" he got from the work, using the same word Tom Dunn used interchangeably with "fun" to characterize his previous job as an IT recruiter.

61. Gershon, *Down and out in the New Economy*, 219–20.

62. See also Bellah et al., *Habits of the Heart*, 20, 154 on Americans' "second languages"; that is, discourses of commitments to a larger community that are alternatives to the "first language" of individualist discourses in the United States.

63. One ambiguous example was Amber Washington's comment about her job for a state department of human services. One of her responsibilities was to appear regularly on television to introduce viewers to a foster child ready for adoption. She said, "That was fun. I loved it." I do not know whether what Amber enjoyed was being on television or helping the foster children. Perhaps it was both. To further complicate matters, volunteer work, the point of which is to contribute to society, could be described as fun. For example, Lisa Rose described her unpaid leadership role in a social change group as "very creative and fun." Perhaps volunteer work was sometimes considered fun because it did not require as many hours and carried fewer responsibilities than paid work. I saw the same pattern with side hustles. Some of my participants described these part-time, less stressful ways of making money as fun. For example, Stacie McCarthy, the loan processor who had made her work her life, sold Avon cosmetics on the side. She said, "It's fun. It's a hobby. That's all it is right now." While Ann Lopez was out of work as an inventory analyst for a telecommunications company, she took a few jobs as a limo driver: "I said, 'Hey, it's some money in my pocket. I'll try it,' you know. And it's been fun."

64. Quoted in Kirsten Weir, "More than Job Satisfaction," *Monitor on Psychology* 44, no. 11 (December 2013), https://www.apa.org/monitor/2013/12/job-satisfaction.

65. Bellah et al., *Habits of the Heart*, 66; Wrzesniewski et al., "Jobs, Careers, and Callings," 22.

66. Martha Wolfenstein, "Fun Morality: An Analysis of Recent American Child Training Literature," in *The Children's Culture Reader*, ed. Henry Jenkins (1955; New York: New York University Press, 1998), 199.

67. Wolfenstein, "Fun Morality," 205, 199.

68. See also Strauss, "Positive Thinking about Being out of Work in Southern California following the Great Recession."

69. Drawing on her fieldwork among hard-partying North American archaeologists, Leighton argues it is "the *lack of boundaries* between what a person is and does in their private life, and what they are and do in their professional capacity, that we should question." I fully agree, but that is different from the kinds of fun my participants found in their jobs. Leighton, "Myths of Meritocracy, Friendship, and Fun Work," 453.

70. Kenneth L. Pike, "Etic and Emic Standpoints for the Description of Behavior," in his *Language in Relation to a Unified Theory of the Structure of Human Behavior*, Janua Linguarum, Series Maior (Berlin: De Gruyter Mouton, 2015), 37–72.

71. On "covert categories," see Brent Berlin, Dennis E. Breedlove, and Peter H. Raven, "Covert Categories and Folk Taxonomies," *American Anthropologist* 70, no. 2 (1968), https://doi.org/10.1525/aa.1968.70.2.02a00050, and Terence E. Hays, "An Empirical Method for the Identification of Covert Categories in Ethnobiology," *American Ethnologist* 3, no. 3 (1976), https://doi.org/10.1525/ae.1976.3.3.02a00070.

72. Nor do these findings fit standard economistic thinking according to which work is a disutility. This point is emphasized by Schwartz, *Why We Work*. I discuss that point further in the last chapter.

7. A Post-Pandemic Update and the Future of Work

1. Kohls, "The Values Americans Live By," 6.

2. Charlie Warzel, "What If People Don't Want 'a Career?'" Galaxy Brain, August 30, 2021, https://warzel.substack.com/p/what-if-people-dont-want-a-career?s=r.

3. Joshua Montes, Christopher Smith, and Juliana Dajon, "'The Great Retirement Boom': The Pandemic-Era Surge in Retirements and Implications for Future Labor Force Participation" (Finance and Economics Discussion Series 2022–081, Board of Governors of the Federal Reserve System, Washington, DC, 2022), https://www.federalreserve.gov/econres/feds/files/2022081pap.pdf.

4. "Civilian Unemployment Rate, Seasonally Adjusted," US Bureau of Labor Statistics, accessed May 25, 2021, https://www.bls.gov/charts/employment-situation/civilian-unemployment-rate.htm.

5. "Out of Work in America," *New York Times*, October 23, 2020, https://www.nytimes.com/interactive/2020/10/22/us/pandemic-unemployment-covid.html.

6. The average nationwide is replacement of 40% of former wages. Michele Evermore, "Unemployment Insurance during COVID-19: The CARES Act and Role of UI during the Pandemic," Testimony June 9, 2020. National Employment Law Project, https://www.nelp.org/publication/unemployment-insurance-covid-19-cares-act-role-ui-pandemic/. In California, the maximum benefit during my research was $450 a week. California Employment Development Department, "A Guide to Benefits and Employment Services," 9.

7. Damaske, *Tolls of Uncertainty*, 217.

8. Normally, to be eligible for unemployment benefits, workers must be laid off by an employer that has paid into the federal and state unemployment insurance funds; thus, gig workers and the self-employed have not qualified. Alison Doyle, "Collecting Unemployment Benefits for Self-Employed Workers," The Balance Careers, updated on December 13, 2022, https://www.thebalancecareers.com/can-i-collect-unemployment-if-i-m-self-employed-2064148.

9. Peter Ganong et al., "Ch. 2, Lessons Learned from Expanded Unemployment Insurance during COVID-19," in *Recession Remedies: Lessons Learned from the US Economic Policy Response to COVID-19*, ed. Wendy Edelberg, Louise Sheiner, and David Wessel (Washington, DC: Brookings Institution, 2022), 49.

10. There is federal legislation providing for an automatic extended benefit period in states with a high level of unemployed workers. In addition, the US Congress typically votes to provide federal unemployment benefits beyond the period of state benefits during a national recession.

11. Gay Gilbert, "4 Things to Know about Unemployment Benefits under the CARES Act," US Department of Labor blog, May 11, 2020, https://blog.dol.gov/2020/05/11/4-things-to-know-about-unemployment-benefits-under-the-cares-act.

12. Sources disagree about whether the average was based on the mean or the median national weekly wage at that time. Both were just under $1,000, while the average weekly unemployment benefit was $387. US Bureau of Labor Statistics, "Usual Weekly Earnings of Wage and Salary Workers First Quarter 2020" (Washington, DC, April 15, 2020), https://www.bls.gov/news.release/archives/wkyeng_04152020.pdf; "US Average Weekly Earnings," YCharts, https://ycharts.com/indicators/us_average_weekly_earnings, accessed July 25, 2022; Center on Budget and Policy Priorities, "Policy Basics: Unemployment Insurance,"1. Other sources cite a slightly different figure for the average unemployment benefit.

13. For the occupations most affected, see Maximiliano A. Dvorkin, "Which Jobs Have Been Hit Hardest by COVID-19?" (Federal Reserve Bank of St. Louis, August 17, 2020), https://www.stlouisfed.org/publications/regional-economist/third-quarter-2020/jobs-hit-hardest-covid-19. By January 2021, unemployment rates were more than 20% for the lowest-paid quarter of workers but less than 5% for the top quarter. Cameron Jenkins, "Fed's Brainard: Unemployment for Lowest Paid Workers 'Likely above 20 Percent,'" *The Hill*, January 13, 2021, https://thehill.com/homenews/news/534122-feds-brainard-unemployment-for-lowest-paid-workers-likely-above-20-percent.

14. If nonwage compensation and taxes are taken into account, then 69% of the unemployed were economically better off than they had been while working, thanks to the enhanced unemployment benefits. Peter Ganong, Pascal Noel, and Joseph S. Vavra, "US Unemployment Insurance Replacement Rates during the Pandemic" (Becker Friedman Institute Working Paper, University of Chicago, Chicago, August 24, 2020), 2, https://bfi.uchicago.edu/working-paper/2020-62/.

15. Karen Rouse, "How Shame and Stigma Influence the Debate over Extending $600 a Week Pandemic Assistance," *Gothamist*, August 7, 2020, https://gothamist.com/news/how-shame-and-stigma-influence-debate-over-extending-600-week-pandemic-assistance?mc_cid=8fa2808bad&mc_eid=eb68fbbd80.

16. Greg Iacurci, "Covid Relief Bill Offers 11 Weeks of Extra Unemployment Benefits, $300 Boost and a Supplement for Some Gig Workers," CNBC, December 21, 2020, https://www.cnbc.com/2020/12/21/covid-relief-bill-extends-and-enhances-unemployment-benefits.html; Lauren Bauer and Adrianna Pita, "Congress Extended Unemployment Benefits: What Should Come Next?" Podcast, Brookings, March 12, 2021, https://www.brookings.edu/podcast-episode/congress-extended-unemployment-benefits-what-should-come-next/.

17. Neil Irwin, "Unemployment Is High: Why Are Businesses Struggling to Hire?" *New York Times*, April 16, 2021, https://www.nytimes.com/2021/04/16/upshot/unemployment-pandemic-worker-shortages.html.

18. Tom Taylor, owner of Sammy Malone's pub in Baldwinsville, New York, quoted in Irwin, "Unemployment Is High: Why Are Businesses Struggling to Hire?"

19. Ganong et al., "Lessons Learned," 49.

20. "Governor Gordon Withdraws Wyoming from COVID-Era Unemployment Programs," State of Wyoming, May 12, 2021, https://governor.wyo.gov/media/news

-releases / 2021-news-releases / governor-gordon-withdraws-wyoming-from-covid-era
-unemployment-programs.

21. Armstrong Williams, "It's Time for Americans to Get Back to Work," The Hill, May 6, 2021, https: // thehill.com / opinion / finance / 551734-its-time-for-americans-to-get -back-to-work.

22. A more sophisticated rational choice model would consider nonfinancial work benefits and costs of specific jobs, but the simpler version that assumes working is always a cost dominates commentaries about unemployment benefits as a work disincentive. For a critique of rational choice assumptions governing unemployment benefit levels, see McKowen, "Substantive Commitments."

23. These two cultural models can merge in practice with the argument that if people continue to receive sufficient income from other sources, they will eventually lose the habit of supporting themselves.

24. Schwartz specifically addresses the argument that unemployment benefits are a work disincentive. Schwartz, *Why We Work*, 80–81.

25. "UI supplements decreased the new job-finding rate by just 0.6 to 1.1 percentage points," according to Ganong et al., "Lessons Learned," 67. See also Sarah Chaney Cambon and Danny Dougherty, "States That Cut Unemployment Benefits Saw Limited Impact on Job Growth," *Wall Street Journal*, September 1, 2021, https: // www.wsj.com / articles / states-that-cut-unemployment-benefits-saw-limited-impact-on-job-growth -11630488601; Jordan Weissman, "Cutting off Unemployment Benefits Didn't Fix the Economy, It Turns Out," *Slate*, September 24, 2021, https: // slate.com / business / 2021 / 09 / unemployment-insurance-benefits-economy-jobs-hiring.html.

26. "53 percent of jobless workers who received the $600 supplement returned to work before the $600 supplement expired," Ganong et al., "Lessons Learned," 64; Ganong, Noel, and Vavra, "US Unemployment Insurance Replacement Rates during the Pandemic," 2. The economist Ernie Tedeschi reported that approximately 70% of unemployment recipients who resumed working had been receiving more from benefits than from their prior wage. Catherine Rampell, "Opinion: The Myth of Unemployment Benefits Depressing Work," *Washington Post*, August 3, 2020, https: // www.washingtonpost .com / opinions / the-myth-of-unemployment-benefits-depressing-work / 2020 / 08 / 03 / 54cca9f4-d5ba-11ea-9c3b-dfc394c03988_story.html. See also Nicolas Petrosky-Nadeau and Robert G. Valletta, "Did the $600 Unemployment Supplement Discourage Work?" (FRBSF Economic Letter, Federal Reserve Bank of San Francisco, September 21, 2020), https: // www.frbsf.org / wp-content / uploads / sites / 4 / el2020-28.pdf.

27. Timothy P. Carney, "Op-Ed: Demographic Autumn: Our Working-Age Population Is Already Shrinking," American Enterprise Institute, December 16, 2021, https: // www.aei.org / op-eds / demographic-autumn-our-working-age-population-is-already -shrinking /; Paul Krugman, "What Ever Happened to the Great Resignation?" *New York Times*, April 5, 2022, https: // www.nytimes.com / 2022 / 04 / 05 / opinion / great-resignation -employment.html?searchResultPosition=1; Derek Thompson, "Why U.S. Population Growth Is Collapsing," *The Atlantic*, March 28, 2022, https: // www.theatlantic.com / newsletters / archive / 2022 / 03 / american-population-growth-rate-slow / 629392 /.

28. "Number of Unemployed Persons per Job Opening, Seasonally Adjusted," US Bureau of Labor Statistics, accessed February 16, 2023, https: // www.bls.gov / charts / job-openings-and-labor-turnover / unemp-per-job-opening.htm.

29. Eli Rosenberg, "These Businesses Found a Way around the Worker Shortage: Raising Wages to $15 an Hour or More," *Washington Post*, June 10, 2021, https://www.washingtonpost.com/business/2021/06/10/worker-shortage-raising-wages/.

30. Jennifer Elias and Amelia Lucas, "Employees Everywhere Are Organizing: Here's Why It's Happening Now," *CNBC*, updated May 7, 2022, https://www.cnbc.com/2022/05/07/why-is-there-a-union-boom.html.

31. Damaske proposes a 100% replacement for low-income workers, with lower replacement rates for those whose previous income was higher. Damaske, *Tolls of Uncertainty*, 217. Ganong et al. state, "Replacement rates of 60–70 percent would be on par with international standards." Ganong et al., "Lessons Learned," 83. See also Thelen on "embedded flexibilization" as a response of some European countries; for example, Denmark's "flexicurity" supports employer flexibility but provides retraining for workers and generous unemployment benefits. Kathleen Thelen, "Varieties of Capitalism: Trajectories of Liberalization and the New Politics of Social Solidarity," *Annual Review of Political Science* 15 (2012), https://doi.org/10.1146/annurev-polisci-070110-122959.

32. Bryce Covert, "What to Do Now to Prepare for the Next Recession," *New York Times*, July 2, 2022, https://www.nytimes.com/2022/07/02/opinion/recession-government-economy.html.

33. Ammar Farooq, Adriana D. Kugler, and Umberto Muratori, "Do Unemployment Insurance Benefits Improve Match and Employer Quality? Evidence from Recent U.S. Recessions" (NBER Working Paper 27574, revised April 2022), 2–5, http://www.nber.org/papers/w27574.

34. Weeks, *Problem with Work*, 59.

35. See, for example, Lord William Beveridge, *Full Employment in a Free Society: A Report* (1944; repr. London: Routledge, 2014); Leibfried, "Towards a European Welfare State?"

36. Fadhel Kaboub, "Honoring Dr. King's Call for a Job Guarantee Program," New Economic Perspectives, posted August 28, 2013, http://neweconomicperspectives.org/2013/08/honoring-dr-kings-call-for-a-job-guarantee-program.html. According to one historian, "In the push to make the march 'respectable' rather than offensive to the administration and much of white America, the original economic focus of the march was lost." Jessie Kindig, "March on Washington for Jobs and Freedom (August 28, 1963)," BlackPast.org, December 11, 2007, https://www.blackpast.org/african-american-history/march-washington-jobs-and-freedom-august-28-1963/. Farah Stockman makes the same point in *American Made*, 9.

37. Opportunity America/AEI/Brookings Working Class Study Group, *Work, Skills, Community: Restoring Opportunity for the Working Class* (Washington, DC: Opportunity America, 2018), 10–11, 14, https://opportunityamericaonline.org/wp-content/uploads/2018/10/WCG-final_web.pdf.

38. Opportunity America, *Work, Skills, Community*, 14.

39. Weeks, *Problem with Work*, 15.

40. As Weeks explains, post-work theorists draw upon the autonomist Marxist tradition (represented, for example, by Antonio Negri) that arose with Italian social movements in the 1960s and 1970s. This movement brought together "workers, students, feminists, and unemployed people" in an effort to expand the category of the "working class" as the collective subject of revolutionary struggles. Weeks, *Problem with Work*,

92–95. An early post-work polemic cited by Weeks (p. 98) was Paul Lafargue, *The Right to Be Lazy*, trans. Charles Kerr (1883; Forgotten Books, Lafargue Internet Archive, marxists.org, 2000), https://rowlandpasaribu.files.wordpress.com/2013/09/paul-lafargue-the-right-to-be-lazy.pdf. Lafargue's provocative tract is worthy of an in-depth analysis I do not have space to pursue here.

41. Weeks, *Problem with Work*, 97, 99.

42. Amanda Novello, "Commentary: Universal Basic Income versus Jobs Guarantee—Which Serves Workers Better?" Century Foundation, December 17, 2018, https://tcf.org/content/commentary/universal-basic-income-versus-jobs-guarantee-serves-workers-better/?agreed=1.

43. Weeks, *Problem with Work*, 1.

44. Weeks, *Problem with Work*, 145.

45. Charles Murray, "A Guaranteed Income for Every American," *Wall Street Journal*, June 3, 2016, https://www.wsj.com/articles/a-guaranteed-income-for-every-american-1464969586, and Murray, *In Our Hands*.

46. Aronowitz and DiFazio, *Jobless Future*, 335.

47. Weeks, *Problem with Work*, 37, 38.

48. Kathryn Edin and Laura Lein, *Making Ends Meet: How Single Mothers Survive Welfare and Low-Wage Work* (New York: Russell Sage Foundation, 1997); Fouksman, "The Moral Economy of Work"; McKowen, "Substantive Commitments"; Weisner et al., "'I Want What Everybody Wants,'" 151.

49. Fischer, *Good Life*; Jeske, *Laziness Myth*.

50. Roger Vincent, "A 32-Hour Workweek with 40-Hour Pay? It's Happening at Some Companies," *Los Angeles Times*, updated December 20, 2022, https://www.latimes.com/california/story/2022-12-16/four-day-workweeks-not-as-crazy-as-it-sounds.

51. Alison Doyle, "Difference between an Exempt and a Non-Exempt Employee," The Balance Careers, updated November 22, 2020, https://www.thebalancecareers.com/exempt-and-a-non-exempt-employee-2061988. See also Nick Hanauer, "America Gave up on Overtime—And It's Costing Workers $35,451 a Year," *Time*, updated April 21, 2022, https://Time.Com/6168310/Overtime-Pay-History/.

52. Freyssinet and Michon, "Overtime in Europe." See also Fischer, *Good Life*, 107–8, on the cultural value of *Feierabend* (quitting time) in Germany.

53. Adewale Maye, "No-Vacation Nation, Revised" (Center for Economic and Policy Research, Washington, DC, May 2019), https://www.cepr.net/report/no-vacation-nation-revised/.

54. Economist Lawrence Jeff Johnson, quoted in Steven Greenhouse, "Americans' International Lead in Hours Worked Grew in 90's, Report Shows," *New York Times*, September 1, 2001, https://www.nytimes.com/2001/09/01/us/americans-international-lead-in-hours-worked-grew-in-90-s-report-shows.html?searchResultPosition=1.

55. See chap. 2 and Damaske, *Tolls of Uncertainty*, 157.

56. Williams, "It's Time for Americans to Get Back to Work."

57. Bakke, *Citizens without Work*, 155.

58. James Bernard Murphy, *The Moral Economy of Labor: Aristotelian Themes in Economic Theory* (New Haven: Yale University Press, 1993); Sayer, "Contributive Justice and Meaningful Work," 1–2. See also Graeber, *Bullshit Jobs*.

59. Daron Acemoglu, Andrea Manera, and Pascual Restrepo, "Does the US Tax Code Favor Automation?" (Brookings Papers on Economic Activity, Spring 2020), https://www.brookings.edu/wp-content/uploads/2020/12/Acemoglu-FINAL-WEB .pdf; Chris Warhurst, Chris Mathieu, and Sally Wright, "*Vorsprung durch Technik*: The Futures of Work, Digital Technology, and the Platform Economy," in *The Many Futures of Work: Rethinking Expectations and Breaking Molds*, ed. Peter A. Creticos et al. (Philadelphia: Temple University Press, 2021), 179–95. ProQuest Ebook Central, https://ebookcentral.proquest.com/lib/claremont/detail.action?docID=28810809.

60. I am following Roose's use of these terms "as a catch-all term for various digital processes that carry out tasks that were previously done by humans." Kevin Roose, *Futureproof: 9 Rules for Humans in the Age of Automation* (New York: Random House, 2022), xviii.

61. Antonio Regalado, "Engineering the Perfect Baby," *MIT Technology Review*, March 5, 2015, https://www.technologyreview.com/2015/03/05/249167/engineering -the-perfect-baby/.

62. Luca Ventura, "Unemployment Rates around the World 2020," Global Finance, October 22, 2020, https://www.gfmag.com/global-data/economic-data/worlds -unemployment-ratescom.

63. Derek Thompson, "A World without Work," *The Atlantic*, July/August 2015, https://www.theatlantic.com/magazine/archive/2015/07/world-without-work /395294/.

64. Carl Benedikt Frey and Michael A. Osborne, "The Future of Employment: How Susceptible Are Jobs to Computerisation?" (Working Paper, Oxford Martin School, University of Oxford, 2013), https://www.oxfordmartin.ox.ac.uk/downloads/academic /future-of-employment.pdf; Melanie Arntz, Terry Gregory, and Ulrich Zierahn, "The Risk of Automation for Jobs in OECD Countries: A Comparative Analysis" (OECD Social, Employment and Migration Working Papers, No. 189, 2016), http://dx.doi.org /10.1787/5jlz9h56dvq7-en; McKinsey Global Institute, *Jobs Lost, Jobs Gained: Workforce Transitions in a Time of Automations* (McKinsey Global Institute, 2017), https://www .mckinsey.com/~/media/mckinsey/industries/public%20and%20social%20sector /our%20insights/what%20the%20future%20of%20work%20will%20mean%20 for%20jobs%20skills%20and%20wages/mgi%20jobs%20lost-jobs%20gained_report _december%202017.pdf; Kevin Roose, "We Need to Talk about How Good A.I. Is Getting," *New York Times*, August 24, 2022, https://www.nytimes.com/2022/08/24 /technology/ai-technology-progress.html.

65. Dawson makes a similar point regarding self-employment in South Africa. Hannah Dawson, "'Be Your Own Boss': Entrepreneurial Dreams on the Urban Margins of South Africa," in *Beyond the Wage: Ordinary Work in Diverse Economies*, ed. William Monteith, Dora-Olivia Vicol, and Philippa Williams (Bristol, UK: Bristol University Press, 2021), 116.

66. James Ferguson and Tania M. Li, "Beyond the 'Proper Job': Political-Economic Analysis after the Century of Labouring Man" (PLAAS Working Paper 51, Cape Town: University of the Western Cape, April 2018). For a definition of "standard employment," see Franoise Carr, "Destandardization: Qualitative and Quantitative," in *The SAGE Handbook of the Sociology of Work and Employment,* ed. Stephen Edgell, Heidi Gottfried, and Edward Granter (London: SAGE, 2015), 386.

67. Kasmir, "The Anthropology of Labor"; Monteith et al., "Work beyond the Wage," 3–4. See also Jeske, *Laziness Myth*. Note that the "informal" sector as the ILO defines it does not apply to all the alternative forms of work in the regulated formal sector.

68. David Weil, *The Fissured Workplace: Why Work Became So Bad for So Many and What Can Be Done to Improve It* (Cambridge, MA: Harvard University Press, 2014); Mary L. Gray and Siddharth Suri, *Ghost Work: How to Stop Silicon Valley from Building a New Global Underclass* (Boston: Houghton Mifflin, 2019), xvii.

69. Weil, *Fissured Workplace*; Carr, "Destandardization"; Warhurst et al., "Vorsprung durch Technik," 181.

70. "Employment, Hours, and Earnings from the Current Employment Statistics Survey (National): All Employees, Thousands, Temporary Help Services, Seasonally Adjusted, 2010–2019," US Bureau of Labor Statistics, https://data.bls.gov/timeseries/CES6056132001.

71. André Dua et al., "Freelance, Side Hustles, and Gigs: Many More Americans Have Become Independent Workers" (McKinsey & Company, August 2022), 2–3, https://www.mckinsey.com/~/media/mckinsey/featured%20insights/future%20of%20america/freelance%20side%20hustles%20and%20gigs%20many%20more%20americans%20have%20become%20independent%20workers/freelance-side-hustles-and-gigs-many-more-americans-have-become-independent-workers-final.pdf.

72. Intuit QuickBooks, *Gig Economy and Self-Employment Report* (Washington, DC: Gallup, 2019), https://quickbooks.intuit.com/self-employed/report/.

73. Department for Professional Employees, AFL-CIO, "Misclassification of Employees as Independent Contractors" (AFL-CIO, June 15, 2016), 3, https://www.dpeaflcio.org/factsheets/misclassification-of-employees-as-independent-contractors; John Schmitt et al., "The Economic Costs of Worker Misclassification" (Economic Policy Institute, January 25, 2023), https://www.epi.org/publication/cost-of-misclassification/.

74. Claudia Strauss, "Seeking Attachment in the Fissured Workplace: External Workers in the United States," in *Beyond the Wage: Ordinary Work in Diverse Economies*, ed. William Monteith, Dora-Olivia Vicol, and Philippa Williams (Bristol, UK: Bristol University Press, 2021), 71–92.

75. Miriam A. Cherry and Antonio Aloisi, "Dependent Contractors in the Gig Economy: A Comparative Approach," *American University Law Review* 66, no. 3 (February 2017), http://dx.doi.org/10.2139/ssrn.2847869.

76. Warhurst et al., "Vorsprung durch Technik," 187ff.

77. Cherry and Aloisi, "Dependent Contractors in the Gig Economy"; Tanya Goldman and David Weil, "Who's Responsible Here? Establishing Legal Responsibility in the Fissured Workplace," *Berkeley Journal of Employment and Labor Law* 42, no. 1 (2021), https://doi.org/10.36687/inetwp114.

78. "Major Achievements," Freelancers Union, https://www.freelancersunion.org/about/achievements/, accessed February 14, 2023; Phyllis Moen, "Bending the Futures and Meanings of Work, Careers, and Life-Course Pathways," in *The Many Futures of Work: Rethinking Expectations and Breaking Molds*, ed. Peter A. Creticos et al. (Philadelphia: Temple University Press, 2021), 269–87, especially 282.

79. Eurofound, *Exploring Self-Employment in the European Union* (Luxembourg: Publications Office of the European Union, 2017), https://www.european-microfinance

.org/sites/default/files/document/file/exploring-self-employment-in-the-european -union.pdf; 4. "Labour Market Regulation 4.0: Protecting Workers in a Changing World of Work," in *OECD Employment Outlook 2019: The Future of Work* (Paris: OECD Publishing, 2019), https://doi.org/10.1787/9ee00155-en; Etsy, *Economic Security for the Gig Economy: A Social Safety Net That Works for Everyone Who Works* (Brooklyn: Fall 2016), https://extfiles.etsy.com/advocacy/Etsy_EconomicSecurity_2016.pdf.

80. Nele De Cuyper et al., "Literature Review of Theory and Research on the Psychological Impact of Temporary Employment: Towards a Conceptual Model," *International Journal of Management Reviews* 10, no. 1 (2008), https://doi.org/10.1111/j.1468 -2370.2007.00221.x.

81. Alex Rosenblat, *Uberland: How Algorithms are Rewriting the Rules of Work* (Oakland: University of California Press, 2018).

82. Strauss, "Seeking Attachment in the Fissured Workplace," 86–87. See also Gideon Kunda, Stephen R. Barley, and James Evans, "Why Do Contractors Contract? The Experience of Highly Skilled Technical Professionals in a Contingent Labor Market," *Industrial and Labor Relations Review*, 55, no. 2 (2002), https://doi.org/10.2307/26 96207.

83. Brand's review of research on job loss also highlights the heterogeneity of the experience. Brand. "The Far-Reaching Impact of Job Loss and Unemployment."

84. Bakke, *Citizens without Work*, 155.

85. Ho, *Liquidated: An Ethnography of Wall Street*, especially chap. 3; Lane, *Company of One*; Lane, "Man Enough to Let My Wife Support Me," 685–86.

86. Friedman, "Shame and the Experience of Ambivalence on the Margins of the Global"; Marie Jahoda, Paul F. Lazarsfeld, and Hans Zeisel, *Marienthal: The Sociography of an Unemployed Community*, trans. by the authors (1933; repr. Chicago: Aldine Atherton, 1971); Pappas, *Magic City*; Walley, *Exit Zero*; Yang, *Unknotting the Heart*.

87. "All Employees, Total Nonfarm [PAYEMS]," US Bureau of Labor Statistics, retrieved from FRED, Federal Reserve Bank of St. Louis, April 8, 2023, https://fred .stlouisfed.org/series/PAYEMS. If we take population growth into account, the recovery period was even longer. Diane Whitmore Schanzenbach et al., "The Closing of the Jobs Gap: A Decade of Recession and Recovery" (Hamilton Project, Brookings Institution, August 4, 2017), https://www.brookings.edu/research/the-closing-of-the -jobs-gap-a-decade-of-recession-and-recovery/#:~:text=The%20average%20rate%20 of%20recovery,Great%20Recession%20are%20entirely%20healed.

88. Mains, *Hope Is Cut*, 4. See also Clark, "Unemployment as a Social Norm"; Lane, "Man Enough to Let My Wife Support Me."

89. Roose, *Futureproof*, 194.

90. Gray and Suri, *Ghost Work*, x–xi, 12.

91. Brian Merchant, "Minimum Wage 'Ghosts' Keep Google and Microsoft's AI Arms Race from Becoming a Nightmare," *Los Angeles Times*, February 16, 2023, https:// www.latimes.com/business/technology/story/2023-02-16/column-google-microsoft -chatgpt-bard-raters.

92. Jose Maria Barrero, Nicholas Bloom, and Steven J. Davis, "Why Working from Home Will Stick" (NBER Working Paper 28731, updated August 2022), https:// wfhresearch.com/wp-content/uploads/2022/08/WFHResearch_updates_August 2022.pdf.

93. Cevat Giray Aksoy et al., "Working from Home around the World" (Brookings Papers on Economic Activity Conference Drafts, September 8–9, 2022), Aksoy-et-al-Conference-Draft-BPEA-FA22.pdf (brookings.edu); Don Lee, "Surge in Remote Working due to COVID Fuels Record Employment for People with Disabilities," *Los Angeles Times*, December 15, 2022.

94. Sheela Subramanian, "A New Era of Workplace Inclusion: Moving from Retrofit to Redesign," Futureforum.com, posted March 11, 2021, https://futureforum.com/2021/03/11/dismantling-the-office-moving-from-retrofit-to-redesign/.

95. Morgan Smith, "The No. 1 Perk That Will Bring Gen Z and Millennials into the Office, According to Microsoft," CNBC, September 30 2022, https://www.cnbc.com/2022/09/30/no-1-perk-that-will-bring-workers-back-to-office-microsoft-report.html; see also Bloom, "How Working from Home Works Out," 2.

96. Norbert Hedderich, "German-American Inter-Cultural Differences at the Workplace: A Survey," *Global Business Languages* 2 (2010), http://docs.lib.purdue.edu/gbl/vol2/iss1/14.

97. Bennett Cyphers and Karen Gullo, "Inside the Invasive, Secretive 'Bossware' Tracking Workers," Electronic Frontier Foundation, June 30, 2020, https://www.eff.org/deeplinks/2020/06/inside-invasive-secretive-bossware-tracking-workers.

98. Lina Vyas, "'New Normal' at Work in a Post-COVID World: Work-Life Balance and Labor Markets," *Policy and Society* 41, no. 1 (2022): 157, https://doi.org/10.1093/polsoc/puab011.

99. Fischer, *Good Life*, 108.

100. Hochschild, *Time Bind*. Park talked to young Korean women garment workers (employees at others' home factories) who said going to work allowed them to escape onerous domestic responsibilities. Seo Young Park, *Stitching the 24-Hour City* (Ithaca, NY: Cornell University Press, 2021), 68.

101. Park, *Stitching the 24-Hour City*.

102. J. K. Gibson-Graham, *A Postcapitalist Politics* (Minneapolis, MN: University of Minnesota Press, 2006). See also Jeske, *Laziness Myth*; Marco Di Nunzio, "Work, Development, and Refusal in Urban Ethiopia," *American Ethnologist* 49, no. 3 (2022), https://doi.org/10.1111/amet.13091.

103. See chap. 3. Chen found the same among some of the blue-collar workers he interviewed after they were laid off. Chen, *Cut Loose*, 216.

104. Ortner, "On Key Symbols."

105. Brand, "The Far-Reaching Impact of Job Loss and Unemployment," 366.

106. Peter Frase, *Four Futures: Life after Capitalism* (London: Verso, 2016). Some researchers in political studies worry that chronic high unemployment levels will lead to higher crime and political unrest. Guy Standing, *The Precariat: The New Dangerous Class* (London: Bloomsbury, 2011). That need not happen, however, if there are other ways for people to usefully occupy their time and they form social bonds. John P. Murphy, "The Rise of the Precariat? Unemployment and Social Identity in a French Outer City," in *Anthropologies of Unemployment: New Perspectives on Work and Its Absence*, ed. Jong Bum Kwon and Carrie M. Lane (Ithaca, NY: Cornell University Press), 96

107. Fischer, *Good Life*, 2.

108. Weeks, *Problem with Work*, 1, 11, 2, 38ff.

109. Irv Katz, "Are We Tending to the Future of Volunteerism?" *International Journal of Volunteer Administration* 24, no. 3 (2007).

110. Moen, "Bending the Futures and Meanings of Work, Careers, and Life-Course Pathways," 275. See also Richard N. Bolles, *The Three Boxes of Life and How to Get out of Them: An Introduction to Life/Work Planning*, 2nd ed. (Berkeley: Ten Speed Press, 1981).

111. See also Caitrin Lynch, *Retirement on the Line: Age, Work, and Value in an American Factory* (Ithaca, NY: Cornell University Press, 2012), https://doi.org/10.7591/9780801464096.

112. Heather Long, "Opinion: This Isn't the 'End of Ambition' for Young Americans: It's a Redefining of It," *Washington Post*, February 19, 2023, https://www.washingtonpost.com/opinions/2023/02/19/american-workers-sabbatical-time-off/.

113. See chap. 2.

Bibliography

Abu-Lughod, Lila. "Writing against Culture." In *Recapturing Anthropology: Working in the Present*, edited by Richard G. Fox, 137–62. Santa Fe: School of American Research Press, 1991.

Acemoglu, Daron, Andrea Manera, and Pascual Restrepo. "Does the US Tax Code Favor Automation?" Brookings Papers on Economic Activity, Spring 2020. https://www.brookings.edu/wp-content/uploads/2020/12/Acemoglu-FINAL-WEB.pdf.

Agan, Amanda, and Sonja Starr. "Ban the Box, Criminal Records, and Racial Discrimination: A Field Experiment." *Quarterly Journal of Economics* 133, no. 1 (2017): 191–235. https://doi.org/10.1093/qje/qjx028.

Agius Vallejo, Jody. *Barrios to Burbs: The Making of the Mexican American Middle Class.* Stanford, CA: Stanford University Press, 2012.

Aksoy, Cevat Giray, Jose Maria Barrero, Nicholas Bloom, Steven J. Davis, Mathias Dolls, and Pablo Zarate. "Working from Home around the World." Brookings Papers on Economic Activity Conference Drafts, September 8–9, 2022, Aksoy-et-al-Conference-Draft-BPEA-FA22.pdf (brookings.edu).

Allison, Anne. *Precarious Japan.* Durham, NC: Duke University Press, 2013.

Ameri, Mason, Lisa Schur, Meera Adya, F. Scott Bentley, Patrick McKay, and Douglas Kruse. "The Disability Employment Puzzle: A Field Experiment on Employer Hiring Behavior." *ILR Review* 71, no. 2 (2018): 329–64. https://doi.org/10.1177/0019793917717474.

Arnett, Jeffrey Jensen. "Emerging Adulthood: A Theory of Development from the Late Teens through the Twenties." *American Psychologist* 55, no. 5 (2000): 469–80. https://doi.org/10.1037/0003-066X.55.5.469.

Arnold, Dennis, and Joseph R. Bongiovi. "Precarious, Informalizing, and Flexible Work: Transforming Concepts and Understandings." *American Behavioral Scientist* 57, no. 3 (2013): 289–308. https://doi.org/10.1177/0002764212466239.

Arntz, Melanie, Terry Gregory, and Ulrich Zierahn. "The Risk of Automation for Jobs in OECD Countries: A Comparative Analysis." OECD Social, Employment and Migration Working Papers No. 189, 2016. http://dx.doi.org/10.1787/5jlz9h56dvq7-en.

Aronowitz, Stanley, and William DiFazio. *The Jobless Future: Sci-Tech and the Dogma of Work.* Minneapolis: University of Minnesota Press, 1994.

Autor, David, and Melanie Wasserman. "Wayward Sons: The Emerging Gender Gap in Labor Markets and Education." Discussion paper, Blueprint Labs, Massachusetts

Institute of Technology. March 2013. https://seii.mit.edu/research/study/wayward-sons-the-emerging-gender-gap-in-labor-markets-and-education/.

Baehr, Peter. "The 'Iron Cage' and the 'Shell as Hard as Steel': Parsons, Weber, and the *Stahlhartes Gehäuse* Metaphor in *The Protestant Ethic and The Spirit of Capitalism*." *History and Theory* 40 (May 2001). https://doi.org/10.1111/0018-2656.00160.

Baert, Stijn. "Hiring Discrimination: An Overview of (Almost) All Correspondence Experiments since 2005." IZA Discussion Papers No. 10738. Institute of Labor Economics (IZA), Bonn, 2017. https://docs.iza.org/dp10738.pdf.

Bailey, Martha J., and Thomas A. DiPrete. "Five Decades of Remarkable but Slowing Change in U.S. Women's Economic and Social Status and Political Participation." *RSF: The Russell Sage Foundation Journal of the Social Sciences* 2, no. 4 (2016): 1–32. https://doi.org/10.7758/rsf.2016.2.4.01.

Bakke, E. Wight. *Citizens without Work: A Study of the Effects of Unemployment upon the Workers' Social Relations and Practices*. New Haven, CT: Yale University Press, 1940.

Barrero, Jose Maria, Nicholas Bloom, and Steven J. Davis. "Why Working from Home Will Stick." NBER Working Paper 28731. https://wfhresearch.com/wp-content/uploads/2022/08/WFHResearch_updates_August2022.pdf.

Basbug, Gokce, and Ofer Sharone. "The Emotional Toll of Long-Term Unemployment: Examining the Interaction Effects of Gender and Marital Status." *RSF: The Russell Sage Foundation Journal of the Social Sciences* 3, no. 3 (2017). https://doi.org/10.7758/rsf.2017.3.3.10.

Bateman, Nicole, and Martha Ross. "Why Has COVID-19 Been Especially Harmful for Working Women?" Brookings Institution, October 2020. https://www.brookings.edu/essay/why-has-covid-19-been-especially-harmful-for-working-women/.

Bauer, Lauren, and Adrianna Pita. "Congress Extended Unemployment Benefits: What Should Come Next?" Podcast, Brookings, March 12, 2021. https://www.brookings.edu/podcast-episode/congress-extended-unemployment-benefits-what-should-come-next/.

Bauman, Zygmunt. *Work, Consumerism and the New Poor*, 2nd ed. Berkshire, UK: Open University Press, 2005.

Beckman, Christine M., and Melissa Mazmanian. *Dreams of the Overworked: Living, Working, and Parenting in the Digital Age*. Stanford, CA: Stanford University Press, 2020. ProQuest Ebook Central.

Bellah, Robert. "Reflections on the Protestant Ethic Analogy in Asia." In his *Beyond Belief: Essays on Religion in a Post-Traditionalist World*, 53–63. Berkeley: University of California Press, 1970.

Bellah, Robert N., Richard Madsen, William M. Sullivan, Ann Swidler, and Steven M. Tipton. *Habits of the Heart: Individualism and Commitment in American Life*. Berkeley: University of California Press, 1985.

Bellezza, Silvia, Neeru Paharia, and Anat Keinan. "Conspicuous Consumption of Time: When Busyness and Lack of Leisure Time Become a Status Symbol." *Journal of Consumer Research* 44, no. 1 (2017): 118–38. https://doi.org/10.1093/jcr/ucw076.

Berlant, Lauren. *Cruel Optimism*. Durham, NC: Duke University Press, 2011.

Berlin, Brent, Dennis E. Breedlove, and Peter H. Raven. "Covert Categories and Folk Taxonomies." *American Anthropologist* 70, no. 2 (1968): 290–99. https://doi.org/10.1525/aa.1968.70.2.02a00050.

Bernard, Jessie. "The Good-Provider Role: Its Rise and Fall." *American Psychologist* 36, no. 1 (1981): 1–12. https://doi.org/10.1037/0003-066X.36.1.1.

Bertrand, Marianne, and Sendhil Mullainathan. "Are Emily and Greg More Employable than Lakisha and Jamal? A Field Experiment on Labor Market Discrimination." *American Economic Review* 94, no. 4 (2004): 991–1013. https://doi.org/10.1257/0002828042002561.

Beveridge, Lord William. *Full Employment in a Free Society: A Report*. London: Routledge, 2014. First published 1944.

Bishaw, Alemayehu, and Kayla Fontenot. "Poverty: 2012 and 2013." US Census Bureau, Washington, DC, September 2014. https://www2.census.gov/library/publications/2014/acs/acsbr13-01.pdf.

Bloom, Nicholas. "How Working from Home Works Out." Stanford Institute for Economic Policy Research, June 2020. https://siepr.stanford.edu/research/publications/how-working-home-works-out.

Blustein, David L. "The Role of Work in Psychological Health and Well-Being: A Conceptual, Historical, and Public Policy Perspective." *American Psychologist* 63, no. 4 (2008): 228–40. https://doi.org/10.1037/0003-066X.63.4.228.

Board of Governors of the Federal Reserve System. *Report on the Economic Well-Being of U.S. Households in 2018*. Washington, DC: Board of Governors of the Federal Reserve System, May 2019. https://www.federalreserve.gov/publications/2019-economic-well-being-of-us-households-in-2018-dealing-with-unexpected-expenses.htm.

Bolen, Ed, and Stacy Dean. "Waivers Add Key State Flexibility to SNAP's Three-Month Time Limit." Center on Budget and Policy Priorities, Washington, DC, updated February 6, 2018. https://www.cbpp.org/research/food-assistance/waivers-add-key-state-flexibility-to-snaps-three-month-time-limit.

Bolles, Richard N. *The Three Boxes of Life and How to Get out of Them: An Introduction to Life/Work Planning*, 2nd ed. Berkeley, CA: Ten Speed Press, 1981.

Bolton, Sharon C., and Maeve Houlihan. "Are We Having Fun Yet? A Consideration of Workplace Fun and Engagement." *Employee Relations* 31, no. 6 (2009): 556–68. https://doi.org/10.1108/01425450910991721.

Bonacich, Edna, and Juan David De Lara. "Economic Crisis and the Logistics Industry: Financial Insecurity for Warehouse Workers in the Inland Empire." IRLE Working Papers, Institute for Research on Labor and Employment, UCLA, 2009. https://escholarship.org/uc/item/8rn2h9ch.

Bourdieu, Pierre. *Distinction: A Social Critique of the Judgement of Taste*. Translated by Richard Nice. Cambridge, MA: Harvard University Press, 1984.

——. *Outline of a Theory of Practice*. Translated by Richard Nice. Cambridge: Cambridge University Press, 1977.

——. *Travail et Travailleurs en Algérie: Étude Sociologique*. Paris: Editions de la Maison des sciences de l'Homme, 1963. Quoted in John A. Garraty, *Unemployment in History: Economic Thought and Public Policy*. New York: Harper & Row, 1978.

Bowler, Kate. *Blessed: A History of the American Prosperity Gospel*. Oxford: Oxford University Press, 2013.

Brand, Jennie E. "The Far-Reaching Impact of Job Loss and Unemployment." *Annual Review of Sociology* 41 (2015): 359–75. https:// doi.org/ 10.1146/ annurev-soc -071913-043237.

Broder, Tanya, and Gabrielle Lessard. "Overview of Immigrant Eligibility for Federal Programs." National Immigration Law Center, Los Angeles, updated March 2023. https:// www.nilc.org/ issues/ economic-support/ overview -immeligfedprograms/ .

Brynjolfsson, Erik, and Andrew McAfee. *The Second Machine Age: Work, Progress, and Prosperity in a Time of Brilliant Technologies*, 2nd ed. New York: W. W. Norton, 2016.

Budd, John W. *The Thought of Work*. Ithaca, NY: Cornell University Press, 2011.

Bunderson, J. Stuart, and Jeffery A. Thompson. "The Call of the Wild: Zookeepers, Callings, and the Double-Edged Sword of Deeply Meaningful Work." *Administrative Science Quarterly* 54, no. 1 (2009): 32–57. https:// doi.org/ 10 .2189/ asqu.2009.54.1.32.

Byrne, Rhonda. *The Secret*. New York: Atria, 2006.

Calhoun, Michael. "Lessons from the Financial Crisis: The Central Importance of a Sustainable, Affordable and Inclusive Housing Market." Brookings Center on Regulation and Markets, September 5, 2018. https:// www.brookings.edu / research/ lessons-from-the-financial-crisis-the-central-importance-of-a -sustainable-affordable-and-inclusive-housing-market/ .

California Employment Development Department. "A Guide to Benefits and Employment Services." DE 1275A Rev. 49 (2–12), California Employment Development Department, Sacramento, CA. https:// www.edd.ca.gov/ pdf _pub_ctr/ de1275a.pdf.

California Senate Office of Research. "A Statistical Picture of Latinos in California: 2017 Update." California Senate Office of Research, Sacramento, CA, July 2017. https:// latinocaucus.legislature.ca.gov/ sites/ latinocaucus .legislature.ca.gov/ files/ forms/ Statistical%20Picture%20of%20Latinos%20 in%20California%20-%202017%20Update.pdf.

Calzada, Esther J., Catherine S. Tamis-LeMonda, and Hirokazu Yoshikawa. "*Familismo* in Mexican and Dominican Families from Low-Income, Urban Communities." *Journal of Family Issues* 34, no. 12 (2013): 1696–724. https:// doi .org/ 10.1177/ 0192513X12460218.

Carnevale, Anthony P., Nicole Smith, and Artem Gulish. "Women Can't Win: Despite Making Educational Gains and Pursuing High-Wage Majors, Women Still Earn Less than Men." Center on Education and the Workforce, Georgetown University, Washington, DC, 2018. http:// hdl.handle.net/ 10822 / 1049530.

Carr, Franoise. "Destandardization: Qualitative and Quantitative." In *The SAGE Handbook of the Sociology of Work and Employment*, edited by Stephen Edgell, Heidi Gottfried, and Edward Granter, 385–405. London: Sage, 2015.

Center on Budget and Policy Priorities. "Policy Basics: Temporary Assistance for Needy Families." Center on Budget and Policy Priorities, Washington, DC,

updated March 1, 2022. https: // www.cbpp.org / research / family-income
-support / temporary-assistance-for-needy-families.

——. "Policy Basics: Unemployment Insurance." Center on Budget and Policy
Priorities, Washington, DC, updated October 4, 2021. https: // www.cbpp.org
/ research / economy / unemployment-insurance.

Chen, Victor Tan. *Cut Loose: Jobless and Hopeless in an Unfair Economy.* Oakland:
University of California Press, 2015.

Cherry, Miriam A., and Antonio Aloisi. "Dependent Contractors in the Gig Economy: A Comparative Approach." *American University Law Review* 66, no. 3
(February 2017): 635–89. http: // dx.doi.org / 10.2139 / ssrn.2847869.

Chung, Heejung, and Tanja Van der Lippe. "Flexible Working, Work-Life Balance,
and Gender Equality: Introduction." *Social Indicators Research* 151, no. 2
(2020): 365–81. https: // doi.org / 10.1007 / s11205-018-2025-x.

Clark, Andrew E. "Unemployment as a Social Norm: Psychological Evidence from
Panel Data." *Journal of Labor Economics* 21, no. 2 (2003): 323–51. https: // doi
.org / 10.1086 / 345560.

Cohn, D'Vera, Juliana Horowitz, Rachel Minkin, Richard Fry, and Kiley Hurst.
"Financial Issues Top the List of Reasons U.S. Adults Live in Multigenerational Homes." Pew Research Center, Washington, DC, March 2022.
https: // www.pewresearch.org / social-trends / 2022 / 03 / 24 / the-demographics
-of-multigenerational-households /.

Collins, Samuel Gerald. "Working for the Robocracy: Critical Ethnography of
Robot Futures." *Anthropology of Work Review* 39, no. 1 (2018): 5–9. https: // doi
.org / 10.1111 / awr.12131.

Coontz, Stephanie. *The Way We Never Were: American Families and the Nostalgia Trap.*
New York: Basic Books, 1992.

Cooper, Marianne. *Cut Adrift: Families in Insecure Times.* Berkeley: University of
California Press, 2014.

Correll, Shelley J., Stephen Bernard, and In Paik, "Getting a Job: Is There a Motherhood Penalty?" *American Journal of Sociology* 112, no. 5 (2007): 1297–339.
https: // doi.org / 10.1086 / 511799.

Council of Economic Advisors. *Expanding Work Requirements in Non-Cash Welfare
Programs.* Washington, DC: Council of Economic Advisors, July 2018.
Expanding-Work-Requirements-in-Non-Cash-Welfare-Programs.pdf (archives
.gov).

Cowen, Emory L. "In Pursuit of Wellness." *American Psychologist* 46, no. 4 (1991):
404–8. https: // doi.org / 10.1037 / 0003-066X.46.4.404.

Cullen, Jim. *The American Dream: A Short History of an Idea That Shaped a Nation.*
Oxford: Oxford University Press, 2003.

Cunningham, Evan. "Great Recession, Great Recovery? Trends from the Current
Population Survey." *Monthly Labor Review* 141, no. 4 (April 2018): 1–27.
https: // doi.org / 10.21916 / mlr.2018.10.

Dai, Wenqian. "Dual-Earner Couples in the United States." In *Encyclopedia of Family
Studies.* 2016. https: // doi.org / 10.1002 / 9781119085621.wbefs406.

Damaske, Sarah. *The Tolls of Uncertainty: How Privilege and the Guilt Gap Shape
Unemployment in America.* Princeton, NJ: Princeton University Press, 2021.

Darolia, Rajeev, Cory Koedel, Paco Martorell, Katie Wilson, and Francisco Perez-Arce. "Race and Gender Effects on Employer Interest in Job Applicants: New Evidence from a Resume Field Experiment." *Applied Economics Letters* 23, no. 12 (2016): 853–56. https://doi.org/10.1080/13504851.2015.1114571.

Darrah, Charles N., James M Freeman, and J. A. English-Lueck. *Busier than Ever! Why American Families Can't Slow Down.* Stanford, CA: Stanford University Press, 2007.

Davenport, David, and Gordon Lloyd. "Rugged Individualism: Dead or Alive?" Defining Ideas, Hoover Institution, Stanford University, Stanford, January 10, 2017. https://www.hoover.org/research/rugged-individualism-dead-or-alive-0.

Dawson, Hannah. "'Be Your Own Boss': Entrepreneurial Dreams on the Urban Margins of South Africa." In *Beyond the Wage: Ordinary Work in Diverse Economies*, edited by William Monteith, Dora-Olivia Vicol, and Philippa Williams, 115–37. Bristol, UK: Bristol University Press, 2021.

Dean, Jennifer Asanin, and Kathi Wilson. "'Education? It Is Irrelevant to My Job Now. It Makes Me Very Depressed . . .': Exploring the Health Impacts of Under/Unemployment among Highly Skilled Recent Immigrants in Canada." *Ethnicity & Health* 14, no. 2 (2009): 185–204. https://doi.org/10.1080/13557850802227049.

De Cuyper, Nele, Jeroen De Jong, Hans De Witte, Kerstin Isaksson, Thomas Rigotti, and René Schalk. "Literature Review of Theory and Research on the Psychological Impact of Temporary Employment: Towards a Conceptual Model." *International Journal of Management Reviews* 10, no. 1 (2008): 25–51. https://doi.org/10.1111/j.1468-2370.2007.00221.x.

De Lara, Juan D. *Inland Shift: Race, Space, and Capital in Southern California.* Oakland: University of California Press, 2018.

Department for Professional Employees, AFL-CIO. "Misclassification of Employees as Independent Contractors." AFL-CIO, June 15, 2016. https://www.dpeaflcio.org/factsheets/misclassification-of-employees-as-independent-contractors.

DeWitt, Larry. "The Decision to Exclude Agricultural and Domestic Workers from the 1935 Social Security Act." *Social Security Bulletin* 70, no. 4 (2010): 49–68. https://www.ssa.gov/policy/docs/ssb/v70n4/v70n4p49.html.

Di Nunzio, Marco. "Work, Development, and Refusal in Urban Ethiopia." *American Ethnologist* 49, no. 3 (2022): 401–12. https://doi.org/10.1111/amet.13091.

Dua, André, Kweilin Ellingrud, Bryan Hancock, Ryan Luby, Anu Madgavkar, and Sarah Pemberton. "Freelance, Side Hustles, and Gigs: Many More Americans Have Become Independent Workers." McKinsey & Company, August 2022. https://www.mckinsey.com/~/media/mckinsey/featured%20insights/future%20of%20america/freelance%20side%20hustles%20and%20gigs%20many%20more%20americans%20have%20become%20independent%20workers/freelance-side-hustles-and-gigs-many-more-americans-have-become-independent-workers-final.pdf.

Dudley, Katherine M. *The End of the Line: Lost Jobs, New Lives in Postindustrial America.* Chicago: University of Chicago Press, 1994.

Dvorkin, Maximiliano A. "Which Jobs Have Been Hit Hardest by COVID-19?" Federal Reserve Bank of St. Louis, August 17, 2020. https://www.stlouisfed .org/publications/regional-economist/third-quarter-2020/jobs-hit-hardest -covid-19.

Edin, Kathryn, and Laura Lein. *Making Ends Meet: How Single Mothers Survive Welfare and Low-Wage Work*. New York: Russell Sage Foundation, 1997.

Ehrenreich, Barbara. *Bait and Switch: The (Futile) Pursuit of the American Dream*. New York: Henry Holt, 2005.

——. *Bright-Sided: How the Relentless Promotion of Positive Thinking Has Undermined America*. New York: Metropolitan Books, 2009.

——. *The Hearts of Men: American Dreams and the Flight from Commitment*. Garden City, NY: Anchor Press/Doubleday, 1983.

English-Lueck, J. A. *Being and Well-Being: Health and the Working Bodies of Silicon Valley*. Stanford, CA: Stanford University Press, 2010.

English-Lueck, J. A., and Miriam Lueck Avery. "Intensifying Work and Chasing Innovation: Incorporating Care in Silicon Valley." *Anthropology of Work Review* 38, no. 1 (2017): 40–49. https://doi.org/10.1111/awr.12111.

Etsy. *Economic Security for the Gig Economy: A Social Safety Net That Works for Everyone Who Works*. Brooklyn: Etsy, Fall 2016. https://extfiles.etsy.com/advocacy/Etsy _EconomicSecurity_2016.pdf.

Eurofound. *Exploring Self-Employment in the European Union*. Luxembourg: Publications Office of the European Union, 2017. https://www.european -microfinance.org/sites/default/files/document/file/exploring-self -employment-in-the-european-union.pdf.

Farooq, Ammar, Adriana D. Kugler, and Umberto Muratori. "Do Unemployment Insurance Benefits Improve Match and Employer Quality? Evidence from Recent U.S. Recessions." NBER Working Paper 27574, Revised April 2022. http://www.nber.org/papers/w27574.

Federal Reserve Bank of St. Louis. "Unemployment—The Economic Lowdown Podcast Series, Episode 5." Federal Reserve Bank of St. Louis, accessed May 25, 2021. https://www.stlouisfed.org/education/economic-lowdown -podcast-series/episode-5-unemployment.

Feldman, Stanley, and Marco R. Steenbergen. "The Humanitarian Foundation of Public Support for Social Welfare." *American Journal of Political Science* 45, no. 3 (2001): 658–77. https://doi.org/10.2307/2669244.

Ferguson, James, and Tania M. Li. "Beyond the 'Proper Job': Political-Economic Analysis after the Century of Labouring Man." PLAAS Working Paper 51, University of the Western Cape, Cape Town, April 2018.

Fischer, Edward. *The Good Life: Aspiration, Dignity, and the Anthropology of Wellbeing*. Stanford, CA: Stanford University Press, 2014.

Flanagan, Christine, and Mary Schwartz. "Rental Housing Market Condition Measures: A Comparison of U.S. Metropolitan Areas From 2009 to 2011." US Census Bureau, Washington, DC, April 2013. https://www2.census.gov /library/publications/2013/acs/acsbr11-07.pdf.

Flaherty, Michael G. "Time Work: Customizing Temporal Experience." *Social Psychology Quarterly* 66, no. 1 (2003): 17–33. https://doi.org/10.2307/3090138.

Fleming, Peter, and Andrew Sturdy. "'Being Yourself' in the Electronic Sweatshop: New Forms of Normative Control." *Human Relations* 64, no. 2 (2011): 177–200. https://doi.org/10.1177/001872671037548.

Ford, Robert C., Frank S. McLaughlin, and John W. Newstrom. "Questions and Answers about Fun at Work." *Human Resource Planning* 26, no. 4 (2003): 18–33. http://homepages.se.edu/cvonbergen/files/2012/12/Questions-and-Answers-about-Fun-at-Work1.pdf.

Fouksman, E. "The Moral Economy of Work: Demanding Jobs and Deserving Money in South Africa." *Economy and Society* 49, no. 2 (2020): 287–311. https://doi.org/10.1080/03085147.2019.1690276.

Frank, Kristyn, and Feng Hou. "Over-Education and Well-Being: How Does Education-Occupation Mismatch Affect the Life Satisfaction of University-Educated Immigrant and Non-Immigrant Workers?" *Ethnicity & Health* 23, no. 8 (2018): 884–901. https://doi.org/10.1080/13557858.2017.1316832.

Frase, Peter. *Four Futures: Life after Capitalism.* London: Verso, 2016.

Fraser, Nancy. "After the Family Wage: A Postindustrial Thought Experiment." In her *Justice Interruptus: Critical Reflections on the "Postsocialist" Condition,* 41–66. New York: Routledge, 1997. First published in *Political Theory* 22, no. 4 (November 1994).

Fraser, Nancy, and Linda Gordon. "Contract versus Charity: Why Is There No Social Citizenship in the United States?" *Socialist Review* 22, no. 3 (1993): 45–67.

Fraser, Nancy, and Linda Gordon. "A Genealogy of Dependency: Tracing A Keyword of the US Welfare State." *Signs: Journal of Women in Culture and Society* 19, no. 2 (1994): 309–36. https://doi.org/10.1086/494886.

Frederick, Marla F. *Between Sundays: Black Women and Everyday Struggles of Faith.* Berkeley: University of California Press, 2003.

Frey, Carl Benedikt, and Michael A. Osborne. "The Future of Employment: How Susceptible Are Jobs to Computerisation?" Working Paper, Oxford Martin School, University of Oxford, 2013. https://www.oxfordmartin.ox.ac.uk/downloads/academic/future-of-employment.pdf.

Freyssinet, Jacques, and François Michon. "Overtime in Europe." Eurofound, Luxembourg, June 30, 2003. https://www.eurofound.europa.eu/publications/report/2003/overtime-in-europe.

Friedman, Avi, and David Krawitz. *Peeking through the Keyhole: The Evolution of North American Homes.* Montreal: McGill-Queen's University Press, 2002.

Friedman, Jack R. "Shame and the Experience of Ambivalence on the Margins of the Global: Pathologizing the Past and Present in Romania's Industrial Wastelands." *Ethos,* 35, no. 2 (2007): 235–64. https://doi.org/10.1525/eth.2007.35.2.235.

Furnham, Adrian. "The Protestant Work Ethic: A Review of the Psychological Literature." *European Journal of Social Psychology* 14, no. 1 (January/March 1984). https://doi.org/10.1002/ejsp.2420140108.

Gamson, William A., and Andre Modigliani. "Media Discourse and Public Opinion on Nuclear Power: A Constructionist Approach." *American Journal of Sociology* 95, no. 1 (1989): 1–37. https://doi.org/10.1086/229213.

Ganong, Peter, Fiona Greig, Pascal Noel, Daniel M. Sullivan, and Joseph Vavra. "Ch.2, Lessons Learned from Expanded Unemployment Insurance during

COVID-19." In *Recession Remedies: Lessons Learned from the US Economic Policy Response to COVID-19*, edited by Wendy Edelberg, Louise Sheiner, and David Wessel, 49–90. Washington, DC: Brookings Institution, 2022.

Ganong, Peter, Pascal Noel, and Joseph S. Vavra. "US Unemployment Insurance Replacement Rates during the Pandemic." Becker Friedman Institute Working Paper, University of Chicago, Chicago, August 24, 2020. https://bfi .uchicago.edu/working-paper/2020-62/.

Garraty, John A. *Unemployment in History: Economic Thought and Public Policy*. New York: Harper & Row, 1978.

Garrett-Peters, Raymond. "'If I Don't Have to Work Anymore, Who Am I?': Job Loss and Collaborative Self-Concept Repair." *Journal of Contemporary Ethnography* 38, no. 5 (2009): 547–83. https://doi.org/10.1177/089124160 9342104.

Garson, Barbara. *All the Livelong Day: The Meaning and Demeaning of Routine Work*. Garden City, NY: Doubleday, 1975.

Gershon, Ilana. *Down and Out in the New Economy: How People Find (or Don't Find) Work Today*. Chicago: University of Chicago Press, 2017.

Gerson, Kathleen. *The Unfinished Revolution: Coming of Age in a New Era of Gender, Work, and Family*. New York: Oxford University Press, 2010.

Ghayad, Rand. "The Jobless Trap." Northeastern University, Boston, 2013. http:// citeseerx.ist.psu.edu/viewdoc/download?doi=10.1.1.692.6736&rep =rep1&type=pd.

Giattino, Charlie, Esteban Ortiz-Ospina, and Max Roser. "Working Hours." OurWorldInData.org, revised December 2020. https://ourworldindata.org /working-hours.

Gibson-Graham, J. K. *A Postcapitalist Politics*. Minneapolis: University of Minnesota Press, 2006.

Giddens, Anthony. *Beyond Left and Right: The Future of Radical Politics*. Stanford, CA: Stanford University Press, 1994.

Gilens, Martin. *Why Americans Hate Welfare: Race, Media, and the Politics of Antipoverty Policy*. Chicago: University of Chicago Press, 1999.

Glassdoor. *Which Countries in Europe Offer the Fairest Paid Leave and Unemployment Benefits?* Mill Valley, CA: Glassdoor, 2016. https://www.glassdoor.com /research/app/uploads/sites/2/2016/02/GD_FairestPaidLeave_Final-2 .pdf.

Godofsky, Jessica, Carl Van Horn, and Cliff Zukin. *American Workers Assess an Economic Disaster*. New Brunswick, NJ: John J. Heldrich Center for Workforce Development, Rutgers University, 2010.

Goldman, Tanya, and David Weil. "Who's Responsible Here? Establishing Legal Responsibility in the Fissured Workplace." *Berkeley Journal of Employment and Labor Law* 42, no. 1 (2021): 55–116. https://doi.org/10.36687/inet wp114.

Gonzalez-Barrera, Ana. "More Mexicans Leaving than Coming to the U.S." Pew Research Center, Washington, DC, November 19, 2015. https://www .pewresearch.org/hispanic/wp-content/uploads/sites/5/2015/11/2015-11-19 _mexican-immigration__FINAL.pdf.

Gorz, André. *Reclaiming Work: Beyond the Wage-Based Society*. Translated by Chris Turner. Cambridge: Polity Press, 1999.

Graeber, David. *Bullshit Jobs*. New York: Simon & Schuster, 2018.

Gray, Mary L., and Siddharth Suri. *Ghost Work: How to Stop Silicon Valley from Building a New Global Underclass*. Boston: Houghton Mifflin, 2019.

Grund, Francis. *The Americans in Their Moral, Social and Political Relations: Two Volumes in One*. New York: Augustus M. Kelly, 1971. First published 1837 by Marsh, Capen, and Lyon (Boston).

Grusky, David B., Bruce Western, and Christopher Wimer. "The Consequences of the Great Recession." In their *The Great Recession*, 3–20. New York: Russell Sage Foundation, 2011.

Guest, David E. "Perspectives on the Study of Work-Life Balance." *Social Science Information* 41, no. 2 (2002): 255–79. https://doi.org/10.1177/0539018402 04100200.

Hansan, John E. "Poor Relief in Early America." VCU Libraries Social Welfare History Project, Virginia Commonwealth University, 2011. https://socialwelfare.library.vcu.edu/programs/poor-relief-early-amer/.

Hardt, Michael. "Affective Labor." *Boundary 2*, 26, no. 2 (1999): 89–100. https://www.jstor.org/stable/303793.

Harvey, David. *The Condition of Postmodernity: An Inquiry into the Conditions of Cultural Change*. Oxford: Blackwell, 1989.

Hays, Sharon. *The Cultural Contradictions of Motherhood*. New Haven, CT: Yale University Press, 1996.

Hays, Terence E. "An Empirical Method for the Identification of Covert Categories in Ethnobiology." *American Ethnologist* 3, no. 3 (1976): 489–507. https://doi.org/10.1525/ae.1976.3.3.02a00070.

Hedderich, Norbert. "German-American Inter-Cultural Differences at the Workplace: A Survey." *Global Business Languages* 2 (2010). http://docs.lib.purdue.edu/gbl/vol2/iss1/14.

Heelas, Paul. "Work Ethics, Soft Capitalism and the 'Turn to Life.'" In *Cultural Economy: Cultural Analysis and Commercial Life*, edited by Paul Du Gay and Michael Pryke, 78–96. London: Sage, 2002.

Heiman, Rachel, Carla Freeman, and Mark Liechty, eds. *The Global Middle Classes: Theorizing through Ethnography*. Santa Fe: School for Advanced Research Press, 2012.

Hendriks, Martijn. "The Happiness of International Migrants: A Review of Research Findings." *Migration Studies* 3, no. 3 (2015): 343–69. https://doi.org/10.1093/migration/mnu053.

Hirschfeld, Robert R., and Hubert S. Field. "Work Centrality and Work Alienation: Distinct Aspects of a General Commitment to Work." *Journal of Organizational Behavior* 21, no. 7 (2000). https://doi.org/10.1002/1099-1379(200011)21:73.0.CO;2-W.

Ho, Karen. *Liquidated: An Ethnography of Wall Street*. Durham, NC: Duke University Press, 2009.

Hochschild, Arlie Russell. *The Time Bind: When Work Becomes Home and Home Becomes Work*. New York: Metropolitan Books, 2000. First published 1997.

Horowitz, Daniel. *The Anxieties of Affluence: Critiques of American Consumer Culture, 1939–1979.* Amherst: University of Massachusetts Press, 2004.

Howard, Christopher, Amirio Freeman, April Wilson, and Eboni Brown. "The Polls-Trends: Poverty." *Public Opinion Quarterly* 81, no. 3 (2017): 769–89. https://doi.org/10.1093/poq/nfx022.

Hsu, Francis L. K. "Rugged Individualism Reconsidered." In his *Rugged Individualism Reconsidered: Essays in Psychological Anthropology,* 3–17. Knoxville: University of Tennessee Press, 1983.

Huizinga, Johan. *Homo Ludens: A Study of the Play-Element in Culture.* Boston: Beacon, 1955.

Intuit QuickBooks. *Gig Economy and Self-Employment Report.* Washington, DC: Gallup, 2019. https://quickbooks.intuit.com/self-employed/report/.

Jacobs, Jerry A., and Kathleen Gerson. *The Time Divide: Work, Family, and Gender Inequality.* Cambridge, MA: Harvard University Press, 2004.

Jahoda, Marie. "Work, Employment, and Unemployment: Values, Theories, and Approaches in Social Research." *American Psychologist* 36, no. 2 (1981): 184–91. https://doi.org/10.1037//0003-066X.36.2.184.

Jahoda, Marie, Paul F. Lazarsfeld, and Hans Zeisel. *Marienthal: The Sociography of an Unemployed Community.* Translated by the authors. Chicago: Aldine Atherton, 1971. First published 1933.

Jefferson, Anna. "'Not What It Used to Be': Schemas of Class and Contradiction in the Great Recession." *Economic Anthropology* 2, no. 2 (2015): 310–25. https://doi.org/ 10.1002/sea2.12033.

Jeffrey, Craig. *Timepass: Youth, Class, and the Politics of Waiting in India.* Stanford, CA: Stanford University Press, 2010.

Jeske, Christine. *The Laziness Myth: Narratives of Work and The Good Life in South Africa.* Ithaca, NY: Cornell University Press, 2020.

Jonsson, Hjorleifur. "Serious Fun: Minority Cultural Dynamics and National Integration in Thailand." *American Ethnologist* 28, no. 1 (Feb. 2001): 151–78. https://doi.org/10.1525/ae.2001.28.1.151.

Kaiser Family Foundation/NPR. "Long-Term Unemployed Survey." Henry J. Kaiser Family Foundation, Menlo Park, CA, 2011. https://www.kff.org/other/poll-finding/long-term-unemployed-survey/.

Kandiyoti, Deniz. "Bargaining with Patriarchy." *Gender & Society* 2, no. 3 (1988): 274–90. https://doi.org/10.1177/089124388002003004.

Kang, Sonia K., Katherine A. DeCelles, András Tilcsik, and Sora Jun. "Whitened Résumés: Race and Self-Presentation in the Labor Market." *Administrative Science Quarterly* 61, no. 3 (September 2016): 469–502. https://doi.org/10.1177/0001839216639577.

Kasmir, Sharryn. "The Anthropology of Labor." In *Oxford Research Encyclopedia of Anthropology.* Oxford: Oxford University Press, 2020. https://doi.org/10.1093/acrefore/9780190854584.013.97.

Katz, Irv. "Are We Tending to the Future of Volunteerism?" *International Journal of Volunteer Administration* 24, no. 3 (2007): 54–57.

Katz, Michael B. *The Undeserving Poor: America's Enduring Confrontation with Poverty.* 2nd ed. Oxford: Oxford University Press, 2013.

Kindig, Jessie. "March on Washington for Jobs and Freedom (August 28, 1963)." BlackPast.org, December 11, 2007. https://www.blackpast.org/african -american-history/march-washington-jobs-and-freedom-august-28-1963/.

Kluckhohn, Clyde. *Mirror for Man*. New York: McGraw-Hill, 1949. Quoted in Myers, Robert. "Nuf and E-Nuf among the Nacirema." In *Reflecting on America: Anthropological Views of U.S. Culture*, edited by Clare Boulanger, 175–84. New York: Pearson Education, 2008.

Kochhar, Rakesh. "The American Middle Class Is Stable in Size, but Losing Ground Financially to Upper-Income Families." Pew Research Center, September 6, 2018. https://pewrsr.ch/2FxKvLs.

Kohls, L. Robert. "The Values Americans Live By." Meridian Intercultural Orientation Program, Washington, DC, 1984.

Komarovsky, Mirra. *The Unemployed Man and His Family: The Effect of Unemployment upon the Status of the Man in Fifty-Nine Families*. New York: Dryden Press, 1940.

Kunda, Gideon, Stephen R. Barley, and James Evans. "Why Do Contractors Contract? The Experience of Highly Skilled Technical Professionals in a Contingent Labor Market." *Industrial and Labor Relations Review* 55, no. 2 (2002): 234–61. https://doi.org/10.2307/2696207.

Lacy, Karyn R. *Blue-Chip Black: Race, Class, and Status in the New Black Middle Class*. Berkeley: University of California Press, 2007.

Lafargue, Paul. *The Right to Be Lazy*. Translated by Charles Kerr. Forgotten Books, Lafargue Internet Archive, marxists.org, 2000. https://rowlandpasaribu.files .wordpress.com/2013/09/paul-lafargue-the-right-to-be-lazy.pdf. First published Charles Kerr and Co, Co-operative, 1883.

Lakoff, George, and Mark Johnson. *Metaphors We Live By*. Chicago: University of Chicago Press, 1980.

Lamont, Michèle. *The Dignity of Working Men: Morality and the Boundaries of Race, Class, and Immigration*. New York: Russell Sage Foundation, 2000.

Lane, Carrie M. "Man Enough to Let My Wife Support Me: How Changing Models of Career and Gender Are Reshaping the Experience of Unemployment." *American Ethnologist* 36, no. 4 (2009): 681–92. https://doi.org/10.1111/j.1548 -1425.2009.01203.x.

Lane, Carrie M. *A Company of One: Insecurity, Independence, and the New World of White-Collar Unemployment*. Ithaca, NY: Cornell University Press, 2011.

Lane, Carrie M. "The Limits of Liminality: Anthropological Approaches to Unemployment in the United States." In *Anthropologies of Unemployment: New Perspectives on Work and Its Absence*, edited by Jong Bum Kwon and Carrie M. Lane, 18–33. Ithaca, NY: Cornell University Press, 2016.

Lareau, Annette. *Unequal Childhoods: Class, Race, and Family Life*. Berkeley: University of California Press, 2011.

Leibfried, Stephan. "Towards a European Welfare State? On Integrating Poverty Regimes into the European Community." In *Social Policy in a Changing Europe*, edited by Zsuzsa Ferge and Jon Eivind Kolberg, 245–79. Frankfurt am Main: Campus Verlag, 1992.

Leighton, Mary. "Myths of Meritocracy, Friendship, and Fun Work: Class and Gender in North American Academic Communities." *American Anthropologist* 122, no. 3 (2020): 444–58. https://doi.org/10.1111/aman.13455.

Leppel, Karen. "Labour Force Status and Sexual Orientation." *Economica* 76, no. 301 (2009): 197–207. https://doi.org/10.1111/j.1468-0335.2007.00676.x.

Lesko, Nancy. "Individualism and Community: Ritual Discourse in a Parochial High School." *Anthropology & Education Quarterly* 17 (1986): 25–39. https://doi.org/10.1525/aeq.1986.17.1.05x0977o.

Levanon, Gad, Amy Lui Abel, Allen Li, and Calvin Rong. "Job Satisfaction 2021." Conference Board, New York, 2021. https://www.conference-board.org/research/job-satisfaction.

LeVine, Robert A. *Culture, Behavior, and Personality: An Introduction to the Comparative Study of Psychosocial Adaptation*, 2nd ed. New Brunswick, NJ: Aldine Transaction, 1982.

Lewis, Oscar. "The Culture of Poverty." *Scientific American* 215, no. 4 (1966): 19–25.

Lewis, Suzan, Richenda Gambles, and Rhona Rapoport. "The Constraints of a 'Work–Life Balance' Approach: An International Perspective." *International Journal of Human Resource Management* 18, no. 3 (2007): 360–73. https://doi.org/10.1080/09585190601165577.

Linkon, Sherry Lee. *The Half-Life of Deindustrialization: Working-Class Writing about Economic Restructuring*. Ann Arbor: University of Michigan Press, 2018.

Linqvist, Erik, Robert Östling, and David Cesarini. "Long-Run Effects of Lottery Wealth on Psychological Well-Being." NBER Working Paper No. 24667, May 2018. https://doi.org/10.3386/w24667.

Little, Beverly, and Philip Little. "Employee Engagement: Conceptual Issues." *Journal of Organizational Culture, Communications and Conflict* 10, no. 1 (2006): 111–20.

Lopez, Steven H., and Lora A. Phillips. "Unemployed: White-Collar Job Searching after the Great Recession." *Work and Occupations* 46, no. 4 (2019): 470–510. https://doi.org/10.1177/0730888419852379.

Los Angeles County Economic Development Corporation. *Manufacturing: Still a Force in Southern California*. Los Angeles: Los Angeles County Economic Development Corporation, 2011.

Los Angeles Department of City Planning. *Housing Element 2013–2021*. Los Angeles: Department of City Planning, 2013. https://planning.lacity.org/odocument/05b5d571-9bde-43c7-99e4-1aa6b656a7e9/HousingElement_20140321.pdf.

Luhrmann, Tanya. *When God Talks Back: Understanding the American Evangelical Relationship with God*. New York: Vintage, 2012.

Lynch, Caitrin. *Retirement on the Line: Age, Work, and Value in an American Factory*. Ithaca, NY: Cornell University Press, 2012.

Lynch, Caitrin, and Daniel Mains. "Epilogue: Rethinking the Value of Work and Unemployment." In *Anthropologies of Unemployment: New Perspectives on Work and Its Absence*, edited by Jong Bum Kwon and Carrie M. Lane, 212–28. Ithaca, NY: Cornell University Press, 2016.

Mains, Daniel. *Hope Is Cut: Youth, Unemployment, and the Future in Urban Ethiopia*. Philadelphia: Temple University Press, 2012.

Margo, Robert A. "Employment and Unemployment in the 1930s." *Journal of Economic Perspectives* 7, no. 2 (1993): 41–59. https://doi.org/10.1257/jep.7.2.41.

Marshall, Thomas Humphrey. "Citizenship and Social Class." Excerpted in *Citizenship and Social Class*, Vol. 2, ed. Thomas Burton Bottomore and Thomas Humphrey Marshall, 30–39. London: Pluto Press, 1992. First published 1950.

Mather, Mark, and Diana Lavery. "In U.S., Proportion Married at Lowest Recorded Levels." Population Reference Bureau, September 28, 2010. https://www.prb.org/usmarriagedecline/.

Marx, Karl. *Grundrisse: Foundations of the Critique of Political Economy (Rough Draft)*. Translated by Martin Nicolaus. London: Penguin Books, 1973.

Mauss, Marcel. *The Gift: Forms and Functions of Exchange in Archaic Societies*. Translated by Ian Cunnison. New York: W. W. Norton, 1967. First published 1925.

Maye, Adewale. "No-Vacation Nation, Revised." Center for Economic and Policy Research, Washington, DC, May 2019. https://www.cepr.net/report/no-vacation-nation-revised/.

McCracken, Grant. *Culture and Consumption: New Approaches to the Symbolic Character of Consumer Goods and Activities*. Bloomington: Indiana University Press, 1988.

McGillivray, David. "Fitter, Happier, More Productive: Governing Working Bodies through Wellness." *Culture and Organization* 11, no. 2 (2005): 125–38.

McKinsey & Company. *Women in the Workplace:2020*. McKinsey & Company, 2020. https://www.mckinsey.com/featured-insights/diversity-and-inclusion/women-in-the-workplace.

McKinsey Global Institute. *Jobs Lost, Jobs Gained: Workforce Transitions in a Time of Automation*. McKinsey Global Institute, 2017. https://www.mckinsey.com/~/media/mckinsey/industries/public%20and%20social%20sector/our%20insights/what%20the%20future%20of%20work%20will%20mean%20for%20jobs%20skills%20and%20wages/mgi%20jobs%20lost-jobs%20gained_ssreport_december%202017.pdf.

McKowen, Kelly. "Substantive Commitments: Reconciling Work Ethics and the Welfare State in Norway." *Economic Anthropology* 7, no. 1 (2020): 120–33. https://doi.org/10.1002/sea2.12169.

Mead, Lawrence M. *The New Politics of Poverty: The Nonworking Poor in America*. New York: Basic Books, 1992.

Mendoza-Denton, Norma, and Aomar Boum. "Breached Initiations: Sociopolitical Resources and Conflicts in Emergent Adulthood." *Annual Review of Anthropology* 44 (2015): 295–310. https://doi.org/10.1146/annurev-anthro-102214-014012.

Meneley, Anne. "Consumerism." *Annual Review of Anthropology* 47 (2018): 117–32. https://doi.org/10.1146/annurev-anthro-102116-041518.

Mian, Atif, and Amir Sufi. *House of Debt: How They (and You) Caused the Great Recession, and How We Can Prevent It from Happening Again*. Chicago: University of Chicago Press, 2014.

Miller, Daniel. "Consumption as the Vanguard of History." In *Acknowledging Consumption: A Review of New Studies*, edited by Daniel Miller, 1–52. London: Routledge, 1995.

Miller, Daniel. "Consumption Studies as the Transformation of Anthropology." In *Acknowledging Consumption: A Review of New Studies*, edited by Daniel Miller, 263–92. London: Routledge, 1995.

Mishel, Emma. "Discrimination against Queer Women in the U.S. Workforce: A Résumé Audit Study." *Socius: Sociological Research for a Dynamic World* 2 (2016): 1–13. https://doi.org/10.1177/2378023115621316.

Moen, Phyllis. "Bending the Futures and Meanings of Work, Careers, and Life-Course Pathways." In *The Many Futures of Work: Rethinking Expectations and Breaking Molds*, edited by Peter A. Creticos, Larry Bennett, Laura Owen, Costas Spirou, and Maxine Morphis-Riesbeck, 269–87. Philadelphia: Temple University Press, 2021. ProQuest Ebook Central, https://ebookcentral.proquest.com/lib/claremont/detail.action?docID=28810809.

Moffatt, Michael. *Coming of Age in New Jersey: College and American Culture*. New Brunswick, NJ: Rutgers University Press, 1989.

Molstad, Clark. "Choosing and Coping with Boring Work." *Urban Life* 15, no. 2 (1986): 215–36. https://doi.org/10.1177/089124168601500204.

Monteith, William, Dora-Olivia Vicol, and Philippa Williams, eds. *Beyond the Wage: Ordinary Work in Diverse Economies*. Bristol, UK: Bristol University Press, 2021.

Monteith, William, Dora-Olivia Vicol, and Philippa Williams. "Work beyond the Wage." In *Beyond the Wage: Ordinary Work in Diverse Economies*, edited by William Monteith, Dora-Olivia Vicol, and Philippa Williams, 1–19. Bristol, UK: Bristol University Press, 2021.

Montes, Joshua, Christopher Smith, and Juliana Dajon. "'The Great Retirement Boom': The Pandemic-Era Surge in Retirements and Implications for Future Labor Force Participation." Finance and Economics Discussion Series 2022–081, Board of Governors of the Federal Reserve System, Washington, DC, 2022. https://www.federalreserve.gov/econres/feds/files/2022081pap.pdf.

MOW International Research Team. *The Meaning of Working*. London: Academic Press, 1987.

Muehlebach, Andrea, and Nitzan Shoshan. "Post-Fordist Affect: Introduction." *Anthropological Quarterly* 85, no. 2 (2012): 317–43.

Murphy, James Bernard. *The Moral Economy of Labor: Aristotelian Themes in Economic Theory*. New Haven, CT: Yale University Press, 1993.

Murphy, John P. "The Rise of the Precariat? Unemployment and Social Identity in a French Outer City." In *Anthropologies of Unemployment: New Perspectives on Work and Its Absence*, edited by J. B. Kwon and Carrie M. Lane, 71–96. Ithaca, NY: Cornell University Press, 2016.

Murray, Charles. *In Our Hands: A Plan to Replace the Welfare State*. Washington, DC: American Enterprise Institute for Public Policy Research, 2016.

Murray, Charles. *Losing Ground: American Social Policy, 1950–1980*. New York: Basic Books, 1984.

Myers, Robert. "Nuf and E-Nuf Among the Nacirema." In *Reflecting on America: Anthropological Views of U.S. Culture*, edited by Clare Boulanger, 175–84. New York: Pearson Education, 2008.

Neumark, David, Ian Burn, and Patrick Button. "Is It Harder for Older Workers to Find Jobs? New and Improved Evidence from a Field Experiment." *Journal of

Political Economy 127, no. 2 (April 2019): 922–70. https://doi.org/10.1086/701029.

Newman, Katherine S. *The Accordion Family: Boomerang Kids, Anxious Parents, and the Private Toll of Global Competition.* Boston: Beacon Press, 2012.

——. *Falling from Grace: Downward Mobility in the Age of Affluence.* Berkeley, CA: University of California Press, 1988.

Nichols, Austin, Josh Mitchell, and Stephan Lindner. "Consequences of Long-Term Unemployment." Urban Institute, Washington, DC, 2013. https://www.urban.org/sites/default/files/publication/23921/412887-Consequences-of-Long-Term-Unemployment.PDF.

Oates, Wayne E. *Confessions of a Workaholic: The Facts about Work Addiction.* New York: World, 1971. Quoted in Wilmar B. Schaufeli, Toon W. Taris, and Arnold B. Bakker, "Dr. Jekyll or Mr. Hyde? On the Differences between Work Engagement and Workaholism." In *Research Companion to Working Time and Work Addiction*, edited by Ronald J. Burke, 193–217. Cheltenham, UK: Edward Elgar, 2006.

OECD. "4. Labour Market Regulation 4.0: Protecting Workers in a Changing World of Work." In *OECD Employment Outlook 2019: The Future of Work.* Paris: OECD Publishing, 2019. https://doi.org/10.1787/9ee00155-en.

Ong, Aihwa. "Cultural Citizenship as Subject-Making: Immigrants Negotiate Racial and Cultural Boundaries in the United States [and Comments and Reply]." *Current Anthropology* 37, no. 5 (1996): 737–62. https://doi.org/10.1086/204560.

Opportunity America/AEI/Brookings Working Class Study Group. *Work, Skills, Community: Restoring Opportunity for the Working Class.* Washington, DC: Opportunity America, 2018. https://opportunityamericaonline.org/wp-content/uploads/2018/10/WCG-final_web.pdf.

Ortiz-Ospina, Esteban, and Max Roser. "Marriages and Divorces." Our World in Data. 2020. https://ourworldindata.org/marriages-and-divorces.

Ortner, Sherry B. "Identities: The Hidden Life of Class." *Journal of Anthropological Research* 54, no. 1 (1998): 1–17. https://doi.org/10.1086/jar.54.1.3631674.

——. "On Key Symbols." *American Anthropologist* 75, no. 5 (1973): 1338–46. https://doi.org/10.1525/aa.1973.75.5.02a00100.

Pappas, Gregory. *The Magic City: Unemployment in a Working-Class Community.* Ithaca, NY: Cornell University Press, 1989.

Park, Seo Young. "Stitching the Fabric of Family: Time, Work, and Intimacy in Seoul's Tongdaemun Market." *Journal of Korean Studies* 17, no. 2 (2012): 383–406. https://doi.org/10.1353/jks.2012.0023.

——. *Stitching the 24-Hour City.* Ithaca, NY: Cornell University Press, 2021.

Parker, Kim, Juliana Horowitz, and Rachel Minkin. "How the Coronavirus Outbreak Has—and Hasn't—Changed the Way Americans Work." Pew Research Center, December 2020. https://www.pewresearch.org/social-trends/2020/12/09/how-the-coronavirus-outbreak-has-and-hasnt-changed-the-way-americans-work.

Patton, Wendy, and Ross Donohue. "Coping with Long-Term Unemployment." *Journal of Community & Applied Social Psychology* 8, no. 5 (1998): 331–43. https://doi.org/10.1002/(SICI)1099-1298(1998090)8:53.0.CO;2–6.

Paul, Karsten I., and Klaus Moser. "Unemployment Impairs Mental Health: Meta-Analyses." *Journal of Vocational behavior* 74, no. 3 (2009): 264–82. https://doi.org/10.1016/j.jvb.2009.01.001.

Perin, Constance. *Everything in its Place: Social Order and Land Use in America.* Princeton, NJ: Princeton University Press, 1977.

Petrosky-Nadeau, Nicolas, and Robert G. Valletta. "Did the $600 Unemployment Supplement Discourage Work?" FRBSF Economic Letter, Federal Reserve Bank of San Francisco, September 21, 2020. https://www.frbsf.org/wp-content/uploads/sites/4/el2020-28.pdf.

Pew Research Center. "From the Age of Aquarius to the Age of Responsibility: Baby Boomers Approach Age 60." Pew Research Center, Washington, DC, December 8, 2005.

Pike, Kenneth L. "Etic and Emic Standpoints for the Description of Behavior." In his *Language in Relation to a Unified Theory of the Structure of Human Behavior,* 37–72. Janua Linguarum. Series Maior. Berlin: De Gruyter Mouton, 2015. First published 1967.

Pirog, Maureen, Edwin Gerrish, and Lindsey Bullinger. "TANF and SNAP Asset Limits and the Financial Behavior of Low-Income Households." A Report to the Pew Charitable Trusts, May 2017. http://www.pewtrusts.org/~/media/Assets/2017/09/TANF_and_SNAP_Asset_Limits_and_the_Financial_Behavior_of_Low_Income_Households.pdf.

Portes, Alejandro, and Rubén G. Rumbaut. *Immigrant America: A Portrait.* Berkeley: University of California Press, 2014.

Potuchek, Jean L. *Who Supports the Family? Gender and Breadwinning in Dual-Earner Marriages.* Stanford CA: Stanford University Press, 1997.

Quinn, Naomi, ed. *Finding Culture in Talk: A Collection of Methods.* New York: Palgrave, 2005.

Quinn, Naomi, and Dorothy Holland. "Culture and Cognition." In *Cultural Models in Language and Thought,* edited by Dorothy Holland and Naomi Quinn, 3–40. Cambridge: Cambridge University Press, 1987.

Rank, Mark R. "A View from the Inside Out: Recipients' Perceptions of Welfare." *Journal of Sociology & Social Welfare* 21, no. 2 (May 1994): 27–47.

Rank, Mark Robert, Thomas A. Hirschil, and Kirk A. Foster. *Chasing the American Dream: Understanding What Shapes Our Fortunes.* Oxford: Oxford University Press, 2014.

Rao, Aliya Hamid. *Crunch Time: How Married Couples Confront Unemployment.* Oakland: University of California Press, 2020.

Rayman, Paula. "Women and Unemployment." *Social Research* 54, no. 2 (1987): 355–76.

Roose, Kevin. *Futureproof: 9 Rules for Humans in the Age of Automation.* New York: Random House, 2022.

Rosen, Ellen Israel. *Bitter Choices: Blue-Collar Women in and out of Work.* Chicago: University of Chicago Press, 1987.

Rosenbaum, Susanna. *Domestic Economies: Women, Work, and the American Dream in Los Angeles.* Durham, NC: Duke University Press, 2017.

Rosenblat, Alex. *Uberland: How Algorithms are Rewriting the Rules of Work.* Oakland: University of California Press, 2018.

Rothstein, Frances Abrahamer. "Labor on the Move: Kinship, Social Networks, and Precarious Work among Mexican Migrants." In *Anthropologies of Unemployment: New Perspectives on Work and Its Absence*, edited by Jong Bum Kwon and Carrie M. Lane, 155–70. Ithaca, NY: Cornell University Press, 2016.

Rotolo, Thomas. "Trends in Voluntary Association Participation." *Nonprofit and Voluntary Sector Quarterly* 28, no. 2 (June 1999): 199–212. https://doi.org/10.1177/0899764099282005.

Sahlins, Marshall. "The Original Affluent Society." In *Stone Age Economics*, 1–39. Chicago: Aldine, 1972.

Salanova, Marisa, Mario Del Líbano, Susana Llorens, and Wilmar B Schaufeli. "Engaged, Workaholic, Burned-Out or Just 9-To-5? Toward a Typology of Employee Well-Being." *Stress and Health* 30, no. 1 (2014): 71–81. https://doi.org/10.1002/smi.2499.

Sayer, Andrew. "Contributive Justice and Meaningful Work." *Res Publica* 15 (2009): 1–16. https://doi.org/10.1007/s11158-008-9077-8.

Schanzenbach, Diane Whitmore, Ryan Nunn, Lauren Bauer, and Audrey Breitwieser. "The Closing of the Jobs Gap: A Decade of Recession and Recovery." Hamilton Project, Brookings Institution, August 4, 2017. https://www.brookings.edu/research/the-closing-of-the-jobs-gap-a-decade-of-recession-and-recovery/#:~:text=The%20average%20rate%20of%20recovery,Great%20Recession%20are%20entirely%20healed.

Schaufeli, Wilmar B., Toon W. Taris, and Arnold B. Bakker. "Dr. Jekyll or Mr. Hyde? On the Differences between Work Engagement and Workaholism." In *Research Companion to Working Time and Work Addiction*, edited by Ronald J. Burke, 193–217. Cheltenham, UK: Edward Elgar, 2006.

Schaufeli, Wilmar B., Toon W. Taris, and Arnold B. Bakker. "It Takes Two to Tango: Workaholism Is Working Excessively and Working Compulsively." In *The Long Work Hours Culture: Causes, Consequences and Choices*, edited by Ronald J. Burke and Cary L. Cooper, 203–26. Bingley, UK: Emerald, 2008.

Schlozman, Kay Lehman, and Sidney Verba. *Injury to Insult: Unemployment, Class, and Political Response*. Cambridge, MA: Harvard University Press, 1979.

Schmitt, John, Heidi Shierholz, Margaret Poydock, and Samantha Sanders. "The Economic Costs of Worker Misclassification." Economic Policy Institute, January 25, 2023. https://www.epi.org/publication/cost-of-misclassification/.

Schor, Juliet B. *The Overspent American: Why We Want What We Don't Need*. New York: Harper, 1998.

Schott, Liz. "State General Assistance Programs Very Limited in Half the States and Nonexistent in Others, despite Need." Center on Budget and Policy Priorities, Washington, DC, updated July 2, 2020. https://www.cbpp.org/research/family-income-support/state-general-assistance-programs-very-limited-in-half-the-states.

Schulte, Brigid. *Overwhelmed: Work, Love, and Play When No One Has the Time*. New York: Sarah Crichton Books, 2014.

Schwartz, Barry. *Why We Work*. New York: Simon & Schuster, 2015.

Schwartz, Christine R., and Robert D. Mare. "Trends in Educational Assortative Marriage from 1940 to 2003." *Demography* 42, no. 4 (2005): 621–46. https://doi.org/10.1353/dem.2005.0036.

Seitz, Benjamin M., Athena Aktipis, David M. Buss, Joe Alcock, Paul Bloom, Michele Gelfand, Sam Harris, Debra Lieberman, Barbara N. Horowitz, Steven Pinker, et al. "The Pandemic Exposes Human Nature: 10 Evolutionary Insights," *PNAS* 117, no. 45 (November 10, 2020): 27767–76. https://doi.org/10.1073/pnas.2009787117.

Sennett, Richard. *The Corrosion of Character.* New York: W. W. Norton, 1998.

———. *The Culture of the New Capitalism.* New Haven, CT: Yale University Press, 2006.

Serneels, Pieter. "The Nature of Unemployment among Young Men in Urban Ethiopia." *Review of Development Economics* 11, no. 1 (2007). https://doi.org/10.1111/j.1467-9361.2007.00389.x.

Sharone, Ofer. *Flawed System/Flawed Self: Job Searching and Unemployment Experiences.* Chicago: University of Chicago Press, 2014.

Shaw, Hannah, and Chad Stone. "Key Things to Know about Unemployment Insurance." Center on Budget and Policy Priorities, Washington, DC, updated December 20, 2011. https://www.cbpp.org/research/key-things-to-know-about-unemployment-insurance.

Shimazu, Akihito, Wilmar B Schaufeli, Kimika Kamiyama, and Norito Kawakami. "Workaholism vs. Work Engagement: The Two Different Predictors of Future Well-Being and Performance." *International Journal of Behavioral Medicine* 22, no. 1 (2015): 18–23. https://doi.org/10.1007/s12529-014-9410-x.

Shklar, Judith N. *American Citizenship: The Quest for Inclusion.* Cambridge, MA: Harvard University Press, 1991.

Slaughter, Anne-Marie. *Unfinished Business: Women Men Work Family.* New York: Random House, 2015.

Smith-Morris, Carolyn, Daisy Morales-Campos, Edith Alejandra Castañeda Alvarez, and Matthew Turner. "An Anthropology of Familismo: On Narratives and Description of Mexican/Immigrants." *Hispanic Journal of Behavioral Sciences* 35, no. 1 (2013): 35–60. https://doi.org/10.1177/0739986312459508.

Standing, Guy. *The Precariat: The New Dangerous Class.* London: Bloomsbury, 2011.

Steger, Michael F., Bryan J. Dik, and Ryan D. Duffy. "Measuring Meaningful Work: The Work and Meaning Inventory (WAMI)." *Journal of Career Assessment* 20, no. 3 (2012): 322–37. https://doi.org/10.1177/1069072711436160. Cited in Sarah J. Ward and Laura A. King, "Work and the Good Life: How Work Contributes to Meaning in Life," *Research in Organizational Behavior* 37 (2017). https://doi.org/10.1016/j.riob.2017.10.001.

Stevenson, Betsey, and Justin Wolfers. "Economic Growth and Subjective Well-Being: Reassessing the Easterlin Paradox." Brookings Papers on Economic Activity, no. 14282, 2008. https://users.nber.org/~jwolfers/papers/EasterlinParadox.pdf.

Stockman, Farah. *American Made: What Happens to People When Work Disappears.* New York: Random House, 2021.

Stone, Chad. "Congress Should Renew Emergency Unemployment Compensation before the End of the Year." Center on Budget and Policy Priorities, Washington, DC, updated November 21, 2013. https://www.cbpp.org/research/congress-should-renew-emergency-unemployment-compensation-before-the-end-of-the-year.

Stone, Chad, Danilo Trisi, Arloc Sherman, and Jennifer Beltrán. "A Guide to Statistics on Historical Trends in Income Inequality." Center on Budget and Policy Priorities, Washington, DC, updated January 13, 2020. https://www.cbpp.org/research/poverty-and-inequality/a-guide-to-statistics-on-historical-trends-in-income-inequality.

Stone, Pamela. *Opting Out? Why Women Really Quit Careers and Head Home.* Berkeley: University of California Press, 2007.

Strauss, Claudia. "The Complexity of Culture in Persons." In *Advances in Culture Theory from Psychological Anthropology*, edited by Naomi Quinn, 109–38. New York: Palgrave, 2018.

——. "Cultural Standing in Expression of Opinion." *Language in Society* 33, no. 2 (2004): 161–94. https://doi.org/10.1017/S004740450433201X.

——. "Engaged by the Spectacle of Protest: How Bystanders Became Invested in Occupy Wall Street." In *Political Sentiments and Social Movements: The Person in Politics and Culture*, edited by Claudia Strauss and Jack Friedman, 33–60. New York: Palgrave, 2018.

——. *Making Sense of Public Opinion: American Discourses about Immigration and Social Programs.* New York: Cambridge University Press, 2012.

——. "Not-So Rugged Individualists: U.S. Americans' Conflicting Ideas about Poverty." In *Work, Welfare, and Politics: Confronting Poverty in the Wake of Welfare Reform*, edited by Frances Fox Piven, Joan Acker, Margaret Hallock, and Sandra Morgen, 55–69. Eugene, OR: University of Oregon Press, 2002.

——. "Positive Thinking about Being out of Work in Southern California after the Great Recession." In *Anthropologies of Unemployment: New Perspectives on Work and Its Absence*, edited by Jong Bum Kwon and Carrie M. Lane, 171–90. Ithaca, NY: Cornell University Press, 2016.

——. "Seeking Attachment in the Fissured Workplace: External Workers in the United States." In *Beyond the Wage: Ordinary Work in Diverse Economies*, edited by William Monteith, Dora-Olivia Vicol, and Philippa Williams, 71–92. Bristol, UK: Bristol University Press, 2021.

——. "'That Was Just Fun': Small Work Pleasures, Precarious Jobs, and Well-Being." Under review, *Economic Anthropology*, special issue on Well-Being.

——. "What Makes Tony Run? Schemas as Motives Reconsidered." In *Human Motives and Cultural Models*, edited by Roy G. D'Andrade and Claudia Strauss, 197–224. Cambridge: Cambridge University Press, 1992.

Strauss, Claudia, and Naomi Quinn. *A Cognitive Theory of Cultural Meaning.* Cambridge: Cambridge University Press, 1997.

Sullivan, Oriel. "An End to Gender Display through the Performance of Housework? A Review and Reassessment of the Quantitative Literature Using Insights from the Qualitative Literature." *Journal of Family Theory and Review* 3 (2011): 1–13. https://doi.org/10.1111/j.1756-2589.2010.00074.x.

Susser, Ida. "The Construction of Poverty and Homelessness in US Cities." *Annual Review of Anthropology* 25, no. 1 (1996): 411–35. https://doi.org/10.1146/annurev.anthro.25.1.411.

Suzman, James. *Work: A Deep History, from the Stone Age to the Age of Robots.* New York: Penguin Press, 2021.

Terkel, Studs. *Working.* New York: New Press, 2004.

Thelen, Kathleen. "Varieties of Capitalism: Trajectories of Liberalization and the New Politics of Social Solidarity." *Annual Review of Political Science* 15 (2012): 137–59. https://doi.org/10.1146/annurev-polisci-070110-122959.

Thompson, E. P. "Time, Work-Discipline, and Industrial Capitalism." *Past & Present* 38 (1967): 56–97.

Tilcsik, András. "Pride and Prejudice: Employment Discrimination against Openly Gay Men in the United States." *American Journal of Sociology* 117 (2011): 586–626. https://doi.org/10.1086/661653.

Tocqueville, Alexis de. *Democracy in America.* Translated by George Lawrence, edited by J. P. Mayer. Garden City, New York: Doubleday, 1969. First published 1835 (Vol. 1) and 1840 (Vol. 2).

Toossi, Mitra. "A Century of Change: The U.S. Labor Force, 1950–2050." *Monthly Labor Review* (May 2002): 15–28. https://www.bls.gov/opub/mlr/2002/05/art2full.pdf.

Townsend, Nicholas W. *The Package Deal: Marriage, Work and Fatherhood in Men's Lives.* Philadelphia: Temple University Press, 2002.

Traub, Amy. *Discredited: How Employment Credit Checks Keep Qualified Workers out of a Job.* New York: Dēmos, 2014. https://www.demos.org/research/discredited-how-employment-credit-checks-keep-qualified-workers-out-job.

US Bureau of Labor Statistics. "Usual Weekly Earnings of Wage and Salary Workers First Quarter 2020." US Bureau of Labor Statistics, Washington, DC, April 15, 2020, https://www.bls.gov/news.release/archives/wkyeng_04152020.pdf.

US Department of Health and Human Services, Office of the Assistant Secretary for Planning and Evaluation. *Poverty in the United States: 50-Year Trends and Safety Net Impacts,* by Ajay Chaudry, Christopher Wimer, Suzanne Macartney, Lauren Frohlich, Colin Campbell, Kendall Swenson, Don Oellerich, and Susan Hauan. Washington, DC: March 2016. https://aspe.hhs.gov/system/files/pdf/154286/50YearTrends.pdf.

US Department of the Treasury. "COBRA Insurance Coverage since the Recovery Act: Results from New Survey Data." US Department of the Treasury, Washington, DC, May 2010. https://home.treasury.gov/system/files/226/COBRA_Insurance_Coverage_since_the_Recovery_Act_Results_from_New_Survey_Data_MAY2010.pdf.

US Government Accountability Office. "Unemployed Older Workers: Many Experience Challenges Regaining Employment and Face Reduced Retirement Security." Report to the Chairman, Special Committee on Aging, US Senate, Washington, DC, May 15, 2012. https://www.gao.gov/products/gao-12-445.

US Immigration and Naturalization Service. "Field Guidance on Deportability and Inadmissibility on Public Charge Grounds." *Federal Register* 64, no. 101 (March 26, 1999). https://www.govinfo.gov/content/pkg/FR-1999-05-26/pdf/99-13202.pdf.

Van Hook, Jennifer, and Frank D. Bean. "Explaining Mexican-Immigrant Welfare Behaviors: The Importance of Employment-Related Cultural Repertoires." *American Sociological Review* 74, no. 3 (2009): 423–44. https://doi.org/10.1177/000312240907400305.

Veblen, Thorstein. *The Theory of the Leisure Class*. Mineola, NY: Dover, 1994. First published 1899 by Macmillan (New York).

Vyas, Lina. "'New Normal' at Work in a Post-COVID World: Work-Life Balance and Labor Markets." *Policy and Society* 41, no. 1 (2022): 155–67. https://doi.org/10.1093/polsoc/puab011.

Walley, Christine J. *Exit Zero: Family and Class in Postindustrial Chicago*. Chicago: University of Chicago Press, 2013.

Wang, Wendy, and Kim Parker. "Record Share of Americans Have Never Married." Pew Research Center, Washington, DC, September 24, 2014. http://www.pewsocialtrends.org/2014/09/24/record-share-of-americans-have-never-married/#fn-19804-2.

Ward, Sarah J., and Laura A. King. "Work and the Good Life: How Work Contributes to Meaning in Life." *Research in Organizational Behavior* 37 (2017): 59–82. https://doi.org/10.1016/j.riob.2017.10.001.

Warhurst, Chris, Chris Mathieu, and Sally Wright. "*Vorsprung durch Technik*: The Futures of Work, Digital Technology, and the Platform Economy." In *The Many Futures of Work: Rethinking Expectations and Breaking Molds*, edited by Peter A. Creticos, Larry Bennett, Laura Owen, Costas Spirou, and Maxine Morphis-Riesbeck, 179–95. Philadelphia: Temple University Press, 2021. ProQuest Ebook Central, https://ebookcentral.proquest.com/lib/claremont/detail.action?docID=28810809.

Weber, Max. *The Protestant Ethic and the Spirit of Capitalism*. Translated by Talcott Parsons. New York: Charles Scribner's Sons, 1958. First published 1904–5.

Weeks, Kathi. *The Problem with Work: Feminism, Marxism, Antiwork Politics, and Postwork Imaginaries*. Durham, NC: Duke University Press, 2011.

Weil, David. *The Fissured Workplace: Why Work Became So Bad for So Many and What Can Be Done to Improve It*. Cambridge, MA: Harvard University Press, 2014.

Weir, Kirsten. "More than Job Satisfaction." *Monitor on Psychology* 44, no. 11 (December 2013). https://www.apa.org/monitor/2013/12/job-satisfaction.

Weisner, Thomas S., Hirokazu Yoshikawa, Edward D. Lowe, and Faye Carter. "'I Want What Everybody Wants': Goals, Values, and Work in the Lives of New Hope Families." In *Making It Work: Low-Wage Employment, Family Life, and Child Development*, edited by Hirokazu Yoshikawa, Thomas S. Weisner, and Edward D. Lowe, 147–72. New York: Russell Sage Foundation, 2005.

Weisshaar, Katherine. "Earnings Equality and Relationship Stability for Same-Sex and Heterosexual Couples." *Social Forces* 93, no. 1 (2014): 93–123. https://doi.org/10.1093/sf/sou065.

White, Lynn, and Stacy J. Rogers. "Economic Circumstances and Family Outcomes: A Review of the 1990s." *Journal of Marriage and Family* 62, no. 4 (2000): 1035–51. https://doi.org/10.1111/j.1741-3737.2000.01035.x.

Willott, Sara, and Christine Griffin. "'Wham Bam, Am I a Man?' Unemployed Men Talk about Masculinities." *Feminism & Psychology* 7, no. 1 (1997): 107–28. https://doi.org/10.1177/0959353597071012.

Wolfenstein, Martha. "Fun Morality: An Analysis of Recent American Child Training Literature." In *The Children's Culture Reader*, edited by Henry Jenkins, 199–208. New York: New York University Press 1998. First published 1955.

Wright, Bradley R. E., Michael Wallace, John Bailey, and Allen Hyde. "Religious Affiliation and Hiring Discrimination in New England: A Field Experiment." *Research in Social Stratification and Mobility* 34 (2013): 111–26. https://doi.org/10.1016/j.rssm.2013.10.002.

Wrzesniewski, Amy, Clark McCauley, Paul Rozin, and Barry Schwartz. "Jobs, Careers, and Callings: People's Relations to Their Work." *Journal of Research in Personality* 31, no. 1 (March 1997): 21–33. https://doi.org/10.1006/jrpe.1997.2162.

Yang, Jie. *Unknotting the Heart: Unemployment and Therapeutic Governance in China.* Ithaca, NY: Cornell University Press, 2015.

Young, Alford A. "New Life for an Old Concept: Frame Analysis and the Reinvigoration of Studies in Culture and Poverty." *Annals of the American Academy of Political and Social Science* 629 (May 2010): 53–74. https://doi.org/10.1177/0002716209357145.

Index

Note: Page numbers in *italic* refer to illustrative matter.

www.ingramcontent.com/pod-product-compliance
Lightning Source LLC
Chambersburg PA
CBHW030915270326
41929CB00008B/710